WEBSTER'S NEW WORLD™

Letter Writing Handbook

Robert W. Bly

Wiley Publishing, Inc.

Webster's New World™ Letter Writing Handbook

Copyright © 2004 by Wiley Publishing, Inc., Indianapolis, Indiana

Published by Wiley Publishing, Inc., Indianapolis, Indiana
Published simultaneously in Canada

For general information on our other products and services or to obtain technical support please contact our Customer Care Department within the U.S. at 800-762-2974, outside the U.S. at 317-572-3993 or fax 317-572-4002.
Wiley also publishes its books in a variety of electronic formats. Some content that appears in print may not be available in electronic books.

Library of Congress Cataloging-in-Publication Data is available from the publisher.

Manufactured in the United States of America

10 9 8 7 6 5 4 3 2 1

ACKNOWLEDGMENTS

Thanks to my agents, Bob Diforio and Marilyn Allen, for bringing to me the opportunity to write this book, and to my editors, Roxane Cerda, Helen Chin, and Suzanne Snyder, for making this manuscript much better than it was when it first crossed their desks.

Thanks also to the many organizations and individuals who gave me permission to reprint their letters in this book.

DEDICATION

For Bob Diforio and Marilyn Allen.

TABLE OF CONTENTS

LETTER WRITING IN THE INTERNET AGE

What is the state of letter writing in the age of the Internet? Is the ability to write clear, concise letters no longer important? Has e-mail rendered paper letters obsolete? Is there a completely different style for writing e-mail versus on paper?

The answer is a resounding 'No!' The Internet has revolutionized the speed at which we communicate, and the ease of getting your message into the hands of other people. But it hasn't — at least not yet — dramatically altered the English language.

With the advent of e-mail, people probably write more than they used to. If anything, the Internet has increased our preference for written communication versus verbal (e.g., sending e-mails instead of making phone calls). That would seem to call for more of an emphasis on writing skills, not less. In fact, recent research says that written communications are one of the ten most important traits of leaders and successful people.

Professionals today definitely *type* more than they used do. As recently as a decade or so ago, most managers dictated or wrote by hand. Secretaries typed their letters. No self-respecting manager had a keyboard on his or her desk. Now, computer literacy — including a working knowledge of Word and Excel — is a basic requisite for managers. So is English literacy: being able to express oneself clearly in simple, direct language.

There have been, in my opinion, three important changes in written communication within the last few years affecting the art of letter writing:

First, we are universally acknowledged to be busier than we were 10 or 20 years ago. Part of that is the relentless pressure of communications technology: beepers, pagers, PCs, e-mail, fax machines, voice mail, cell phones, and personal digital assistants means we are constantly bombarded with messages from people who want our attention. Because of time pressures and information overload, you have to work harder than ever to get and keep the reader's attention. Online marketers know that simply changing the subject line can double response to an e-mail marketing message. How many e-mails do you delete each day without even opening them? How many letters do you open, read, but not respond or react to — because you are too busy?

The second major change in writing is also related to information overload and time pressures: the shrinking of letter size. Not the size of the paper, but the size of the message, the key being: The shorter, the better. If you read books that reprint historically important letters (e.g., those of Lincoln), or books that collect the correspondence of nineteenth-century writers, you may be struck by how incredibly elegant, detailed, and long these letters are. The modern reader, however, has neither the time nor the patience for long letters (with a few notable exceptions discussed later in the book).

Conciseness has always been a virtue in writing — and an enviable skill to be acquired. Philosopher and mathematician Blaise Pascal is often quoted as saying to a correspondent: "Forgive me for the long letter; I did not have time to write a short one." But in the twenty-first century, being concise has graduated from being a virtue to a necessity: If you don't get to the point quickly, and get your message across in the fewest possible words, you'll turn off your reader.

The third major change in letter writing is that correspondence has become less formal and increasingly conversational in style. Conversational style, like conciseness, has also long been a virtue in writing. But the advent of e-mail has accelerated the acceptance of conversational style and the banishment of "corporatese." We don't get buzzword laden messages about "thinking outside the box" or "shifting our paradigms" when we zing off our e-mails — we get right to the point: "Marketing plans are due today at 3:00 p.m., please add information focusing on new product development."

The sample letters in *Webster's New World Letter Writing Handbook* — and the guidelines for adapting them for your own use — reflect the modern style of letter writing: to the point, concise, and conversational. Although some can be copied merely verbatim, more often these sample letters can serve as models on which to base your own letters.

The specifics of your situation may require making changes — sometimes substantial — to the sample letters in this book. But the tone, style, pace, and organization of the sample letters should help you say what you want in most situations, most of the time, faster and with less effort than composing your own letters from scratch. After all, why reinvent the wheel when the tires have already been perfected in the laboratory, thoroughly inspected for quality control, and field tested in thousand of situations?

INTRODUCTION

The right letter can make all the difference. From getting the right job to closing the sale, from obtaining a scholarship to offering thanks gracefully, letters leave a lasting impression. Packed with hundreds of examples that fulfill almost any goal, *Webster's New World Letter Writing Handbook* is the most modern and up-to-date reference for writing effective letters.

No one has time to craft and redraft letters from scratch. The expert guidance in *Webster's New World Letter Writing Handbook,* partnered with hundreds of examples, helps readers quickly write letters that get results.

Containing more than just cover letters and thank-you notes, this title also covers such common correspondence as wishing congratulations, apologizing, expressing sympathy, fundraising, asking favors, requesting and providing information, job hunting, selling, making and responding to complaints, giving feedback, refusals, or reprimands, and even collecting past-due payments.

Webster's New World Letter Writing Handbook starts with the nuts and bolts of letter writing but doesn't stop there. Going beyond the essentials, this title helps you:

- Craft attention-grabbing introductions.
- State your case effectively.
- Sway your reader's opinion.
- Close with a clincher.
- Make a lasting impression.
- Generate the desired response or reaction from the recipient.

Webster's New World Letter Writing Handbook covers all the essentials with expert guidance and offers hundreds of examples. Here's how the book is organized:

- *Part I* covers such letter-writing basics as understanding your reader, achieving the proper tone and style, prewriting planning, how to write clearly, and letter format and layout.
- *Part II* contains sample letters with guidelines for adaptation to cover personal correspondence of all kinds, from thanking someone for a gift to expressing condolences.
- *Part III* deals with letters relating to your job and career. You are shown how to reply to help-wanted ads and how to create cover letters when sending out résumés to potential employers. Employers are given the letters they need to communicate with potential candidates, reject unsuitable candidates, and to write letters of recommendation and introduction.
- *Part IV* presents letters for general business correspondence, from common business requests and information transmittals, to handling difficult situations, such as announcing mergers or bankruptcies.

- *Part V* gives you numerous examples of memos written for internal communication, showing you how to instruct, educate, persuade, and collaborate with others within your organization.
- *Part VI* focuses on letters to customers. Special attention is given to handling dissatisfied customers, resolving complaints, and getting customers to renew contracts and subscriptions, or continue ordering products.
- *Part VII* gives you letters for the sale force to use in customer contact and prospecting, as well as direct mail letters for the marketing department. You can use these letters to generate leads, make quotas, and gain appointments.
- *Part VIII* is devoted to credit, collection, and billing correspondence. The objective is to get customers to pay what they owe promptly while retaining their business and goodwill.
- *Part IX* gives you many model letters for communicating with your vendors. The goal here is to get what you want, yet motivate the vendor to give you good service and make them feel positive about doing business with you.
- While the model letters in Parts I through VIII can easily be adapted to e-mail, *Part X* gives guidance on writing effective online messages and formatting e-mails correctly and for maximum open rates. Similarly, *Part X* covers the special requirements of fax correspondence.

As you go through the book, you might argue that a letter found in one category or part belongs in another. This is the natural result of the crossover between functional areas in modern business. A customer service letter can also have a selling purpose, while a collection letter — designed to bring back a check — also serves the customer service function of retaining the buyer's goodwill.

Whether for business or personal reasons, everyone has to write letters, but barely anyone has the time to start from scratch every time. From busy executives to disgruntled consumers, everyone needs a one-stop source for quick, effective letter writing. Now you have it in your hands. Enjoy!

PART I

LETTER WRITING BASICS

Wherever you are today as a letter writer — good, bad, or indifferent — you can take your level of skill to the next level in a relatively short time.

The benefit of doing so is that you will write more effective letters: Letters that get your message across without the reader calling you for clarification. Letters that persuade your readers to accept your point of view, or take the actions you want them to take. Letters that get you the results — business and personal — you desire.

In this part, we cover some rules and tools for effective letter writing. They may seem like a lot of work right now — and maybe they will be, for now. But soon they will become a reflexive part of your letter-writing process. You won't have to think about most of them; you will just use them to make your letters sharper, clearer, and more convincing than ever.

Prewriting Planning

You would not start building an addition onto your home until you had an architect make a drawing to show you what it would look like, would you? And a manager in charge of a division or product line would not start marketing the products without a marketing plan, would she?

In the same way, doing some preliminary preparation — rather than just turning on the PC and starting to type, can help you craft better letters. Of course writing a letter is not as big a job as planning a marketing campaign or building a family room. But it is important. As the saying goes, "Anything worth doing is worth doing well."

Besides, the "planning" you do for a small writing job, like a letter, need not and should not be elaborate or time-consuming. A few minutes spent thinking and following the steps that follow can help you write a better letter, and may actually save time rather than take more time.

Here are some simple steps to take when planning a letter or other communication of any significance:

1. Do a SAP (subject, audience, and purpose) analysis as outlined in the sections that follow.
2. Gather the information you need and do whatever additional research is required to complete the letter.
3. Make a simple 1-2-3 outline of the points you need to cover, in the order you want to present them.
4. Now sit down, and start writing!

SAP: SUBJECT, AUDIENCE, PURPOSE

SAP analysis is a process that quickly enables you to pin down the content and organization of your letter. The process requires you to ask and answer three questions:

- What is the subject (topic) of your letter?
- Who is your audience? (Who will be receiving your letter?)
- What is the purpose of your letter?

Subject

What is the subject (topic) of the letter? Make it as narrow and specific as possible. For instance, "marketing product X" is too broad for a letter; you'll need a report or other longer document to cover it. But "approving copy for product X in our next catalog" is narrow and specific; there's room in a letter to cover it.

Audience

Who is your reader? Well, you know who your reader is, but do you know what he or she thinks, likes, and worries about? Or what he or she wants, hopes, dreams, and desires? Most of us spend too much time thinking about what we want, and not enough time thinking about what the reader wants. Written communications are most effective when they are *personal*. Your writing should be built around the needs, interests, desires, and profit of the reader. The better you understand the other person, the more effectively you can communicate with him or her.

Crafting a letter that fits the reader is relatively easy when you are writing a personal letter to a friend or relative you know well. In the case of a business letter, it makes sense to ask yourself, "Who is my reader? What does he or she know about this subject? What is my relationship with the reader — subordinate, superior, colleague, or customer? How can I get the message across so that the reader will understand and agree?" When writing business letters, here are some things you want to know about your reader:

- **Job title.** Mechanics are interested in your compressor's reliability and serviceability, while the purchasing agent is more concerned with cost. A person's job colors his perspective of your product, service, or idea. Are you writing for plant engineers? Office managers? CEOs? Shop foremen? Make the tone and content of your writing compatible with the professional interests of your readers.
- **Education.** Is your reader a PhD or a high-school dropout? Is he a chemical engineer? A doctor? A carpenter? A senior citizen? Write simply enough so that the least technical and educated of your readers can understand you completely. When in doubt, err on the side of simplicity. You will never have a recipient of your letter complain to you that it was too easy to read.
- **Industry.** When chemical producers buy a reverse-osmosis water-purification system for a chemical plant, they want to know every technical detail down to the last pipe, pump, fan, and filter. Marine buyers, on the other hand, have only two basic questions: *What does it cost? How reliable is it?* The weight and size are also important, since the system must be carried onto and bolted onto the floor of a boat.
- **Level of interest.** A prospect who has responded to your ad is more likely to be receptive to a salesman's call than someone who the salesman calls on "cold turkey." Is your reader interested or disinterested? Friendly or hostile? Receptive or resistant? Understanding the reader's state of mind helps you tailor your message to meet his needs.

Often, however, when writing business letters and longer documents — articles, papers, manuals, reports, and brochures — you are writing for many readers, not an individual. Even though you may not know the names of your readers, you still need to develop a picture of who they are — their job titles, education, industry, and interests.

Purpose

What is the purpose of your letter? You might be tempted to say, "to transmit information." Sometimes merely transmitting information is the letter's sole purpose, but often it is more than that. Is there a request you want the reader to comply with, or a favor you are hoping they will grant? Keep your goal in mind as you write, so that you may persuade the reader to agree with your point of view.

GATHER INFORMATION

In order to write an effective letter and save time in doing so, you need to have all your information at hand, such as copies of previous correspondence on the topic, customer records, service orders, and so on. If you don't have all the information you need, do the necessary research. For instance, if you are answering a technical question for a customer, and you do not know the answer, ask someone in engineering to explain it to you. Or if you are writing a letter to your insurance company explaining

The 3-Step Writing Process

Often when people write, they're afraid to make mistakes, and so they edit themselves word by word, inhibiting the natural flow of ideas and sentences. But professional writers know that writing is a process consisting of numerous drafts, rewrites, deletions, and revisions.

Rarely does a writer produce a perfect manuscript on the first try. The task ideally should be divided into three steps: writing, rewriting, and polishing.

1. **Writing.** Most professional writers go through a minimum of three drafts. The first is this initial "go with the flow" draft where the words come tumbling out.

   When you sit down to write, let the words flow freely. Don't worry about style, syntax, punctuation, or typos — just write. You can always go back and fix it later. By "letting it all out," you build momentum and overcome inhibitions that block your ability to write and think.

2. **Rewriting.** In the second draft — the rewriting step — you take a critical look at what you've written. You edit for organization, logic, content, and persuasiveness. Using your PC, you add, delete, and rearrange paragraphs. You rewrite jumbled passages to make them clear.

3. **Polishing.** In the third draft, you give your prose a final polishing by editing for style, syntax, spelling, and punctuation. This is the step where you worry about things like consistency in numbers, units of measure, equations, symbols, abbreviations, and capitalization.

why you think they were wrong in refusing to pay for your treatment, it really helps to have all the facts in front of you — dates and costs of your exams, test results, doctors seen, and a copy of your policy, so you can reference the part that supports your argument.

MAKE A SIMPLE OUTLINE

For any document longer than a short e-mail, an outline can make the writing easier and ensure that all key points are covered. The outline also helps you keep your points in a logical order and transition smoothly between them. A letter requesting a scholarship or financial aid, for instance, might be organized along the following lines:

1. Describe your educational goals and ambitions.
2. Explain why you need financial aid to attain these goals.
3. Say why you deserve to be given the aid.
4. Cite specific evidence (e.g., community service, extracurricular activities, grade point average, honors and awards).
5. Ask for the specific amount of money you need.

Here's the outline for a memo requesting budget approval from your supervisor at work:

1. List what you want to buy.
2. Describe the item and its function or purpose.
3. Give the cost.
4. Explain why you need it and how the company will come out ahead (e.g., how much time or money will it save?).
5. Do a cost/benefit analysis showing projected return on investment and payback period.
6. Ask for authorization or approval.

Twelve Rules for Better Letter Writing

Better writing can result in proposals that win contracts, advertisements that sell products, instruction manuals that users can follow, billboards that catch a driver's attention, stories that make us laugh or cry, and letters, memos, and reports that get your message across to the reader. Here are 12 tips on style and word choice that can make writing clear and persuasive.

1. PRESENT YOUR BEST SELF

Your moods vary. After all, you're only human. But while it is sometimes difficult to present your best self in conversation, which is spontaneous and instant, letters are written alone and on your own schedule. Therefore, you can and should take the time to let your most pleasant personality shine through in your writing.

Be especially careful when replying to an e-mail message you have received. The temptation is to treat the message as conversation, and if you are irritated or just outrageously pressured and busy, the tendency is to reply in a clipped and curt fashion — again, not showing you at your best.

The solution? Although you may be eager to reply immediately to e-mail so you can get the message out of your inbox, a better strategy for when your reply is important is to set it aside, compose your answer when you are not so time pressured, and read it carefully before sending.

> A Tip: Never write a letter when angry. If you must write the letter when angry, then put it aside without sending it, and come back to it later. You will most likely want to throw it out and start over, not send it at all, or drastically revise it.

Remember, once you hit the Reply button, it is too late to get the message back. It's out there, and you can't retrieve it. Same thing when you drop a letter in the mailbox (it's actually a felony to reach into the mailbox and try to retrieve the letter!).

2. WRITE IN A CLEAR, CONVERSATIONAL STYLE

Naturally, a memo on sizing pumps shouldn't have the same chatty tone as a personal letter. But most business and technical professionals lean too much in the other direction, and their sharp thinking is obscured by windy, overly formal prose.

The key to success in business or technical writing? *Keep it simple.* I've said this before, but it bears repeating: Write to express — not to impress. A relaxed, conversational style can add vigor and clarity to your letters.

Formal business style	Informal conversational style
The data provided by direct examination of samples under the lens of the microscope are insufficient for the purpose of making a proper identification of the components of the substance.	We can't tell what it is made of by looking at it under the microscope.
We have found during conversations with customers that even the most experienced of extruder specialists have a tendency to avoid the extrusion of silicone profiles or hoses.	Our customers tell us that experienced extruder specialists avoid extruding silicone profiles or hoses.
The corporation terminated the employment of Mr. Joseph Smith.	Joe was fired.

3. BE CONCISE

Professionals, especially those in industry, are busy people. Make your writing less time-consuming for them to read by telling the whole story in the fewest possible words.

How can you make your writing more concise? One way is to avoid redundancies — a needless form of wordiness in which a modifier repeats an idea already contained within the word being modified.

For example, a recent trade ad described a product as a "new innovation." Could there be such a thing as an *old* innovation? The ad also said the product was "very unique." Unique means "one of a kind," so it is impossible for anything to be *very* unique.

By now, you probably get the picture. Some common redundancies are presented below, along with the correct way to rewrite them:

Redundancy	Rewrite as
advance plan	plan
actual experience	experience
two cubic feet in volume	two cubic feet
cylindrical in shape	cylindrical
uniformly homogeneous	homogeneous

Many writers are fond of overblown expressions such as "the fact that," "it is well known that," and "it is the purpose of this writer to show that." These take up space but add little to meaning or clarity.

The following list includes some common wordy phrases. The column on the right offers suggested substitute words:

Wordy phrase	Suggested substitute
during the course of	during
in the form of	as
in many cases	often
in the event of	if
exhibits the ability to	can

4. BE CONSISTENT

"A foolish consistency," wrote Ralph Waldo Emerson, "is the hobgoblin of little minds." This may be so. But, on the other hand, inconsistencies in your writing will confuse your readers and convince them that your information and reasoning are as sloppy and unorganized as your prose.

Good writers strive for consistency in their use of numbers, hyphens, units of measure, punctuation, equations, grammar, symbols, capitalization, technical terms, and abbreviations. Keep in mind that if you are inconsistent in any of these matters of usage, you are automatically wrong at least part of the time.

For example, many writers are inconsistent in the use of hyphens. The rule is: two words that form an adjective are hyphenated. Thus, write: first-order reaction, fluidized-bed combustion, high-sulfur coal, space-time continuum.

The *U.S. Government Printing Office Style Manual*, Strunk and White's *The Elements of Style*, your organization's writing manual, and the appendix of this book can guide you in the basics of grammar, punctuation, abbreviation, and capitalization.

5. USE JARGON SPARINGLY

Many disciplines and specialties have a special language all their own. Technical terms are a helpful shorthand when you're communicating within the profession, but they may confuse readers who do not have your special background. Take the word, "yield," for example. To a chemical engineer, yield is a measure of how much product a reaction produces. But to car drivers, yield means slowing down (and stopping, if necessary) at an intersection.

Other words that have special meaning to chemical engineers but have a different definition in everyday use include: vacuum, pressure, batch, bypass, recycle, concentration, mole, purge, saturation, catalyst.

A good working definition of jargon is, "Language more complex than the ideas it serves to communicate." Use legitimate technical terms when they communicate your ideas precisely, but avoid using jargon just because the words sound impressive. In other words, do not write that material is "gravimetrically conveyed" when it is simply dumped. If you are a dentist, do not tell patients you have a procedure to help "stabilize mobile dentition" when what it really does is keeps loose teeth in place.

6. AVOID BIG WORDS

Some writers prefer to use big, important-sounding words instead of short, simple words. This is a mistake; fancy language just frustrates the reader. Write in plain, ordinary English and your readers will love you for it.

Here are a few frequently occurring big words; the column on the right presents a shorter — and preferable — substitution.

Big word	Substitution
beverage	drink
dentition	teeth
eliminate	get rid of
furnish	give, provide
incombustible	fireproof
prioritize	put in order
substantiate	prove
terminate	end
utilize	use

7. PREFER THE SPECIFIC TO THE GENERAL

Your readers want information — facts, figures, conclusions, and recommendations. Do not be content to say something is good, bad, fast, or slow when you can say *how* good, *how* bad, *how* fast, or *how* slow. Be specific whenever possible.

General	Specific
a tall building	a 20-story building
plant	oil refinery
heavy equipment	equipment weighing over 10 tons
unit	apartment
unfavorable weather conditions	rain (snow, etc.)
structural degradation	a leaky roof
disturbance	riot
high performance	95% efficiency
creature	dog (cat, etc.)
laboratory apparatus	test tubc

8. Break Up Your Writing into Short Sections

Long, unbroken blocks of text are stumbling blocks that intimidate and bore readers. Breaking up your writing into short sections and short paragraphs — as in this book — makes the text easier to read.

If your paragraphs are too long, go through them. Wherever a new thought starts, type a return and start a new paragraph.

In the same way, short sentences are easicr to grasp than long ones. A good guide for keeping sentence length under control is to write sentences that can be spoken aloud without losing your breath (do *not* take a deep breath before doing this test).

9. Use Visuals

Drawings, graphs, and other visuals can reinforce your text. In fact, pictures often communicate better than words; we remember 10 percent of what we read, but 30 percent of what we see.

Visuals can make your technical communications more effective. The different types of visuals and what they can show are listed below:

Type of visual	This shows . . .
Photograph or illustration	. . . what something looks like
Map	. . . where it is located
Exploded view	. . . how it is put together
Schematic diagram	. . . how it works or is organized
Graph	. . . how much there is (quantity)
	. . . how one thing varies as a function of another
Pie chart	. . . proportions and percentages
Bar chart	. . . comparisons between quantities
Table	. . . a body of related data
Mass and energy balances	. . . what goes in and what comes out

In the days when letters were written on typewriters, the idea of using visuals was out of the question. Today, software makes it relatively easy to add a chart, table, or graph to your letter. Why not do so, if it helps get your point across in a clearer and more persuasive fashion?

10. USE THE ACTIVE VOICE

Voice refers to the person speaking words or doing an action. An "active verb" stresses the person doing the thing. A "passive verb" stresses the thing being done.

In the active voice, action is expressed directly: "John performed the experiment." In the passive voice, the action is indirect: "The experiment was performed by John."

When possible, use the active voice. Your writing will be more direct and vigorous; your sentences more concise. As you can see in the samples below, the passive voice seems puny and stiff by comparison:

Passive voice	Active voice
Control of the bearing-oil supply is provided by the shutoff valves.	Shutoff valves control the bearing-oil supply.
Grandma's apple pie was enjoyed by everyone in the family.	Everyone in the family enjoyed Grandma's apple pie.
A good time was had by all.	We all had a good time.
Fuel-cost savings were realized through the installation of thermal insulation in the attic.	The installation of thermal insulation in the attic cut fuel costs.

11. ORGANIZATION

Poor organization is the number one problem in letter writing. As editor Jerry Bacchetti points out, "If the reader believes the content has some importance to him, he can plow through a report even if it is dull or has lengthy sentences and big words. But if it's poorly organized — forget it. There's no way to make sense of what is written."

Poor organization stems from poor planning. While a computer programmer would never think of writing a complex program without first drawing a flow chart, he'd probably knock out a draft of a user's manual without making notes or an outline. In the same way, a builder who requires detailed blueprints before he lays the first brick will write a letter without really considering his message, audience, or purpose.

Before you write, plan. As mentioned in the prewriting planning discussion earlier in this part, you should create a rough outline that spells out the contents and organization of your letter, memo, report, or proposal.

By the time you finish writing, some things in the final document might be different from the outline. That's okay. The outline is a tool to aid in organization, not a commandment etched in stone. If you want to change it as you go along — fine.

The outline helps you divide letters and larger writing projects into many smaller, easy-to-handle pieces and parts. The organization of these parts depends on the type of document you're writing.

There are standard formats for writing meeting minutes, travel reports, and many other business memos and letters. You can just follow the models in this book (see Appendix A).

If the format isn't strictly defined by the type of letter you are writing, select the organizational scheme that best fits the material. Some common formats include:

- **Order of location.** For example, a report recommending where to acquire new warehouses and parts depots based on the distance from the central manufacturing operation and the location relative to key accounts.
- **Order of increasing difficulty.** Instructions often start with the easiest material and, as the user masters basic principles, move on to more complex operations.
- **Alphabetical order.** A logical way to arrange a letter about vitamins (A, B, B1, and so on) or a directory of company employees.
- **Chronological order.** Presents the facts in the order in which they happened. Trip reports are sometimes written this way.
- **Problem/solution.** The problem/solution format begins with "Here's what the problem was" and ends with "Here's how we solved it."
- **Inverted pyramid.** The newspaper style of news reporting where the lead paragraph summarizes the story and the following paragraphs present the facts in order of decreasing importance. You can use this format in journal articles, letters, memos, and reports.
- **Deductive order.** Start with a generalization, and then support it with particulars. A lawyer might use this method in preparing to argue a case before a judge.
- **Inductive order.** Begin with specific instances, and then lead the reader to the idea or general principles the instances suggest. A minister might talk about different problems in the church caused by flaws in the building before asking for contributions to build a new roof.
- **List.** This section is a list because it describes, in list form, the ways to organize written material. A recent mailing from an electric company to its business customers contained a sheet titled "Seven Ways to Reduce Your Plant's Electric Bill."

Once you have an outline with sections and subsections, you can organize your information by putting it on index cards. Each card gets a heading outline. Or — using your personal computer — you can cut and paste the information within a word-processing file.

12. LENGTH

Whenever possible, keep your letter to one page. Today's busy readers really appreciate seeing that everything is on one side of a sheet of paper. Even Winston Churchill used to require of those serving under him that they express their concerns on no more than one side of a single sheet of paper.

If you have more to say, you can go to a second page, and possibly a third. No more than that. Exceptions include sales letters marketing products by mail (those can run four to eight pages or more) and family Christmas/holiday letters.

For ordinary business correspondence, if your letter is taking up more than one side of two or three sheets, consider splitting the content between a shorter letter and an attachment or enclosure, such as a report.

The art of being concise in your letter writing can require considerable effort in the rewriting and editing stage. Philosopher Blaise Pascal once wrote to a friend and apologized for sending a long letter. He said, "I would have written a shorter letter, but I didn't have the time."

Proofreading Tips

It may be unfair, but people judge you by the words you use. They also judge you by whether you spell those words correctly, which is why proofreading is so important.

In today's computer age, nearly everyone has spell-checking capability — often as part of an e-mail or word-processing program. You should run your copy through the spell-checker, but doing that alone is not enough. Recently an executive at a Big Six accounting firm sent a letter he had spell-checked to an important client, only to discover that he had described himself as a "Certified Pubic Accountant"!

Proof everything you write, but be aware that the more times you write and rewrite a document, the less able you become to proof it effectively. For this reason, you should have "volunteer proofreaders" lined up — coworkers, assistants, and colleagues — who can proof your letters on short notice.

If you have to proofread a document you have already written, rewritten, and read several times, here's a way to catch typos despite your reading fatigue: Proofread the document *backward.* Doing so forces you to read each word individually, and eliminates the natural tendency to concentrate on the whole sentence and its content. Result: You proof each word more carefully, and catch more typos.

Tone

The best way to write your letters is in your own natural style. Having said that, there may be occasions during which you want to modify your natural style to better fit the occasion and your audience. For instance, if you are a naturally upbeat, cheery person, you would want to use a more somber tone in a condolence note.

Let's look at four basic options for letter tone — forceful, passive, personal, and impersonal — including how and when to use each.

FORCEFUL TONE

Forceful tone is used when addressing subordinates or others who, basically, have to do what you tell them to do. You are not asking them; you are ordering them in no uncertain terms — which you can do, because you have the power.

This does not, however, give you license to be cavalier or crude. Indeed, the real skill is in getting people to follow your commands without harboring ill will toward you. To achieve a forceful tone in your writing:

1. Use the active voice.
2. Be direct.
3. Take a stand.
4. Avoid hedge phrases and weasel words — language that equivocates rather than speaks plainly and directly (e.g., "might," "may," "perhaps").
5. Be clear.
6. Be positive.
7. Don't qualify or apologize.

[*For examples of forceful tone, see the section titled* Collection Series *in Part VIII.*]

PASSIVE TONE

Passive tone is used when addressing superiors and others who, basically, you have to listen to and please — bosses, customers, clients. To achieve a passive tone in your writing:

1. Suggest and imply.
2. Do not insist or command.
3. Use the passive voice when possible.
4. Do not pinpoint cause and effect (e.g., solve the problem, but do not look to lay blame on the reader or anyone else).
5. Use qualifiers (for example, "might be," "may," "approximately," "roughly").
6. Divert attention from the problem to the solution.
7. Focus on the solution to the problem, rather than assigning blame.

[*For an example of passive tone, see the letter titled* "We Need to Hear From You" *in Part VI.*]

PERSONAL TONE

Personal tone is used when you want to give support or establish or improve a relationship. It is most appropriately used with people you know, rather than strangers, or at least with people whose situations you know about and empathize with. To achieve a personal tone in your writing:

1. Be warm.
2. Use the active voice.
3. Use personal pronouns ("I," "we," "you," and so forth).
4. Use the person's name.
5. Use contractions (we'll, it's, they're, can't).
6. Write in a natural, conversational style.
7. Write in the first person ("I") and in the second person ("you").
8. Vary sentence length.
9. Let your personality shine through in your writing.

[*There are many examples of personal tone in Part II, Personal Correspondence.*]

IMPERSONAL TONE

Impersonal tone is used when you either want to keep a relationship on a strictly professional level, or when you want to distance yourself from the other person or the subject at hand. Impersonal tone is also used when the relationship is adversarial, or to stress the urgency and serious nature of the situation being written about. To achieve an impersonal tone in your writing:

1. Do not use the person's name.
2. Avoid personal pronouns when possible.
3. Use the passive voice when possible.
4. Write in the third person (for example, "the company," "the vendor," "the purchasing department," "the client").
5. Write in a corporate or formal style.
6. Be remote and aloof.

[*For examples of impersonal tone, see the letters titled* "Requests for Compliance" *and* "Request for Vendor Tax ID or Social Security" *in Part IX.*]

Layouts and Supplies

The appendix gives illustrations of the various formats and layouts for letters, memos, e-mails, and other documents. You can't go wrong following these models.

Do not overly concern yourself with questions of precise style. The reader does not really care whether the left margin is ½-inch or ¾-inch, as long as the letter is easy to read.

Here are a few quick rules for clear, easy-to-read letter layouts:

- Single-space copy; double-space between paragraphs.
- Indenting the first line of each paragraph five spaces makes the letter easier to read.
- Use generous margins — at least a half-inch bottom, top, and right, and maybe a little more on the left.
- Margins should be flush left and ragged right. Flush left means the first letters of each line are vertically aligned, creating a straight edge on the left. Ragged right means the right-hand border of the text is not neatly lined up.
- Do not try to cram too much text onto the page for the sake of keeping your letter to one page. It's better to either cut copy, or spread the copy out onto a second page.
- Sign in blue ink. It makes the live signature stand out more.
- Enclose your business card, unless you are sending a personal letter.

TYPE STYLES, FONTS, AND SIZES

Use a plain, simple type for body copy. Times Roman is clean and a favorite with many PC users. You can use New Courier or Prestige Elite, which gives the look and feel of a letter typed on an IBM Selectric typewriter. Many older readers associate this look with a personal letter versus computer fonts, which look more impersonal.

Type size depends on the style selected. For New Courier, you can use 9- or 10-point type. For Times Roman, 11- or 12-point type is better.

Boldface and italic fonts can be used for emphasis. Bullets or numbers help set lists apart and make them easy to scan.

For longer documents, you might consider breaking up the text into short sections, each with a boldface subhead.

LETTERHEAD

You can type your name, return address, and other contact information at the top of every letter on a plain sheet, or have letterhead made up by a printer. Many people have personal letterhead; virtually every business also uses preprinted letterhead, adding the company name and logo at the top.

Before you have your business letterhead printed, look at the layout prepared by your graphic artist or printer. Some layouts that take a creative approach may be graphically bold, but take up much space that could otherwise be used for letter text. Therefore you can fit far less copy on a single page than you would like, and are forced to use a second sheet (second page) to continue.

Much better is to have a letterhead design that allows maximum space for letter text. That way even if you have a lot to say, you can fit it comfortably on one page.

"Second sheets" are pages of letterhead designed specifically to be used as the second and third pages in a multipage letter. Some people use the same letterhead for every page, but this is unnecessary, unwieldy, and unusual. Most people use second sheets that have no printing on them, but are of the same paper stock of their letterhead. That way, the first and subsequent pages are all on the same stock.

Speaking of paper stock, your best bet is white, off-white, or cream colored. These light colors allow major contrast between the paper and the black type. Letterhead that is gray, medium brown, red, or another dark color makes it difficult for your reader to photocopy or fax your letter, which many people want to do.

Enclosures

We want to keep most of our letters to one or at most two pages, but sometimes we have a lot more than one or two pages worth of information to convey.

To solve this problem, you may want to limit your letter to an overview or summary, and put the details in one or more enclosures. These may be documents you write. Or you might enclose documents already produced by other sources.

Beware of overwhelming your correspondent with paper and information. People are busy today. Do they really need all that stuff you are cramming into the envelope? Or would it be better to condense it in a one or two-page summary, and offer to send more details if they are interested?

When you are discussing a topic in an e-mail, do not send the "enclosures" or supplementary materials as attached files unless you know the recipient and he knows you. People are rightfully wary of opening up attached files from strangers, for fear of getting a computer virus.

An alternative to attaching files to an e-mail message is to post the supplementary information on a Web site, and then to embed links to the Web site's general URL or, even better, to the specific Web page you want the person to read in the person's e-mail message. They can just click on the link to instantly access the supplementary material.

OUTER ENVELOPES

The most common choice for business correspondence is the #10 [*see Glossary*] envelope. A standard 8½- by 11-inch piece of letterhead, folded twice horizontally into three sections, fits perfectly in a #10 envelope.

If you have bulky enclosures, you may want to use a "jumbo," or 9- by 12-inch envelope. This allows you to enclose literature and other materials without having to fold them.

For personal mail, you can use either a #10 envelope or a smaller, Monarch [*see Glossary*] envelope. The Monarch envelope has a slightly more personal touch, since businesses rarely use it. Monarch envelopes and stationery work well for short letters; for longer correspondence, standard #10 letterhead (fitting #10 envelopes) give more room for text.

On the back flap or in the upper left corner of the front of your envelope (known as the "corner card"), have your name and address for your personal letterhead. For your business letterhead, have your company name and address.

When you are sending correspondence or enclosed material that the customer requested, use a red rubber stamp with the words "Here is the information you requested" on the front of the envelope. This is an indication that the recipient asked you to send the letter and it is not unsolicited.

STAMPS, METERS, PREPRINTED INDICIAS

There are three ways to handle the postage for your letter: stamps, meters, and preprinted indicias (preprinted postal permits).

The main thing when sending business letters is you want your letters to look like individual correspondence, not direct mail. The reason? Personal mail gets read, while promotional mail often gets tossed in the trash.

The postage stamp is the best choice for doing this. If you want to get extra attention, try using an unusual stamp, such as a commemorative. Another technique that gains attention is to use several stamps of smaller denominations instead of a single stamp for the correct amount.

Second-best to stamps is a postage meter. Enough businesses use postage meters for individual correspondence that it has an acceptable look and does not smack of advertising.

Least desirable is a preprinted indicia. Since so many mass mailers use indicias in their direct mail campaigns, your reader might think your personal letter is direct mail (if you have used an indicia) and mistakenly toss it.

Even if your letter is direct mail and you are sending it bulk rate, a little-known fact is that you can use a third-class stamp instead of an indicia. This gives your direct mail a more personalized look, and hence a better chance of being opened and read.

Overcoming Writer's Block

Writer's Block isn't just for professional writers; it can afflict executives and managers too. Writer's Block is the inability to start putting words on paper, and it stems from anxiety and fear of writing.

Here are a few tips to help you overcome Writer's Block:

- Break up the writing into short sections, and write one section at a time. Tackling many little writing assignments seems less formidable a task than taking on a large project all at once.
- Write the easy sections first. If you can't get a handle on the main argument of your report or paper, write the close. This will get you started and help build momentum.
- Write abstracts, introductions, and summaries last. Although they come first in the final document, it doesn't make sense to try to sum up a paper that hasn't been written yet.
- Avoid grammar-book rules that inhibit writers. One such rule says every paragraph must begin with a topic sentence (a first sentence that states the central idea of the paragraph). By insisting on topic sentences, teachers and editors throw up a block that prevents you from putting your thoughts on paper. Professional writers don't worry about topic sentences (or sentence diagrams or grammatical jargon or ending a sentence with a preposition). Neither should you.
- Sleep on it. Put your draft in a drawer and come back to it the next morning. Refreshed, you'll be able to edit and rewrite more effectively and with greater ease.

Letter-Writing Advice from Lewis Carroll

Lewis Carroll is best known as the author of *Alice in Wonderland*, but he was also an avid letter writer, especially personal letters to friends and colleagues.

In 1890, he wrote a small pamphlet with his advice on how to write better letters. An abbreviated and slightly edited version appears below.

Some of his advice, dated and charming, will give the twenty-first century reader a chuckle. But much of the author's letter-writing advice is still relevant and useful more than a century later.

How to Begin a Letter

If the letter is to be in answer to another, begin by getting out that other letter and reading it through, in order to refresh your memory, as to what it is you have to answer, and as to your correspondence's present address.

Next, address and stamp the envelope. "What! Before writing the letter?"

Most certainly. And I'll tell you what will happen if you don't. You will go on writing till the last moment, and, just in the middle of the last sentence, you will become aware that time's up!

Then comes the hurried wind-up-the wildly-scrawled signature . . . the hastily-fastened envelope, which comes open in the post . . . the address, a mere hieroglyphic . . . the horrible discovery that you've forgotten to replenish your stamp supply . . . the frantic appeal, to every one in the house, to lend you a stamp . . . the headlong rush to the post office, arriving, hot and gasping, just after the box has closed . . . and finally, a week afterwards, the return of the letter, from the Dead-Letter Office, marked "address illegible."

Next, put your own address, in full, as the top of the note-sheet. It is an aggravating thing — I speak from bitter experience — when a friend, staying at some new address, heads his letter "Dover," simply, assuming that you can get the rest of the address from his previous letter, which perhaps you have destroyed.

Next, put the date in full. It is another aggravating thing, when you wish, years afterwards, to arrange a series of letters, to find them dated "Feb. 17", "Aug. 2", without any year to guide you as to which comes first. And never, never put "Wednesday," simply, as the date. That way madness lies!

How to Go on With a Letter

Here is a golden rule to begin with. Write legibly. The average temper of the human race would be perceptibly sweetened, if everybody obeyed this rule!

A great deal of the bad writing in the world comes simply from writing too quickly. Of course you reply, "I do it to save time." A very good object, no doubt: but what right have you to do it at your friend's expense? Isn't his time as valuable as yours?

Years ago, I used to receive letters from a friend — and very interesting letters too — written in one of the most atrocious hands ever invented.

It generally took me about a week to read one of his letters! I used to carry it about in my pocket, and take it out at leisure times, to puzzle over the riddles which composed it — holding it in different positions, and at different distances, till at last the meaning of some hopeless scrawl would flash upon me, when I at once wrote down the English under it; and, when several had been thus guessed, the context would help one with the others, till at last the whole series of hieroglyphics was deciphered. If all one's friends wrote like that, life would be entirely spent in reading their letters!

This rule applies, specially, to names of people or places — and most specially, to names of people or places — and most especially to foreign names. I got a letter once, containing some Russian names, written in the same hasty scramble in which people often write "yours sincerely." The context, of course, didn't help in the least: and one spelling was just as likely as another, so far as I knew: it was necessary to write and tell my friend that I couldn't read any of them!

My second rule is, don't fill more than a page and a half with apologies for not having written sooner!

The best subject, to begin with, is your friend's last letter. Write with the letter open before you. Answer his questions, and make any remarks his letter suggests. Then go on to what you want to say yourself.

This arrangement is more courteous, and pleasanter for the reader, than to fill the letter with your own invaluable remarks, and then hastily answer your friend's questions in a postscript. Your friend is much more likely to enjoy your wit, after his own anxiety for information has been satisfied.

In referring to anything your friend has said in his letter, it is best to quote the exact words, and not to give a summary of them in your words, A's impression, of what B has said, expressed in A's words, will never convey to B the meaning of his own words.

This is especially necessary when some point has arisen as to which the two correspondents do not quite agree. There ought to be no opening for such writing as "You are quite mistaken in thinking I said so-and-so. It was not in the least my meaning," which tends to make a correspondence last for a lifetime.

A few more rules may fitly be given here, for correspondence that has unfortunately become controversial:

- Don't repeat yourself. When once you have said your say, fully and clearly, on a certain point, and have failed to convince your friend, drop that subject: to repeat your arguments, all over again, will simply lead to his doing the same; and so you will go on, like a circulating [repeating] decimal. Did you ever know a circulating decimal to come to an end?
- When you have written a letter that you feel may possibly irritate your friend, however necessary you may have felt it to so express yourself, put it aside till the next day.
- Then read it over again, and fancy it addressed to yourself. This will often lead to your writing it all over again, taking out a lot of the vinegar and pepper, and putting in honey instead, and thus making a much more palatable dish of it!
- If, when you have done your best to write inoffensively, you still feel that it will probably lead to further controversy, keep a copy of it. There is very little use, months afterwards, in pleading "I am almost sure I never expressed myself as you say: to the best of my recollection I said so-and-so". Far better to be able to write "I did not express myself so; these are the words I used."

- If your friend makes a severe remark, either leave it unnoticed, or make your reply distinctly less severe: and if he makes a friendly remark, tending towards 'making up,' let your reply be distinctly more friendly. If, in picking a quarrel, each party declined to go more than three-eighths of the way, and if, in making friends, each was ready to go five-eighths of the way — why, there would be more reconciliations than quarrels!

- Don't try to have the last word! How many a controversy would be nipped in the bud, if each was anxious to let the other have the last word! Never mind how telling a rejoinder you leave unuttered: never mind your friend's supposing that you are silent from lack of anything to say: let the thing drop, as soon as it is possible without discourtesy: remember 'speech is silvern, but silence is golden'!

- If it should ever occur to you to write, jestingly, in dispraise of your friend, be sure you exaggerate enough to make the jesting obvious: a word spoken in jest, but taken as earnest, may lead to very serious consequences. I have known it to lead to the breaking-off of a friendship.

  Suppose, for instance, you wish to remind your friend of a sovereign you have lent him, which he has forgotten to repay — you might quite mean the words "I mention it, as you seem to have a conveniently bad memory for debts", in jest: yet there would be nothing to wonder at if he took offence at that way of putting it.

  But, suppose you wrote "Long observation of your career, as a pickpocket and a burglar, has convinced me that my one lingering hope, for recovering that sovereign I lent you, is to say 'Pay up, or I'll summons yer'" he would indeed be a matter-of-fact friend if he took that as seriously meant!

- When you say, in your letter, "I enclose cheque for $5", or "I enclose John's letter for you to see", leave off writing for a moment — go and get the document referred to — and put it into the envelope. Otherwise, you are pretty certain to find it lying about, after the post has gone!

How to End a Letter

If doubtful whether to end with 'yours faithfully', or 'yours truly', or 'yours most truly', etc. (there are at least a dozen varieties, before you reach 'yours affectionately'), refer to your correspondent's last letter, and make your winding-up at least as friendly as his: in fact, even if a shade more friendly, it will do no harm!

A postscript is a very useful invention: but it is not meant to contain the real gist of the letter: it serves rather to throw into the shade any little matter we do not wish to make a fuss about.

For example, your friend had promised to execute a commission for you in town, but forgot it, thereby putting you to great inconvenience: and he now writes to apologize for his negligence.

It would be cruel, and needlessly crushing to make it the main subject of your reply. How much more gracefully it comes is "P.S. Don't distress yourself any more about having omitted that little matter in town. I won't deny that it did put my plans out a little, at the time: but it's all right now. I often forget things, myself: and 'those, who live in glass-houses, mustn't throw stones', you know!"

Persuasion in Print

A recent TV commercial informed viewers that the U.S. Post Office handles 300 million pieces of mail every day. That's a lot of letters. And letters are an important part of communicating with your customers, coworkers, and colleagues.

But how many letters actually get their messages across and motivate the reader? Surprisingly few. In direct-mail marketing, for example, a 2 percent response rate is exceptionally high. So a manufacturer mailing 1,000 sales letters expects that fewer than 20 people will respond to the pitch. If high-powered letters written by ad-agency copywriters produce such a limited response, you can see why letters written by busy business executives (who are not professional writers) may not always accomplish their objectives.

Failure to get to the point, technical jargon, pompous language, misreading the reader — these are the poor stylistic habits that cause others to ignore the letters we send. Part of the problem is that many managers and support staff don't know how to write persuasively.

There is a solution, stated as a formula first discovered by advertising writers, and it's called **AIDA.** AIDA stands for Attention, Interest, Desire, and Action — a sequence of psychological reactions that happen in the mind of the reader who is being sold on your idea. Briefly, here's how it works.

1. First, the letter gets the reader's attention with a hard-hitting lead paragraph that goes straight to the point or offers an element of intrigue.
2. Then, the letter hooks the reader's interest: The hook is often a clear statement of the reader's problems, needs, or wants. For example, if you are writing to a customer who received damaged goods, acknowledge the problem and then offer a solution.
3. Next, create desire. Your letter is an offer of something: a service, a product, goodwill, an agreement, a contract, a compromise, a consultation. Tell the reader how she will benefit from your offering. That creates a desire to cooperate with you.
4. Finally, call for action. Ask for the order, the signature, the donation, the assignment.

What follows are actual examples of how each of these steps has been used in business letters.

ATTENTION

Getting the reader's attention is a tough job. If your letter is boring, pompous, or says nothing of interest, you'll lose the reader. Fast!

One attention-getting technique used by successful writers is to open with an intriguing question or statement — a "teaser" that grabs the readers' attention and compels them to read on. Here's an opening teaser from a letter written by a freelance public relations writer to the head of a large PR firm:

> Is freelance a dirty word to you?

Even if you hate freelancers, you can't help but be curious about what follows. And what follows is a convincing argument to hire the writer:

> Is freelance a dirty word to you?
> It really shouldn't be, because in public relations, with its crisis-lull-crisis rhythm, really good freelancers can save you money and headaches. Use them when you need them. When you don't, they don't cost you a cent.
> Use me. I am a public-relations specialist with more than 20 years' experience in all phases of the profession. MY SERVICES ARE AVAILABLE TO YOU ON A FREELANCE BASIS . . .

Another freelance writer might use a more straightforward approach:

> Dear Mr. Mann:
> Congratulations on your new business. May you have great success and pleasure from it.
> I offer my services as a freelance public relations writer specializing in medical and technical subjects.

Here, the writer gets attention by opening with a subject that has a built-in appeal to the reader namely, the reader's own business. Most of us like to read about ourselves. And just about everybody would react favorably to the good wishes expressed in the second sentence.

INTEREST

Once you get the reader's attention, you've got to provide a "hook" to create real interest in your subject and keep them reading. This hook is a promise — a promise to solve problems, answer questions, or satisfy needs.

The hook is often written in a two-paragraph format: The first paragraph is a clear statement of the reader's needs, while the second shows how the writer can satisfy these needs. Here's the hook from a letter written by a job seeker to the vice president of one of the television networks:

> To stay ahead, you need aggressive people willing to take chances. People who are confident, flexible, dedicated. People who want to learn who are not afraid to ask questions.
> I am one of those people — one of the people you should have on your staff. Let me prove it. Start by reading my résumé. It shows I can take any challenge and succeed.

What better way to hold people's interest than to promise to solve their problems?

Here's an example of a two-paragraph (two-line) hook from a successful fundraising letter:

> Some day, you may need the Red Cross.
> But right now, the Red Cross needs you.

A principal rule of persuasive writing is: Remember that the reader isn't interested in you. The reader is interested in *the reader*. And because we want to hear about ourselves, the following letter was particularly effective in gaining and holding this author's interest:

> As you may already know, we have been doing some work for people who have the same last name as you do. Finally, after months of work, my new book, **THE AMAZING STORY OF THE BLYS IN AMERICA**, is ready for printing and you are in it!
> The Bly name is very rare and our research has shown that less than two one thousandths of one percent of the people in America share the Bly name . . . .

DESIRE

Get attention. Hook the reader's interest. Then create the desire to buy what you're selling, or do what you are asking.

This is the step where many businesspeople falter. Their corporate backgrounds condition them to write business letters in "corporatese," so they fill paragraphs with pompous phrases, jargon, clichés, and windy sentences. Here's a real-life example from a major investment firm:

> All of the bonds in the above described account having been heretofore disposed of, we are this day terminating same. We accordingly enclose herein check in the amount of $22,000 same being your share realized therein, as per statement attached. Not withstanding the distribution to you of the described amount, you shall remain liable for your proportionate share.

Don't write to impress — write to express. State the facts, the features, and the benefits of your offer in plain, simple English.

Give the reader reasons why he or she should buy your product, give you the job, sign the contract, or approve the budget. Create a desire for what you're offering. Here's how the manager in charge of manufacturing persuaded the president to sign a purchase order for a $20,000 machine.

> I've enclosed a copy of my report, which includes an executive summary.
> As you can see, even at the low levels of production we've experienced recently, the T-1000 Automatic Wire-Wrap Machine can cut production time by 15 percent. At this rate, the machine will pay for itself within 14 months including its purchase price plus the cost of training operators.
> We've already discussed the employees' resistance to automation in the plant. As you know, we've held discussion groups on this subject over the past three months. And, an informal survey shows that 80 percent of our technicians dislike manual wire-wrap and would welcome automation in that area.

Benefits are spelled out. Anxieties are eliminated. The reader is given the reasons why the company should buy a T-1000. (And the president signed the order.)

ACTION

If you've carried AIDA this far, you've gained attention, created interest, and turned that interest into desire. The reader wants what you're selling, or at least has been persuaded to see your point of view. Now comes the last step — asking for action.

If you're selling consulting services, ask for a contract. If you want an interview, ask for it. If you're writing a fundraising letter, include a reply envelope and ask for a donation. In short, if you want your letter to get results, you have to ask for them.

Here's a letter from a customer who purchased a defective can of spray paint. Instead of just complaining or venting anger, she explains the problem and asks for a response:

> Recently, I purchased a can of your Permaspray spray paint. But when I tried using it, the nozzle broke off. I cannot reattach this nozzle, and the can, though full, will have to be thrown away.
> I am sure your product is generally well packaged; my can was probably a one-in-a-million defect. Would you please send a replacement can of white Permaspray? I would greatly appreciate it.

An exchange of business letters is usually an action-reaction situation. To move things along, determine the action you want your letter to generate and tell the reader about it.

Formulas have their limitations, and you can't force-fit every letter or memo into the AIDA framework. Short interoffice memos, for example, seldom require this degree of persuasiveness.

But when you're faced with more sophisticated writing tasks — a memo to motivate the sales force, a mailer to bring in orders, a letter to collect bad debts — AIDA can help. Get attention. Hook the reader's interest. Create a desire. Ask for action. And your letters will get better results.

Special Considerations for Writing about Technology

The modern business writer today is virtually forced to write about technology and technical matters because we live in a technological age. Three situations generally exist that are troublesome in this regard.

1. The first is a technician, such as an engineer or scientist, writing for a nontechnical reader, such as a consumer, patient, or executive. The main error is to assume the layperson has the same level of education, understanding, and interest in the topic as would a fellow technician.

    Technicians are interested in technical details. Executives don't care about the technical details; they are more focused on bottom-line results.

2. When writing scientist-to-scientist, overuse of jargon is not an insurmountable problem (though it may make for dull reading), because the recipient of the letter knows the same language you do.

    Or do they? Technology is so specialized today that the knowledge and background of one computer programmer versus another, or one civil engineer versus another, that technician A is not familiar with half the concepts and terms used by technician B. Do not assume that the reader knows everything you do. It is better to overexplain and be absolutely clear, than to underexplain and risk leaving the reader in the dark.

3. The third situation is a layperson writing to a scientist.

    The problem here: The writer does not understand the technology, and spends a lot of time teaching it to himself. Not desiring to put that education to waste, he explains it to the reader.

    Problem is, the reader already knows it. Technical people want technical information, not popular science. You need to find out what is new and important, and communicate that; the techie already has the foundation.

Below are time-tested tips for writing about technical subjects in a variety of situations:

- **Be technically accurate.** Being accurate means being truthful. Technical readers are among the most sophisticated of audiences. Technical know-how is their forte, and they'll be likely to spot any exaggerations, omissions, or "white lies" you make.

  Being accurate also means being specific. Writing that a piece of equipment "can handle your toughest injection molding jobs" is vague and meaningless to a technician; but saying that the machine "can handle pressures of up to 12,000 pounds" is honest, concrete, and useful.

  And, just as a stain on a sleeve can ruin the whole suit, a single technical inaccuracy can destroy the credibility of the entire promotion. All the persuasive writing skill in the world won't motivate the industrial buyer if he feels that you don't know what you're talking about.

- **Check the numbers.** Many of us were relieved to finish school because it meant we could finally get *away* from having to deal with numbers; all the math whizzes in our class went on to become computer programmers, accountants, and media buyers. But to write about many technical subjects, you've got to approach those members with a new-found respect.

  Just think of the disaster that would result if a misplaced decimal in a sales letter offered a one-year magazine subscription at $169.50, ten times the actual price of $16.95. You can see why this would stop sales cold.

  Well, the same goes for technical writing. Only, in technical writing, a misplaced decimal or other math mistake is less obvious to us, since the material is so highly technical.

  You would suspect an error in a mailer that advertised a $169.50 magazine subscription. But could you say, at a glance, whether the pore size in a reverse osmosis filter should be 0.005 or 0.00005 or 0.0005 microns? (How many of us even know what a micron is?) Yet, to the chemical engineer, the pore size of the filter may be as crucial as the price of the magazine subscription. Get it wrong, and you've lost a sale.

  All numbers in technical writing should be checked and double-checked by the writer, and ideally also by your technical people.

- **Be concise.** Engineers and managers are busy people. They don't have the time to read all the papers that cross their desks, so make your message brief and to the point.

  As Strunk and White point out in *The Elements of Style*, conciseness "requires not that the writer . . . avoid all detail and treat his subjects only in outline, but that *every word tell*."

Avoid redundancies, run-on sentences, wordy phrases, and other poor stylistic habits that take up space but add little to meaning or clarity. For example, don't write "water droplets condensed from atmospheric vapor and sufficiently massive to fall to earth's surface" when what you're talking about is "rain."

- **Simplify.** The key to good technical writing is to explain complex concepts and products clearly and directly. Avoid overly complicated narratives; write in plain, simple English. In the first draft of a letter about a pollution control device, the author wrote:

  > It is absolutely essential that the interior wall surface of the conduit be maintained in a wet condition, and that means be provided for wetting continually the peripheral interior wall surface during operation of the device, in order to avoid the accumulation of particulate matter about the interior surface area.

  Here's how, after rewriting, he simplified this bit of technical gobbledygook to make it more readable:

  > The interior wall must be continually wetted to avoid solids buildup.

- **Understand what is really important to the reader.** By talking with a few knowledgeable engineers, you can quickly grasp what aspects of a technical topic are of greatest interest to your audience.

  Because the subject matter is highly technical, you can't rely on your own feelings and intuition to select the key points. The benefits of buying a kitchen appliance or joining a record club are obvious, but how can a layman say what features of a multistage distillation system are important to the chemical engineer, and which are trivial?

- **Know how much to tell.** As discussed, different types of readers seek different levels of technical information. If you're writing for top management, keep it short and simple, and pile on the benefits. If you're pitching to technicians, be sure to include plenty of meaty technical information.

  Here's a description of a "Dry FGD System" (a large piece of industrial equipment) from a promotion aimed at plant engineers:

  > The average SO2 emission rate as determined in the outlet duct was 0.410 lb/106 Btu (176 ng/J). All emission rates were determined with F-factors calculated from flue gas analyses obtained with an Orsat analyzer during the course of each test run.

This will satisfy the technically curious buyer who wants to know *how* you determined your product specifications, not just what they are. But managers have little time or interest in the nitty-gritty; they want to know how the product can save them money and help improve their operations.

By comparison, a letter on this same Dry FGD System aimed at management takes a lighter, more sales-oriented tone:

> The Dry FCD System is a cost-effective alternative to conventional wet scrubbers for cleaning flue gas in coal-fired boilers. Fly ash and chemical waste are removed as an easily handled dry powder, not a wet sludge. And with dry systems, industrial and utility boilers can operate cleanly and reliably.

- **Don't forget the features.** By all means, stress benefits when writing to executives. But don't forget to include technical features as well. In the industrial marketplace, a pressure rating or the availability of certain materials of construction often mean the difference between a use or no-use decision.

  Although these features may seem boring or meaningless to you, they are important to the technical reader. Yes, discuss the bottom-line benefits. But be clear about what features deliver these benefits. Features and their benefits are often presented in "cause and effect" statements, such as:

  > Because the system uses L-band frequency and improved MTI (moving target indication), it can detect targets up to 50 times smaller than conventional S-band radars.
  > No mechanical systems or moving parts are required, which means that Hydro-Clean consumes less energy and takes less space than conventional pump driven clarifiers.
  > The geometric shape of the seal ring amplifies the force against the disc. As the pressure grows, so does the valve's sealing performance.

A tip: If you routinely write about a technical topic in which you are not an expert, go to the bookstore and buy a children's book on the subject. It will make everything crystal clear and understandable to you. Most specialized disciplines also have dictionaries of their terms; purchase one of these as well.

PART II

PERSONAL CORRESPONDENCE

If you read the personal letters of literary and historical figures, you'll notice three things:

- The leisurely tone and pace of the letters
- The length of the letters
- The large volume of correspondence sent and received

As recently as the 1950s, writing personal letters was an important communications vehicle for intelligent, educated people. Even many "average folk" — farmers, factory workers, day laborers, and homemakers — routinely wrote letters to friends and relatives. People looked forward to letters: writing them, sending them, receiving them, and reading them. Getting letters was an unexpected, welcome event, like unwrapping packages on Christmas Day.

Today, personal letter writing is a declining art. The stories of our lives are now told in short, abrupt, unliterary, and ungrammatical e-mails instead of thoughtfully written letters penned in elegant handwriting. Yet people still write letters: brothers write sisters, college students write home to Mom and Dad, parents write loving letters to children who are spending their first summer at sleep-away camp. Letters can still warm the heart, wash away fear and loneliness, and put a smile on Grandmother's face.

The overriding instruction for personal letters: Write from the heart in a positive, caring, giving tone. Warm letters have always had a powerful ability to build goodwill. And in an age of computers and e-mail, the old-fashioned personal letter stands out even more.

Letters that Strengthen Relationships

Some letters are written not merely to inform, but to strengthen the bond between you and the reader. Letters of congratulations, thank-you letters, acknowledgments, "get well" letters, letters of condolence and sympathy, letters from the heart: All of these go beyond mere routine correspondence; if done well, they are written straight from the heart and create an emotional response (e.g., gratitude, pleasure, and warm feelings) in the reader.

In today's mass-communicated society, the greeting card industry has moved to relieve time-pressured consumers of the responsibility of writing relationship-strengthening messages by writing generic messages in preprinted greeting cards. As appreciated as greeting cards may be — sending one is a thoughtful gesture — personalize the message by inserting your own letter into the store-bought card.

Another plus of writing letters by mail: Because most people wite e-mail messages today rather than letters, sending a personal letter makes you stand out and has greater impact than other more expedient forms of communication.

CONGRATULATIONS LETTERS

Achievement of a milestone — a birthday or anniversary, birth of a new child, getting a new job, buying a home, winning an award, getting married, an anniversary — is an ideal reason to send someone a letter of congratulations. The reader will be pleased that you remembered the event and took the time to acknowledge it in writing.

Format: [*See Appendix A:* Fig. A-1. Simple format for letters and memos.] Handwritten or typed/word-processed. Personal letterhead unless writing to a business colleague or acquaintance, in which case use company letterhead.

Style/Tone/Voice: Informal or formal, depending upon the occasion. Personal tone: friendly and enthusiastic, warm, and caring. Active voice. [*See Part I for more on these subjects.*]

Structure: (1) Offer congratulations, (2) Identify the event or reason, (3) Express a personal thought, (4) Restate congratulations.

Handy Phrases: I was thrilled to hear; Congratulations; You deserve it; I'm so happy for you.

See Also: *Part V:* Congratulations to an Individual or a Team.

Dear Parrish,

Wow! You've done it again. Congratulations!

I just read in NEPA Hotline that the direct mail package you wrote for Second Opinion just won a Gold Award for best promotion — your third time, I believe.

The client also gave you a wonderful plug in the article, noting that your DM packages for him have always been winners. That's an enviable track record few copywriters have ever achieved.

You must feel great, and I'm sure your clients are impressed, too. This should bring you a lot of new business — not that you need it.

Job well done, Parrish. I always learn a lot from you.

Sincerely,

Ben Carter

Tips for Writing Congratulations Letters

- Congratulate the reader for her achievement, accomplishment, anniversary, new child, or whatever.
- Tell her where you learned about the accomplishment.
- Add a comment of a personal nature (e.g., if the reader is a former teacher, tell him how much being in his class meant to you).

THANK-YOU LETTERS

In our fast-paced society, the polite act of writing thank-you letters has become increasingly rare. Many people prefer to thank people with a quick phone call or e-mail, rather than take the time to write and send a personal letter. *A note of advice:* Take the time. The extra effort will be appreciated and make you stand out from the crowd.

If you don't write thank-you letters, start now. Thank-you letters are critical to maintaining good relationships. Conversely, not sending a thank-you letter when one is called for can harm a relationship. You may think that other people don't care if you send a thank-you letter — but they do.

A wide variety of occasions are appropriate for sending thank-you letters. The most obvious is when you have received a gift. You should also thank people for favors, friendship, and effort expended on your behalf.

Format: [*See Appendix A:* Fig. A-1. Simple format for letters and memos.] Handwritten or typed/word-processed. Personal letterheads unless related to business; then use company letterhead.

Style/Tone/Voice: Informal or formal. Personal tone: Warm and cordial. Active voice. [*See Part I for more on these subjects.*]

Structure: (1) Begin with the words "thank you," (2) Tell the readers what you are thanking them for, (3) Express how much their gift or help has meant to you, (4) Close by thanking them a second time.

Handy Phrases: Thank you; Thanks so much; I appreciate; I am grateful.

See also: *Part II:* Acknowledgments; *Part IV:* Donation Thank-You Letters; *Part VI:* Holiday Season Thank-Yous to Valued Customers.

Dear Bernie,

Lisa and I are still talking about the great afternoon and evening you gave us in New York. It is an occasion that we will long remember.

Although you probably take New York in stride, everything we saw and did was a grand adventure: the boat trip around Manhattan Island, cocktails at the Stork Club, dinner at the Four Seasons, the famous cheesecake at Lindy's.

The buying trip was very successful, and my boss was immensely pleased with my selections. Never again will I believe the old adage, "You can't mix business with pleasure." You provided the pleasure — and, incidentally some of the business. Thank you!

Here's a letter you might send if you had asked for contributions to make the holiday season more special for an underprivileged girl or boy.

Dear Ms. Jones,

Thank you for sharing the holiday spirit with your sponsored child, Riquelina! Your generous gift of $25.00 will help us make this a memorable time of year for her, as well as for all sponsored children.

I'm happy to share with you what presents you have helped provide. These gifts have been carefully chosen, with input from the children and their families, to ensure the boys and girls receive items they will use and appreciate all year long.

Riquelina will receive a new shirt and a pair of pants. New clothing is always needed and appreciated, especially by older children. They're learning to take care with their appearance at this age, and new clothing helps raise their self-esteem.

Thank you, Ms. Jones, for remembering Riquelina this holiday season. Your caring support means so much! It's through the efforts of dedicated friends like you that we can continue to make a long-term, positive impact on the children's lives.

Sincerely,

James R. Cook
President

Tips for Writing Thank-You Letters

- Don't view writing a thank-you letter as a chore, as so many children do every year at Christmas and their birthday.
- Be enthusiastic and genuine. Even if you don't like something, there is always at least one nice thing you can find to say about it. So find it — and say it.
- Be warm. Write in a friendly, personal style.

ACKNOWLEDGMENTS

A specific category of thank-you is the acknowledgment of a gift given or a contribution made. An acknowledgment letter is similar to a thank-you note. If there is a difference, a thank-you note typically focuses on one short-term action, such as a birthday present you have received. An acknowledgment usually signifies something long term, such as the support a friend or relative has given you during a particularly difficult period.

Thank-you letters are event driven; for instance when your father co-signs for the loan on your first condo. An acknowledgment is emotion driven; for example, you feel an overwhelming need to thank your dad for all the love he has given you as a parent.

Both thank-you letters and acknowledgments cement your bond with the reader. But an acknowledgment may be even more powerful because it is not expected. Acknowledgment is a spontaneous act, compared with thanks, which are expected as the social norm.

Format: [*See Appendix A:* Fig. A-1. Simple format for letters and memos.] Handwritten or typed/word-processed. Personal letterhead unless sent to a boss or colleague; then use company letterhead.

Style/Tone/Voice: Informal or formal. With sincerity and a touch of humbleness. Active voice. [*See Part I for more on these subjects.*]

Structure: (1) Tell them why you are writing (remember, your letter is unexpected), (2) State what the readers have done for you, (3) Thank the readers, (4) Explain the positive effect the readers or their actions have had in your life, (5) Repeat the thank you in the close.

Handy Phrases: Thank you; I wanted to let you know; You may not be aware; Here's why I'm writing you today.

See also: *Part II:* Thank-You Letters; *Part IV:* Letters of Confirmation and Acknowledgement; *Part VI:* Order Acknowledgment.

Dear Amy, Bob, Alex, Stephen,

Thank you for the beautiful flowers. It brought so many ooohs and aahs from everyone who passed my room. They brought me such pleasure and really picked up my spirits.

Thank you for being so thoughtful, caring and wonderful — not only now, but as the most wonderful cousins I could ever hope to have.

Family is important, and your love and concern continue to give me joy and strength during my long recuperation.

Best wishes, love, and again — thanks!

Bill

Tips for Writing Acknowledgments

- Be sincere and, if appropriate, even emotional.
- Talk about only positive things; do not bring up any past conflicts or problems.
- Recall specific events, deeds, and reasons why you are acknowledging the reader.
- Indicate the beneficial effect the reader's actions have had on your life.

GET-WELL LETTERS

Social custom dictates that you send a get-well letter to anyone close to you who has suffered a prolonged or serious illness, is or has been hospitalized, or is recovering from an accident or surgery. If you send a get-well card, you can slip a letter inside it to add the more personal touch.

In addition to the obvious benefit of bringing a smile to the face of a person who needs to smile more, your letter may actually help bring about their recovery. Numerous studies have identified a clear link between attitude and wellness: Stress can make you sick, and positive emotions (faith, humor, happiness) can make you well.

Format: [*See Appendix A:* Fig. A-1. Simple format for letters and memos.] Handwritten or typed/word-processed. Personal letterhead.

Style/Tone/Voice: Informal and personal. Active voice. [*See Part I for more on these subjects.*]

Structure: (1) Say hello — greet the readers, (2) Acknowledge that they have not been feeling well, (3) Say that you hope they are doing/feeling better, (4) Express your wishes for a speedy and full recovery.

Handy Phrases: I was so sorry to hear; Thinking of you; Hoping for a speedy recovery; Get well soon; Can't wait to hear you're up and about.

See also: *Part II:* Letters of Condolence and Sympathy.

Dear Uncle Ira,

I'm glad you are home from the hospital and doing better.

An ulcer is not fun, but I know you are relieved that the doctors have ruled out anything more severe.

I suppose you will have to give up hot peppers and chili — not easy — but that's a small price to pay for staying out of the doctor's office.

Get well soon, so you can come and see the kids again.

Love,

Jeff

Tips for Writing Get-Well Letters

- Keep it brief.
- Do not minimize their condition or suffering.
- Wish for their fast and full recovery.
- Do not diagnose the reader's illness or give unsolicited medical advice — especially regarding supplements, untested treatments, or alternative medicine — unless you are a doctor.

LETTERS OF CONDOLENCE AND SYMPATHY

Misery does not always love company, but when people have problems, they can get by a little better with some help — or at least a shoulder to lean on — from their friends.

A letter of sympathy is also a letter of empathy, helping people get through tough times by showing them that they are not alone. They gain strength from knowing another person (you, the writer) has gone through something similar and survived, or at least understand what is happening and how they feel about it.

A condolence letter is a specialized form of sympathy. It is sent on the grimmest of occasions: when a loved one has passed away. Words usually fail at such a time, yet we must try to succeed with them anyway.

Condolence Letters

A condolence letter expresses feelings of sympathy, care, empathy, and concern when a person close to the reader has recently passed away. Since there is nothing you can really say to make things right, say as little as possible. A few words from the heart and the fact that you took the time to send a personal note are the appropriate communication here.

Format: [*See Appendix A:* Fig. A-1. Simple format for letters and memos.] Handwritten or typed/word-processed. Personal letterhead.

Style/Tone/Voice: Informal. Personal. Passive or active voice. [*See Part I for more on these subjects.*]

Structure: (1) Give the reader your sympathies, (2) Recall a personal anecdote involving the deceased, (3) Tell the reader how your life — and everyone else's — was made better for having known the person.

Handy Phrases: I was saddened to hear; I'm so sorry; I have many fond memories of [name]; You have my condolences; I'm thinking of you; My thoughts are with you.

See also: *Part II:* Sympathy Letters.

Dear Bert,

Dad told me about Sy's passing. I am so sorry. You have my condolences.

Sy was a great guy and one of the smartest men I have ever known. I will never forget when he tried out for the TV game show "Who, What, Where, and When" but wasn't selected because, while he knew every last fact about WW II, he didn't know the names of Donald Duck's nephews.

As a kid, I loved coming into Paterson to my dad's office and stopping by Sy's pawn shop to see all the watches, coins, and trinkets, which fascinated Sy and me too.

We will all miss him. He is at peace.

Tips for Writing Condolence Letters

- Remember, you are writing not for the dead person, but for the loved ones he or she left behind.
- Share a personal story or pleasant memory about the deceased.
- Do not make any negative comment about the deceased.
- Do not minimize the reader's grief or sorrow, or the tragedy of the deceased's passing.

Sympathy Letters

As discussed earlier, a letter of sympathy is also a letter of empathy, helping other people get through difficult periods by showing that you understand and are there for them. Occasions that call for a sympathy letter can include personal injury or illness, separation or divorce, loss of a job or going out of business, failing a grade or dropping out of college, or any other unpleasant or negative occurrence.

Format: [*See Appendix A:* Fig. A-1. Simple format for letters and memos.] Handwritten or typed/word-processed. Personal letterhead.

Style/Tone/Voice: Informal. Personal tone. Passive or active voice. [*See Part I for more on these subjects.*]

Structure: (1) Identify the problem or event warranting the sympathy, (2) Say how you came to know about it, (3) Express sympathies, (4) Put as positive a spin on the event as possible, without making light of it, (5) Share a relevant inspirational anecdote if applicable, (6) Close with an offer to help the person in some specific way.

Handy Phrases: You have my sympathies; I'm sorry; You are not alone in this; You're in my prayers; You will make it through this; All life experiences can be used as learning experiences to make us stronger; It's hard to be encouraged at a time like this, but; With my sincere concern.

See also: *Part II:* Condolence Letters; *Part III:* Letter to Unsuccessful Candidate.

Dear Arnie,

Your brother told me that, despite a great audition, you didn't get the lead in the senior play.

But as the understudy, you should learn the role as if you did have the lead. After all, people get sick. (They even break legs — hence the show-business expression, "Break a leg!")

And even if you do not act in this show, mastering such a difficult role as Robespierre will serve you well in your future acting endeavors.

I had a similar situation in school, though in a different area: I wanted to be editor of the school paper, but the teacher in charge picked another student.

I was crushed, but kept writing — and as you know, I now have a regular column in my industry trade paper. So persistence pays!

By the way, it's time you came into New York to see your old uncle. Pick whichever Broadway show you want. The tickets, and a great dinner, are on me — my treat.

Feel better, smile, and keep up your spirits. *You* are great, and that's all that matters!

Sincerely,

Uncle Andy

Tips for Writing Sympathy Letters

- Acknowledge the negativity, pain, and suffering the person may be enduring.
- Point out any positives that may result or be seen in the situation without minimizing the negatives.
- Offer your help — as generously as you are willing and feel comfortable.

LETTERS FROM THE HEART

Perhaps the best and finest use of personal letters is one sent from the heart, from one human being to another, as an act of kindness, with a message of hope, and a tone of warmth and caring. Often, such notes are sent on meaningful days or events, such as Valentine's Day, Mother's Day, or graduation day; but they are also appropriate any time the spirit moves you.

Format: [*See Appendix A:* Fig. A-1. Simple format for letters and memos.] Handwritten or typed/word-processed. Personal letterhead.

Style/Tone/Voice: Informal. Personal tone. Active voice. [*See Part I for more on these subjects.*]

Structure: Varies. No standard format.

Handy Phrases: None. Say what your heart tells you to say.

See also: None.

The letter below was written by a woman to a shy child who attended her granddaughter's birthday party.

Dear Craig,

It was such a great pleasure to meet you; I have hardly been able to stop thinking of you. Even though you needed to leave the party early, God allowed us to talk for quite some time.

You are a very special and wonderful boy, Craig, and I know as I write, that you will be lifted up in your life, and enjoy many happy times.

I hope you will feel free to write back, as I am so glad to know you. Please let me know how school is coming along and how your holidays are going.

With love and hugs,

Tips for Writing Letters from the Heart

- Allow your personality to shine through in your writing.
- Show your feelings. Express love, concern, and empathy.
- Offer to help the other person achieve their goal or attain greater happiness.

Information Letters

Unlike business letters, which are written mostly to inform or persuade, personal letters are usually not a primary medium for dissemination of information, although part of the content of any personal letter is often information (e.g., "Aunt Bess won first prize in the pie-baking contest at the county fair").

Two exceptions are personal update letters and the long-copy annual holiday letters sent by many families as a tradition to their relatives and friends.

HOLIDAY LETTERS

Many families send an annual holiday letter with or instead of a greeting card during December. Richard and Sharon Armstrong put an unusual twist on their annual Christmas letter: it is always signed (and allegedly written by!) one of the pets in the Armstrong household. The pet author refers to Richard and Sharon as "Mom and Dad" in the letter.

Format: [*See Appendix A:* Fig. A-1. Simple format for letters and memos.] Handwritten or typed/word-processed. Personal letterhead.

Style/Tone/Voice: Informal. Personal. Active tone [*See Part I for more on these subjects.*]

Structure: (1) Introduce the letter as your annual holiday message, (2) Relate the highlights of the year in some kind of structured order (e.g., chronological or in order of importance), (3) Close by wishing the reader a happy holiday.

Handy Phrases: Season's greetings; Happy holidays; Merry Christmas; Happy Hanukkah; It's that time of year again; I can't believe another whole year has passed.

See Also: *Part II:* Information Letters; *Part IV:* Cordial Contacts; *Part VI:* Holiday Season Thank-Yous to Valued Customers.

Dear Friends and Family,

Don't worry, Scooter is not dead. (Yet.) But he is fifteen years old, and let's face it, he won't be writing this Christmas newsletter forever. So this is what you might call a "transition" phase.

My name is Cicco (pronounced Cheek-oh). I'm a cockatiel. Since cockatiels have a life expectancy of twenty years or more, and since I'm only ten months old at the moment, I'm going to be the editor of this publication for quite a while, so you'd better start getting used to it.

Yes, old Scooter is quite out of his mind these days. He's sleeping 22 hours a day, and the two hours he's not sleeping just happen to fall between 2:00 AM and 4:00 AM each night, during which time he barks, growls, whines, paces, stares into space, and generally does a good imitation of a 10-week-old puppy — except for the loving and affectionate part, which he can't seem to muster up anymore. By combining a new canine senility drug called "Anipryl" with an old favorite called "Valium," we have attained just enough chemical equilibrium in the household to keep him happily alive for a while longer.

But other than Scooter's "long goodbye," the year 2000 has been a good one in the Armstrong household. Mom, in particular, had what professional athletes sometimes describe as a "career year" because . . . well, she ended her career. Or at least the part of it that required her to dress in nice clothes, put an ID badge around her neck, and head off to work each morning. She is now a "consultant," which should come as no surprise, and what's more, she is a *successful* one. In just three months on her own, she has replaced her previous income, taken on scads of new clients, is working around the clock, and (this is new) seems to be enjoying every minute of it!

Dad, by contrast, begins to look more and more "retired" with each passing year. He's hanging around the church a lot, volunteering for odd jobs and committee assignments. His "work" consists of going into the office for a few hours each day, answering correspondence, and talking on the phone. He watches the stock ticker a lot (at least he did until April, now he can't bear to watch it). He plays a ton of golf. When people ask him when he plans to retire, he says, "I'm retired now." And truthfully, this has taken a lot of pressure off him.

Whew! Writing the Christmas letter is a big responsibility. I can see now why Scooter was so reluctant to give it up. But look, we live in a democratic system. I won the election fair and square. If Scooter wants to contest it in the courts, he's free to do so. But for now, I am newsletter editor-elect. And that gives me the privilege and honor of wishing each and every one of you a Merry Christmas and a Happy New Year!

Love,

Cicco

Tips for Writing Holiday Letters

- Have fun.
- Mention as many people on the distribution list as you can. People like to see their own name in print.
- When bragging a bit about accomplishments, use a bit of self-effacing humor to balance ego with humility.
- Mail the letter early, to compensate for the heavy workload of the post office during the holidays.
- Think about everyone receiving your letter. Do not say anything that would offend even one person or make them feel bad.

PERSONAL UPDATES

Perhaps the most common type of personal letter is the update letter. This is a letter that tells the reader what you have been up to since the last time the two of you communicated.

Format: [*See Appendix A:* Fig. A-1. Simple format for letters and memos.] Handwritten or typed/word-processed. Personal letterhead.

Style/Tone/Voice: Informal. Personal. Active voice. [*See Part I for more on these subjects.*]

Structure: (1) Greet the recipient, (2) Tell him there is no special reason you are writing and this is just a letter to keep in touch, (3) Update him on what's been going on, (4) Close with a conclusion or by encouraging the person to write back.

Handy Phrases: Just a short note to say "hi"; Hadn't heard from you in a while, so I thought I'd drop you a line; Hope things are well with you; write back when you can.

See also: *Part II:* Information Letters; *Part VI:* Cordial Contact; *Part VII:* After the Sale Letters.

October 22, 2002

Dear Jim,

I thought I'd drop you a line to tell you what's going on here. In a couple of minutes I will be heading toward the Recreation Center to at least lift some weights. I have given up riding the bicycle for a couple of weeks till my body can begin to deal with all the excess medications I am carrying. Since walking is a rather slow and laborious process right now, riding a bike is rather difficult.

I still go into the University every day and do my teaching and all other activities. I tell you, when I get home I am ready for bed. Still, I have kept up with my reading and some light home-improvement projects.

The weather has turned very nasty. A cold front has moved in bringing with it freezing drizzle along with a little snow. I had to scrape off the windows of the Subaru before taking Lillian to work. The ice was on in a solid mass so I chipped off what I could, ran the car with the defroster on, and set the heating elements for the rear window. I suppose we're in for another brutal Chicago winter.

Hope to hear from you soon,

Scott

Tips for Writing Update Letters

- Organize your points. Chronological order is often easiest and best. Or, you can present information in order of importance.

- Letters often get left lying around on the kitchen table. Don't write anything you wouldn't want other people in the reader's household to see.

- Include news of friends, relatives, and other people you have seen or spoken with that the reader knows.

FORMAL INFORMATION LETTERS

A formal information letter is a letter of a personal nature written to someone who is either a stranger or someone who you know, but not well.

Formal letters of information can introduce people to your group, inform them about an upcoming event, or announce important news.

Format: [*See Appendix A:* Fig. A-1. Simple format for letters and memos.] Typed or word-processed. Personal letterhead.

Style/Tone/Voice: Formal. Active tone. [*See Part I for more on these subjects.*]

Structure: (1) Open with brief synopsis of event or situation, (2) Convey all necessary information — the hows, whys, whens, wheres — as clearly and succinctly as possible, (3) Provide a means for the reader to gain additional information if he/she so desires (phone numbers of people to contact, Web sites to consult, etc.).

Handy Phrases: Here are the facts; You may not know that.

See also: *Part II:* Information Letters; *Part IV:* FYI Letters; *Part VI:* Relationship-Building Letters.

Dear Parent,

This year, as an enrichment opportunity through the SAGE program, Woodside School's fourth and fifth graders will have the opportunity to participate in the National Geographic Bee, between November 23 and January 13. This is a nationwide contest for schools in the United States. There are three levels of competition: school, state, and national. The winning student at Woodside must take a written, multiple choice "Qualifying Test," in order to compete for advancement to the state level. (The first place winner at the state level will proceed to the national level.)

Questions will require knowledge of place names or of the location of cultural and physical features. Students may be asked about cultural and physical regions or about physical phenomena, such as landforms, climate, bodies of water, soils, flora, and fauna. Tools geographers use, such as maps, instruments, graphs, and statistics, may be the subject of other questions.

If you would like to bone up on your geography skills you can visit one of these sites.

- GeoBee Challenge Game: Test yourself with five National Geographic Bee questions every day at http:www.nationalgeographic.com/geobee/
- GeoSpy Game: Can you find your way around a blank map? You are given the place-name, and have to click the correct location to win at http:www.nationalgeographic.com/kids/geospy/
- MapMachine Flags and Facts: Quick! What language do they speak in Malta? Find the answer in Flags and Facts — plus country and state profiles, statistics, flags, and maps. Go to http.plasma.nationalgeographic.com/mapmachine/ to learn more.

- Current Events: Listen to the news or read the newspaper to stay up to date on world-wide happenings.

Have fun!!!

Mrs. Wolf

Tips for Writing Formal Information Letters

- Omit needless detail. Tell the readers only what they need to know.
- Give just the important facts, not the whole background or history.
- Enclose or offer additional information for those readers who want detail, or refer them to a Web site where more information can be found.
- When a program, event, or other thing is new, say so.

ALUMNI LETTERS

One of the forms of writing that has the greatest potential for boredom and bad writing is the college alumni letter. Mature adults sometimes suddenly feel the need to pretend they have gone back in time, and write as they imagine a spirited, carefree 19-year-old would. As a result, many alumni letters are written in a cornball tone that decidedly fails to capture the spirit of college life as it was. Everyone is better served when you write in your natural voice of today, and limit the recall of yesteryear to the facts rather than the style.

Format: [*See Appendix A:* Fig. A-1. Simple format for letters and memos.] Typed/word-processed. Personal or business letterhead.

Style/Tone/Voice: Informal, even chummy. Active. [*See Part I for more on these subjects.*]

Structure: Varied. No standard format.

Handy Phrases: Greetings; It's been a while; It's me again.

See also: *Part II:* Information Letters; *Part IV:* FYI Letters.

Dear Classmates:

Two major events influence my current writing. The first was the class agents' meeting on September 16 and the second was our 45th reunion celebrations at the Sofitel and the next day at Gustavus the weekend of September 29–30.

First, the class agents' meeting. I was struck by the range of ages of the class agents all the way from young kids to the venerable sages of bygone eras. It reminded me of the broad continuum of affection and dedication to the Gustavus ideal that persists.

Currently Gustavus ranks 39th of 160 colleges in percentage of alumni giving. About 3,000 donors lapse each year! You may have heard of Guslink. That is a group of selected students who make calls on behalf of the Gustavus Fund. There are simply not enough callers from the alumni to cover all of our fellow Gustie grads. So please, give the Guslink callers a cordial welcome for their efforts in behalf of the Fund.

One other special note from the meeting. If you have news that you would like to have considered for the Gustavus *Quarterly*, send it directly to the *Quarterly*. Alumni news that agents receive is not automatically considered for the *Quarterly*.

My thanks go to Don "Swannie" Swanson for his planning and conducting of the reunion dinner at Sofitel. Although I was unable to be there, I heard rave reviews. The evening was highlighted by brief speeches from Eileen Eckberg Scott, George Torrey, Joan Bonn Wright, Phil Hall, Carol Roberg Lind, Einar Satter, Homer Russ, Phil Eckman, and Pat Hall.

On Saturday, Robert "Esby" Esbjornson honored and entertained us with his reflections on his career at Gustavus, much of which involved us. His remarks were framed in the context of a letter to a granddaughter, a clever device. The tear-filled eyes and loud applause attested to his eloquence. Certainly, the mentorship of professors like Esby has much to do with our continuing affection.

Swannie will be given the prestigious George Haun award presented by the MSHSCA. He will be given the award at the annual Hall of Fame awards banquet to be held on November 11 at the Four Points Sheraton Hotel in Minneapolis. Congratulations Swannie!

I wish you all an exciting fall and happy holiday season. Keep your cards and e-mails coming. So long for now.

Dick DeRemee

1955 Class Agent

Tips for Writing College Alumni Letters

- Name as many fellow alumni as you can in every letter of bulletin. People like to read their name in print.
- Publicize the activities and accomplishments of fellow alumni.
- Announce upcoming events
- Identify the needs of the school (funds, mentors for students, intern opportunities) and ask for help.

Requests

A request is a letter asking the recipient to do something he or she does not have to do, may not have time to do, or may not want to do. Therefore, pay particular attention to the structure given for each letter; these are time-tested formulas for persuasive writing that have been proven to work.

FAVOR REQUESTS

A letter is an ideal medium for requesting a favor. Making the request in writing allows the other person to think it over in the privacy of her own home or office, without the pressure of you standing there waiting for an answer, or the potential for embarrassment (for both of you) if you are turned down.

Format: [*See Appendix A:* Fig. A-1. Simple format for letters and memos.] Typed/word-processed. Personal letterhead.

Style/Tone/Voice: Formal. Active voice. [*See Part I for more on these subjects.*]

Structure: (1) Identify yourself if the reader does not already know you, (2) State the reason you are writing, (3) Say exactly what the request is, (4) Show the reader why it behooves him to comply with your request, (5) Address and answer any objections he is likely to have, (6) Ask for the specific action, including what you want done and by when.

Handy Phrases: Please; Thank you; I'd sure appreciate it if; I would be in your debt; I would be grateful if.

See also: *Part III:* Inquiring about a Job Opening; *Part IV:* Requests for Information; *Part V:* Requesting a Meeting; *Part VIII:* Requesting Credit; *Part IX:* Request for Estimate.

Ms. Helen Cornell, CAE, CMP
Executive Director
CFCE Education Foundation
Senior Vice President, Education
CFCE
1300 East Eight Mile, Suite 110
Pontiac, MI 43320

Dear Helen:

I'm the author of *Last Minute Meetings, a* book I hope you'll consider for possible inclusion in your catalog and offerings.

Last Minute Meetings provides numerous up-to-date resources and ideas to help plan a meeting — quickly, if need be, and on budget.

This book would be an excellent fit with your current offerings. For people new to the industry, it explains in simple language the details involved in planning a successful event — giving lots of real-life examples and forms. Industry veterans can use the book as a resource guide to find vendors as well as definitive "best sources".

I have enclosed a review copy. *Last Minute Meetings* is published by Career Press (Franklin Lakes, NJ; December 2000) and retails for $11.99. I've included a few recent book reviews as well as a brief bio.

I look forward to the possibility of working together to bring this book into your offering.

Regards.

Fern Dickey, CMP

Tips for Requesting a Favor

- Ask politely. Do not demand or threaten.
- Show the reader what's in it for her. Prove your case.
- Say exactly what you hope she will do for you.

INVITATIONS TO EVENTS

An invitation is a request to attend an event. It could be an invitation to a barbecue, a night at the theater, your child's violin recital, a birthday or anniversary party, a housewarming, a wedding, or a bar/bat mitzvah, to name just a few possibilities. It could be a formal event or a casual one, even a religious event.

Format: [*See Appendix A:* Fig. A-1. Flier.] Handwritten, typed/word-processed, or desktop-published. Preprinted invitation or card.

Style/Tone/Voice: Informal. Active voice. [*See Part I for more on these subjects.*]

Structure: What, when (be specific), where (include address; also a map, if necessary), charge (if any), R.S.V.P., dress (casual, costume, etc.)

Handy Phrases: R.S.V.P.

See also: *Part IV:* Invitations; *Part VII:* Selling By Invitation.

TO: Jeffrey Cohen

WHAT: Stephen Cammito's 10th birthday party.

WHEN: Saturday, October 9, 3pm–5pm

WHERE: SportWorld Amusements, 345 Arcadia Road, Anytown, USA

* Games
* Rides
* Laser tag
* Indoor mini-golf
* Pizza and soft drinks+
* Birthday cake+

+ For parents, too!

Casual dress — wear something comfortable!

R.S.V.P.! 555-5555

Here is another informal invitation example:

> Dear Dr. and Mrs. Davidson,
>
> We will be celebrating Paula and Steve's thirtieth year of ministry with a dinner at the Flori-bunda Commons Restaurant, Saturday, November 29th, at 8:00 p.m. Please let us know by Monday the 24th if you can join us on this happy occasion.
>
> With love,

Tips for Writing Invitations to Events

- Describe the event.
- Be sure to cover the details: location, time, date, dress, directions.
- Provide a reply card, e-mail address, or phone number for responding.

Because there are many good and widely available sources for examples of wedding invitations — a specific type of formal invitation that carries with it certain codes of etiquette — this section will cover other formal invitations relating to the celebrations of "life milestones," such as significant anniversaries, bar/bat mitzvahs, and so forth.

Format: [*See Appendix A:* Fig. A-1. Flier.] Handwritten, word-processed, or desktop published; engraved or preprinted invitation or card. R.S.V.P. (usually on separate card)

Style/Tone/Voice: Formal. Active or passive voice. [*See Part I for more on these subjects.*]

Structure: (1) State the occasion, (2) State when (be specific), where (include address; also a map, if necessary), (3) R.S.V.P., (4) Other information, e.g. a luncheon will be held, formal dress is required (white/black tie, etc.)

Handy Phrases: R.S.V.P.; We invite you to share our joy; Request the pleasure of your company.

See also: *Part IV:* Invitations; *Part VII:* Selling By Invitation.

The following invitation could be easily adapted to a bar mitzvah as well.

> We invite you to share our joy and love as our daughter
>
> Esther Hannah
>
> is called to the Torah as a Bat Mitzvah
>
> January 25, 2003 at 10:30 in the morning.
>
> Congregation Beth Zion
>
> Jackson, New Jersey
>
> Kiddush following services
>
> Mr. and Mrs. Samuel Silverstein

Formal invitations are often sent out for significant milestones, such as a fiftieth wedding anniversary.

> Twila Lockard Davis and Gladys Lockard
>
> invite you to an
>
> Open House
>
> celebrating the fiftieth wedding anniversary of our parents,
>
> Thomas and Susannah Lockard
>
> Saturday, May 25th, 2002
>
> from 3:00 to 5:00 p.m.
>
> at the home of
>
> Dr. and Mrs. David Hasbro
>
> 4776 Wailing Wind Dr.
>
> Indiana, Pennsylvania
>
> Please no presents, just your presence!

They may also be used for significant events, such as the opening of a new enterprise, as seen in the sample that follows.

Rita Fiorentino

requests the pleasure of your company

at

The Grand Opening Celebration

of

The Gathering Together

Sunday, the ninth of November, two thousand and three

from

three o'clock until seven o'clock in the evening

202 N. Elm St.

Locust Valley, IN

Tips for Writing Formal Invitations

- The phrase "request(s) the honour of your presence" is reserved for wedding invitations; however the phrase "request(s) the pleasure of your company" is appropriate in any formal invitation.

- If you must cancel a formal invitation, use the same format and style as that of the original invitation (if you have time to do so; otherwise phone the invited guests).

- Send invitations well in advance (six weeks is not too early), particularly if you have invited out-of-town guests to the event.

LOCAL FUNDRAISING REQUESTS

Communities often get involved in raising funds for worthy causes, and some day you may be asked to write a letter to help solicit donations. You may also be writing on your own to support a cause you believe in. You could also be writing on behalf of a church group or club.

Format: [*See Appendix A:* Fig. A-1. Simple format for letters and memos.] Typed/word-processed. Personal letterhead.

Style/Tone/Voice: Informal or formal. Active voice. [*See Part I for more on these subjects.*]

Structure: (1) Identify your organization, (2) State the purpose or cause for which you are raising money, (3) Say exactly what the money will be used for, (4) Make an appeal to both the readers' emotions and logical side to persuade them to contribute, (5) Ask for the money, and (6) Thank them in advance for their generosity.

Handy Phrases: Can you help us?; Our need is urgent; We need your help; Your support is important to us.

See also: *Part IV:* Funding and Donation Requests; *Part VII:* Non-Profit Fundraising.

Dear Friends and Colleagues,

As many of you know, this past March my father-in-law underwent a kidney transplant. This fall I will be taking part in the **Walk 5 to Win the Fight Against Diseases of the Kidney.** I am participating in recognition of everything he has gone through over the course of this year and in appreciation for all of the support he has enjoyed from organizations, hospitals, and individuals.

The walk is offered in support of the **State Chapter of the Foundation for Kidney Research.** The foundation seeks to raise funds in support of their three main goals: to increase public awareness of kidney diseases, to promote and implement medical education programs, and to establish nationwide research programs.

The walk will be held on October 4, 2004 and I am writing to you to solicit pledges for my walk. Any pledge amount would be greatly appreciated. I need to raise at least $100 to participate in the walk, but have set a personal goal of contributing $250. I will be collecting pledges from now until October 3rd. You can show your support by dropping by or e-mailing me with your pledge amount.

Thanks to all of you for taking the time to consider my request. Diseases of the kidneys are devastating and I am pleased to be able to help in some small way to further research and education for this cause.

Sincerely,

Tips for Writing Local Fundraising Letters

- Identify yourself as a member of the reader's community or a local organization.
- Say how the donation will help improve the lives of people in the area or enhance community life, if this is the case.
- Tell the reader whom to make the check out to and where to send it. Give a deadline for doing so.

REFUSING A REQUEST

A letter is also an ideal medium for refusing requests as well as making them. When you say "no" to someone in person, they can employ a variety of techniques that at best are uncomfortable and at worst can pressure you to change your mind. But a letter doesn't bend in the face of pleading or sad faces; its "no" stands firm.

Format: [*See Appendix A:* Fig. A-1. Simple format for letters and memos.] Typed/word-processed. Personal or business letterhead.

Style/Tone/Voice: Formal. Passive or active voice. [*See Part I for more on these subjects.*]

Structure: (1) Thank the writer for her request, (2) Turn her down gently, (3) Give the reasons why you are doing so, (4) If appropriate, offer her an alternative to her original request.

Handy Phrases: Thanks for your interest; Thanks for your concern; I appreciate your offer; I'm flattered; Unfortunately; I'm afraid I'm unable.

See also: *Part III:* Letter to Unsuccessful Candidate; *Part IV:* Refusing Business Requests; *Part VIII:* Turning Down a Request for Credit; *Part IX:* Notification of Loss to Losing Bidder.

Dear Mr. Dennison:

Thanks for thinking of me as a sponsor of your boycott.

Like you, Mr. Dennison, I want our children to grow up in a moral society, But I'm afraid I can't give you permission to use my name as a supporter for Parents for Library Censorship.

The fact is, you and I are on different sides of this issue — namely, I am *for* freedom of speech and *against* censorship in any form.

While I agree with you that some of the books on the list are of questionable quality and taste, I also feel just as strongly that no one person or organization has the right to determine what is "suitable" literature for other people.

I spoke out very strongly against library censorship at a recent parent-teachers meeting and I will do likewise when I have the opportunity.

Very truly yours,

Tips for Refusing a Request

- To put an end to the matter and avoid further discussion, say no emphatically. Don't beat around the bush.
- Give the reasons why you are refusing the request.
- Make it clear that your refusal is not a reflection on the character of the reader or the worthiness of his request; it is just the best decision for you at this time.

LETTER GRANTING A REQUEST

A more pleasant writing task is composing a letter granting a request. Your job is easy, because you are delivering happy news.

Format: [*See Appendix A:* Fig. A-1. Simple format for letters and memos.] Handwritten or typed/word-processed. Personal letterhead.

Style/Tone/Voice: Informal or formal. Active voice. [*See Part I for more on these subjects.*]

Structure: (1) Give the good news in the first paragraph, (2) Say what you are doing, (3) Say why you are doing it, (4) Offer any advice or instruction you may wish to give, (5) Wish the reader luck, and (6) Ask for a progress report or other feedback, if you are interested.

Handy Phrases: I have some good news for you; I'm writing in response to your request for; It's my pleasure; I'm happy to be able to; I'm delighted to be able to help you.

continued

continued

See also: *Part III:* Offering a Candidate a Position; *Part IV:* Responding to Business Requests; *Part VI:* Order Acknowledgment; *Part VII:* Sales Agreements; *Part IX:* Letters Regarding Bids, Contracts, and Agreements.

Dear Mr. Hatch:

I received your letter today, and I am happy to grant permission for you to reprint my father's war diaries, in whole or in part, in the book you are writing on World War II.

While Dad was not a talkative man, I know he had some extraordinary experiences during the war, and it pleases me that you feel they are of historical importance.

If you wish, I can arrange for you to go through his medals, memorabilia, and other personal files, although I am not sure anything there will be of use to you.

Good luck with your book project! Please let me know when it is published.

Thanks,

Axel Andersson

Tips for Granting a Request

- Be specific about what you are agreeing to and what you are not.
- Don't be afraid to ask for something in return. Remember, you are doing the other person a favor.
- Follow up on your promises. If your letter promises an action, do what you said you would do.

LETTERS TO YOUR LANDLORD

A common problem for tenants is repeatedly asking the landlord or super to fix things in the apartment, only to get the runaround. If this persists, send a letter.

Format: [*See Appendix A:* Fig. A-1. Simple format for letters and memos.] Typed/word-processed. Personal letterhead. ***Note:*** If you have your own business and work at home, do not use your business letterhead, lest you alert the landlord that you are running a business in his building.

Style/Tone/Voice: Formal. Polite but firm. Active voice. [*See Part I for more on these subjects.*]

Structure: (1) State the problem, (2) Remind the landlord of your previous communications concerning this problem, if applicable, (3) List the negative consequences of the problem as it relates to the landlord's needs and concerns (e.g., a leaky roof is damaging the building), (4) Ask him to fix the problem, (5) Give a time frame by which you expect this work to be completed.

Handy Phrases: I need to hear from you; When may I expect this problem to be resolved; I think you'll agree I've always been a model tenant.

See also: *Part IV:* Business Requests; *Part V:* Internal Requests; *Part VI:* Sensitive Customer Correspondence; *Part IX:* Letters Requesting Information.

Dear NAME,

This letter is to inform you that the following conditions in my apartment are in need of repair:

_____

_____

_____

The Ohio Landlord-Tenant Law (ORC 5321.04) requires you to keep this rental unit in a fit and habitable condition and to make all repairs.

If the above conditions are not corrected within a reasonable time, not to exceed thirty days, I may exercise my right to deposit my rent with the Clerk of Municipal Court, or apply to the Court for an order to correct the conditions, or terminate my rental agreement as provided for in Section 5321.07 of the Ohio Revised Code.

I think you'll agree I've been a model tenant, but these problems must be fixed. Thank you for your cooperation. I am sure that you will take care of these conditions so that no further action is necessary.

Sincerely,

Bob Jones

Tips for Writing to Your Landlord

- Check your lease and understand your rights before lodging a complaint.

- In a series of letters, start gently, and then get increasingly insistent if you do not get a positive response (the letter above was sent only after three other letters failed to get the landlord's attention).

- Send the letter certified mail, return receipt requested, for proof of delivery. Mail it at the post office. Do not drop it off.

- Do not browbeat the landlord, insult him, or trade barbs. If you anger the landlord, he will take every legal means to evict you, and you may find yourself looking for a new home.

Letters that Require Special Handling

No, this heading doesn't mean you'll require a special postal sticker on your envelope. We're talking instead about letters that deal with sensitive and delicate situations: apologies, complaints, and advice.

Apologies are difficult because we may not feel we were wrong, but making a "partial apology" is ineffective. Complaints are difficult because people often react negatively to criticism.

Advice and motivation are also problematic. If the advice is unsolicited, you may think twice about giving it — unsolicited suggestions are frequently poorly received. If the advice is solicited, be aware that the recipient may not really want to know the truth, but rather have you confirm his opinion or conclusion, whether it's right or not.

One universal tip for all of the special situation letters shown in this section: After writing the letter, put it aside. Sleep on it. Read the letter again the next morning. Then, if you are still confident in your copy, send it along.

LETTER OF APOLOGY

When you have had difficulty or a conflict with a person, a letter of apology can be effective in setting things right. Apologizing by letter permits the other person to accept your apology, without argument or waffling. It also eliminates your desire to want to retract part of it or argue over the history of the incident.

At the same time, do not turn to letters simply to distance yourself from a difficult situation or protect yourself from a situation that may become confrontational. The advantage of letter writing is that you can take your time composing your thoughts, and the recipient can similarly take her time considering your message and deciding how to respond.

Format: [*See Appendix A:* Fig. A-1. Simple format for letters and memos.] Handwritten or typed/word-processed. Personal letterhead.

Style/Tone/Voice: Formal. Active voice. [*See Part I for more on these subjects.*]

Structure: (1) Recall the specific incident, (2) Apologize unconditionally, but (3) Let the reader know about any mitigating circumstances, if they exist, (4) Repeat your apology, and (5) Close by saying you look forward to continuing the relationship.

Handy Phrases: Sincere regrets; I'm sorry; I was wrong; I made a mistake.

See also: *Part VI:* Resolving Problems.

Dear Steven:

My comments about your playing last Thursday had only the best intention. Any suggestions I make are only to make you a better player. You're already so good, I didn't think my suggestion would upset you.

I am sorry my words upset you. From now on, I'll think more carefully about how I say things before I say them. My job is to teach *and* motivate you, and obviously I let you down in the latter. My apologies.

Sincerely,

Tips for Writing Letters of Apology

- Apologize unconditionally.
- Admit you were wrong. Accept the blame even if the other person is not in fact blameless.
- Be the bigger person. Don't be petty or search for ways in which they previously did you wrong as a way of compensating for today's apology.

LETTER OF COMPLAINT

Unfortunately, there are many things to complain about in the world today, from poor service in a restaurant or store, to the high price of gasoline and rising income taxes.

Complaints are often most effective when made in writing. There are two advantages to writing a complaint letter rather than talking about it. First, you feel better. And second, the person or organization causing the problem takes you much more seriously when you commit your thoughts to paper.

Format: [*See Appendix A:* Fig. A-1. Simple format for letters and memos.] Typed/word-processed. Personal letterhead.

Style/Tone/Voice: Formal. Cool and collected, but serious in your resolve. Active voice. [*See Part I for more on these subjects.*]

Structure: (1) Recall the specific incident, (2) State your specific complaint, (3) Give appropriate, specific details, (4) Enclose and cite any backup proof or documents (e.g., a previous letter from the reader), (5) Say what you expect the reader to do, if appropriate, (6) Close by saying you look forward to a speedy resolution and to continuing the relationship.

Handy Phrases: I want to bring [blank] to your attention; Are you aware that; You may not be aware that; Do you think; Do you feel.

See also: *Part II:* Letters to Editors; Letters to Elected Officials; *Part IX:* Letters Expressing Dissatisfaction.

September 10, 2004
Mr. Roger Beecher
Learn It Now! Network
Anytown, USA

Dear Roger:

I attended "Cold-Calling for the Non-Salesperson" last night and thoroughly enjoyed the session. However, I did want to bring something to your attention. The session's description (copy attached) listed Stephen Carter — a well-known guru and the reason I registered for the session — as the seminar presenter. In reality, Stephen gave a half-hour presentation and then turned the program over to his colleague, Michael Snyder.

Michael was terrific. I was engaged, I took copious notes, I walked away satisfied with the content. But I felt I was misled by the description in your catalog.

I'm taking Carol Connor's "Clutter-Free Basement" session on October 10 and since she's also a guru, I'm leery of the possibility of having the same experience I did last night.

Again, "Cold-Calling" was a great session and I understand that it's difficult to monitor every course, so I did want to let you know about my experience.

Sincerely,

Fern Dickey

Tips for Writing Letters of Complaint

- Before giving a negative, start with a positive. Say what you liked before gelling to what you didn't like.
- Make a specific rather than a general complaint. Focus on the part that was defective. Isolate and confine your complaint to that part.
- Be courteous in tone throughout.
- Don't threaten. As the adage goes, "You catch more flies with honey than with vinegar."
- Say what action you want the reader to take, if any.

MOTIVATION

Your child is away at college and getting a D in freshman chemistry. Your brother got passed over for a big promotion. Your best friend's dot.com crashed and his stock is worth as much as a roll of toilet paper.

A pep talk can help in situations like these. Communication vehicles of choice can include a face-to-face talk, phone call, letter, or e-mail. The advantage of sending a letter is that the recipient can keep it for rereading and inspiration; some readers have saved especially meaningful personal letters for their entire lifetime.

Format: [*See Appendix A*: Fig. A-1. Simple format for letters and memos.] Handwritten or typed/word-processed. Personal letterhead.

Style/Tone/Voice: Informal. Active voice. [*See Part I for more on these subjects.*]

Structure: (1) Say why you are writing, (2) Identify the problem and how you know about it, (3) Offer your advice, (4) Close with an offer of additional help and support.

Handy Phrases: You can do it; Believe in yourself; I have faith in you.

See also: *Part II:* Giving Advice; *Part V:* Offering Advice.

Dear Peggy:

Some career paths are more difficult than others, and certainly public speaking is one of the toughest. I know you've had a tough time securing clients lately

But may I share a secret with you?

I have heard many great speakers in my career — men and women who are highly paid to stand before groups of businesspeople and motivate or instruct them in some useful subject.

You are as good as many I have heard.

You can succeed in this business! The key is persistence.

Keep at it. Don't give up. If a prospect chooses another speaker, send 10 more letters to potential clients offering your services.

Success in business is basically a numbers game. If the numbers are high enough — the number of cold calls you make, or letters you send — you will get the response you need to make a good living in your field.

We have known each other for 10 years, and you have everything you need to make a handsome income as a professional speaker already inside you. As Winston Churchill once said in a graduation speech at Oxford, "Never give up!"

If you don't give up, you will make it. Of that I have no doubt.

Sincerely,

Bill

P.S. If you want to send me your promotional mailing, I'd be glad to take a look at it and see what we can do to make it stronger.

Tips for Writing Letters of Motivation

- Share success strategies only if you have reason to believe they will work.
- If you have overcome a similar problem, or know of someone else who has, say so.
- Point the reader to resources that may help (e.g., an attorney or counseling center).

GIVING ADVICE

Many people do not want or need to be motivated. Their hearts are in the right place, and they go at things with enthusiasm. It's just that their approaches don't work.

Stepping in and providing them with guidance is an act of kindness on your part, but the recipient may not always see it as such. That's why letters of advice need to take a gentle hand, and not be arrogant or dictatorial.

Format: [*See Appendix A:* Fig. A-1. Simple format for letters and memos.] Typed/word-processed. Personal letterhead.

Style/Tone/Voice: Informal or formal. Active voice. [*See Part I for more on these subjects.*]

Structure: (1) Identify the specific situation on which you are advising the readers, (2) If they asked for your opinion, remind them of the facts, (3) Present your advice, (4) Convince the readers to follow your recommendations.

Handy Phrases: This is just my opinion; In my opinion; May I make a suggestion.

See also: *Part V:* Warning an Employee; Offering Advice.

Dear Manny,

I'm sorry that Shirley overheard comments you did not intend for her to hear, and is taking it out on you, excluding you from the planning committee.

Could this be avoided in the future? I think so, and here is my suggestion:

It's impossible in business, as in life, not to talk about other people. In business especially, it sometimes has to be done. The rule I've used to keep my comments discreet is to assume that the person about whom I am talking is listening in. This rule has kept me from making statements that could come back to haunt me.

In the meantime, why don't you call Shirley, eat some humble pie, and see if you can sit down with her to straighten things out. Worth a try, if the project is really important to you.

Sincerely,

Ellis

Tips for Giving Advice

- When the advice is solicited, you can be brutally honest; when it is unsolicited, think about how your reader is going to react emotionally to your butting in.
- Criticism should also be specific ("you don't get to your main theme until page 7") rather than general ("your paper is weak").
- Don't just tell the reader what she is doing wrong; tell her how to fix her mistakes and start doing it right.

LETTERS TO THE EDITOR

Letters to the editor are freedom of speech in action. You can express your views in a large public forum, and it won't cost you a dime.

You are free to write your letter to the editor poorly or well. If done poorly, your letter risks being unpublished and, even if published, unread. Write well and your ideas see a better chance of getting into print and influencing the people you want to reach.

Format: [*See Appendix A:* Fig. A-1. Simple format for letters and memos.] Typed/word-processed. Personal letterhead.

Style/Tone/Voice: Formal. Active voice. [*See Part I for more on these subjects.*]

Structure: (1) Reference any earlier letter to the editor or article you are responding to, if such is the case, (2) Sum up the issue or the point made in the other letter or article, (3) State your point of view, (4) Give facts to support your conclusions and recommendations.

Handy Phrases: A matter of opinion; We can agree to disagree; Contrary to what [name of person] said.

See also: *Part II:* Letters to Elected Officials.

Dear Editor:

So columnist Phillip Schwindley believes animals have no rights — and that animal abusers should be let off with a slap of the wrist.

Is it true then, Mr. Schwindley, that the strong, who have power over the weak, have the right to exert that power, just because they can?

The kind of person you are is largely defined by how kind you are to others even if there is no benefit in it for you. And yes, "others" refers to all animals — four legged as well as two legged.

Sincerely,

Ed Flanders

Tips for Letters to the Editor

- Back up your opinions with facts.
- Say what you want to say in the fewest words possible.
- Avoid insults or name-calling.

LETTERS TO ELECTED OFFICIALS

Lots of people write congressmen, senators, mayors, and other elected officials to make suggestions, complain, or voice an opinion concerning how the national, local or state government is run.

Does the elected official actually read these letters? In the case of a small-town mayor, maybe. In the case of the governor, probably a staff member is reading and replying to your letter. But his job is to keep the boss in office, so attention will be paid to what you say.

Do you want your letter to really make a difference? Then don't just grouse. Suggest a specific course of action you want your elected official to take, and urge him with all your persuasive powers to take it.

Format: [*See Appendix A:* Fig. A-1. Simple format for letters and memos.] Typed/word-processed. Personal letterhead.

Style/Tone/Voice: Formal. Active voice. [*See Part I for more on these subjects.*]

Structure: (1) Identify the issue you are writing about, (2) State your position on the issue, (3) Tell the readers what you want them to do, (4) Prove your argument, (5) Request a specific action (e.g., voting in favor of a bill).

Handy Phrases: Please vote; It is important; My concern; Your constituency; The voters.

See also: *Part II:* Letters to the Editor.

Dear Representative Smith:

Recently, a bill (H.R. 207) was introduced that classifies a number of popular nutritional supplements, a few of which I take for my health, as controlled substances. As I depend on these products to maintain my health, I am gravely concerned about the consequences of this bill.

The bill represents blatant disregard for the meaning and purpose of the controlled substance act, which was designed to protect the American public from illegal and dangerous drugs, not from vitamins, herbs, and minerals whose use goes back to ancient times. As an advocate of alternative medicine, I suspect that the lobbying efforts of the American Medical Association and Pharmaceutical Manufacturers of America are the reason for the introduction of this bill.

H.R. 207 should not be passed. If the government believes nutritional supplements are unsafe, and wishes to restrict their use, it should do so through already established legitimate means. The government should be required to produce evidence that these supplements are a risk to public health and safety, or that they fit the legal and scientific criteria required for classification as a controlled substance.

If the bill is passed, it will directly affect the health of millions of Americans, including mature individuals who use these supplements to maintain good health. Please vote NO on H.R. 207!

Thanks for your time and consideration.

Sincerely,

Cole Sebastian

Tips for Writing to Elected Officials

- Type the letter on your personal letterhead, and personalize it with the official's name. Do not send a photocopied or mimeographed form letter.

- Come across as a rational and reasonable human being, not as a fanatic or lunatic.

- If you are writing about a piece of legislation, be specific about which bill, law, act, or case you are referring to.

PART III

CAREER AND EMPLOYMENT LETTERS

With high unemployment, human resources departments are flooded with résumés. Microsoft, for example, gets 45,000 résumés a month.

A decade or two ago, you could be assured of at least a form letter response if a company had no openings or was not interested in you. Now, you may get nothing but silence. According to a survey by the Society of Human Resources Managers, 55 percent of companies do not bother to respond in writing to unsolicited résumés, and 14 percent throw such résumés into the trash.

In such a job market, the need to write effective career and employment-related letters is perhaps greater than ever. The good news: An effective, persuasive cover letter can make your résumé stand out from the crowd, and increase your chances of getting that phone call you want — the one that says, "We got your résumé; when can you come in for an interview?"

Companies still need to hire. They need workers with specific skills. In short, they need you. Let them know it in your cover letter, and the job can be yours!

Cover Letters and Job Inquiries

A cover letter is a personal letter to a potential employer, mailed along with a copy of your résumé. The objective is to convince the reader that it would be in his best interest to hire you or, more specifically, to at least invite you in for a job interview.

Below are examples of four basic types of cover letters: experience-oriented, achievement-oriented, benefit-oriented, and creative. I include guidelines not only on how to write each type of letter, but also how to determine which is best suited to your situation based on your work history and education.

I also provide models for such common job-hunting situations as responding to help-wanted ads, inquiring about job openings, networking, and follow up. When in doubt about whether to write and send a letter, err on the side of being proactive and send it. As a rule, the more frequently you contact potential employers, the sooner you will get a new job.

EXPERIENCE-ORIENTED COVER LETTERS

An experience-oriented cover letter stresses your work history, and is a good choice when you have a long history of employment in responsible positions with good companies in the industry where you are seeking employment.

In writing the experience-oriented cover letter, play to your strong points. For instance, if you are an experienced professional, and your experience matches closely the position and the hiring organization, stress those strengths in your cover letter. If you are highly experienced in the field, industry, or occupation for which you are applying, stress your credentials — education, vocational training, certifications, what you have done, who you have done it for, and the results you have achieved.

Format: [*See Appendix A:* Fig. A-1. Simple format for letters and memos.] Typed/word-processed. Personal letterhead.

Style/Tone/Voice: Formal. Active voice. [*See Part I for more on these subjects.*]

Structure: (1) State the position you are applying for, (2) Say why you are especially qualified, (3) Mention two of your previous positions most relevant to the current opportunity, (4) Highlight any special skills that make you a good fit for the job requirements, (5) Ask for the interview.

Handy Phrases: In response to your help-wanted ad, I am writing to inquire about job openings; May I be of help to you?; Would it make sense for us to get together?; I know I can make a positive contribution.

See also: *Part III:* Cover Letters and Job Inquiries; *Part IV:* Letter of Transmittal.

Dear Mr. Ha-Keim:

I saw in yesterday's *New York Times* that you are looking for a concierge for your new condominiums at Center Plaza. My background is so wonderfully matched with your requirement that I am taking the opportunity to write to you immediately.

You ask for fluency in seven languages because people of all nations occupy your buildings. I am of Danish birth, brought up by a Danish father and Greek mother in Paris, and schooled in French. After attending the French Lycee, I moved with my family to Italy and later to Russia, where my father was employed in the foreign service of Denmark.

I was fortunate to be able to continue my studies in the United States and have therefore an excellent knowledge of English. I studied both Italian and Spanish and acquired fluency both written and spoken. Thus I have good command of seven languages. I worked several years as an "animateur" for the Club Mediterranean, and later as manager of a small clothing boutique in Auteuil.

I enjoy working with different cultures. I am experienced with budgets, schedules, and general coordination of routines, and I consider myself to have good judgment of people and situations. I feel confident that the position of concierge, which you describe, is one for which I am suited and which would give me great pleasure.

I am enclosing some references for you, and I shall try to contact you next week. I find your position challenging and exciting, and I would like to talk with you about the feasibility of working at Center Plaza.

Yours sincerely,

Tips for Writing Experience-Oriented Cover Letters

- Reference the specific ad you responded to or the specific position you are applying for.
- Show how your experience, background, and skills match the employer's requirements.
- Demonstrate a high level of expertise and proficiency (e.g., you just didn't take courses in the skills; you have used them successfully in previous jobs).

EXPERIENCE/ACHIEVEMENT-ORIENTED COVER LETTERS

The combination "experience/achievement" cover letter combines great qualifications for the job with great results achieved in previous positions. Use this format when you are not only qualified for the job, but have proven your ability to generate results while working in similar positions for other employers.

Format: [*See Appendix A:* Fig. A-1. Simple format for letters and memos.] Typed/word-processed. Personal letterhead.

Style/Tone/Voice: Formal. Active voice. [*See Part I for more on these subjects.*]

continued

continued

Structure: (1) State the position you are applying for, (2) Say why you are especially qualified, (3) Mention two of your previous positions most relevant to the current opportunity and highlight any special skills that make you a good fit for the job, (4) Discuss with details specific achievements you've had that correlate directly with the job to which you are applying, (5) Ask for the interview.

Handy Phrases: In response to your help-wanted ad; I am writing to inquire about job openings; May I be of help to you?; Would it make sense for us to get together?; I know I can make a positive contribution; I have been awarded; I was able to contribute/ achieve; Helped my previous employer gain [some tangible goal]; I increased my divisions/employer's [revenue, customer base, recognition]; Want to offer you some of these same results.

See also: *Part III:* Cover Letters and Job Inquiries; *Part IV:* Letter of Transmittal.

Dear Mr. Fitzpatrick:

For the past five years I have been successfully handling construction management in a very large general contracting business. I am now changing positions, and I feel that your organization might need my services.

I know both construction management and construction engineering. Among my accomplishments are these:

- With Atlas Construction Co. during the past five years, I've had personal direct charge at the job site for building construction worth $50 million.
- I know the techniques of maintaining construction on schedule.
- I have years of contract administration success.
- I understand the value of cost control and the necessity for profit in building construction.

If you will let me talk with you for about 20 minutes, I believe I can assure you of my value. I am available upon normal notice. My résumé is enclosed.

For your current or future need, may I come in?

Very truly yours,

Carl Messer

Tips for Writing Experience/Achievement-Oriented Cover Letters

- Show how your experience, background, and skills match the employer's requirements.
- Talk about past accomplishments that will give the employer confidence that you can perform well in the position being offered.
- Talk about what is important to the employer and why you can meet those needs.

BENEFIT-ORIENTED COVER LETTERS

What if you are a novice, a recent college graduate, or are switching fields? You probably don't have much relevant job experience. When you are a beginner, it is better to say what you *can* and *will* do for the employer, rather than what you *have* done for others.

Format: [*See Appendix A:* Fig. A-1. Simple format for letters and memos.] Typed/word-processed. Personal letterhead.

Style/Tone/Voice: Formal. Active voice. [*See Part I for more on these subjects.*]

Structure: (1) Identify the position you're applying for, (2) Present all relevant experience and credentials, (3) Do not state that your experience is weak or thin (let the reader draw that conclusion for himself, or not, as the case may be), (4) Ask for the interview.

Handy Phrases: I'm interested in; I am applying for; I am writing to find out whether [enthusiasm, commitment, interest] is a good fit.

See also: *Part III:* Cover Letters and Job Inquiries; *Part IV:* Letter of Transmittal.

Dear Ms. Sevres-Babylon:

I would like to be considered a candidate for the position of Project Coordinator in the federally funded program to increase the representation of women in technical education. This is an area that has long deserved attention and it is an area which I have given much thought.

Recently, I assumed full directorship of a nonprofit agency dealing with professional level career changers and job seekers. Prior to assuming full, overall supervision of the agency, my specific organizational responsibilities were coordinating, scheduling, supervising, staffing, planning, and evaluating a workshop program geared to participants ranging from college to retirement age. In addition, I have played a major role in outreach/publicity, editing the agency's newsletter and appearing on television and radio to impart information concerning the organization and its programs.

To your project I can bring:

- A strong commitment to women's concerns
- Demonstrated ability in organizational administration
- Solid experience in program planning and development
- Familiarity with the structure of today's job/career environment
- A working knowledge of methods of outreach to business and the community at large
- Excellent written and oral communication skills

I would be happy to meet with you in order to discuss my background and experience relative to your needs, and will call your office early next week to see if we can find a time.

Sincerely,

Jeannette Montparnasse Bienvenue

Tips for Writing Benefit-Oriented Cover Letters

- Play up what limited experience or credentials you have now. Put the most aggressive, positive spin on it that you can.
- List all the things you can think of that you can and will do for the employer if you are hired. Spell these out in your letter.
- Do not volunteer that you are relatively inexperienced or apologize for your lack of credentials in any way. If the employer is going to conclude that you are not qualified, let her come to this conclusion on her own; do not help her toward it.

CREATIVE COVER LETTERS

A "creative" cover letter uses direct-mail copywriting techniques to grab the reader's attention. Typically, it stresses a need the employer's organization has and how you can help fill that need, rather than target a specific opening or position.

The advantage of a creative letter is that it may indeed succeed in luring the reader in where a dry, conventional cover letter might have failed.

The disadvantage is that it may come across as gimmicky, making the reader think you emphasize style over substance.

Format: [*See Appendix A:* Fig. A-1. Simple format for letters and memos.] Typed/word-processed. Personal letterhead.

Style/Tone/Voice: Formal. Active voice. [*See Part I for more on these subjects.*]

Structure: (1) State the reader's problem, (2) Show that the services you would perform as an employee of the firm can solve that problem, (3) Give proof, (4) Suggest that you meet with the reader to explore your proposal further.

Handy Phrases: Solve your problem; Meet your needs; Here's how I can help you; I may be able to help; That's right up my alley; This is what I do best.

See also: *Part III:* Cover Letters and Job Inquiries; *Part IV:* Letter of Transmittal.

Dear Mr. Peterson:

Time enough is still a problem, isn't it? Not scarcity of printout data, but time.

Has a corporate or division president anything more important to do than taking the time for good decision-making? Can some of the things he does, or wants to do, be handled by an assistant having similar experience, maturity, and profit orientation?

This is what I can offer you to help build corporate profit:

- Comprehension of the essential elements in your business with the ability to establish, improve, or implement programs that contribute to corporate performance.
- Experience in saving substantial sums through operational and market analysis and the resulting improved management controls.
- Intelligence and skill in working harmoniously and productively with and through others at all levels.

My résumé is enclosed in great confidence, as my present company is not aware of my decision to consider a change. May I talk to you?

Very truly yours,

Wayne C. Powell

Tips for Writing Creative Cover Letters

- Carefully craft an opening line designed to get the reader's attention. To do this, your lead must highlight a concern or problem the reader has, but say it in a fresh and compelling way.

- Position yourself and your skills as the solution to this concern or problem — a solution the reader can obtain only by hiring you.

- Suggest a next step, such as a meeting or interview.

RESPONDING TO HELP-WANTED ADS

Traditionally, sending a letter to a post office box or street address shown in a help-wanted ad is a usual method of response. Enclose a résumé with your cover letter.

More and more ads include fax numbers or e-mail addresses for response. It's easy enough to fax your résumé with a cover letter, but be careful about e-mail: Many people will not open an attached file from someone they do not know, so if you attach your résumé as a file, the recipient may not see it. Solution: Paste the résumé into your e-mail.

Format: [*See Appendix A:* Fig. A-1. Simple format for letters and memos.] Typed/word-processed. Personal letterhead.

Style/Tone/Voice: Formal. Active voice. [*See Part I for more on these subjects.*]

Structure: (1) Specify which ad you are responding to, including the newspaper it ran in and the position being advertised, (2) Say how your experience, education, and credentials make you a strong candidate for the position, (3) Refer the reader to your enclosed résumé for more detail, (4) Ask for the interview.

Handy Phrases: I am writing in response to your ad; In response to the ad; As my résumé shows; As my experience demonstrates; I am interested in the position you advertised; Your ad in the [name of newspaper] caught my eye.

See also: *Part III:* Cover Letters and Job Inquiries; *Part IV:* Letter of Transmittal.

Dear Ms. Bishop;

I am responding to the part-time marketing position that was advertised in *The Record* newspaper on Nov. 17th. I had the opportunity to meet with you and Tom McKeon last November when this position was previously advertised. I was very impressed with both

Thompson Industries and the Marketing Department and would like the opportunity to reapply for this position.

Enclosed is an updated résumé that highlights my job experiences. I have progressively acquired and improved upon my marketing-related skills, many of which are in line with the requirements of this position. I produced brochures and flyers to promote training programs, which included writing copy and coordinating details with the printer, mail house, and list manager. In addition, I was involved in the advertising process, which included using various media such as bulk mailings, e-mail, telephone, and fax campaigns. I developed all aspects of a company tour as a marketing tool for the public. This tour later became the basis for a company video used for public relations purposes. Through my experiences I have developed exceptional organization and communication skills, the ability to juggle multiple tasks and work independently with limited supervision. I have a high level of proficiency in Microsoft Office (Word, Excel, and PowerPoint).

My salary requirements are within your stated range of $17.00–$21.00/hour. When we first met last November, I was very excited about the prospect of working for Thompson Industries in the Marketing Department and I still feel that way today. Please reconsider my qualifications for the part-time marketing position. I hope to hear from you soon.

Sincerely,

Robyn Waage

In the letter above, the writer already has a relationship with the reader, having previously applied for a job with the company. The more common situation, as addressed in the letter below, is to respond to a classified ad not knowing the name of the person to write to — forcing you to use a job title instead of a name in the salutation.

Dear Human Resources Manager:

I am responding to the October 2nd advertisement in *The Record* newspaper for the Administrative Assistant position. Based on the job responsibilities listed, I feel that this is both an opportunity to use skills that I have mastered through previous job experiences, as well as allow me to continue to grow professionally.

My position as Program Coordinator for 42's Conferences and Seminars Department required exceptional organization and communication skills and the ability to juggle multiple tasks. The detailed nature of event planning requires a great deal of coordination and teamwork to insure that each program runs smoothly and successfully. Additionally, there are elements of that job, such as writing copy for collateral material to promote our programs, that required the ability to adhere to deadlines and work independently.

My most recent salary was $17/hour. I am very interested in this position and would welcome the opportunity to explore how my qualifications and skills can benefit Hunter Photo Imaging.

Sincerely,

Robyn Waage

Tips for Responding to Help-Wanted Ads

- Reference the specific ad: the newspaper, the day the ad ran, and the position being advertised.

- Provide everything the employer asked for in the ad. If they ask whether you can use a particular computer program, say so. If they ask your current salary, give it.

- In addition to the information the employer asks for, include other qualifications, education, experiences, and facts that make you seem ideally qualified for the position being advertised.

INQUIRING ABOUT A JOB OPENING

Not all positions are advertised. In fact, some experts estimate that 80 percent of jobs are unadvertised. People find out about them through referral, word of mouth, and proactively canvassing local companies and inquiring about job opportunities. Naturally, much of this canvassing can be done by letter.

Format: [*See Appendix A:* Fig. A-1. Simple format for letters and memos.] Typed/word-processed. Personal letterhead.

Style/Tone/Voice: Formal. Active voice. [*See Part I for more on these subjects.*]

Structure: (1) Say why you are contacting the reader and where you got her name, (2) If you know for a fact they are looking to fill a position, name the position and tell how you know about it, (3) Relate your qualifications to the requirement of the position, (4) Ask for the interview.

Handy Phrases: The reason I am writing; Do you need?; Inquiring about an opening; Join your team.

See also: *Part II:* Requests; *Part III:* Cover Letters and Job Inquiries; Query Letters; *Part IV:* Business Requests.

Dear Mr. Carter,

Nancy Kreeger of Green & Associates Advertising suggested I contact you regarding a possible public relations opening in your firm.

As an editor/writer for Waterford's city magazine, I've developed my talent and experience as a public relations writer. Because the staff is very small, I've worn a number of hats, including: developing the editorial format and individual story concepts, writing numerous articles, editing copy, laying out the magazine, and supervising production.

Prior to my current position, I was highly involved in the public relations industry, working for Jones & Jones, where I prepared numerous press releases and media guides, as well as managed several major direct-mail campaigns.

My previous employers who have quickly promoted me to positions of greater responsibility have recognized my high degree of motivation; I was promoted from assistant editor to editor *of Waterford Monthly* after only five months.

I am eager to talk with you about the contribution I could make to your firm. I will call you the week of April 25th to see if we can find a mutual time and date to get together and discuss the possibility.

Your consideration is greatly appreciated.

Cordially,

Mary Standish

Tips for Writing Letters of Inquiry

- If you know that the employer is looking to fill a specific job, say what the job is and how you know about it.
- Highlight your qualifications for the position.
- Ask for the job interview.

NETWORKING LETTERS

One strategy for job hunting is to write networking letters. Instead of seeking employment with the reader's organization, ask the reader to share knowledge, contacts, and observations about the field or industry into which you are moving.

Networking letters often get higher response than job applications because there is less pressure: The person doesn't want anything from you except a few minutes of your time. At worst, you are granted that time, and walk away with some tips or knowledge gained from the meeting. At best, you impress the person enough to make him either recommend you to someone for a job, or hire you himself.

Format: [*See Appendix A:* Fig. A-1. Simple format for letters and memos.] Typed/word-processed. Personal letterhead.

Style/Tone/Voice: Formal. Active voice. [*See Part I for more on these subjects.*]

Structure: (1) Say where you got the reader's name, (2) Explain who you are, (3) Tell why you are writing, (4) Make a specific request (e.g., a 20-minute meeting, advice, a referral).

Handy Phrases: Pick your brain; May I ask a favor of you?; Can you help me?; As someone highly respected in the industry.

See also: *Part II:* Requests; *Part III:* Cover Letters and Job Inquiries; Letters of Recommendation and Introduction; Query Letters; *Part IV:* Networking Business Letters; Business Requests

March 15, 2001

Mr. Benjamin Tenney
Curriculum Design Department
InfoSoft
732 Fifth Avenue
Kansas City, MO 64100

Dear Mr. Tenney:

Barry Childers, whom I met at a recent meeting of the Association of Instructional Designers, suggested that I contact you about my interest in entering the instructional design field.

I'm currently a systems analyst, but I did some instructional design as the result of teaching a class at Permafrost Community College. I am extremely intrigued by the field, especially the possibilities that Web-based instruction presents.

I would be very grateful for any suggestions you might have.

I'd like to contact you in the near future to "pick your brain." I won't take much of your time and will greatly appreciate any advice you can offer.

Sincerely,

John Philips

Tips for Writing Networking Letters

- Tell the person where you got his name. Were you referred by a mutual acquaintance? Are you both members of a club or the local chapter of your trade association?

- Give a brief summary of who you are, what you have done, and what you want to do now.

- Be clear that you are not after a job, but would appreciate any information, advice, and guidance the person is willing to give. Assure them that you understand how busy they are, and that if they offer help, you won't abuse the privilege.

FOLLOW-UP LETTERS

When you network, you will now and then uncover a hot, live job opportunity. After talking to the right person in the company about it, immediately follow up by mail, e-mail, or fax.

Format: [*See Appendix A:* Fig. A-1. Simple format for letters and memos.] Typed/word-processed. Personal letterhead.

Style/Tone/Voice: Formal. Active voice. [*See Part I for more on these subjects.*]

Structure: (1) Say how you know about the position or job opening, (2) Enclose your résumé, (3) Highlight key experience, (4) Ask for the interview.

Handy Phrases: My résumé is enclosed; As my résumé indicates; I am interested in; My background; My qualifications.

See also: *Part III:* Cover Letters and Job Inquiries; *Part IV:* Post-Meeting Follow-Up Letters; *Part VII:* Lead Inquiry-Fulfillment Follow-Ups; After-Sale Follow Up Letters.

Dear Andrea,

As we discussed over the phone this morning, I am faxing a copy of my résumé for your consideration.

I am interested in temporary or permanent employment in an administrative assistant or project coordinator position. My background includes extensive experience with most Microsoft Office programs with specific expertise in Excel and Word.

I would welcome the opportunity to meet with you so that we may discuss my qualifications in more detail.

Sincerely,

Gail Leiniger

Tips for Writing Follow-Up Letters

- Remind the person of who you are, when you talked, and the position you discussed.
- Say you are strongly interested in the position.
- Enclose your résumé and highlight the points on the résumé that most closely match the requirements of the job.

Résumés

While a cover letter makes the persuasive case why the reader should grant you an interview, the résumé presents the detailed facts of your employment history in an easy-to-scan format. The four basic types of résumé that this section provides are: executive, novice, chronological, and functional.

EXECUTIVE RÉSUMÉS

For an experienced executive who has accumulated his or her share of gray hair, the challenge is to compress a long job history into a one- or two-page résumé. Two techniques work well here: clear organization and concise writing.

Format: [*See Appendix A:* Fig. A-6. Résumé format.] Typed/word-processed.

Style/Tone/Voice: Formal. Passive voice. [*See Part I for more on these subjects.*]

Structure: (1) Name, address, and phone number, (2) Career objective or goal, (3) Areas of expertise, (4) Education, experience, (5) Additional information.

Handy Phrases: Managed; Created; Achieved; Produced; Results; Responsibilities.

See also: *Part III:* Résumés.

JOHN WILSON
5555 Parkside Avenue
New York, NY 02166
Telephone: (212) 555-5555

OBJECTIVE	<u>Regional Director</u> or <u>Vice President, Group Sales</u> — Insurance Industry
AREAS OF KNOWLEDGE	Group Life Insurance Sales Individual Life Insurance Sales Management Accident and Health Insurance Sales Training Medical Care Insurance Administration
EDUCATION	DePaul University, Chicago, Illinois - B.S. Degree: Business Administration Minor: Marketing

EXPERIENCE

1966 to Present	NO-FAULT INSURANCE COMPANY, one of the very largest in the United States, offering complete coverage with all forms of life, health, hospital, and medical care insurance.
1977 to Present	<u>Position</u>: Group Account Executive (Regional Office) after promotion from Group Sales Supervisor. Report to Vice President. <u>Responsibilities</u>: – To personally manage and serve the extremely large group accounts annual premium range from $250,000 to many millions. – To maintain and build Company relations with Brokers and Insurance Consultants. – To represent the Company at the highest levels. <u>Achievements</u>: – Successfully handled complicated claim negotiations to the satisfaction of major policyholders and the Company. – Assisted in the underwriting and administration areas, involving the most important clients. – In 1977, qualified as 4th leading Account Executive, although in the position only a few months.
1968–1977	<u>Position</u>: Group Sales Supervisor (Chicago, Cleveland Offices) after promotion from Sales Supervisor/Sales Trainee.

Responsibilities:

– Initially, to develop Group Life Sales to new accounts, substantially opening the Illinois and Ohio areas.

– Since promotion to Chicago (1972), responsible for maintenance of large and vital Group accounts.

– To train and assist Company agents in building Group Sales through prospect development.

Achievements:

– In 1974, was 18th leading Company Sales Representative in the United States.

– Sold over $221 million of new life insurance in 1975, climbing to No. 2 in the country.

– Ranked first in the United States in 1976; $102 million of life insurance and $863 thousand of disability premium produced.

– Built a reputation for achievement in personal sales along with an excellent conservation record and underwriting performance.

1967–1968	Position: Service Supervisor/Sales Trainee (Chicago Office), after promotion from Insurance Agent.
1966–1967	Position: Insurance Agent (Jasper, Indiana Office).
TRAVEL	Agreeable to any amount required to handle the position effectively.
LOCATE	Readily willing to relocate anywhere.
AVAILABILITY	30 days after final hiring commitment.
EMPLOYER CONTACT	Present employer is not aware of decision to change. Do not contact before hiring commitment.
REFERENCES	Business and personal references immediately available upon request.

Tips for Writing Executive Résumés

- Find the organizational scheme that works best for your job history: chronological, or by function or achievement.
- Hit the highlights. Save the detail for the interview.
- Use bullets instead of paragraphs for easy scanning.

NOVICE RÉSUMÉS

When you are a recent college graduate or otherwise lack extensive job experience, compression is not your problem. Your challenge instead is to make what little you have seem like a lot. Unlike the 20-year veteran who has to shrink his experience to fit it all on one or two pages, you have to elaborate and embellish on your background and credentials to make the résumé seem solid.

Format: [*See Appendix A:* Fig. A-6. Résumé format.] Typed/word-processed.

Style/Tone/Voice: Formal. Passive voice. [*See Part I for more on these subjects.*]

Structure: (1) Name, address, and phone number, (2) Key attributes, knowledge, of areas of expertise, (3) Education, (4) Work experience.

Handy Phrases: Creative; Analytical; Problem-solving; Teamwork; Efficient; Effective; Results-oriented.

See also: *Part III:* Résumés.

JUDE LAWLER
6372 Breaker Street, Cleveland, Ohio 12345
(216) 555-5555

STRENGTHS

- **Finance:** Finance emphasis in both graduate and undergraduate studies. Broad base of knowledge and skills in a wide variety of finance applications. Strong desire to apply education to real-world situations.
- **Analytical Skills:** Analytical by nature. Solid problem-solving abilities. Research and investigation skills, including sourcing and fact-checking.
- **Personal Attributes:** Strong leadership skills. Decisive and goal-oriented. Effective in both individual and team competitive situations.
- **Communications:** Articulate, persuasive and quick thinking. Trilingual English/Mandarin/Indonesian. Computers: IBM PC. Experienced with DOS, Lotus 1-2-3, dBase, WordPerfect.

EDUCATION

Norfolk State University, Norfolk, Virginia   1989–1992
M.S.B.A., Finance Emphasis (GPA: 3.9/4.0)

Coursework included:

- **Finance:** Financial Management; Financial Reporting and Analysis; Financial Markets and Institutions; International Corporate Finance
- **Banking:** Bank and Thrift Management; International Banking

- **Investments:** Portfolio Management; Investments
- **Management:** Business Development; Managerial Analysis and Communication; Business Policy and Strategy

Accomplishments/Affiliations

- **Treasurer, Minority Student Association.** Managed revenues and funds. Developed and implemented programs to promote cooperation and friendship between MSA members, the university, and the community.
- **Member,** Asian Business Association.
- **Member,** Finance Student Association.
- **Member,** Phi Alpha Delta.
- **Member,** American Management Association.

Oregon State University, Corvallis, Oregon   1986–1989
B.A., Finance Emphasis in Banking and Investment, Minor in Chinese. (GPA: 3.8/4.0)

Coursework included:

- **Finance:** International Financial Management, Management of Financial Institutions.
- **Banking:** Monetary and Banking Theory
- **Investments:** Security Analysis & Portfolio Management; Real Estate Investments.
- **Management:** Business & Its Environment; Business Policy; Management Information Systems.

Accomplishments/Affiliations

Vice President, Permias (Indonesian Student Association).

- Member of team to unite Indonesian students.
- Helped create/implement programs to introduce Permias to the University Community.

REFERENCES
Provided upon request.

Tips for Writing Novice Résumés

- Brainstorm. Think about your life. Make a list of every experience and skill that will make you valuable to potential employers.

- College students should stress major and minor, extracurricular activities, internships, part-time jobs held during school, and summer jobs.

- Point out the benefit of an experience if not obvious (e.g., "Dormitory resident advisor — managed housing for 300 students of diverse cultural and ethnic backgrounds").

CHRONOLOGICAL RÉSUMÉS

The most common method of organization for your résumé and presenting your job experience is in chronological order. You begin by listing your current job — company, title, job description — and then go back from there, listing all jobs held since you graduated school.

The chronological method works well if you have been working steadily for a long period, have not been unemployed between jobs, and tend to stay in jobs relatively long rather than job hop.

Format: [*See Appendix A:* Fig. A-6. Résumé format.] Typed/word-processed.

Style/Tone/Voice: Formal. Passive voice. [*See Part I for more on these subjects.*]

Structure: (1) Name, address, phone number, (2) Work experience in reverse chronological order, (3) Education, (4) Personal data (optional).

Handy Phrases: Managed; Designed; Planned; Created; Achieved; Produced; Results; Responsibilities; Attained; Succeeded in.

See also: *Part III:* Résumés.

SAMUEL TAYLOR
55 North Drive
Suburbia, Illinois 68301
Telephone: (312) 555-5555

Quality Control Manager, Electronics, Northwestern States

PROFESSIONAL EXPERIENCE

December 19— to Present	Department Head, Quality Control, Camfer Electronics Company. Responsible for customer acceptance of electronic components and airframe for air-to-air missile. Plan, schedule, and ensure timely completion of tasks of 200 employees. Report directly to Plant Manager.
June 19— to December 19—	Supervisor, Quality Audit, Camfer Electronics. 10 employees. Responsible for adequate quality control procedures, all aspects of production, from purchasing to shipping. Reported to Head of Quality Control Department.

May 19— to June 19—   Chief, Quality Control Procedures, Camfer Electronics. Edited and directed the work of five employees, providing all quality control procedures. Reported to Head of Quality Control Department.

August 19— to May 19—   Technical Writer, Morrow Electronics Corporation Prepared, published, and distributed test procedures for test stations and assembly operations. Coordinated management procedures.

PROFESSIONAL AFFILIATIONS

Member, American Society for Quality Control since 19—, President local chapter 19— Member, Society of Technical Writers and Publishers since 19—, Senior member since 19—, President local chapter 19—, Secretary 19—.

EDUCATION

B.S. Industrial Management, Podunk University, 19—.

Postgraduate studies include evening courses in Quality Control Concepts, Management Problems, Elements of Supervision, Engineering Statistics, and Labor Relations Problems.

PERSONAL

Will negotiate salary. Available within 30 days. Résumé submitted in confidence.

Tips for Writing Chronological Résumés

- Use a layout that allows the reader to see the entire chronology of dates in advance. One good method is to put dates in the left-hand column, with the company, your title, and job description to the right.

- Make sure there are no gaps in your timeline. You don't want a potential employer asking, "Well, what did you do from February 2002 to September 2002 if you were out of work during those 8 months." (If you have such a gap, consider using the functional résumé below.)

- Use bold, italic, or all-cap heading to separate the sections (e.g., AWARDS, PUBLICATIONS, EDUCATION).

FUNCTIONAL RÉSUMÉS

The functional résumé lists work experience by job title, job description, or work performed. It does not show chronology. Use a functional résumé when there are large gaps in your employment history (e.g., you spent a year hiking in Europe) or when you have job-hopped frequently (e.g., you worked for three dot.coms in two years).

Format: [*See Appendix A:* Fig. A-6. Résumé format.] Typed/word-processed.

Style/Tone/Voice: Formal. Passive voice. [*See Part I for more on these subjects.*]

Structure: (1) Name, address, phone number, (2) Experience, (3) Results achieved, (4) Education, (5) Personal data (optional).

Handy Phrases: Managed; Designed; Planned; Created; Achieved; Produced; Results; Responsibilities; Attained; Succeeded in.

See also: *Part III:* Résumés.

SAMUEL TAYLOR
55 North Drive
Suburbia, Illinois 68301
Telephone: (312) 555-5555

Quality Control Manager Electronics

EXPERIENCE

<u>Quality Control Department Head</u>, Camfer Electronics Company. Manage 200 employees in a firm with a gross sales of $3.5 million. Familiar with all facets of quality control to electronics industry, having served in the present position for the past four years. Joined Camfer In 19 — as Chief Quality Control Procedures.

- Eliminated inspection bottlenecks by procedures change, saving $40,000 per year.
- Directed fabrication methods studies, reducing costs by 20 percent.
- Reduced inspection costs 20 percent while reducing rejection rate saved $160,000.

PREVIOUS EXPERIENCE

Supervisor of Quality Audit, Camfer Electronics, 19— to 19—.

Chief of Quality Control Procedures, Camfer Electronics, 19— to 19—.

Technical Writer, Morrow Electronics Corporation, 19— to 19—.

OTHER QUALIFICATIONS

Received B.S. in Industrial Management from Podunk University 19—; graduated in upper third of class. Postgraduate studies include evening courses in Quality Control Concepts,

Management Problems, Engineering Statistics, Labor Relations, and Supervision. President on local chapter of ASQC.

PERSONAL

Enjoy outdoors. Available with in 30 days; do not contact employer.

Tips for Writing Functional Résumés

- Be consistent in how you organize and categorize work experience. Is it by tasks performed? Job title? Industry? Department?
- Keep descriptions short — two or three sentences per job.
- Highlight what you did and the results you achieved.

After the Interview

You might think that once your résumé gets you in the door for an interview, the letter writing is done. On the contrary: There are many more letters to write in search of a job. After the interview, these can include a thank-you letter for the interview, a letter accepting or declining an offer, a letter notifying your boss about your new job, or a letter to the interviewer to show you handle rejection well.

THANK-YOU LETTERS TO INTERVIEWERS

In Part II, we discussed what a rarity thank-you letters are becoming and how, as a result, sending a thank-you letter makes you stand out and creates a strong, memorable impression.

This is especially true and important when you are job hunting. Only a fraction of candidates bother to send a thank-you letter to the recruiter or hiring manager who interviewed them.

What a mistake! That person has given up valuable time to give you a valuable opportunity. They deserve to be thanked. Not doing so is rude. Doing so raises you a notch or two in their minds, giving you a better chance of becoming one of the finalists for the position.

The first model letter is a thank-you letter sent to a Mr. Belfry who granted the writer a networking interview — some time to benefit from Mr. Belfry's knowledge and experience in his industry, even though no specific job opening was on the table.

Format: [*See Appendix A:* Fig. A-1. Simple format for letters and memos.] Typed/word-processed. Personal letterhead.

Style/Tone/Voice: Formal. Active voice. [*See Part I for more on these subjects.*]

Structure: (1) Thank the person for the interview or favor, (2) Express your sincere gratitude, (3) Tell the reader what you learned or how you benefited, (4) Say what you want to happen next.

Handy Phrases: Thanks for your time; Thank you for seeing me; Thanks for the interview; I appreciate your time and consideration; If there's anything I can do for you please let me know.

See also: *Part II:* Thank-You Letters; *Part IV:* Donation Thank-You Letters; *Part VI:* Holiday Season Thank Yous to Valued Customers.

Dear Mr. Belfry,

Thank you for the time and consideration you extended to me during my interview with you yesterday.

I greatly appreciated the opportunity to speak with you about my experience in related fields and my future goals. Thank you again for your courtesy. I look forward to hearing from you.

Very truly yours,

Sandy Brixton

In the following letter, the writer is thanking Alison, the recipient, for granting an interview specifically to discuss employment with her firm.

Dear Alison,

Thank you for taking the time to meet with me last Friday to discuss the opportunity for employment with Minnesota Bearings.

When interviewing for a job, it is always a challenge to try and learn enough information about the company and its culture in a short time to be able to determine if that job would be a "good fit." Your explanation of the benefits was very thorough and the positive comments about your personal experience as a Minnesota Bearings employee painted a picture of exactly the kind of company that I am seeking.

It was a pleasure to meet with you and I thank you again for your time and attention. I look forward to hearing from you soon.

Sincerely,

Grant Streit

The next example is also discussing an interview for a specific position; however, in this letter the writer discusses the events of the interview in more detail.

Dear Charles,

Thank you for taking the time to meet with me last Tuesday to discuss the details of the Administrative Coordinator position at NYM, Inc.

The initial tour through the facility and your thorough explanation of the job requirements provided me with a solid grasp of the demands of this position. During the interview with you and Brian, I came to understand that being part of your department would provide a challenging and varied work environment, which is exactly what I am looking for. I feel that my past work experience has given me the necessary skills to be a valuable asset in meeting the challenges of your department for 2004 and beyond. I would welcome the opportunity to help make the day-to-day operations run smoothly.

Once again, thank you for your time and attention and I look forward to hearing from you soon.

Sincerely,

David Evans

Tips for Writing Thank-You Letters to Interviewers

- Remind them of when the meeting took place and the position you were interviewing for.
- Thank them for their time and consideration.
- Express again your enthusiasm for the position.
- Restate why you think you are the right person for the job — and they should, too.

ACCEPTING JOB OFFERS

When you accept a job offer, confirm the offer and your acceptance in writing. Many companies do not use employment contracts, so if you are not given a contract, or the offer is not made in writing, your acceptance letter will document the terms and other particulars. This way, you have written proof of your position in case a dispute should arise.

If the offer is made verbally, take notes on what is said. Repeat back what you hear to make sure you have heard it correctly. Then sum it up in a letter to your new boss. Keep a copy for your files, and confirm both receipt of the letter and agreement to its terms and conditions.

Format: [*See Appendix A:* Fig. A-1. Simple format for letters and memos.] Typed/word-processed. Personal letterhead.

Style/Tone/Voice: Formal. Passive or active voice. [*See Part I for more on these subjects.*]

Structure: (1) Repeat the job offer, (2) Thank the reader for the offer, (3) Accept, (4) List salary, benefits, and other particulars, (5) Thank the reader again, and (6) Close by discussing your start date and any requirements concerning it.

Handy Phrases: Thanks; I'm delighted; I am happy to accept; This is a great opportunity.

See also: *Part IV:* Letters of Confirmation and Acknowledgment; *Part VI:* Order Acknowledgement; *Part IX:* Letters Regarding Bids, Contracts, and Agreements; Confirmation of Order.

Dear Mike:

Thanks for your call the other night.

To get right to the point, I am thrilled to be offered the advertising manager position and am delighted to accept.

To sum up our discussion:

- I will be responsible for managing Kresge Engineering's marketing communications program, including trade advertising and the content on the Web site.
- My salary will be $47,000 a year plus a performance bonus to be determined after my 6-month review.
- My immediate supervisor will be you.
- Kresge Engineering will pay all my moving expenses from Baltimore to Wichita.
- I will have a private office equipped with a PC and fast Internet connection.

Mike, I am excited about this opportunity and looking forward to working with you, beginning on May 1. Thanks again for your confidence in me. I, too, am confident that together we can achieve a significant increase in Kresge's return on its advertising investments.

Sincerely,

Wayne Roberts

Tips for Accepting Job Offers

- Express your gratitude multiple times.
- State all agreed-upon terms of employment that are important to you (e.g., having a company car).
- Start the relationship off on a positive note.
- Do not discuss specific work issues or problems. Save that for when you start the job.

DECLINING JOB OFFERS

When turning down a job offer, do it in writing. This way, there are no hurt feelings, awkward moments, or heated arguments. Also, why burn bridges? Maintain a positive relationship with the recipient of your letter. He/she may be a future employer, employee, vendor, or customer.

Format: [*See Appendix A:* Fig. A-1. Simple format for letters.] Typed/word-processed. Company or personal letterhead.

Style/Tone/Voice: Informal or formal. Active voice. [*See Part I for more on these subjects.*]

Structure: (1) Identify the position under discussion, (2) Decline the offer, (3) Give your reasons why, (4) Thank the reader for the offer.

Handy Phrases: With regrets; I must respectfully decline; After careful consideration; I gave it a lot of thought; I'm going to pass.

See also: *Part II:* Refusing a Request; *Part IV:* Refusing Business Requests; Declining an Invitation to Serve; Refusing a Donation Request; *Part VI:* Sensitive Customer Correspondence; *Part VIII:* Refusing to Pay a Bill; Turning Down a Request for Credit; *Part IX:* Vendor Gift Policy.

Dear Dave,

With regards to the Assistant Manager position within the STL Group, I respectfully decline your offer for the new position.

I am thankful for the opportunity offered and for the confidence in my abilities to support the STL business. However, after careful consideration, I have decided to return to school full time in January to finish my M.B.A.

Again, thanks for the consideration and opportunity afforded me by Concord Industrial Industries. I hope that after I attain my degree, you will consider me for future positions within the company.

Sincerely,

Tim Sullivan

Tips for Declining Job Offers

- Say you are flattered they have offered the job, but after giving it careful thought, have decided not to take it.
- Give the reason why you are passing on this opportunity. Is it that the work really doesn't interest you, or that you have a better offer, or prefer not to relocate after all?
- Thank the person for the time and effort expended in considering you for the position.

NOTIFYING YOUR PRESENT EMPLOYER THAT YOU ARE TAKING A NEW JOB

When you take a new job, you must break the news to those in your current organization, particularly your direct supervisor who should be notified first. Later, to avoid having to tell the same story 20 different times to 20 different people, you can recast the same text in a memo and distribute to all concerned.

Format: [*See Appendix A:* Fig. A-1. Simple format for letters and memos.] Typed/word-processed. Business letterhead.

Style/Tone/Voice: Formal. Active voice. [*See Part I for more on these subjects.*]

Structure: (1) Say that you have accepted a job offer, (2) Say what it is, (3) If appropriate, say why, (4) Thank your current company, (5) Wish them well.

Handy Phrases: My last day; I have accepted.

See also: *Part II:* Information Letters; *Part V:* Announcements.

To: John Ferguson, AC Department Manager

I am pleased to announce that I have accepted a position with BulboTech Corporation's Telecommunications and TV Components Group effective February 10, 2004. My last day in the Air Conditioning Department will be February 7, 2004.

I have enjoyed working with you during my 6½ years in the Air Conditioning Department, and it is not without regret that I move on. However, I believe this is a positive change and will provide new challenges and opportunities in my career.

Working with the AC department here has given me a great deal of experience as well as pleasure. I have thoroughly enjoyed working with you and would like to take this opportunity to thank you for everything you have done to make my tenure successful. I also wish you every success in your future endeavors.

I look forward to working with you again in the future.

Kindest personal regards,

Bill

Tips for Notifying Your Present Company That You Are Taking a New Job

- Come right out and say it: You have accepted a new job as a [POSITION] with [COMPANY] and your last day is [DATE].
- Be courteous. Say how much you enjoyed working with them.
- Do not take this as an opportunity to vent pent-up anger. Leave them with a good feeling about you.

RESPONDING TO A REJECTION NOTICE AFTER AN INTERVIEW

Why would you write back to an employer who rejects you? Not to argue — you're not going to change their minds — but to build goodwill and leave the door open for future opportunities. Since the majority of rejected candidates are never heard from again, writing a gracious letter thanking the interviewer for his or her time makes you stand out from the crowd in a positive, pleasing manner.

Format: [*See Appendix A:* Fig. A-1. Simple format for letters and memos.] Typed. Business letterhead.

Style/Tone/Voice: Formal. Active voice. [*See Part I for more on these subjects.*]

Structure: (1) Acknowledge the rejection, (2) Thank the reader for taking the time to interview you and consider your application, (3) Express your ongoing interest in their company, (4) Suggest the possibility that the reader might reevaluate you as a potential employee in the future.

Handy Phrases: Thanks so much; Thanks for considering me; Thanks for taking the time the other day; I'm sorry that.

See also: *Part III:* After the Interview.

Dear Mr. Frisch:

Thanks for your letter.

While I'm sorry I wasn't chosen for the opening in your production department, I appreciate your taking the time to consider me for the position. I still am very interested in working for WebCam Limited.

During our interview, you said my work experience fit the job well, but noted my lack of familiarity with the X-1500 Digital PrePress Package — the system you use for your prepress work.

I want you to know I have signed up for training to become a certified X-1500 operator. When I get my certificate this May, I will recontact you to see if you still need a qualified prepress specialist who can operate this package.

Thanks again for your time and consideration.

Sincerely,

Florence Rubin

Tips for Writing to an Interviewer Who Rejects You

- Never say the reader was wrong or that he made a bad decision.
- Do not disparage other candidates.
- If appropriate, let the reader know you want him to be successful in filling the position, whether it is with you or someone else.

Letters from Employers to Potential Employees

At times, the shoe will be on the other foot, and you will be the employer in search of a candidate to fill a position. Your recruitment effort will be accompanied by various documentation including job descriptions, job offers, and rejection letters.

JOB DESCRIPTION

When you want to hire an employee, start by writing a memo containing a job description for the position. You will use this to communicate with internal staff, your human resources department, headhunters, even job candidates. Such memos are often posted in company cafeterias and lounges to inform employees of the opening.

Format: [*See Appendix A:* Fig. A-1. Memo format.] Typed/word-processed or desktop-published.

Style/Tone/Voice: Formal. Active voice. [*See Part I for more on these subjects.*]

Structure: (1) Identify the document as a job description, (2) State the position, (3) Describe the job, (4) Outline the qualifications and experience required.

Handy Phrases: Not applicable.

See also: *Part V:* Announcements; *Part IX:* Letters Regarding Bids, Contracts, and Agreements.

TO: Terry Dawson
FROM: Pat Riley
SUBJECT: Job Description
POSITION: Securities Trader
DUTIES: To buy and sell various investments securities including stocks, bonds, options, and commercial paper. Other responsibilities include:

- Maintaining a trade log
- Maintaining a brokerage commission budget
- Recording pertinent market data on a daily basis
- Preparing a weekly written report on market activity.

NATURE OF THE JOB: Extremely fast-paced and intense during market trading hours. The trader is usually working on several trades at any given time. Almost all work is done on the telephone. The trader is constantly in contact with other traders, brokers, and outside sources of information, conducting trades and maintaining an overall picture of what the markets are doing and where they are going. Can be very stressful at times.

POSITION WITHIN THE FIRM: Trader reports directly to Chief Investment Officer. Because the firm's portfolio managers and analysts work closely with the trader, their evaluation of the trader is weighed heavily in all performance reviews.

REQUIREMENTS: Candidates must have a Bachelor's degree, preferably in finance, and some experience in the financial markets. Attention to detail, organization, and ability to work in high-pressure situations are essential. Some experience with computers and programs such as Lotus 1-2-3 helpful.

COMPENSATION: Includes a competitive salary and benefits package. Supplemented by an annual bonus based on individual performance and overall firm profitability.

Tips for Writing Job Descriptions

- Keep the description to one side of a sheet of paper (for posting on bulletin boards).

- Explain what the job entails. What will the person be doing during the 8 or 10 hours a day she is working for you?

- Outline the requirements the successful candidate must possess, including experience, skills, knowledge, education, and licenses or certifications.

LETTER TO POTENTIAL CANDIDATE AFTER INTERVIEW

Another situation that calls for written communication is following up with the candidate after the interview but before you have made a decision. You do not want to start off your relationship with a potential employee by leaving him hanging about such important news, so he should get a letter from you within a few days of the interview to let him know where he stands and what the next step is.

Here is a sample of a letter sent to a candidate after an interview. The company is still deciding who is still in the running for the position.

Format: [*See Appendix A:* Fig. A-1. Simple format for letters.] Typed/word-processed. Business letterhead.

Style/Tone/Voice: Formal. Active voice. [*See Part I for more on these subjects.*]

Structure: (1) Refer to the position for which the reader interviewed, (2) Thank the reader for his interest in employment with your organization, (3) Say where you are in the hiring process, (4) Spell out the next steps — his and yours.

continued

continued

Handy Phrases: Thanks for your interest; We are still reviewing; Under consideration; The next steps; We appreciate.

See also: *Part III:* Cover Letters and Job Inquiries; *Part IV:* Post-Meeting Follow-Up Letters; *Part VII:* Lead Inquiry-Fulfillment Follow-Ups; After-Sale Follow Up Letters.

Dear [applicant]:

Thank you for your interest in the [insert position title here] position. We have begun the process of screening applications received and hope to complete the process by [enter date here], at which time we will contact those applicants who we would like to consider further.

Again, we appreciate your interest and will communicate with you in the near future regarding the status of your application.

Sincerely,

Hiring Official (or designee)

Tips for Writing Post-Interview Letters to Potential Candidates

- Thank the candidate for their interest in the position.
- Let the person know they are still being considered for the position.
- Spell out what is going to happen next.

LETTER TO UNSUCCESSFUL CANDIDATE

People get their hopes up after a job interview, and when a letter comes in an envelope with your company's logo, they tear it open with bated breath. If the news is negative, let them down gently.

There are two cases in which you write rejection letters. The first is to someone who has sent a résumé, but based on your review of that résumé, you deem is not qualified.

Format: [*See Appendix A:* Fig. A-1. Simple format for letters and memos.] Typed/ word-processed. Business letterhead.

Style/Tone/Voice: Formal. Passive or active tone. [*See Part I for more on these subjects.*]

Structure: (1) Thank the candidate for applying or interviewing for the job, (2) State that the candidate is not in the running for the position, (3) Make a positive comment about their qualifications or the interview, (4) Thank the reader once more for the time and interest expressed in your organization.

Handy Phrases: Thanks for your interest; Unfortunately; A difficult decision; After careful consideration; Weighing all the factors.

See also: *Part II:* Refusing a Request; *Part IV:* Refusing Business Requests; Declining an Invitation to Serve; Refusing a Donation Request; *Part VI:* Sensitive Customer Correspondence; *Part VIII:* Refusing to Pay a Bill; Turning Down a Request for Credit; *Part IX:* Vendor Gift Policy.

Dear Applicant:

I would like to express my appreciation to you for your interest in our recruitment for [insert job title here].

We have identified candidates for interviews, and you have not been selected for interview. Although your experience is impressive, the résumés of other candidates more closely match the requirements of our position, and will be considered further.

Again, thank you for your interest in our position, and for taking the time to submit your résumé. If you wish to be considered for other positions at the University, please contact ASU's Human Resources Department, phone (555) 555-2454 or fax (555) 555-5544, office located at 1313 Ball Street, Albuquerque, NM 12345.

Sincerely,

Hiring Official [or designee]

The second case is when the person is being rejected after the interview. This may be more painful, since the candidate may take it as a personal rejection (e.g., they worry that you didn't like them based on your seeing and speaking with them — which may, unfortunately, be true but which you should never say).

Dear Candidate:

Thank you for your interest in our current recruitment for a [insert position title here], and for taking the time to speak with us about your qualifications and interest in the position.

You have many skills and abilities to bring to an organization. We had a number of qualified final candidates for the position and our decision was a difficult one. We have selected another candidate whose experience, education, and training more closely matches the requirements of the position and needs of our department.

If you wish to be considered for other positions at the University, please contact ASU's Human Resources Department, phone (555) 555-2454 or fax (555) 555-5544, office located at 1313 Ball Street, Albuquerque, NM 12345.

We wish you the best in your future endeavors.

Sincerely,

Hiring Official

Tips for Writing Rejection Letters

- Thank them for their time and interest.
- Praise their skills, credentials, poise, and whatever else about them impressed you.
- Give the reason they did not get the job, which is typically that you found someone who was a better fit for that particular position.

OFFERING A CANDIDATE A POSITION

Although you may want to call the candidate to tell her the good news in person, you should also send a letter; people like to have job offers in writing.

Format: [*See Appendix A:* Fig. A-1. Simple format for letters.] Typed/word-processed. Business letterhead.

Style/Tone/Voice: Formal. Active voice. [*See Part I for more on these subjects.*]

Structure: (1) Let the reader know immediately you are offering the job to him, (2) State the job title, (3) Give a brief summary of the job description, (4) Summarize the terms and conditions of the offer, (5) Ask for a response.

Handy Phrases: Congratulations; I'm pleased; I have some good news for you; We are offering you.

See also: *Part II:* Congratulations Letters; *Part III:* Accepting Job Offers; *Part V:* Congratulations to an Individual or Team; *Part IX:* Notification of Winning Bid.

Mr. Alan Rogers
1234 NW Springville Ct
Portland, OR 12345

Dear Alan:

On behalf of ABC Industrial Company's Applied Technologies Group, I am pleased to offer you the position of Sales Engineer, reporting to Bill Simmons, Business Unit Manager, beginning on May 1. This position is to be compensated in the following manner:

- Monthly Exempt Pay Rate: $5,666.67/month
- You will participate in the PIC Sales Incentive Program
- You will participate in the Company Automobile Program
- You are eligible to participate in the Company Benefit Program as described in the literature provided to you

This offer is contingent upon you satisfying the Company pre-employment drug testing, education, and reference verification requirements.

Please understand that this employment offer and any other Company documents are in no way to be construed as a contract of employment or any assurance of continued employment. Employment is at will and can be terminated at any time by either party. We look forward to welcoming you to ABC Industrial Company.

Sincerely,

Jon Trautman
Assistant Manager, Regional Personnel

I accept the terms of employment and will start_____

Date_____

Signature_____Date_____

Tips for Offering Someone a Job Via Letter

- Congratulate the person for beating a number of tough competitors for the job.
- Be clear about the offer — salary, vacation, benefits, job description, and starting date.
- Ask the reader to notify you either in person, by phone, or in writing of their acceptance of your offer.

Letters of Recommendation and Introduction

You will invariably be asked sometime in your life to write a letter of recommendation for someone seeking a job. If someone asks you in advance whether she can use you as a reference or have you write a referral letter, and you cannot in good conscience recommend her, say so. People who ask you to be references or write referral letters assume you will say positive things; after all, they are trying to get a job. Intending to write a less-than-glowing letter and not informing the person who asked you of your intention is like an ambush. If you cannot write a good letter of recommendation, decline.

There are two specific types of letters of recommendation. In the first type, a friend or colleague asks you to write a "generic" letter of recommendation. It is not for a specific job or employer, but meant to be a general reference she can show to interviewers if asked for such a letter.

In the second type, the employer asks the candidate for references, and the candidate gives your name. The employer then asks you whether you recommend the person, and why.

A letter of introduction works a bit differently. Let's say Sally asks John to help her get an interview with Marvin at Biotech Industries. John writes a letter to Marvin telling him about Sally. In the letter, he asks Marvin to grant Sally an interview or consider hiring her to work at Biotech.

GENERIC LETTERS OF RECOMMENDATION

If you have agreed to serve as a reference for a friend or acquaintance seeking a job, you may not want to write a separate letter for each position your friend is applying for. You can solve this problem by writing a blanket recommendation that the job seeker can show all potential employers.

Format: [*See Appendix A:* Fig. A-1. Simple format for letters and memos.] Handwritten or typed. Personal or business letterhead.

Style/Tone/Voice: Informal or formal. Active voice. [*See Part I for more on these subjects.*]

Structure: (1) State who you are and who you are with, (2) Explain how you know the person you are recommending, (3) Give the reasons why you think she would be a good person to hire, (4) Suggest to the reader that it would be a good idea to at least interview the candidate for consideration.

Handy Phrases: I highly recommend; Enthusiastic; A valuable team member; Results-oriented; Self-starter; Hard-working; Leadership qualities; Quick study; Articulate; Bright; Personable; Eager to succeed; Extremely knowledgeable; Experienced.

See also: *Part III:* Letters of Recommendation and Introduction; *Part IV:* Introductions; *Part IX:* Vendor Referral.

Prospective Employer:

I am the Partner-In-Charge of Zephyr Industries, and am writing to recommend Tracy Graduate. I have known Tracy Graduate through her work experience with our firm during the past summer, when she served as an Auditor Intern in our New York office.

Tracy became immediately involved in the annual audit of Zephyr Industries, conducting much of the historical accounting research required for the audit. In addition to gathering the financial information, Tracy was instrumental in the development of the final certification report. Tracy also participated in several other smaller audits, including her instrumental role in the quarterly audit of ABC Bank, where she developed several Excel macros to audit the inputs at the PC level. She later further developed these macros for use in future audits, which we have integrated into our Auditors Toolkit.

Tracy has shown the kind of initiative that is necessary to be successful over the long term in the public accounting field. She has excellent forensic skills, yet remains focused on the overall needs of the client. I believe she will be a strong Auditor and has an excellent future in the public accounting field. She is a conscientious worker and has an excellent work ethic. We would gladly have hired Tracy upon graduation if she were open to the New York City area.

I recommend Tracy to you without reservation. If you have any further questions with regard to her background or qualifications, please do not hesitate to call me.

Sincerely,

Terry Thompson
Partner-in-Charge

SPECIFIC LETTERS OF RECOMMENDATION

Here's another common situation: You agree to let someone use you as a reference, and when she does, the organization to which she is applying for a job contacts you for verification. To maximize the person's chance of getting the job, you want to write a letter of recommendation that is specific, positive, and concise.

Format: [*See Appendix A:* Fig. A-1. Simple format for letters.] Typed/word-processed. Business or personal letterhead.

Style/Tone/Voice: Formal. Active voice. [*See Part I for more on these subjects.*]

Structure: (1) Reference the reader's original request for your opinion, (2) Explain how you know the person you are recommending, (3) Give the reasons why you think he would be a good person to hire, (4) Suggest to the reader that it would be a good idea to at least interview the candidate for consideration.

Handy Phrases: Enthusiastic; A valuable team member; Results-oriented; Self-starter; Hard-working; Leadership qualities; Quick study; Articulate; Bright; Personable; Eager to succeed; Extremely knowledgeable.

See also: *Part III:* Letters of Recommendation and Introduction; *Part IV:* Introductions; *Part IX:* Vendor Referral.

Dear Mr. Villas:

This is in response to your recent request for a letter of recommendation for Maria Ramírez who worked for me up until two years ago.

Maria Ramírez worked under my direct supervision at Extension Technologies for a period of six years ending in October 2000. During that period, I had the great pleasure of seeing her blossom from a junior marketing trainee at the beginning, into a fully functioning Marketing

Program Co-Coordinator in her final two years with the company. That was the last position she held before moving on to a better career opportunity elsewhere.

Ms. Ramírez is a hard-working self-starter who invariably understands exactly what a project is all about from the outset, and how to get it done quickly and effectively. During her two years in the Marketing Co-Coordinator position, I cannot remember an instance in which she missed a major deadline. She often brought projects in below budget, and a few were even completed ahead of schedule.

Ms. Ramírez is a resourceful, creative, and solution-oriented person who was frequently able to come up with new and innovative approaches to her assigned projects. She functioned well as a team leader when required, and she also worked effectively as a team member under the direction of other team leaders.

On the interpersonal side, Ms. Ramírez has superior written and verbal communication skills. She gets along extremely well with staff under her supervision, as well as colleagues at her own level. She is highly respected, as both a person and a professional, by colleagues, employees, suppliers, and customers alike.

In closing, as detailed above, based on my experience working with her, I can unreservedly recommend Maria Ramírez to you for any intermediate or senior marketing position. If you would like further elaboration, feel free to call me at (555) 555-4293.

Sincerely,

Georgette Christenson
Director, Marketing and Sales

Tips for Writing Letters of Recommendation

- Say how you know the person. Are you a former boss, colleague, or employee?

- Base your letter on first-hand knowledge and personal observation (e.g., the employer already knows from the résumé that the candidate can use Word, but you can say how fast he got your correspondence done).

- Cover both technical skills and people skills. The potential employer wants to know: Is she good at her job? Will she get along with the people I already have?

LETTERS OF INTRODUCTION

As discussed, a letter of introduction does just what its name implies: introducing one person to another person, but for the specific purpose of convincing the reader that the person being introduced in the letter would make a good addition to an organization.

Format: [*See Appendix A:* Fig. A-1. Simple format for letters.] Typed/word-processed. Business or personal letterhead.

Style/Tone/Voice: Informal or /formal. Passive or active voice. [*See Part I for more on these subjects.*]

Structure: (1) Give the name of the person to be introduced and a few personal details, (2) State how you know the person and what your relationship is or has been [e.g., teacher, mentor, boss, relative, fellow alumni], (3) Discuss the candidate's qualifications, be specific and enthusiastic, (4) Explain your reasons for introducing this person and how you know what you know about this person.

Handy Phrases: Put the two of you in touch; Can heartily recommend; Have observed continued professionalism/performance/maturity; Have worked with/known for X years; I hope the two of you can benefit from the acquaintance.

See also: *Part III:* Letters of Recommendation and Introduction; *Part IV:* Introductions; *Part IX:* Vendor Referral.

Dear Mr. Greenstreet:

Ann Morgan, a young engineer who took my process design seminar given for AIChE last summer, has asked me whether I can put the two of you together, so that you might consider granting her an interview for a position in your process control department.

You know that I am a rather tough instructor, so it means something when I tell you that Ms. Morgan has an exceedingly strong grasp of process design and control — especially considering she is just two years out of college. By the way, she showed me her transcript, and was a solid B+ student at Brightwater Tech, which, as you know, has one of the best programs on the East Coast.

My department is overstaffed and, since the acquisition, half of our work is being moved to the California location. If this were not the case, and we were looking to add personnel, I would make Ms. Morgan an offer tomorrow.

Whether she would be an ideal fit with your group I cannot say, although I know that technically she can handle a Process Engineer position with extreme competence. As for whether she'd be a good addition to your team (which I suspect she would), why don't you give her an interview and find out for yourself?

Sincerely,

Tips for Writing Letters of Introduction

- Say how you know the person. Are you a former boss, colleague, professor, or employee?

- Point out the candidate's qualifications in a specific and enthusiastic manner.

- Explain how you know what you know about this person. Why are you so confident in your recommendation?

Query Letters

A query letter is a proposal to a publisher that you write an article or book for them. There are two categories of people who need to write query letters. The first consists of professional writers, who write books and articles for a living.

The larger category is businesspeople, who write articles and books to promote themselves and their organizations. They write not for pay, but for the credibility being a published author generates as well as the inquiries resulting from this free publicity.

ARTICLE QUERY LETTERS

A smart way to promote yourself or your company is by writing articles. One method of getting published is to write short articles and send them to editors with a cover letter. Sending the manuscript with the letter works best when the article is a short item — say, 500 words or less. The cover letter says why you are writing, what the article is about, and why you are qualified to write it.

Format: *See Appendix A:* Fig. A-1. Simple format for letters. Typed/word-processed. Personal or business letterhead.

Style/Tone/Voice: Informal or formal. Active voice. [*See Part I for more on these subjects.*]

Structure: (1) Refer to the enclosed manuscript, (2) State the word length, (3) Say in a sentence or two what the article is about, including why it is relevant to the editor's publication, (4) Present a brief bio of the author.

continued

continued

Handy Phrases: Enclosed for your consideration; Might be right for you; A good fit; A timely topic; Your readers.

See also: *Part III:* Cover Letters and Job Inquiries; *Part VII:* Types of Sales Letters; Lead-Generating Letters.

September 1, 2000

Joe Smith, Editor
Communication Briefings

Dear Mr. Smith,

I love your "Communication Briefings" and thought the following short item below, 180 words, might fit in the newsletter.

I've adapted it from a piece I wrote, "Five Tips to Improve Your Technical Writing," which appeared in *How to Write Online* in February 2000.

I am a freelance writer and computer professional with over twenty articles published in the computer and technical press. I've also published one computer book.

Regards,

Doug Nickerson

For articles of 500 words and above, you should not send the manuscript. Instead, before you write the article, write and send a query letter.

You may also want to discuss how you will research the article. For instance, if you are writing about kidney stones because you had them, your personal experience is not enough. You also have to interview doctors.

Give an approximate length for the article and note how quickly you can write it. Then ask the editor for the go-ahead.

Mr. James Frank, Editor
NYT Express
34 East 51st St.
New York, NY 12345

Dear Mr. Frank:

Is this letter a waste of paper?

Yes — *if* it fails to get the desired result.

In business, most letters and memos are written to generate a specific response, close a sale, set up a meeting, get a job interview, make a contact. Many of these letters fail to do their job.

Part of the problem is that business executives and support staff don't know how to write persuasively. The solution is a formula first discovered by advertising copywriters, a formula called AIDA. AIDA stands for Attention, Interest, Desire, Action.

First, the letter gets attention . . . with a hard-hitting lead paragraph that goes straight to the point, or offers an element of intrigue.

Then, the letter hooks the reader's interest. The hook is often a clear statement of the reader's problems, his needs, his concerns. If you are writing to a customer who received damaged goods, state the problem. And then promise a solution.

Next, it creates desire. You are offering something — a service, a product, an agreement, a contract, a compromise, a consultation. Tell the reader the benefit he'll receive from your offering. Create a desire for your product.

Finally, call for action. Ask for the order, the signature, the check, the assignment.

I'd like to write a 1,500-word article on "How to Write Letters that Get Results." The piece will illustrate the AIDA formula with a variety of actual letters and memos from insurance companies, banks, manufacturers, and other organizations. I can deliver the piece by May 1.

This letter, too, was written to get a specific result — an article assignment from the editor of *NYT Express.*

Did it succeed?

Regards.

Doug Wilson

Tips for Writing Article Query Letters

- Read the magazine before proposing an article for it. Editors are good at sensing when a writer proposing an article is unfamiliar with their publication.
- Keep your query letter to one page if possible, no more than two. If you have a detailed outline for the article, consider sending it as an attachment.
- Do not try to exert any leverage or pressure to get the editor to take the article. For instance, don't say your company is an advertiser. Editors resent such pressure and it makes them more inclined to say no.
- Make the query letter sparkling, sharp, and crisp. The editor judges whether you can write the article or not by how well your query letter is written.

BOOK QUERY LETTERS

If articles are a great self-promotion for your business, a book is even more so: Marketing consultant Jeffrey Lant says that "a book is a brochure that will never be thrown away." But in your book query letter, don't hint that you are doing it as a self-promotion; publishers want a solid, informative, objective book they can profitably sell to book buyers.

Your book query can go to one of two audiences: either a literary agent or an editor at a publishing house. In today's market, we recommend engaging the services of a literary agent to sell your book; the majority of publishers today will not consider looking at unagented manuscripts (you do not need an agent to sell your articles).

Format: [*See Appendix A:* Fig. A-1. Simple format for letters.] Typed/word-processed. Personal or business letterhead.

Style/Tone/Voice: Informal or formal. Active voice. [*See Part I for more on these subjects.*]

Structure: (1) Tell the reader where you got her name, (2) State the title or topic of the book you propose to write, (3) Explain its contents, purpose, and intended audience, (4) Give your qualifications to write a book on this topic, (5) Offer to send a more detailed proposal and outline of the book.

Handy Phrases: May I send you a proposal; Is the ideal market for this book; I am uniquely qualified to write this book because; Readers of this book would include; The assets I can bring to this endeavor are.

See also: *Part III:* Cover Letters and Job Inquiries; *Part VII:* Types of Sales Letters; Lead-Generating Letters.

Mr. John Jones
XYZ [Publishers/Literary] Agency

Dear Mr. Jones:

I notice you are the [editor/agent] for *How to Raise Poodles for Fun and Profit* by Sue Smith. Would you consider looking at a proposal for a poodle book that focuses on health, obedience, and grooming?

For 12 years, I have been the owner of Oodles of Poodles, a boutique specializing in poodle care. We do haircuts, styling, bathing, nail trimming, and poodle "charm school," and I am uniquely qualified to offer poodle owners a lot of valuable how-to advice on these subjects.

May I send you a proposal for a nonfiction, do-it-yourself book, aimed at poodle owners, on taking care of their pet poodles? A self-addressed stamped envelope is enclosed for your reply.

Thanks,

Dick Smithers

P.S. Poodles owned by our clients have won 65 "Best of Show" blue ribbons at dog shows since 1995.

Tips for Writing Book Query Letters

- Address your letter to the agent or editor by name — not "dear agent/editor."
- Show familiarity with the other books the reader represents or publishes, especially those in the same field as yours.
- Say what makes your book different or better than other books on the same topic.
- Keep your letter brief — ideally a page at most.

SCRIPT QUERY LETTERS

If you have ambitions of writing for stage, screen, or television, query letters will also be in your future. Navigating the waters of Hollywood is beyond the scope of this book, but I can provide you with the following model letter as a guide.

Format: [*See Appendix A:* Fig. A-1. Simple format for letters.] Typed/word-processed. Personal or business letterhead.

Style/Tone/Voice: Informal or formal. Active voice. [*See Part I for more on these subjects.*]

Structure: (1) Say who you are (i.e., writer, producer, actor, director), (2) Explain the project, (3) Give any relevant credentials or connections, (4) Offer to send the script.

Handy Phrases: In development; In collaboration; In partnership.

See also: *Part III:* Cover Letters and Job Inquiries; *Part VII:* Types of Sales Letters; Lead-Generating Letters.

RE: *Backstage at Guffaw's*

Dear Ms. Zeichner:

I am a producer who has collaborated with comedian Peter Fogel on a project called *Back-stage at Guffaw's.*

It's a very satirical and poignant look at life as a stand-up comedian, done in a documentary ("mockumentary") style; it's *This is Spinal Tap* with comics. We anticipate attaching some of the biggest names in comedy in cameo roles. Toward that end, Richard Jeni and Kevin Meany have already expressed their interest in becoming involved.

At your request, I will be happy to forward you a copy. I look forward to hearing from you.

Sincerely,

Braddon L. Mendelson
Producer

Tips for Writing Script Query Letters

- Sum up the idea in a single sentence or phrase.
- Compare your idea with something successful the reader is already familiar with (e.g., "This is *Driving Miss Daisy* with James Bond as the chauffeur").
- Drop the names of any show business heavyweights with whom you've discussed the project.

PART IV

GENERAL BUSINESS CORRESPONDENCE

In this section I give you model letters for a wide range of business situations, from sending a follow-up letter to a contact you've made while networking at an association meeting, to requesting a favor from someone who has no particular reason to grant it. Most of these models can be used interchangeably as either a letter, a fax, or an e-mail. You can simply fit the text provided into proper letter, fax, or e-mail format as shown in Appendix A.

Most business writers today attempt to fit their entire letter on one side of a single sheet of company letterhead, which necessitates brevity. Second sheets are used only if needed. Keep your faxes and e-mail messages brief — if there is lengthy explanatory or supporting material, send it as an attached file. [*See Part X for more about e-mails and faxes.*] External business communications work best when they communicate one central idea or point. For highly detailed or technical information, you may want to use one or more attachments.

It is highly unlikely that a sample letter in this or any model letter book can be used verbatim for anything but the simplest and most generic situations — although plenty of these situations exist, and you'll find our letters handy for addressing them.

A more practical use of these letters is to guide you in how to say things that you have often had difficulty saying in the past — for example, requesting a favor, giving instructions, saying yes, or saying no. Perhaps in the letters here you will find just the right phrase for those difficult moments, and save time, money, and frustration as a result.

Communicating Business Information

From the casual "FYI" note to the communications campaign that surrounds announcing a merger, the writer should organize the information to be disseminated and work to make sure their communication is readable and easy to digest. Here are samples of how to handle the myriad business writing situations such as simple greetings and "nice to meet you" letters, making and responding to requests, and communicating difficult news your clients and associates don't want to hear.

FYI LETTERS

The abbreviation "FYI" stands for "for your information," and an FYI letter does just that: transmits short bits of information. Typically this is information the reader needs to know now or needs as reference, or is information that you want to tell him. FYIs can be used to discuss current events or something that would impact the reader down the road (e.g., a policy change taking effect the following year). It can be something as simple as a self-stick note stating, "FYI: I thought this article would be of interest" or a letter sent to an association's members alerting them that a new president is being elected.

Say you are an auto dealer. An example of "need to know now" information would be that it's time for the reader to bring his car in for a 30,000-mile inspection. An example of reference is that your dealership will be exhibiting at the auto show next week. An example of information you want him to know is that you have hired two service technicians to reduce wait time in your shop. Retailers often send this kind of information via a postcard.

It is not always necessary to use the term FYI in an FYI letter. Another way to quickly cue the reader into the topic under discussion is to use a "Re:" or "subject" line. In a letter, leave one or two lines after the inside address (the recipient's name and address) and then type the "Re:" line. Then leave another one or two lines and begin with the salutation.

FYI postcards are a most efficient way to alert business associates about a change in your contact information (e.g., address, telephone number). This information can also be sent via e-mail — it's probably a good idea to send it both ways to ensure that your information doesn't get lost in the daily shuffling of paperwork. Formal FYI letters are typically used to alert the reader about changes in credit terms, about factory recalls of products, and about holiday closings.

Format: [*See Appendix A:* Fig. A-1. Simple format for letters and memos.] Typed/word-processed. Business or personal letterhead.

Style/Tone/Voice: Can be informal or formal, depending on the content. Active tone or voice. [*See Part I for more on these subjects.*]

Structure: (1) Call reader's attention, (2) Explain details, (3) Ask for action, if necessary, (4) Ask the reader to contact you with questions or concerns.

Handy Phrases: FYI; For your information; Thought you'd like to know; Please call me if you have any questions.

See also: *Part V:* FYI Internal Memos; *Part X:* E-mail and Fax Correspondence.

Mr. Mike Hernandez
Alchemy Consulting
123 Main Street
Anytown, USA
Re: Liability insurance premiums

Dear Mike:

You're right. The premium for the policy we proposed is higher than the other companies provided you with quotes.

However, our policy gives you broader liability coverage, with a much smaller deductible, as explained in the comparison table attached.

We can offer a policy with equivalent terms to the other insurance companies who quoted you, at approximately the same premium.

The problem is, this level of coverage excludes the precise situations for which you want the most protection!

Please let me know which option you prefer. Thanks.

Sincerely,

Joe Carlson, Agent
Continental Insurance

Enclosure

When you send enclosures, type the word "Enclosure" a line or two below the signature (or the P.S. if you use one).

Tips for FYI Letters

- Don't waste words.
- Avoid going off on tangents or writing about tangential or irrelevant topics, such as the World Series or social plans.
- If you are referring to a previous letter or other document whose details are important to the discussion, consider including it as an enclosure.
- Do not feel compelled to "stretch" your copy or add words because the letter seems too short. If all you want to say is "FYI," then just write "FYI" and sign your name. Your reader will not complain that your letter is too short.

INSTRUCTION LETTERS

Letters may be used to give instructions or confirm them.

Because of the need for brevity and the limitations of the letter format, they are usually restricted to giving simple instructions.

A more complex task might have to be explained on the phone or in a personal meeting. Procedures, such as how to operate or repair equipment, are usually communicated in manuals or on CD-ROM.

Format: [*See Appendix A:* Fig. A-1. Simple format for letters and memos.] Typed/word-processed. Business or personal letterhead.

Style/Tone/Voice: Informal or formal (or can be both). Active tone or voice. [*See Part I for more on these subjects.*]

Structure: (1) Open with brief synopsis of situation, (2) State instructions in bullet form, (3) If you are correcting problems, outline as Problem A, Solution A, Problem B, Solution B; if you are not correcting problems, proceed to step 4, (4) Ask for cooperation, (5) Let them know what steps to take if they have questions or problems.

Handy Phrases: As discussed last week, we will discontinue xxx; When we place orders, please follow the process outlined below; Attached is a proposal to simplify our xxxx process; In reviewing our project list we've agreed on the following course of action.

See also: *Part V:* Human Resources (HR) Policies

June 4, 2002

Ms. Kathryn Wilson
Director-Consumer Information Center
American Retail Corporation
1330 North R Street
Anytown, USA

Dear Ms. Wilson:

This will confirm my telephone instructions to Mr. George Hopkins concerning the diversion of ASDS 87778.

This order, shipped from North Washington, Delaware, by Star Chemical Company via AmRail direct, was originally consigned to ABC Chemicals Corporation at Nutley, New Jersey. Please arrange to divert ASDS 87778 to Monmouth Chemical Company at Kearney, New Jersey, via AmRail direct. Any charges connected with this diversion should be sent to me.

Sincerely,

Frederick Loosey
Senior Transportation Analyst

Tips for Writing Instruction Letters

- Write instructions in the imperative, active voice (e.g., "Turn the valve to the right," not "The valve should be turned to the right" or "You must turn the valve to your right"). See Part I for more discussion of the imperative, active voice.

- Any warnings (e.g., "Wear safety goggles when handling cylinders") should be highlighted in boldface or placed in a box so the warning stands out on the page.

- You may want to explain why it is important to follow the instructions you have provided — either the benefits of doing so or the problems that can arise when they are not followed. People dislike reading instructions and must often be motivated to do so.

- Provide a resource the reader can contact if she has questions and encourage her to do so.

LETTER OF TRANSMITTAL

Cover letters are typically informational in nature and straightforward in content. They serve recipients in two ways. First, they help the reader save time by telling them what is enclosed without making them read through several documents. If the enclosures have value to the reader and are being given at no cost, the cover letter also may be used to stress their utility, importance, and value. Second, they help the reader get into the right mindset to read the accompanying material. One of the most common uses of letters today is as cover notes to accompany more detailed material—reports, proposals, manuals, product samples, and so on. Cover letters for employment are written to highlight achievements, refer the reader to important points on an attached résumé, and ask for an interview. [*See Part III for more about employment cover letters.*]

Format: [*See Appendix A:* Fig. A-1. Simple format for letters and memos.] Typed/word-processed. Business or personal letterhead.

Style/Tone/Voice: Informal or formal (or can be both). Active tone or voice. [*See Part I for more on these subjects.*]

Structure: (1) The lead of the letter should list what documents are attached/enclosed (give titles and brief descriptions), (2) The body should summarize the contents of the enclosure, why they are of interest, and what, if anything, the reader should do with the materials, or how he should use them, (3) The close should state any desired response and, as a courtesy to the reader, give a contact the reader can call for more help, to ask questions, or request additional materials.

Handy Phrases: Enclosed is our department's 2004 budget and marketing plan; The following material contains details about the recall of part no. xxx; The attached report describes; Please read and follow the instructions on page xx of the enclosed policy; Please call me if you have any questions.

See also: *Part III:* Cover Letters and Job Inquiries.

January 1, 2003

Mr. Bernie Segal
Laboratory Technician
Laten Chemical Corporation
1234 Trenton Street
Anytown, VA 88898

Dear Mr. Segal:

Enclosed is a technical service report and a laboratory procedure for emulsification of FO-BRAN 55 on a small scale.

The report describes some of FO-BRAN's physical properties, gives examples of sizing results in the field, and explains field emulsification procedure. The laboratory procedure tells you how FO-BRAN emulsion is prepared in smaller amounts.

I hope the information enclosed is sufficient to introduce you to FO-BRAN and allow you to run your evaluations successfully.

If you have any questions, please call me at (555) 555-5555.

Sincerely,

Robin Deere
Paper Development Specialist

Enclosures

Tips for Writing Letters of Transmittal

- If there are multiple enclosures, list them in bullet form with a short explanation of the contents and purpose of each. Also state whether they should be read in any particular order.

- If the enclosed materials are rather technical and the reader is not interested in technical details, use the letter as an executive summary to explain the key points in plain English.

- An effective technique is to highlight interesting content in the enclosures by summarizing it in a paragraph in the cover letter, with a reference to the document and page number on which it is discussed.

DISSEMINATING TECHNICAL INFORMATION

Engineers, doctors, and other specialists must frequently communicate technical information, and they often use letters to do it.

We usually see detailed technical information communicated in media other than letters, such as Web sites, product data sheets, manuals, and technical papers. Letters are most effective when communicating just one or two points of information. For more, you need a longer format.

Format: [*See Appendix A:* Fig. A-1. Simple format for letters and memos.] Typed/word-processed. Business or personal letterhead.

Style/Tone/Voice: Can be either informal or formal. Active tone or voice. [*See Part I for more on these subjects.*]

Structure: (1) Open your letter with your reason for writing, let them know the topic of the technical information you wish to convey, (2) Carefully construct the body of your letter using an outline, go over each technical point in language appropriate to your audience, (3) Close the letter with a brief summary of your main points and offer resources for additional information, which could be separate documentation, a Web site, someone within your company, or a combination of any of these.

Handy Phrases: I wanted to bring to your attention; The following material contains details about; If you'd like further information; To clarify any of the above; Please call me if you have any questions.

See also: *Part V:* Information Technology (IT) Memos.

September 29, 2002

Ms. Ruth Callahan
Barry Chemical Co.
234 Victoria Street
New Octavia, KS 12345

Dear Ms. Callahan:

At your request, I am sending 1.3 Kg 0.2% AGE-modified starch and a Material Safety Data Sheet for your research program.

As I suggested, you should study the effect of AGE on the starch backbone and molecular weight of starch.

Natural Polymer Research will prepare these starches for you.

Please keep me updated on the progress of the starch/graft research.

Regards,

Bonnie Bonnard

Tips for Writing Letters of Technical Information

- An outline is essential to creating a coherent and easy-to-understand document.
- Keep the length under two pages. If you have more information to communicate, you need a separate enclosure.
- State your intended purpose in the lead. Why are you sending the information? Why should the reader read it? What is he expected to do with the information?
- Be aware of your audience. When describing a technical process, you would do it differently depending on whether you were writing to an engineer, a nontechnical executive, or a high school student.
- Think about the most important thing the reader needs to know about this subject, and build your letter around it.

Networking Business Letters

Business networking offers opportunities to share ideas, contacts, and most important, referrals. Most people attend meetings and events but make no effort to build that initial contact into a solid relationship. The following networking business letter samples will help you make the most of your networking efforts.

BUSINESS GREETINGS

When you meet someone online, over the phone, or in person, it's a smart idea to introduce yourself with a bit more detail in a follow-up e-mail or letter. Why? If you did not exchange business cards, the e-mail or letter gives the recipient a record of your contact information: name, e-mail address, phone number, mailing address. If you did exchange business cards, the follow-up greeting allows you to provide information not on the card. It may repeat information you discussed as well as provide details not found on your card.

How many people have you met or talked with this year who you've already forgotten? The follow-up reminds the recipient of the meeting or conversation, creating a more lasting impression of you in his or her mind.

Format: [*See Appendix A:* Fig. A-1. Simple format for letters and memos.] Typed/word-processed. Business or personal letterhead.

Style/Tone/Voice: Can be either informal or formal. Active tone or voice. [*See Part I for more on these subjects.*]

Structure: (1) Include a phrase that it was "a pleasure to meet you", (2) Add a brief reminder of your conversation; comment on the event; and/or enclose a helpful tip, lead, or article, (3) Close with a reason to stay in touch and/or make contact again the future.

Handy Phrases: It was great meeting you at last night's event; I enjoyed sharing war stories about our industry; I look forward to talking again about working with you on the project idea we discussed; Based on our conversation, I thought you might find the enclosed article of interest; My colleague, [name], would be a good prospect for you, when you contact her please let her know I referred you.

See also: *Part III:* Networking Letters.

Bob:

It was great to meet you on the phone just now! I look forward to working with you.

Below is my contact information; please call or e-mail me if you have any questions. Feel free in the next few weeks to send material for me to look over — I'll be happy to send you some feedback.

Sincerely,

Suzanne Davis
Project Editor
Kitsch House Publishing

Tips for Business Greetings

- Send the greeting message within 48 hours after meeting the person. The longer you wait, the less of a positive impression it makes.

- In the lead, remind the person where, how, when, and under what circumstances the two of you first met.

- Be friendly and positive. You are trying to deepen the relationship and get it off to a successful start. Save complaints, concerns, or problems for another communication.

- If needed and relevant, give a capsule summary of who you are, what you do, and why the reader should care.

- Include all relevant contact information. Usually this is transmitted in the letterhead of a business letter or the sig file (*see Part X:* E-mail and Fax Correspondence) of an e-mail.

- Be helpful. Offer support, friendship, services, or whatever else you can do to help the recipient achieve his or her goals.

POST-MEETING FOLLOW-UP LETTERS

Combined, American businesspeople spend thousands of hours every month networking, but much of the benefit from the networking is lost through poor or nonexistent follow-up. Typically, a person collects between 30–50 business cards during a trade show. These usually end up sitting in a drawer, untouched and collecting dust. By creating a couple of letter templates, you'll find it is easy (and worthwhile) to keep in touch.

Take the time to compose a standard response letter you can send out to everyone you meet. Just collect their cards at the meeting; input their name, title, company, and address into the form document; print; and mail.

Format: [*See Appendix A:* Fig. A-1. Simple format for letters and memos.] Typed/word-processed. Business or personal letterhead.

Style/Tone/Voice: Can be either informal/formal depending on the level of the businessperson within his/her company hierarchy (C.E.O., manager, or marketer, etc.) and type of show. Active tone or voice. [*See Part I for more on these subjects.*]

Structure: If you're a vendor: (1) Thank the person for stopping by your booth or for spending time talking with you, (2) Remind the person about your services and how you can help them, (3) Refer them to highlights of any enclosed material, (4) Close by stating next steps.

For other situations, use the same format as for business greetings: (1) Open with a statement saying "it was nice to meet you," (2) Add a brief reminder of your conversation; comment on the event and/or enclose a helpful tip, lead, or article, (3) Close with a reason to stay in touch and/or make contact again in the future.

Handy Phrases: Thanks for stopping by our booth at the Widget Conference; It was a pleasure meeting you; Based on our discussion, I've enclosed some material tailored for your requirements; I've enclosed some preliminary cost estimates; I'll call you later this week to see if you're ready to make a decision; Please call me if you have questions or need additional information.

See also: *Part III:* Follow-Up Letters.

Dear Tim:

Absolutely super to meet you at the most recent meeting. If you are looking for a letter shop organization that delivers throughput-efficiency and cost-effectiveness, then look no further!

Trans-Experian's Letter Shop, Printing and Packaging Services group is the largest letter shop in the country. Whether you need cutting-edge services like poly wrapping, duplex imaging, card affixing; or a traditional package with a personalized letter, lift note and reply envelope, we handle it with meticulous attention to detail.

While Trans-Experian has the resources to handle an individual mailing of 100 million pieces or more, we're also happy to help you with a test drop of 50,000 prior to a roll-out. You will also have access to creative engineering when you have complex needs no one else can meet. For example, we've been building custom equipment for our clients since the 1950s and most recently we devised systems for mass-mailings of CD-ROMs and diapers.

Our continued capital investment in *new* equipment and efficient processing — more than $50 million just in the last three years — means that with Trans-Experian, you'll enjoy greater speed, lower costs, shorter cycle times, and optimal flexibility. Unlike most letter shops in our industry, we can easily accommodate significant growth. In 2001 we assembled and mailed over 2 billion pieces of mail and we are still not at full capacity!

Once you entrust your Letter Shop, Printing and Packaging campaigns to us, a designated customer service representative and I will serve as your contacts, making sure that each step in the process takes place correctly and on time. Through our team approach, we provide a balanced, reliable, fail-safe environment and optimum service. Close working partnerships with clients are the norm at Trans-Experian, so that you'll soon feel as though we are an extension of your own in-house operations.

Enclosed is an overview of our services. If I have not heard from you sooner, I will call next week to find out more about your Letter Shop, Printing and Packaging needs. I look forward to helping your organization achieve its direct marketing goals.

Sincerely,

Hector G. Hernandez
Account Executive

P.S. Ask me how we can help you keep your postage costs down. With our mail commingling and drop entry program and multiple locations across the country, we offer ways to lower your spending while speeding delivery of your material to recipients at the same time.

Tips for Writing Post-meeting Follow-Ups

- State the event at which you met the person. Say you enjoyed meeting them.
- Tell them relevant details about your company, product, or service. Let them know how you can help them.
- Suggest the next step in the relationship, which might be a meeting, presentation, or price quote.

CORDIAL CONTACTS

The main purpose of a cordial contact letter is simply to keep in touch with the reader and let him know you are thinking of him.

Who would you want to keep in touch with? Customers, prospects, inactive accounts, consultants, industry gurus, colleagues, coworkers, employees, friends, relatives, the media, vendors, key suppliers, business partners, and any other people you know and care about or want to know about you.

The holidays are the obvious time when people go through their address book or database and send out cards, gifts, or make calls, but the effort gets lost among all the correspondence your recipient is fielding. Make an effort to send notes and letters to important people all year long; consistency — and not one-shot deals — is the key to building relationships.

Format: [*See Appendix A:* Fig. A-1. Simple format for letters and memos.] Typed/word-processed. Business or personal letterhead.

Style/Tone/Voice: Can be informal or formal. Active tone or voice. [*See Part I for more on these subjects.*]

Structure: (1) Begin with the reason you're writing (e.g., been thinking of you; hope you're enjoying the season; want to thank you for your continued business), (2) Expand on your opening, (3) Express wish for continued relationship, (4) Close with regards/good wishes.

Handy Phrases: Just taking a moment to express our thanks for your business; I was just thinking about you and I hope you and your loved ones can take some time off to enjoy this beautiful summer weather; Thank you for the satisfying relationship we've enjoyed these past xx years; Wishing you continued personal and professional success.

See also: *Part VI:* Relationship-Building Letters.

Dear Randy:

I was flipping through my touch file and noticed your name. It's been too long since we've talked, and I wanted you to know that I we have appreciated your business over the years. I don't see you simply as a customer; I see you as a friend.

I hope that you were satisfied with our prompt handling of your auto claim last August; I pride myself on the company's responsiveness to these types of claims and feel good personally when I know we've gotten you back on the road, so to speak.

If I can do anything else for you, please don't hesitate to call.

Sincerely,

With the advent of the Internet, cordial contacts are often made via e-mail. One resulting effect, letters sent via snail mail have greater impact; people admire the extra effort you've taken to write out your thoughts.

Invest some money in a nice pen and handsome stationery. Keep them near your desk with plenty of stamps. When you're in the midst of the workday and you think of someone or see a name pop up on your database, take a moment to write out a quick note — it will be noticed and appreciated.

For companies that want to keep their name in front of customers and prospects, online promotional newsletters, or e-zines, are the medium of choice. E-zines are sent typically monthly or biweekly. [*See Appendix A for a sample e-zine.*]

For individuals, a good contact method is to periodically send information of interest with a simple "FYI" note as outlined in the earlier section. This information can include your company's annual report, new sales brochures, reprints of articles by or about you, or other industry-specific or general items of interest.

Tips for Cordial Contact Letters

- The tone should be light and friendly (that's why they're called "cordial" contacts).
- Limit the content to two to four short pieces of news or items of interest.
- Recall an old event, a favorite time, a pleasant memory to reinforce your bond with the recipient.
- Add interest. Tell the reader something fascinating or relevant to his life that he does not already know.
- Add a human touch. Connect not just on a business level, but also on a personal one, with your reader.

INTRODUCTIONS

An introduction is similar to a business greeting or a post-meeting follow-up, in that you are making an effort to establish a business relationship. You may be introducing yourself or introducing a person to another person — for instance, letting your customers know about a new salesperson you have hired, or referring a vendor to a colleague. [*See Part IX for more on vendor referral letters.*]

You may even be writing to someone whom you've never met. They may not know who you are, what your company is, what you represent or sell, or why they want to know you.

The goal of the introduction letter is to give the recipient a reason that he/she should want to know you. Your letter can be brief and to the point. Tell the recipient who you are and establish that you are a resource they should want to get to know better.

Your second objective, which is optional, is suggesting a specific course of action, or making a specific offer. Sometimes this works in an introduction letter. In other situations, it may best be saved for a future contact [*see* Requests, *later in this part*].

However, a universal truth is that the reader is always asking, "What's in it for me?" If there is no compelling reason to know you or get to know you — if he perceives that you cannot improve his life or business — he will have little interest in learning who you are or why you are writing.

Format: [*See Appendix A:* Fig. A-1. Simple format for letters and memos.] Typed/word-processed. Business or personal letterhead.

Style/Tone/Voice: Can be informal or formal. Active tone or voice. [*See Part I for more on these subjects.*]

Structure: (1) Make the Introduction, (2) Give some background that will be compelling to the reader, (3) Close with a statement of your confidence that the relationship will be mutually beneficial.

Handy Phrases: It is with great pleasure that I introduce you to; I know you'll enjoy speaking to him; I saw your name in the latest journal and thought you might be interested in.

See also: *Part II:* Requests; *Part III:* Letters of Recommendation and Introduction; *Part IV:* Business Requests; *Part IX:* Vendor Referral.

Here's a letter introducing a new hair colorist. Notice how the letter entices clients to come in to meet the new person by commenting on her experience.

Dear Customers:

It is with great pleasure that I introduce you to our newest hair color specialist, Georgia Hall. We're excited to have Georgia join us — we think you'll enjoy reaping the benefits of her training and experiences in Paris salons.

Give us a call when you're ready for your next hair color appointment and we'll set up a time for you to meet with Georgia.

As always, thank you for your business and we look forward to seeing you soon.

Warm regards,

Here's a common situation — announcing to your clients that you've hired a new sales representative:

Dear [Customer],

Our Industrial Products Department is pleased to announce that Alan Smith has joined us as a Sales Engineer working out of the Portland, Oregon, office. Alan brings over 20 years of experience in engineering and systems sales covering Oregon and other Western states, most recently as a factory representative for Northwest Electronics in Portland.

Alan will take over responsibility for the Northwestern territory, calling on the Office Automation, PC and Telecom markets.

Alan will be contacting you shortly to greet you. We're sure you'll enjoy working with Alan — he's quite knowledgeable and he's a pleasure to talk to. As always, we appreciate our relationship and we're here if you have any questions or concerns.

Sincerely,

Tips for Introduction Letters

- Even though the letter is supposedly about you, keep in mind that it's really about the reader — his needs, desires, interests, and goals.

- The reader only cares about you with respect to how you can help him.

- When telling about yourself, state the facts plainly and concisely. Write a letter, not your autobiography.

- Be humble and self-effacing. No one likes a braggart.

- If you intend to follow up, tell the reader when he may expect to hear from you and what the topic of discussion will be.

- If you want the reader to call or write you, give him a compelling reason to do so, a benefit he will get by contacting you.

GIVING A BUSINESS GIFT

We give personal gifts because we love or like the person, but business gifts are another matter. The not-so-hidden motive behind business gift-giving is to build goodwill and strengthen the relationship. Just as we attend events to network and to build one-to-one relationships that can't be established solely over the phone, giving business gifts, accompanied by a personalized note, makes the recipient feel special without obligating him to reciprocate.

Just sending a gift in a box (especially direct from an Internet shop) can seem cold and impersonal — the opposite of the mood and feeling you are trying to convey. Adding a short handwritten or typed note can make gift-giving much more effective in achieving the results you desire.

Like the FYI letter discussed at the beginning of this section, a cover letter for a business gift should be brief.

Format: [*See Appendix A:* Fig. A-1. Simple format for letters and memos.] Typed/word-processed. Business or personal letterhead.

Style/Tone/Voice: Can be either informal or formal. Active tone or voice. [*See Part I for more on these subjects.*]

Structure: (1) State why you are sending the gift, (2) If applicable, explain why you selected the particular gift, (3) Close with warm wishes.

Handy Phrases: I hope you enjoy the enclosed xxx; After our conversation about xxx, I saw this in the store and had to get it for you; Just a little something for you because I appreciate our relationship.

See also: *Part VI:* Free Gifts; *Part IX:* Vendor Gift Policy.

15 October 2002

Dear Neil,

This is a little present for you — in memory of your stay here in Bonn.

Wishing you all the best!

Best regards,

Christian Boucke

Tips for Writing Short Notes to Accompany a Business Gift

- Don't repeat the product features from the manufacturer's brochure, Web site, or packaging in your letter. You are not selling this product — you are giving it away as a gift.

- The longer and more detailed your letter is about why you are giving the gift, the more you are giving yourself a chance to get in trouble by saying the wrong thing. Let the act of giving the gift do most of the talking.

- Some closing lines that work: "Wising you all the best!" "I value our friendship!" "I value our relationship!" "Here's to a happy — and successful — future!"

- Studies show that business gift-giving is most effective when done randomly and unexpectedly throughout the year, rather than regularly at Christmas time, when the recipient is getting a ton of gifts and yours doesn't stand out.

- Choose gifts individually and personally, based on the interests of your clients and colleagues. You can keep a record of these interests with contact management (e.g., Act, Telemagic, Goldmine) or personal database (e.g., Outlook) software.

- You can also store client and colleague events like birthdays and anniversaries in these programs, and set many of them to remind you when these events are coming up. You can then give a gift for that occasion.

Business Requests

There are many other occasions when you need to ask for information, for a favor (e.g., asking a colleague to refer you to someone you want to meet), for a deadline change, or for permission to reprint something — it's just part of doing business.

REQUESTS FOR BUSINESS FAVORS

Everyone, on occasion, needs help or needs to ask a favor. Examples include requesting a networking interview to learn more about a company or industry when doing a job search; asking for a letter of recommendation or reference; and asking someone for free advice, information, ideas, guidance, or referrals to others. [*See also the "requests" sections of Part II:* Personal Correspondence *and Part III:* Career and Employment Letters, *respectively.*]

In your lead, tell the person why you are writing to them (as opposed to others in similar positions) — in other words, why did you select that person out of all the others in his field? If you admire him or his work, or he is well respected or his organization is well respected, say so. Flattery doesn't get you everywhere, but it's a good start.

Then go right into what you are up to and why you need his help in it. In a few concise sentences, make clear your venture or project, and what you hope he can help you with.

Never ask for general help; such requests overwhelm the reader, and he may fear there will be no escaping you. Instead, ask for a favor that is limited, small, and specific.

Another good idea is to thank him for the time he spent reading your letter, even if he chooses not to help you. The kind, sincere thanks shows you recognize how busy he is, but also may make him feel guilty enough to spend a few minutes on your request.

There may not always be a benefit to the reader you can claim he will receive if he helps you, but usually there is. Think about what that might be and remind him of it in your letter.

If this is not your first request, never criticize the reader for not responding to your earlier letter. He is busy, and while it would have been polite for him to respond, he is under no obligation to do so.

Format: [*See Appendix A:* Fig. A-1. Simple format for letters and memos.] Typed/word-processed. Business or personal letterhead.

Style/Tone/Voice: Can be either informal or formal, depending on the request and the person you are writing to. Use active tone or voice. [*See Part I for more on these subjects.*]

Structure: (1) Acknowledge that you are asking someone to give you something (his time, knowledge, permission), (2) Make the request and give details or circumstances, (3) Explain why the recipient is the best person for this favor, (4) Offer — if possible — to reciprocate the favor, (5) End with a show of gratitude.

Handy Phrases: I have a favor to ask; Could you help us with a small favor?; Would you be willing?; Would it be possible?; Please let me know if you'd be able to; We appreciate your assistance; We look forward to hearing your reply.

See also: *Part II:* Favor Requests.

Dear Fred:

I read your article on the "Intellectual Property Protection Restoration Act" on the Web and was quite impressed.

I would like to reprint it in my company newsletter. (I've attached a copy of the newsletter for your review.) We'll be sure to send you several copies of the newsletter for your files.

If this is okay with you, would you please sign this note and fax it back to me at xxx-xxx-xxxx? If there are any changes, please let me know. Also, we will credit the article as it is bylined on the Web site, unless you have an alternate credit line that you'd like us to use.

Thank you so much for your consideration; I look forward to hearing from you.

Regards,

Sam Duncan

The letter that follows is a bit more flamboyant. It uses the time-tested "I've made a bet" gambit to attract the reader's attention — and, it worked!

Dear Archie,

I have a bet with a master-copy who says I will not get a response from you. I bet him I would. Besides being a marketing genius and successful copywriter, I think deep down you're also a warm and nice guy. (And I promise to keep it our secret.)

So here it goes.

I am a NYC-based comedy writer/copywriter. I'm writing an article and want to do a lecture entitled "The Secret to Effectively using Humor in Direct Mail."

You had mentioned on some lecture tapes that humor works if used correctly. You discussed it a little, but then didn't go much into the subject.

My question is whether there are any statistics or studies done that I could use as proof in my article or lecture? I know how to effectively put humor into a piece that will help the copy — and not hinder it.

BUT, as you know, marketers have a need for concrete proof and numbers crunched. Was there ever a study done on this subject? If you can assist me with this small request I would be most appreciative. I look forward to winning my bet.

Respectfully,

Tony Lipkins

Tips for Requesting a Business Favor

- Remember that the reader does not owe you anything. Do not imply that he does, in any way.

- Acknowledge that he must get many such requests and be far too busy to respond to most of them, and that you understand that. Then give him a reason to respond to yours. This may be flattery or a benefit.

- Always ask. Never demand. Do not use the appeal "didn't you wish someone would have helped you when you were starting out like me?" It falls on deaf ears and only serves to alienate the reader.

- As a show of appreciation, you may want to offer a gift, such as a free membership, free product, or free service as an incentive. The reader will probably not accept the gift, however, especially if taking advantage of it takes time.

- If you have had positive personal dealings with some of the recipient's peers, mentioning their names may help warm the recipient to the idea of helping you.

REQUESTS FOR COOPERATION OR ASSISTANCE

In today's corporate world, few projects of any significant scope are accomplished without the help of others. The challenge is how to get that help, especially from people who may not have the time, inclination, or desire to give it. You'd need, for example, cooperation to set up a meeting, resolve a credit issue, or extend a deadline.

Format: [*See Appendix A:* Fig. A-1. Simple format for letters and memos.] Typed/word-processed. Business or personal letterhead.

Style/Tone/Voice: Depending on the seriousness of subject matter, can be informal or formal. Active tone or voice. [*See Part I for more on these subjects.*]

Structure: (1) Explain who you are (if they don't know you), (2) State your request, (3) Give details, (4) State why you're writing them (i.e., why they were chosen), (5) Ask for their cooperation, (6) State follow-up steps.

Handy Phrases: Your firm has the reputation; Would you be willing?; I'm looking for information; Are you available?; We eagerly await your reply; Would this be of interest?

See also: *Part II:* Requests; *Part IX:* Common or Possible Client-to-Vendor Requests.

Dear Jack:

I have a favor to ask. I'm putting together a schedule for the factory so that we can stay on track with production of our new design.

Since you are the most knowledgeable about the new application for the widgets, I'd love to have our engineers meet with you for about an hour early next week so that we can review your changes and make a final CAD design.

I know that you've got a busy schedule, so if there are any projects we can handle for you in return, we'd be happy to do so.

I hope you'll be able to work with us. I'll call you later this week to see if you're available.

Thanks so much, Jack. You've already given so much to this project and it's much appreciated.

Regards,

Dave Smeltzer

The following is a more formal letter of request. In the example above, the relationship was already established, the writer knew the recipient. In the letter below, the writing is more formal, appropriate if the relationship is not an ongoing one.

TO: Mr. Iishi
FROM: Mark Douglas
RE: Taiwan widgets

CBAC, Inc., is interested in purchasing FB1-type widgets from our Taiwan factory. The factory representative in Japan, Mr. Yamashita, informed CBAC that they would not support this business. Additionally, Mr. Okamura from the overseas sales department also declined to support this business. CBAC is still looking for overseas sales support and would like your group to support this business.

As of today, CBAC purchases motors from Taiwan through your department (Ms. Fujimoto is the sales coordinator). Please advise if your department can help coordinate this business.

CBAC has plans to introduce these products into our distribution network immediately, and we will offer the widget to original equipment manufacturers (OEMs) starting in Q3'99. Our sales target is US$1M in the '99 fiscal year (400–500K pcs.).

We have contacted Mr. Usui at the Taiwan factory directly to confirm the sales route, but have not yet received a reply. Because your group already has a relationship with the Taiwan factory we would appreciate your help in establishing the following:

- Confirmed Sales Route
- Ex-HK FOB Pricing
- Lead Time and Availability

Please advise if you can help CBAC to establish this new business.

Best regards,

Mark Douglas

Tips for Writing Request-for-Cooperation Letters

- Avoid a dictatorial tone, even if the reader is required to help you and comply with your request.
- Show respect for the reader's position, time, and other responsibilities.
- Be clear about what you need and why you feel the reader is the one best qualified to help you.
- Say how you, your organization, the reader, and the reader's organization all benefit from her cooperation.
- Be specific about what happens next. What are you going to do? What do you want them to do? By when?

REQUESTS FOR INFORMATION

Often we cannot complete our work without information from others, inside or outside of our company. Ironically, even when these people provide late or incomplete information, they ultimately blame us for delays and missed deadlines.

Therefore, to serve your own interests and theirs, it is your responsibility to aggressively pursue getting the information you need, but to do so in a manner that doesn't offend.

Since phone calls can be confrontational, or can seem like pestering if too frequent, e-mails and letters are ideal mediums for requesting information. The recipient can post your request on his wall as a reminder to get to the task. The fact that it is a written request adds urgency, and also documents that you repeatedly asked for the information if there are complaints later.

Format: [*See Appendix A:* Fig. A-1. Simple format for letters and memos.] Typed/word-processed. Business or personal letterhead.

Style/Tone/Voice: Can be either informal or formal. Passive/active tone or voice. [*See Part I for more on these subjects.*]

Structure: (1) Make the request specific, (2) Expand on the reason for the request, if necessary, (3) Express your appreciation at their expected cooperation, (4) Add regards.

Handy Phrases: Would you please send me last quarter's sales statements?; Would you mind sharing a copy of the proposal you wrote?; We'd appreciate it if you could take a few moments to fill out the attached questionnaire; I know you're busy and appreciate your time; Thank you, in advance for helping us with this.

See also: *Part IX:* Letters Requesting Information.

Dear Amy:

I have prepared and enclosed, in duplicate, your 2002 estimated tax payments for the third quarter. Please remit the following payments by September 16, 2002.

These payments are based on your 2001 income and tax liability, because I still do not have any information to prepare your 2002 personal and business tax returns. Please expedite the process by forwarding me the bank statements and checkbook register for Bickawalla Center. The home mortgage, property tax payments, interest/dividend income and investment statements can be forwarded to me later.

Thanks in advance for your attention to these payments. If you have any questions, please do not hesitate to contact me.

Sincerely,

Wayne W. Brothers

Enclosures

Tips for Writing Letters Requesting Information

- Tell the reader what you need. List each item separately. Be as specific as possible.

- Tell them why you need it — what it's for, how you will use it, why it is in their best interests to respond in a timely manner.

- Say when you need to receive the information. Give a deadline date.

- Describe any penalties that may be incurred if the material is not received by you on or before the deadline date.

- Acknowledge that you know they are busy, but that this project is a priority with them or someone higher up in the organization, and their cooperation with you is essential to completing it on time.

REQUESTS FOR INTERVIEWS

While a stranger may be resistant to helping you at a distance, many are even more resistant to helping you in person. Therefore you must write even more persuasively if you are requesting an interview, meeting, or other personal contact.

The sample letter below is a good example. The writer is requesting an interview with a busy doctor for an article to be published in a trade journal in which the doctor has no interest. It might be prestigious to be interviewed for a peer-reviewed medical journal or a national story in *USA Today,* but there is little appeal to a doctor to be interviewed in a marketing magazine about his advertising tactics.

The letter writer did some research into the subscriber base of the journal, and based on this, came up with an unusual appeal: Thousands of the journal readers lived in the doctor's geographic market and might be potential patients for his services.

Format: [*See Appendix A:* Fig. A-1. Simple format for letters and memos.] Typed/word-processed. Business or personal letterhead.

Style/Tone/Voice: Tends to be formal. Passive/active tone or voice. [*See Part I for more on these subjects.*]

Structure: (1) Open with a brief statement about who you are, (2) Explain why you are requesting the interview, (3) Expand on point two if necessary, (4) State your desired next step, (5) Express your appreciation at their expected cooperation/add regards.

continued

continued

Handy Phrases: If you would be willing; I know you must be very busy; It would be invaluable to meet with you; I would enjoy the opportunity to speak with you; I would like to share your experience with my audience/organization; Discuss your accomplishments/the success you have had with; Please contact me — if you are too busy to reply I will call you.

See also: *Part II:* Requests; *Part III:* Cover Letters and Job Inquiries.

Dear Dr. Stevens:

Last week I spoke with your assistant Albert to see if you would be willing to be interviewed (via the phone) for an article my associate Bob Randolph is writing for his column in *DM Bimonthly News* — a weekly trade journal for the direct marketing industry — on transit ads. I hadn't heard back and I can only imagine how busy your office is; so I thought I'd put my request in writing.

For some background, *DM Bimonthly News* has 40,000 subscribers — 10,000 of them are in the tri-state area. Bob Randolph is an independent copywriter and consultant with 20 years of experience in business-to-business, high-tech, industrial, and direct marketing. He's also the author of more than 50 books.

If you would be willing to have Bob interview you, you can have someone from your office call Bob directly at 555-555-5555 this week. (Otherwise. I'll try your office on Monday.)

Thanks for your consideration, Dr. Stevens.

Regards,

In the letter below, the writer appeals to the reader's sense of pride.

Dear Don:

I hope this letter finds you well. I hear there's a heat wave in Chicago right now!

I'm writing because we're putting together the next issue of our association newsletter and we'd like to include a column featuring you and your company.

I'd appreciate if you could spare about 20 minutes answering some questions (I've attached them for your review) and if you could mail me the latest corporate brochure.

I'll call you in a few days to see if you're interested (and available). Thanks, Don. We know you've got a busy schedule but we hope you can spare some time for the association.

Best,

Tips for Requesting an Interview

- Assume that the reader dislikes and does not have time for "meetings." Give the specific purpose or nature of the interview.

- Keep the interview short. Reassure the reader that you will need just 20 minutes. If the interview runs longer and he is enjoying it or finds it productive or interesting, he won't hold you to the time limit.

- If the expert gets any publicity out of the interview, or the person's organization benefits in any way, say so.

- Demonstrate that you are familiar with the reader's reputation, work, or organization. He does not want to feel you picked him at random or simply because you thought he'd be available.

REQUESTS FOR ACTION

Letters are a good medium for requesting specific action on the part of the reader. When you ask people to do something verbally, it's easy for them to forget the request, or at least not take it seriously. After all, people say things all the time, and then promptly forget about them.

Requesting action in written form makes the request more formal, more serious, and more urgent. People can ignore conversation, but a piece of paper is more difficult to ignore. You know the pressure of having bills in your in-basket you have to pay. Putting your request in writing exerts a similar pressure for the reader to pay attention and respond.

But whether that response is positive or negative depends on both the tone and content of your letter.

Tone should be respectful and just a touch subservient, rather than superior. After all, you are asking for the favor. They have the power to grant it or refuse. You want to get on their good side, and you do it by being humble.

Format: [*See Appendix A:* Fig. A-1. Simple format for letters and memos.] Typed/word-processed. Business or personal letterhead.

Style/Tone/Voice: Tends to be formal. Active/passive tone or voice. [*See Part I for more on these subjects.*]

continued

continued

Structure: (1) Your lead should say what you want them to do for you, (2) The middle of the letter gives the reasons why they should do it. Focus on how they come out ahead, not on you and your needs, (3) Show what you are willing to do to help make compliance with your request easier for them. Are you flexible? Do you still want their help even if they are willing to do some of what you ask but not all of it? Say so, (4) Thank them for considering your request, (5) State next move, give a desired time-frame for its completion, and provide an incentive for them to act now instead of later.

Handy Phrases: Please consider; We would like to opportunity to; [Name] indicated that you may be able to help us/me; Your assistance would be invaluable; I appreciate the time you have taken to consider this matter; If you would like any further information; If you should have any questions, please feel free to contact me; If there is anything I can do in return.

See also: *Part II:* Requests; *Part V:* Internal Requests; *Part VIII:* Requesting Credit; *Part IX:* Requests for Compliance.

Dear Mr. Kresge:

Wyandotte Mining Company's Precious Metals Smelter respectfully requests nomination for itself in the Fourth Annual Governor's Awards Program for Safety and Health under the category of "Small Private Employer." The Precious Metals Smelter is to be considered separate from the Wyandotte Mine because of its distance from the mining operations and the differing government agency jurisdictions (OSHA vs. MSHA).

In 1993, the smelter was granted an exemption from OSHA-programmed inspections — to the best of our knowledge, it's the only smelter operation in the nation to receive this privilege. It was also the first such exemption granted to a Utah business in several years. This year, the smelter will pursue a renewal of the exemption and is confident it will be granted.

As you may know, the working environment in a smelter, while greatly improved over that of 30 years ago, can be quite hostile to human beings. Therefore, Wyandotte Mining Company's Precious Metals Smelter considers its safety record and low accident rate noteworthy.

Please see the attached nomination form and supporting documentation. We're confident you will agree the Precious Metals Smelter has made the safety and health of our employees top priority in our operation. At this time, we extend to you and to Governor Morrison an invitation to tour our facility and allow us to show you, firsthand, the results of our safety and health program.

Thank you for your consideration and this opportunity to participate in the Awards Program.

Sincerely,

Tips When Requesting Action

- The more the recipient is free not to comply with your request for action, the humbler your tone should be.

- Show how compliance with your request for action satisfies the reader's self-interest, not just yours.

- Provide all the documentation, materials, references, contact information, and resources the reader will need to take the action — or say that you will supply it as soon as they indicate that they want it.

REQUEST TO PARTICIPATE IN A SURVEY

There are some people who love surveys and participate in every survey they get. These folks love to make their voice heard! Although you should provide them with a cover letter that gives clear instructions on how to complete the survey and return it for tallying, survey-lovers really don't need any prompting to fill out the questionnaire.

Some people, on the other hand, hate surveys. They consider them a waste of time and are too busy to participate. No matter how much you plead or persuade in your cover letter, they won't do the survey. But ask anyway. You may get lucky.

Most people fall in between these two extremes, and are the main target of your survey cover letter. They are busy, and filling out surveys takes time. Often they don't feel surveys are worth the bother.

When writing to consumers, you can often get attention by attaching a dollar bill to the survey. While a dollar hardly compensates them for their time, they feel they should comply because you gave them something. In your cover letter say, "I know the enclosed dollar doesn't compensate you for your time filling out this brief survey. But it may brighten the day of a child you know."

When writing to businesspeople, stress how the survey is going to provide information to them that is useful in their business. Offer a free copy of the survey results as soon as they are published, in exchange for their cooperation. If you will be selling the survey, mention the retail price, which makes the free report seem more valuable.

Ensure the reader that their identity will not be revealed, and say by when you need the completed form returned.

Format: [*See Appendix A:* Fig. A-1. Simple format for letters and memos.] Typed/word-processed. Business or personal letterhead.

Style/Tone/Voice: Informal or formal. Active tone or voice. [*See Part I for more on these subjects.*]

Structure: (1) Explain objective, (2) Ask recipient to fill out form (explain how, if necessary), (3) Give a specific deadline and make sure they know how to send the survey back to you, (4) Guarantee confidentiality, (5) Promise, if possible, that they can get a free copy of the results, (6) Thank them for their time and support.

Handy Phrases: We'd love to get your opinion; Our association needs your help; If you respond by [date], you'll receive a free copy of the results.

See also: *Part VI:* Customer Satisfaction Surveys; *Part VII:* Surveys or Questionnaires.

MEMORANDUM

TO: SEPTOK Members
FROM: Patti Freeman
RE: Financial and Operations Benchmarking Survey
URGENT: Response Needed by October 31

Since 1980, the Association has from time to time surveyed its members concerning their financial practices and operations. The purpose, specifically, is to provide select benchmarking data for SEPTOK members to use in evaluating the performance of their own business . . . and to make better-informed business decisions.

We need your help! To make this project most effective, maximum participation is essential. The broader and deeper the range of firms represented, the more useful the benchmarking data will be.

Please commit to completing this survey questionnaire and returning it within ten days. If you return the survey after this deadline, we will be unable to include your opinions.

All firms responding with completed questionnaires will receive, free, a copy of the full analytical benchmarking report. (Those not responding may purchase the report for $895.)

Strict confidentiality is assured. No identifying information will be associated with the data you provide and all results will be reported only in aggregate.

This project exists only to serve you. Please do your part by completing the enclosed survey questionnaire and returning it by October 31, 2002. Thanks so much for your help!

Tips for Writing a Survey Cover Letter

- Stress the importance of returning the survey by the deadline and say their opinions will not be included when the results are tallied unless they meet this deadline.

- To businesspeople, talk about how you value their opinion because they are important and influential in the industry.

- Guarantee confidentiality — you are often requesting privileged information.

- Tell what topics the questions cover and why you are surveying them on these topics.

- Show how they might use the information in the survey results to increase their profits.

SOLICITING A TESTIMONIAL

Testimonials are an incredibly powerful tool for selling and marketing your product or service. Strong testimonials can help overcome skepticism, hesitancy, anxiety, and concern about doing business with you. Conversely, a lack of testimonials may cause the prospect to wonder why you don't have any.

Many businesspeople say they do not have testimonials because no one sent any. But you don't have to wait for people to write to you. You can ask customers for testimonials with a simple letter. Send out a dozen or two and you will rapidly build a file of solid testimonials for your company and product.

Format: [*See Appendix A:* Fig. A-1. Simple format for letters and memos.] Typed/word-processed. Business or personal letterhead.

Style/Tone/Voice: Can be informal or formal, depending on situation. Active tone or voice. [*See Part I for more on these subjects.*]

Structure: (1) Explain why you would like a testimonial from the recipient, (2) Ask reader if he can take a few minutes to write a testimonial about you/your company, (3) If possible, give the reader the option to fax, e-mail, or mail his response, (4) Add a sentence or two that you're interested in constructive comments as well as glowing ratings, (5) Thank the reader for taking time to do this favor.

continued

continued

Handy Phrases: I'm in the process of putting together a list of testimonials; I've enjoyed working with you on recent projects and have a favor to ask you; Would you be willing to write a testimonial for the my Web site?

See also: *Part III:* Letters of Recommendation and Introduction; *Part IX:* Letters that Strengthen the Client/Vendor Relationship.

Mr. Andrew Slotz
President
Hazardous Technograms, Inc.
Anywhere, U.S.A.

Dear Andrew:

I have a favor to ask of you.

I'm in the process of putting together a list of testimonials — a collection of comments about my services from satisfied clients like yourself.

Would you take a few minutes to give me your opinion — good or bad — of my writing services? No need to dictate a letter — just jot your comments on the back of this letter, sign below, and return it to me in the enclosed envelope. (The second copy is for your files.) I look forward to learning what you like about my service ... but I also welcome any suggestions or criticisms, too.

Many thanks, Andrew.

Regards,

Steve Kahn

YOU HAVE MY PERMISSION TO QUOTE FROM MY COMMENTS, AND USE THESE QUOTATIONS IN ADS, BROCHURES, MAIL, AND OTHER PROMOTIONS USED TO MARKET YOUR FREELANCE WRITING SERVICES.

Signature_____ Date_____

Tips for Soliciting Testimonials

- Your best response will come from current customers who you know are satisfied with their latest purchase or experience with you. But you can also get good response mailing to longtime customers, even inactive customers.

- Tell the customer how you intend to use his testimonial. Get him to give you permission in writing.

- Ask for an opinion, not a testimonial. Say that you want to hear both the good and the bad. Of course, you will only use the good in your promotional materials. If there is a problem, fix it.

GETTING PERMISSION TO USE AN UNSOLICITED TESTIMONIAL

Testimonials solicited using the above letter as a model may be used as soon as received, since the customer has signed a release.

If you get an unsolicited testimonial, you should send a copy of it to the customer with a cover letter asking permission to use it.

Do not assume you can use a testimonial just because someone sends you a compliment or praise. Some clients may not want their competitors to know you are their vendor. Others might be personally willing to endorse you, but their company policy does not permit making such endorsements. Getting permission in writing, even if the testimonial is glowing, is the safest bet.

Format: [*See Appendix A:* Fig. A-1. Simple format for letters and memos.] Typed/word-processed. Business or personal letterhead.

Style/Tone/Voice: Can be either informal or formal. Passive/active tone or voice. [*See Part I for more on these subjects.*]

Structure: (1) Thank them for the compliment, (2) Ask permission to use the customer's comments; (3) Explain where and how you will use them, (4) Ask for the permission in writing.

Handy Phrases: Thanks so much for your kind words; May I use your glowing words as a testimonial?; Can I use the following quote from your letter on my Web site?

See also: *Part IX:* Letters Regarding Bids, Contracts, and Agreements.

Mr. Mike Hernandez
Advertising Manager
Technilogic, Inc.
Anytown, U.S.A.

Dear Mike:

I never did get around to thanking you for your letter of 8/15/02 (copy attached). So ... thanks!

I'd like to quote from this letter in the ads, brochures, direct-mail packages, and other promotions I use to market my writing services — with your permission, of course. If this is okay with you, would you please sign the bottom of this letter and send it back to me in the enclosed envelope. (The second copy is for your files.)

Many thanks, Mike.

Regards,

Steve Kahn

YOU HAVE MY PERMISSION TO QUOTE FROM THE ATTACHED LETTER IN ADS, BROCHURES, MAIL, AND OTHER PROMOTIONS USED TO MARKET YOUR FREELANCE WRITING SERVICES.

Signature_____Date_____

Tips for Requesting Permission to Use a Testimonial

- Thank them for the compliment. If you are writing months after the fact, mention that your thank you is belated.
- Ask permission to use the customer's comments.
- Explain where and how you will use them.
- Ask for the permission in writing.

RESPONDING TO BUSINESS REQUESTS

When someone, but especially a customer or potential customer, makes an inquiry of you, the speed of your response is critical. The longer her lead, inquiry, or request waits, the less enthusiastic she becomes.

There is a debate about whether it's best to respond to requests and queries by letter or by e-mail. Both have pros and cons.

Depending on the type of request and the lead time, you may want to send your response via regular mail. You may need to respond to someone asking for a copy of a report you've written and you don't have it on an electronic file. If you need to deny a request, especially one that's solemn or of great importance, a letter is more appropriate, since it is more personal than e-mail. E-mail is much faster; your message reaches the recipient literally in seconds. Send e-mail responses in reply to e-mail requests ("here's the stock quote you needed"), when someone needs an immediate reply, or when you're responding to a very informal request (e.g., "Thanks for inviting me to join you to watch the Somerset Patriot game tonight. Where should we meet?").

An increasingly popular strategy for business today is to respond to important requests and queries both ways, online and offline. An e-mail is sent to immediately answer queries, especially if those queries are made online. Then, optionally, you can follow up with more information in the mail — a nice way to exceed your recipient's expectations.

Format: [*See Appendix A:* Fig. A-1. Simple format for letters and memos.] Typed/word-processed. Business or personal letterhead.

Style/Tone/Voice: Can be informal or formal; follow the tone of the request. Passive/active tone or voice. [*See Part I for more on these subjects.*]

Structure: (1) Thank the recipient for thinking of you, (2) Explain whether you can/can't fulfill the request, (3) Give reasons, timeframes, or constraints, if applicable.

Handy Phrases: Thanks for thinking of me; I'm flattered you've asked me for my advice on [subject]; I regret that I won't be able to; As requested, I've enclosed a copy of [material].

See also: *Part II:* Requests; *Part IX:* Common or Possible Client-to-Vendor Requests.

Dear Sam:

Thanks for contacting Jeff Klein about Trinity Media's mobile video communications project. Jeff would be interested in copywriting and consulting for this project. I've attached his latest fee schedule for your records and I'll be available this afternoon if you want to discuss the project particulars. If John wants to hire Jeff, then we'll send an agreement to you and set up a call between you, John, and Jeff.

As you know, b2b high-tech copy (especially in communications) is Jeff's specialty. John can view some samples of Jeff's work on Jeff's Web site, www.xxx.xxx (click on "Portfolio"), and we can also tailor a package of samples to send to you for John's review — just let me know the types of material he'd like to see (e.g., white papers, dm packages).

Jeff isn't interested in becoming a principal for this project, but we appreciate the request for involvement.

I look forward to speaking with you later.

Regards,

Paul Mazza

Tips for Responding to Requests and Queries

- Time is of the essence. In a week, the person may have forgotten their request or query and not even remember who you are or why they contacted you.
- Enthusiasm is critical. If you want a future assignment, order, job, or contract with the requester, you have to make your response reflect how important his request is to you.
- Address the person's key questions and concerns. You may be able to do this in the letter. Or, you may have to suggest a proposal, meeting, report, committee, or other vehicle for answering the key questions.
- Look for what seems to concern the person most (this is what experts call the "worry point" or "pain"). Give a full or at least preliminary answer to this concern. The more you can lay it to rest or at least reassure the reader you can handle it, the more receptive they will be to further dealings with you.
- If you cannot meet every need or handle the total requirement, tell what portion you can handle. Then suggest resources the reader can use to get the other needs taken care of. If you refer him to help for what you can't do, he is more likely to come to you for the parts you can do.

REFUSING BUSINESS REQUESTS

At times, you will be on the receiving end of requests to which, regrettably, you have to say "no" to.

Many people find saying "no" a difficult and unpleasant task, perhaps because of hearing the word from parents and other adults so many times as a child.

Saying "no" in an e-mail or letter is easier than doing it in person. It removes the fear of a confrontation that might occur if the other person is upset by your refusal. A letter can't argue or cajole.

There is no need to apologize when saying no. In most instances, the fact that you have the power, authority, and right to say no means you are not obligated in any way to say "yes."

Should you give a reason for your refusal? Only if it is both logical and palatable to the reader. If the reader would find your reason unacceptable, or be inclined to want to argue with or disprove it, don't get into it. Sometimes you can't just because you can't, and won't just because you won't.

A common situation is a willingness to do some or most of what a person asks, but not all of it. Here you want to be especially careful that you are clear about what you are willing to do and what part of the request you can't fulfill.

Format: [*See Appendix A:* Fig. A-1. Simple format for letters and memos.] Typed/word-processed. Business or personal letterhead.

Style/Tone/Voice: Can be informal or formal; follow the tone of the request. Active tone or voice. [*See Part I for more on these subjects.*]

Structure: (1) Thank the person/organization for making the request, (2) Offer a short explanation that you are refusing the request, (3) Acknowledge the good work done, if appropriate (e.g., we strongly agree that the Widget Conference is the best in our industry), (4) If possible, offer to do part of the request and/or offer something that might be useful (e.g., refer someone else, make a donation), (5) Close by wishing them good luck.

Handy Phrases: I appreciate your invitation; We carefully study all requests we receive; Unfortunately, my schedule doesn't allow for me to.

See also: *Part II:* Refusing a Request; *Part IV:* Refusing a Donation Request; *Part VIII:* Turning Down a Request for Credit.

Hi Don:

Thank you for your request to speak with Mark. At this point, Mark's schedule is extremely tight and he is available on a very limited basis. Because of that, I can only schedule calls with people who are committing to projects.

The fee for Mark to write a sales letter or two-page flier for you would be approximately $2,000. New clients are required to pay half the fee up front and the remainder is invoiced upon completion of the project. I will send you, under separate cover, a draft of the terms for this project, and you can let me know if you'd like to move ahead.

Once Mark gets your deposit, we will set up a call for you and Mark to discuss the project in detail — to decide if a letter or self-mailer would work best and other strategies for a successful mailing.

I will call you sometime today to discuss this, to find out if you'd like to proceed, and to get some convenient dates/times for you to talk with Mark.

Regards,

What if you are saying "no" to someone because your prior dealings with him or her were less than satisfactory? The "refusing a request" letter is not the place to bring out old baggage. But you may want to give them some indication that there is no future because of the past. If they want clarification, that's the opportunity to review the situation and see if it can be fixed.

Dear Olivia:

Thank you so much for thinking of Kim Spilker. We're going to pass on your offer to publish additional books. We appreciate the offer — and your kind words; but our experience with the process of publishing the customer service e-book was that it took more effort than we anticipated, especially in light of the return we received.

Thanks again, though, Olivia.

Best regards,

Tips for Refusing a Request

- Do not encourage a debate or response. You want the recipient to understand that your "no" is final and the discussion is closed.

- Put yourself in the other person's shoes. Your refusal is a disappointment to them. At least cushion the blow with a gently worded letter. Be as kind and complimentary as possible.

- If you can't say yes to the request, maybe someone else can. Refer the writer to others who might be more willing or able to help.

- Your refusal may be a matter of timing. If that's so, encourage the person to try again when you will be able to give more serious consideration to the matter.

- If you fundamentally disagree with the person's cause, politics, ideas, attitudes, or point of view, no need to get into it with them — unless they are persistent and won't go away.

Invitations

Invitations contain lots of details and information — aside from logistics like time, date, and place, your reader will need to know the details/reasons for the invitation and they will need to know how to respond. Carefully crafted invitations spell out all the specifics and make the recipient feel special.

INVITATIONS TO EVENTS

Professionals active in their industry are often involved with one or more trade groups, associations, or professional societies. If you are, you may have occasion to write letters of invitation for the group — to meetings, seminars, holiday events, and awards banquets. An invitation to a specific event can be an opportunity to promote the association as a whole and create a sense of camaraderie.

The same is true for your business, your church/synagogue, and the volunteer organizations you belong to. We all send and receive requests to attend picnics, holiday functions, fundraising dinners, and other events.

Format: [*See Appendix A:* Fig. A-1. Simple format for letters and memos.] Typed/word-processed. Business or personal letterhead.

Style/Tone/Voice: Can be either formal or informal. Passive/active tone or voice. [*See Part I for more on these subjects.*]

Structure: (1) Open with an invitation to join your group, (2) Give the necessary details — organization, time, place, and any special instructions (e.g., wearing casual clothes at a golf outing). (2a) Talk about the venue if it is a selling point for the event; (3) Give information about how to respond, (4) End by expressing that you look forward to having the reader join you at the event.

Handy Phrases: I hope you'll join us; Don't miss this chance to mix and mingle with old friends and new acquaintances; You're invited to the prestigious annual [name] awards dinner; We look forward to seeing you in July.

See also: *Part II:* Invitations to Events; *Part VII* Selling by Invitation

Dear Direct Marketer,

Please join your friends and colleagues at the Roosevelt Hotel on November 1st to honor seven outstanding marketing professionals who will receive the prestigious Silver Key Award.

This Year's Honorees Are

- Brad Simmons
- Andrew Hertig
- William Zorn
- Brian Meyer
- Joan Sprewell

- Don Crider
- Ray Robinson
- DM Bimonthly News

The Silver Key Awards honor the industry's notable innovators and achievers for 25 years of distinguished service to the New York direct marketing community. It is the landmark event of the year.

You will have an opportunity to honor and applaud the men and women who have broken old rules and new ground and have enhanced the image of direct marketing.

You will also meet and share ideas with industry colleagues including former and future Silver Key Award winners.

We have enclosed all the necessary details. We urge you to take a few moments right now to send in your reservation form because space is limited. We look forward to greeting you at the luncheon.

Cordially,

John Stanley
President

Tips for Writing Invitations to Events

- If there is a fee to attend, offer a discount for those who register early. Give a specific date when this "early bird discount" ends.
- Clearly state what the reader can anticipate will happen at the meeting and what might be expected from the recipient (e.g., they will be asked to make a toast to an award winner).
- Make sure the recipient understands whether the event is mandatory.
- All such events create networking opportunities for attendees. Remind them of this in your letter.
- For a special event, say "If you attend only ONE XYZ Club meeting this year, it should be this one." This increases response from regular members as well as those who go to meetings rarely.
- Ask for an RSVP.

MEMBERSHIP INVITATIONS

Letters in this category include invitations to honorary societies, trade associations, social organizations, clubs, and private institutions. The secret is to offer the reader a "key" to something that is available only to a select few, and flatter them with an offer to join an exclusive group of peers.

Format: [*See Appendix A:* Fig. A-1. Simple format for letters and memos.] Typed/word-processed. Business or personal letterhead.

Style/Tone/Voice: Can be either informal or formal. Active tone or voice. [*See Part I for more on these subjects.*]

Structure: (1) If someone has requested membership interest, begin by thanking them for contacting you; if you are seeking memberships, open with an explanation of the importance of joining your particular group, (2) Extend the invitation, indicating how the reader qualifies for membership, (3) Outline the purpose of the organization and how the reader's interests/qualifications complement that purpose, (4) Make sure to clearly outline costs, levels of commitment, and benefits, and (5) Convey your expectation of the reader's acceptance and your desire to have further involvement with the reader.

Handy Phrases: Extend a warm invitation to you to; I am writing on behalf of; You have been nominated for membership; We congratulate you on . . . and extend to you an invitation to join; We therefore extend a cordial invitation to you to join; Congratulations on . . . ; You now qualify for membership in; We extend an invitation to you; As one of our preferred customers; You are invited to.

See also: *Part II:* Invitations to Events; *Part III:* Invitations; *Part VII:* Selling by Invitation; *Part IX:* Invitation to Exhibit.

To a large extent, Pitt Playbills relies on the generosity of the exceptional individuals who continue to support the Company's mission every year. As our Artistic Director explains it, "These members of our family make it possible to preserve the Company's remarkable artistic legacy.

"Each day in the studios, I am awed by the tremendous talent and dedication of our actors. As I work with them, I am reminded of the many members of the family who came before them. It is this rich creative legacy that makes Pitt Playbills one of the nation's great cultural treasures.

"I hope you will join us in our continued pursuit of artistic excellence. It is only with your support that we can continue to preserve Pitt Playbills' extraordinary heritage and build a future that embodies the finest in classical theatre."

Pitt Playbills offers matching gift programs for companies as an opportunity to increase the value of their charitable giving in support of this magnificent art form. Also, Pitt Playbills will combine company gifts with individual gifts, which may entitle Members to receive the benefits and privileges of a higher membership level.

For further information on Pitt Playbills' Major Donor Programs please contact Simone Martin at simonm@website.com. Find out about the benefits of joining the New York Members, and the advantages to becoming a National Member.

The example below focuses on the benefits of membership, which can be a powerful tactic.

Dear (Name of eligible student),

Congratulations on your academic achievement! As a result of your dedication to scholarly success, the Phi Theta Kappa chapter on this campus extends to you an invitation to accept membership in the International Honor Society of the Two-Year College. Membership eligibility is based on the number of hours you have completed and your outstanding GPA; therefore, membership is a special honor afforded to a small group of outstanding students.

Phi Theta Kappa membership guarantees you access to more benefits than any other student organization. As a member, your academic excellence will be recognized with the Golden Key Membership Pin, membership certificate and identification card, notation of membership on your diploma and transcripts, and the privilege of wearing regalia at graduation that sets you apart as a Phi Theta Kappa member.

Membership also provides exclusive access to a compilation of innovative benefits available to you online. Highlights of the online benefits include the eScholarship Directory, listing information on scholarships designated exclusively for Phi Theta Kappa members; letters of recommendation for scholarships and employment; and press releases announcing your induction into the Society. These benefits, accessible exclusively to Phi Theta Kappa members, give you the academic, scholarship, and employment tools that will help you attain your goals for the future. For a complete listing of membership benefits, refer to the enclosed brochure.

Membership applications are available in (location of your Phi Theta Kappa office). Members pay a one-time membership fee of (amount of your local, regional, and international fees), which enrolls them in the organization on the local, regional, and international levels. After induction, members must simply maintain a GPA of (chapter maintenance GPA) to remain members.

To learn more about the opportunities that accompany Phi Theta Kappa membership, make plans to attend the new member orientation on (date) at (time) in (location) or the orientation on (date) at (time) in (location). If you are unable to attend either orientation session and are interested in membership, please call (office phone number) or e-mail (contact e-mail address) for more information.

Again, I congratulate you on your academic achievements. I encourage you to seize this valuable and rewarding opportunity and look forward to seeing your name among the next list of new Phi Theta Kappa members!

Sincerely,

(Your college president's name and signature)

Tips for Writing Membership Invitations

- In your appeal to the reader, be sure to outline what benefits your membership can offer the reader.

- Be sure to be clear about what you are inviting them to join, discuss the organization.

- Make sure to offer details on how to accept membership. Is attendance at a meeting necessary, or is an RSVP sufficient?

- Finally, be sure to include an outline of membership requirements and dues. The reader doesn't want to find out these details after they've decided to accept.

INVITATIONS TO SERVE

Where do we serve? On associations' advisory committees, on corporate boards of directors; on for-profit and nonprofit boards; on the PTA; on the jury; on our town's council. Here are some tips to writing letters that will excite and entice your readers and make them eager to join your group.

Format: [*See Appendix A:* Fig. A-1. Simple format for letters and memos.] Typed/word-processed. Business or personal letterhead.

Style/Tone/Voice: Can be informal or formal depending on situation. Active tone or voice. [See Part I for more on these subjects.]

Structure: (1) Announce the appointment/position, (2) Explain duties, include specifics about position, (3) Clarify expectations such as time commitment, (4) Include information about next event(s), (5) Close by expressing the group's wish to work together.

Handy Phrases: Great confidence in your ability; Has just been named as; Appointment has a term of; Duties will include; Join with me in welcoming; To working more closely with; Will be a valuable addition to.

See also: *Part II:* Invitations to Events; *Part III:* Invitations; *Part VII:* Selling by Invitation; *Part IX:* Invitation to Exhibit.

Dear [Name]:

We'd like to invite you to participate in the planning of an exciting new and unique seminar that examines the effect of public policy on families. Family Impact Seminars (FIS) have been well received by federal policymakers in Washington, D.C. and by state legislators in Wisconsin. _____ County, with the support of the University of Wisconsin-Extension, is one of several counties throughout Wisconsin that is sponsoring similar seminars for local policymakers.

Based on a growing realization that one of the best ways to help individuals is by strengthening their families, FIS analyzes the consequences an issue, policy, or program may have for families. Family Impact Seminar participants include local policymakers such as local government officials, county agency representatives, school officials, judiciary members, religious leaders, educators, law enforcement officials, and business leaders.

The continuing series of seminars provides research-based, objective, nonpartisan information on current family issues — information intended to assist in the design and implementation of policies that strengthen and support families across the life cycle. Each three-hour seminar is accompanied by an in-depth briefing report that summarizes the latest research on a topic and identifies policy options.

Because you are a community leader in _____ County, we would like you to be a part of the advisory/planning committee for the _____ County Family Impact Seminar. We're targeting [month/year] for the first seminar.

The enclosed information describes the Family Impact Seminars in more detail. Please review them and consider participation as a member of the advisory/planning committee. A member of the executive committee will be calling you in a few days to follow up this letter.

Sincerely,

If a prior relationship exists, your appeal to serve does not need to be as formal.

Bill,

I appreciated your feedback on our service that you sent to me a couple of weeks ago. My assistant manager, Debbie Andrews, has been trying to schedule a meeting for us to come up and discuss these issues with you.

At the same time, I would like to discuss with you about becoming a member of an advisory board I am putting together. This board will assist us in enhancing our service. The first issue we will be addressing is the hotel program. Please let me know when you are available to discuss these issues.

Thank you,

Tips for Writing Invitations to Serve

- Appeal to the reader's ego, let them know why you want them to serve.
- Outline the benefit to the community or the organization from their participation.
- Be specific about what you want them to do. Are you asking them to participate in an activity that will take one afternoon or are you requesting that they become part of a permanent body that meets regularly?

- If applicable, offer resources for them to follow up. Is there a Web site available or are you enclosing additional material?
- In closing be sure to describe how you will be following up.

DECLINING AN INVITATION TO SERVE

It's flattering to be thought of and to receive an invitation to be included and it's difficult to say "no" without offending or disappointing. Letters sent to decline an invitation should be tactful, appreciative, and most importantly, they should not be dismissive.

Include your reasons for declining, but keep it simple. Also be aware that some organizations may follow up with a curtailed role to meet your objections. If you can't or don't want to be a part of the organization at all, you should state this upfront. On the other hand, if you do wish to participate but this role or this instance won't work out for you, include this information.

Format: [*See Appendix A:* Fig. A-1. Simple format for letters and memos.] Typed/word-processed. Business or personal letterhead.

Style/Tone/Voice: Formal or informal. Active voice. [*See Part I for more on these subjects.*]

Structure: (1) Be brief. Express your thanks for the invitation, (2) Let the reader know you're pleased to have been considered, (3) Give your reason for declining in one, perhaps two sentences, (4) Close with a wish for their success and (if you mean it) a hope that you'll be able to join them in the future.

Handy Phrases: Please accept my best wishes for future success; Thank you for thinking of me and best wishes in all your endeavors; I know your organization will continue to make a great contribution to our community; I will be following your activities. Perhaps I will be able to participate in the future; Best wishes!; I hope you will consider me for membership again when circumstances allow; Accept my sincere thanks for; Must regretfully decline; Wish I could accept; Best wishes for your success; Keep up the good work; Thank you once more.

See Also: *Part II:* Refusing a Request; *Part III:* Declining Job Offers; *Part IV:* Refusing Business Requests.

Dear Neighborhood Development Board:

I'm flattered by your recent invitation asking me to participate in the upcoming Business Development Roundtable. The work your organization is doing to improve the stability and quality of our neighborhood is impressive and I appreciate your efforts.

Regrettably, I must decline your invitation. I will be in New York on business the week of the Roundtable. Please keep me in mind for future events.

Sincerely,

Tips for Declining an Invitation to Serve

- Keep your letter simple.
- State the reasons you have for declining, but be considerate.
- Be honest about your inclination to accept future participate in events. It may save you from receiving repeated invitations.
- Make sure to note that you appreciate the invitation.

Special Requests: Sponsorship, Fundraising, and Donation Letters

Although the letters in this section are considered requests, they are very different from the standard, straightforward request letters covered earlier in Part IV. The requests presented here tend to be long, fairly complex documents that outline a project or situation and give lengthy details about the reader's possible involvement.

SPONSORSHIP OPPORTUNITY LETTERS

Sponsorships give companies a relatively prestigious and low-cost way to get their names and products in front of a select audience of potential customers. Sponsorship letters are not considered a part of the traditional sales and marketing genre. While sponsorship letters are similar to direct marketing in that they must be compelling and offer the reader a strong incentive to respond, they are truly a business communication — you are inviting the reader to be a part of your team by donating time, money, and resources.

Sponsorship letters announce an event, alert the reader that there will be sponsorships, and describe the various options, which may range from hosting a hospitality suite to having a booth to being the sponsor of the Friday night happy hour.

Format: [*See Appendix A:* Fig. A-1. Simple format for letters and memos.] Typed/word-processed. Business or personal letterhead.

Style/Tone/Voice: Use informal language, active voice, and a friendly conversational tone. [*See Part I for more on these subjects.*]

Structure: (1) Use a cover letter that begins with a statement of interest to the reader, gives information about the event or situation, and provides brief detail about the type of sponsorships being offered, (2) Include documents that give further details about the event/situation, the benefits of sponsorship, the sponsorship levels (opportunities), (3) Include an agreement.

Handy Phrases: We are offering two sponsorship opportunities; We hope you will be part of this exciting event; Thank you for your; Here's an opportunity to gain exposure while supporting; We need your financial support; I'm counting on friends like you; Please do whatever you can to help; Please consider leaving a bequest to; A bequest enables you to leave a legacy in your name (or that of a loved one); You may receive a valuable charitable income tax deduction; You can avoid capital-gains taxes and save on estate taxes by giving a planned gift.

See also: *Part II:* Local Fundraising Requests; *Part IV:* Funding and Donation Requests; *Part VII:* Non-Profit Fundraising.

February, 2004

Dear Marketing Director:

For the first time ever, the New Hampshire Career Counseling Association (NHCCA), with a membership of 1,500 counselors in private practice, education, community mental health agencies, government, and business and industry, is offering sponsorship opportunities at their annual symposium. You'll be able to reach these professionals in ways that your advertising efforts alone cannot.

My discussions with the members of NHCCA led me to a surprising conclusion. These professionals are surprisingly unaware of many of the products and services specifically designed for the counseling field. Many were stumped when I asked them with whom they did business!

That's why you should consider participating in this sponsorship opportunity. In fact, the Professional Convention Management Association recommends sponsorships as the best way to:

- Create stronger awareness
- Demonstrate, highlight, or launch products, publications, or services
- Reinforce brand awareness
- Create relationships with your target audience

NHCCA's 2004 conference is March 4–6, 2004. Sponsoring organizations will get great exposure to their target audience throughout the conference. (See the enclosed sponsorship opportunities sheet for more details.) Secure your place at this program by faxing the enclosed reservation form to me at xxx-xxx-xxxx.

We look forward to seeing you at the Symposium.

[name]

Sponsorship Manager for NHCCA

The above letter was mailed to a list of potential sponsors to let them know about the sponsorship opportunities. These folks did not request the information; it was sent to them because the association identified them as likely sponsors.

The same basic information, in a slightly modified letter, can be used to respond to inquiries about sponsorship — to give the details to someone who has already expressed some level of interest.

Dear Mr. Pryor,

Thanks for your e-mail. As I mentioned, the American Chiropractic Board is offering suppliers the opportunity to gain valuable face-to-face exposure to an audience that's primed to buy your products, via exhibit tables and sponsorship at the American Chiropractic Board of Sports Physicians' (ACBSP) annual symposium.

An exhibit table and/or sponsorship at the symposium will put your salespeople in contact with more than 200 of the leading sports chiropractors in the United States. According to ACA statistics, sports chiropractors are rapidly increasing their annual purchases of equipment and supplies — in some cases by more than 33% over the last four years. These same doctors also *recommend* to clients, including sports teams, those products they endorse.

The 2000 Chiropractic Sports Sciences Symposium is scheduled for March 8–11 at the Hyatt Regency Baltimore on the Inner Harbor In Baltimore, Maryland. This year's topics include the history of chiropractic involvement in the Olympics; neurology of manipulation; brain tumor versus brain trauma; and a wide range of topics about the shoulder — this year's focus area. Shoulder issues will include radiology, biomechanics of the shoulder, arthroscopic surgery on the shoulder, and functional taping.

Please review the attached sponsorship opportunities and secure your place at the 2004 Chiropractic Sports Sciences Symposium today. It's a great way to position yourself more favorably than your competitors.

We look forward to seeing you at the Symposium.

Sponsorship Manager

Tips for Writing a Sponsorship Letter

- Tell the reader that your organization is well respected in its field, and therefore it creates a good image and visibility for the reader's company to be associated with you.

- Stress the prestige and wide attendance of the specific event for which you are trying to obtain sponsorships.

- Offer many sponsorship options to meet virtually any budget. Spell out these options and costs in the letter or on a separate sheet.

- Be clear about whether the sponsor can actually sell at the event and whether selling is encouraged or frowned upon by the association and its members.

- Include a postscript to attract additional attention and add punch to the end of the letter.

- Have the letter signed by the highest official of the organization.

- Mention a specific use for the donation.

- Describe the type of people who attend — their companies, jobs, and buying authority and power.

FUNDING AND DONATION REQUESTS

A funding request typically asks a partnering company to pay for something the requester is doing that is for the benefit of both parties. If a manufacturer's distributor wants to exhibit at a trade show, it makes sense for the manufacturer to contribute to the cost since they will benefit from the exposure without having to deal with the planning and staffing involved in trade show exhibition.

Donation requests are sent to companies that cannot commit to a sponsorship but agree to provide some lower level of financial assistance.

The donation you request can range from taking a whole table at the luncheon to donating some of their products or time as a door prize. Greyhound Friends, for instance — an organization that rescues retired racing greyhounds — sends letters to corporations asking them to donate their products (e.g., a van to transport dogs from tracks to kennels, free veterinary care for broken legs — which is a common problem, and bulk dry dog food to feed kenneled dogs). If a company can't make a product donation, they're asked to donate a small amount of money ($70) to pay for one week's stay at the kennel for one specific dog.

Format: [*See Appendix A:* Fig. A-1. Simple format for letters and memos.] Typed/word-processed. Business or personal letterhead.

Style/Tone/Voice: Can be informal or formal, depending on the situation. Active tone or voice. [*See Part I for more on these subjects.*]

Structure: (1) Begin with a statement of interest to the reader, (2) Offer an outline of why you need funding (is it a joint event or business interest, or are you asking for a charitable donation?) (3) State the benefit that their participation will bring to bear, (4) Conclude with details on how they can contact you and if applicable, how you will be following up with them.

Handy Phrases: Provides an opportunity for publicity; You can help by; Your assistance will benefit; We would like to be able to include you among our sponsors.

See also: *Part II:* Local Fundraising Requests *Part IV:* Funding and Donation Requests; *Part VII:* Non-Profit Fundraising; *Part IX:* Invitation to Exhibit.

TO: Conference Exhibitors

FROM: [name]
Fax xxx-xxx-xxxx
Phone xxx-xxx-xxxx

RE: Scavenger Hunt

The 2004 NHCCA Conference will be here before we know it and we are excited to report that we have already received more than 180 registrations and fully expect additional registrations within the next two weeks. In an effort to encourage the attendees to visit all of the exhibitors, we will be running a scavenger hunt. Each attendee's registration packet will include a game card that will be validated with a sticker as they visit each exhibitor booth. Once they have visited all of the exhibitor booths and completed their game cards, they will deposit them at the registration desk where they will be included in a drawing for prizes.

Typically, the prizes are promotional items that are donated by the exhibitors, which provides an additional opportunity for publicity for your organization. Prizes can include T-shirts, textbooks, gift certificate for a service, or any item of your choice.

Please let me know what prize you are willing to donate by completing the form below and faxing it back to me by Tuesday. February 27, 2004.

Company Name:_____

Prize Donation:_____

In the previous and following examples, note how the donation is tied to a potential benefit to the company being solicited. In these cases, it is the number of people who will attend the trade show.

> Mike,
>
> I just received the request from the San Jose office to approve the $700.00 they requested for the annual Product Expo. This is a regionally sponsored event that attracted 1,400 customers from the Northern California territory last year.
>
> In a booth format, our vendors are able to feature new products, catalogs, etc., along with a food item of some sort. Customers are encouraged to circulate to all booths through a bingo card stamp available only at that booth, which then makes them eligible for entry to drawings for giveaways.
>
> If you could please acknowledge that these funds are available from your cooperative advertising funds and give me an update on the status of the entire co-op budget available from your firm I would appreciate it.
>
> Thanks,
>
>
> Jane Robinson

Tips for Writing a Funding or Donation Request

- Tell the reader what organization you are from, what the event is, and when.
- Suggest that by giving the small donation or funding that you are asking for, they gain high visibility among members of the association for a nominal cost. (See to it that they get that visibility, or they'll likely not donate again!)
- Say specifically what you would like them to give   company golf balls, sports tickets, a small gift, or their product or service (e.g., for a raffle drawing, a magazine publisher might donate a free quarter-page ad in his publication).
- Ask them to commit by telling you what they are going to donate and by when. Have them call, write, or fill out and return a simple form.

CORPORATE FUNDRAISING LETTERS

Many businesses support philanthropies and employees occasionally find themselves needing to compose a letter to be sent to colleagues and acquaintances, in an attempt to raise money for a cause. Companies often affiliate themselves with a cause or association to get positive exposure or to position themselves more favorably than their competition.

Why do people give money? Many reasons. One is that benevolence and altruism are major human motivations. People feel good about themselves when they give money. They also feel powerful. The ability to write a check for $100 or $1,000 without a second thought and give it away feeds the ego, making the donor feel successful and wealthy.

People also donate to causes they feel ultimately help them, too. For instance, a person with a family history of cancer may donate to cancer research, hoping they find a cure.

Letters in this category appeal to more to our emotions rather than to our logic.

Format: [*See Appendix A:* Fig. A-1. Simple format for letters and memos.] Typed/word-processed. Business or personal letterhead.

Style/Tone/Voice: Usually formal. Active tone or voice. [*See Part I for more on these subjects.*]

Structure: (1) Create an opening that catches the reader's interest, (2) If necessary, identify your organization, (3) Explain how contributions are used — use exact examples (e.g., "Your $100 contribution buys one week of groceries), (4) Close on an upbeat note — include a success story or positive statistics, (5) Tell reader how to respond.

Handy Phrases: On behalf of those; To raise funds for; Have organized a; Every dollar you donate goes toward; Your contribution will; Are so grateful for; donation may be tax-deductible; A volunteer organization; Invite you to; Our matching funds program; Return your donation in the.

See also: *Part II:* Local Fundraising Requests; *Part IV:* Funding and Donation Requests; *Part VII:* Non-Profit Fundraising.

October, 2002

Dear Friend,

When you and I were in college, chemical engineering was the most rigorous program on campus. You'll be glad to know that it still is. From thermodynamics to chemical reactor engineering, coursework remains demanding.

But with the increased number of disciplines, fields, and industries to choose from, today's students and young engineers are bewildered by the career choices available.

To help them, AIChE gives college students the facts they need to make wise choices. We've developed a practical program for college freshmen and sophomores, titled "Careers in Chemical Engineering." Consisting of a video, interactive CD-ROM, and readings, it's an exciting introduction to chemical engineering. It describes opportunities in the industry, functional specialties, salaries, techniques of career planning, and more.

Our Web site features a unique student e-zine, "ChAPTER ONE." It profiles career opportunities in traditional and emerging industries and in functional specialties. And it contains information on product development and hot new technologies like genomics and nanotechnology.

But AIChE doesn't stop there. To give them the career-enhancing skills you never get in school, we teach young professionals and students how to work as team members, meet the expectations of their manager, listen, write, and speak better. Called the John J. McKetta ProjectConnect Program, it's taught through AIChE's 150-plus local sections.

The program also finds mentors for these young people. Available in person, by e-mail and phone, mentors answer questions, help troubleshoot and provide invaluable advice. One student reports, "When my corporate internship fell through, I contacted the local section. Within a week, I had a replacement assignment." Another says, "I spent two days with the owner of a small company, an international consultant, and a petroleum company's senior engineer. They gave me advice on my career that I'd never have gotten in the classroom."

AIChE's Career Services department also advises undergraduates and young professionals by phone (at 555/555-3446) and online. A young engineer reports, "Your résumé suggestions are working. I'm getting interviews which I didn't get with my old résumé." A student says, "I used AIChE's online member directory to network with engineers at a major consumer products company.

"The day of my job interview, I found myself sitting across from one of those contacts at lunch. Did that ever make me relax!"

Wouldn't it have been great if this assistance had been available when you and I began our careers?

Wouldn't it be wonderful if we could expand and enhance these programs to help more young people get started? For as little as $50, we can build the groundwork to set up invaluable networking opportunities for these students.

As I'm sure you know, membership dues alone won't pay for these important programs. We need your help to do that. Won't you consider a generous gift for these and the other urgently needed programs described in this package? I know I can count on you to help.

Sincerely,

James M. Braus
Vice Chair, AIChE Foundation

P. S. Contribute $500 or more and you will be recognized as a member of the Olsen Society, named for the Institute's longtime volunteer and founding member. Of course, gifts in all amounts are most welcome, and will be recognized in our donors' roster and on AIChE's Web site (unless of course you prefer to remain anonymous).

Tips for Writing a Fundraising Letter

- If you are mailing to members of a group, appeal to their interest in the well-being of the group. The previous letter was sent to working chemical engineers to help students training to be chemical engineers. Pride in profession or group is a strong appeal.

- If you are mailing to people who have donated previously, remind them of and thank them for past donations. Describe how their money has been put to good use.

- Explain the work that needs to be done, and how their money will be used.

- Put things in concrete terms. "Your money will feed children in underdeveloped nations" is good. "Your $25 can provide a full week of healthy meals for Emily and her whole family" is better.

DONATION THANK-YOU LETTERS

When you get a donation of any kind, a written thank you is in order. This can be a memo, or a short letter, perhaps inserted within a card. For a nice touch, write the letter on Monarch-size rather than business-size stationary [*see* Glossary].

Format: [*See Appendix A:* Fig. A-1. Simple format for letters and memos.] Typed/word-processed. Business or personal letterhead.

Style/Tone/Voice: Informal/formal. Active tone or voice. [*See Part I for more on these subjects.*]

Structure: (1) Thank the person for the donation, (2) Explain how it made a positive impact, (3) Express appreciation for their time/generosity.

Handy Phrases: Thank you for your generous donation; We are truly grateful for your support; Your donation is an investment in [helping children enjoy the holiday season].

See also: *Part II*: Thank-You and Acknowledgement Letters; *Part VII:* Fundraising Follow Up.

TO:
FROM:
RE: T-shirt donation
DATE: March 9, 2002

Thank you again for your generous contribution of six T-shirts to this year's NHCCA Conference. Although the weather conditions were a bit of an obstacle for some people, the conference was still well received by those who were able to attend.

I am sending you the name and address of the person who won your prize and would appreciate it if you could mail the T-shirts directly to her.

Thanks again, Tony. We hope to work with you again next year.

Regards,

Here's another sample:

Dear Philip:

American Volunteer Symposium received the great baseball trading cards that you so generously donated to the patients at Children's Hospital. The selection was perfect, because it was enjoyed by children of all ages.

The holiday season is a busy time for everyone, and on behalf of all our young patients, we appreciate you taking the time to think of us. You made a lot of children very, very happy.

Thank you again for thinking of us as you always do, and we wish you a happy holiday season!

Best wishes,

Tips for Writing a Thank You for a Donation

- Thank them for their specific gift, and say what they gave.
- Tell them what was done with their donation and how it will be used.
- If you are a nonprofit, remind them that a cash donation may be tax deductible and that they should consult with their accountant.

REFUSING A DONATION REQUEST

There may be times when you are the one being asked for a donation, and either you or your organization is not willing to contribute to that group or cause.

Do not feel guilty. You have limited time and funds. There are many worthy causes competing for your donation. You have to choose which ones you will fund, and naturally some are going to be left out.

The previous paragraph summarizes the logical argument that must be made in the letter refusing a request for a donation: You receive an enormous amount of requests and you cannot give to all of them. You may also want to say your budget for giving has been exceeded or already allocated for the year; their request came too late.

Format: [*See Appendix A:* Fig. A-1. Simple format for letters and memos.] Typed/word-processed. Business or personal letterhead.

Style/Tone/Voice: Usually formal, but can be either formal or informal. Active tone or voice. [*See Part I for more on these subjects.*]

Structure: (1) Open with a "thank you for thinking of me," (2) Say something positive about the requester's organization or cause, (3) Explain why you cannot donate, (4) End with a wish for their success.

Handy Phrases: Please accept my apologies for not being able to donate this year; Thank you for your recent letter requesting; Since we cannot support every request we receive, we have established a; Continued success with this year's campaign.

See also: *Part II:* Refusing a Request; *Part IV: Refusing Business Requests.*

Dear Event Organizer:

On behalf of the Michigan Islanders organization, thank you for your recent correspondence regarding the work of your organization and its ongoing need for support.

As you are aware, the Michigan Islanders views itself as more than just a professional franchise. We believe that our team is an integral part of the community and should participate in a variety of programs that touch the lives of all our residents. The club board reviews a broad spectrum of charitable requests that come to our attention. We grant requests up to a reasonable limit for only Michigan-based charities.

Based on your letter, it is clear that your organization is playing an important role in enhancing our region's quality of life, creating programs that are unique and important. We deeply appreciate that you took the time to bring your efforts to our attention.

Regretfully, given the enormous number of daily requests we receive, the Islanders will be unable to provide your outstanding organization with a contribution at this time for we have reached our maximum donation limit. We are touched and honored, however, that you reached out to the team as you seek the additional resources that will enable you to move forward.

Again, on behalf of everyone at the Michigan Islanders, thank you for your letter and our best wishes for a successful event.

Sincerely,

If applicable, your response can offer an alternative to a direct donation. See the next example.

> Dear Dr. Martin,
>
> We compliment your work to provide a summer camp for young cancer patients. This is indeed a worthy cause. Rather than donating to individual charities, however, our employees donate through payroll donations to the United Way. We suggest that you apply to that organization for additional funding.
>
> Although we can't commit to monetary support at this time, when you are ready for volunteer labor, a number of Widget employees are willing to help. We wish you much success in this worthy cause.
>
> Paul Robinson,
> Corporate Manager
> Widget Corp.

Tips for Refusing a Request to Donate Money

- Unless their cause is evil, immoral, or illegal, do not say that you don't agree with it or support it.
- Thank them for taking the time to explain their activity to you, and express regrets that you can't be of more help, at least not right now.
- Tell them of the other things you do in the community and your extensive good works for worthy causes.

Letters of Confirmation and Acknowledgment

Letters of confirmation are acknowledgment letters sent primarily to confirm details or to put any oral agreements in writing.

Other reasons for confirmation letters vary from acknowledging: an invitation, a resignation, the receipt of a report, a résumé, a suggestion, the anniversary of a customer's company, or to respond to feedback (negative or postive).

CONFIRMATION LETTERS

Appointments, travel, meetings, events, conferences, and other time-specific tasks should be confirmed in writing. A simple memo or e-mail does the trick. Other types of confirmations include reviewing business agreements or decisions, confirming oral agreements, and confirming a decision.

Format: [*See Appendix A:* Fig. A-1. Simple format for letters and memos.] Typed/word-processed. Business or personal letterhead.

Style/Tone/Voice: Can be either informal or formal. Active tone or voice. [*See Part I for more on these subjects.*]

Structure: (1) Refer to the issue, (2) State the details of the decision or agreement, (2a) Review the details of the event (when, where, time), (3) For travel and meetings, summarize related items (e.g, you will be bringing the meeting agenda), (4) Close with next steps (e.g., you are returning any necessary forms or you'll be sending your itinerary.

Handy Phrases:.Thank you for providing; I was pleased to receive; In confirmation of your participation; Am happy to confirm; Your place has been reserved; We will count on seeing you.

See also: *Part II:* Acknowledgments; *Part VI:* Order Acknowledgment.

Dear Irene:

I got your message and I am happy to hear that [NAME] is booked for your March "Night of Novel Approaches" to present his Improving Communications workshop. I want to recap the details:

- Date: Wednesday, March 28, 2004
- Time: 7:30 p.m.
- Location: Books, Books, Books!, Paramus, NJ 07652

I understand from your message that you'll promote the event through a press release and signs at the store. Please let me know if you need additional information from us to help with your promotions.

I'll speak to you soon to go over the details.

Regards,

Confirmation doesn't just cover reservations and appointments. You may find you need to confirm an oral agreement or a consensus just reached as in the following sample.

The events of this past week might have left some ambiguity concerning our priorities. To move forward as a team, we must remove any uncertainties and accept the challenges that lie ahead. Let me restate our decisions. First, we must meet the October 15 deadline. Our holiday sales depend on that date. Second, we must release a quality product. We realize this might require long hours and time away from your families. We want to make it up to your families and are formulating a completion bonus.

We have the best team in the industry. We are close to the finish line and can see the flags waving ahead. We need one last burst of energy and commitment from each of you. For now, stop working, go home, take the remainder of the day off. Tomorrow we'll meet in the main conference room at 8:00 a.m. for a kick-off meeting to begin the last stretch of the race.

Tips for Writing Letters of Confirmation

- Confirm all the details in writing including date, time, place, location, and length of meeting or event.

- Thank the reader for helping you make, or agreeing to participate in, this event.

- Spell out administrative details, what the remaining tasks are that need to be done, and who is responsible for each.

- Tell the reader that if the agreement does not correctly reflect their understanding, they should contact you immediately.

LETTER OF ACKNOWLEDGMENT

As its name implies, the letter of acknowledgment acknowledges a fact, situation, or action that has taken place, usually involving the recipient.

According to *Webster's New World College Dictionary*, "acknowledge" means "to admit to be true, or as stated," but an acknowledgment letter does more than acknowledge; it also responds.

Oftentimes, acknowledgements contain refusals or acceptances, or opinions and reactions.

Your opinion and reaction may be mixed, with both positive and negative thoughts. Whenever stating a critique or opinion, give the positive first. Tell what you like and agree with. Then get to the negatives — what you don't like and what you want changed.

Format: [*See Appendix A:* Fig. A-1. Simple format for letters and memos.] Typed/word-processed. Business or personal letterhead.

Style/Tone/Voice: Can be either informal or formal. Active tone or voice. [*See Part I for more on these subjects.*]

Structure: (1) State the thing or situation you are acknowledging in a sentence or two, (2) The body of the letter outlines your opinion of the thing or situation (if the reader wants your opinion or needs to hear it) and your reaction, (3) Close with a proposal of what to do next.

Handy Phrases: For taking the time to; We're sorry you were; I agree that there is a need to; We are attempting to resolve; if you have any other concerns; Thanks for bringing this to my attention.

See also: *Part II:* Acknowledgments; *Part VI:* Order Acknowledgment.

Hi Marilyn,

I can't believe you were able to get back to me with a great candidate so quickly. You are right, Ira Tamburo sounds ideal. I got your packet this morning and took a look through it. It looks great, please do have him work up a proposal for me.

Attached to this e-mail are the series guidelines that will give him an idea of the series tone, scope, and style. Also attached is my sales introduction sheet, outlining my vision for the book. For a writer who is new to a series, we do ask for the proposed table of contents and a writing sample for the series.

What does Mr. Tamburo's availability look like right now? You note below that he is a fast writer and I would like to get this book off to the printer in February, which would mean receiving 100% of the manuscript in mid-October.

I'd be happy to answer any questions you or Mr. Tamburo have about the project or the proposal which I am very much looking forward to seeing.

Thanks!

In the letter below, the writer is acknowledging an unsolicited suggestion.

Dear Jim:

Thank you very much for the "customer helper" idea. As head of our sales department, I will immediately implement your suggestion of assigning a sales representative to customers planning home improvement. We are sure our customers will appreciate this additional service.

As our stores continue to profit, we know that the store managers will also be grateful for customers like you who help them improve their service.

Tony

Tips for Writing Acknowledgment Letters

- Regardless of whether your feelings are positive or negative, or whether you are accepting of or unreceptive to the situation or proposal before you, always start on a positive note and maintain a polite tone throughout your letter.

- In your acknowledgment, briefly recap the idea or proposal you are acknowledging. Do not repeat its history at length; the reader already knows it.

Tough Situations

In the course of your professional life there will be difficult situations for which you will have to write a letter.

Some situations may have negative financial consequences and/or negative emotional or psychological effects for the reader. You should consider the impact on the reader and prepare them to accept the circumstances contained in the letter.

PROBLEMS WITH BUSINESS PARTNERS

"Business partners" are a step up from vendors, in that your relationship is closer and must be managed at a higher level. You may be able to afford to alienate the vendor who paints the stripes in your parking lot, but not the business partner supplying the key technology that drives your best-selling product.

Format: [*See Appendix A:* Fig. A-1. Simple format for letters and memos.] Typed/word-processed. Business or personal letterhead.

Style/Tone/Voice: Can be either informal or formal. Active tone or voice. [*See Part I for more on these subjects.*]

Structure: (1) Open by explaining that there is a problem, (2) Outline problem — give specifics or backup documents when necessary, (3) State what you would like to see happen or (3a) call for a meeting to negotiate or resolve problem, (4) Close with request that they contact you after reading your letter.

Handy Phrases: I wanted to make you aware; Before this escalates; We've been having some issues; We hope that we can easily resolve; We are very committed; This partnership is important; I think we can come to; Let me know your thoughts; Let's set up a teleconference; Please send your comments to me so I can put together an agenda for our next call; What do you suggest; I look forward to hearing from you.

See also: *Part V:* Resolving Disputes and Disagreements.

Dear Lisa,

After discussion with Suzanne, we thought I should make you aware of a potential problem concerning the Web users seminars.

At a joint meeting in February, Jim, Diane, Michael, and Suzanne agreed on a seminars action plan. Our association took responsibility for editorial coordination and design of the seminars brochure. The partners were given 3/31 as the due date for seminar copy to be sent to me. By mid-April, we had not received copy from Jim's group, but had copy from Diane and Michael's speakers. Already behind schedule (first copy approval was set for 4/12), I started to put together the seminar brochure and the seminar schedule.

On April 18, I expressed concern to Suzanne that we were behind schedule and still had not received copy from Jim. I gave Suzanne the number of remaining rooms available at each time slot. Suzanne called Jim to explain that we needed his speaker's session copy and that all other copy was in. She also gave him the information about room/time slot availability.

I received Jim's copy on April 22. On April 24, Jim's assistant, Margaret, called me and strongly expressed her concern about the time slots left open for their association's speakers. I told her that there were no set procedures for allotting time slots to each association and that it typically was allotted on a first come/first served basis. I reminded her that her association's copy came in one month later than everyone else's; additionally, I accommodated everyone's scheduling requests — and the only scheduling instructions I had received from Jim was for their association's president to be scheduled to give both his sessions on Tuesday.

Margaret and I ended our conversation with the decision that I would fax the schedule to the partners, which I did on May 2 and the partners could discuss scheduling possibilities. I told Margaret it would be helpful if we could see how many sessions she wants to switch around. I also suggested that we set a protocol for scheduling for next year (see notation on attached memo).

After my conversation with Margaret, I called Diane to apprise her of the situation. Diane suggested that perhaps the CBAC Trade Show Company could open up extra rooms on Monday and Tuesday for Jim's group — a good idea, in my opinion.

My initial reaction is that Jim was late with copy and lost his opportunity to choose prime time slots. However, I don't want to make decisions that would jeopardize the current relationship between the two associations.

Please let me know if you'd like the association partners at my management level to work this out, or if you feel intervention on a higher level is appropriate.

Sincerely,

Rexella

Tips for Writing Memos About Business Partner Problems

- As concisely as possible, run through the project history today, stopping to cite every instance where the business partner was uncooperative or let you down in any way.

- Help the reader weigh the importance of maintaining the relationship with the business partner versus the cost and delay of their lack of cooperation and poor performance.

- Ask the reader how she wants the situation handled. Involve the appropriate level of management.

MERGER ANNOUNCEMENTS

If you sell your business or another firm acquires the company you work for, you may be called on to send a letter to your accounts explaining the transaction and what it means to them.

Even if the merger is going to benefit the customers, most will initially be negative for a simple reason: People hate change. Also, people like buying from people they know and like. They know you. They don't know the folks who bought you.

The main objective of the merger announcement is to reassure the recipient. He wants to know that what he likes about doing business with your firm will continue, and that any change will only help improve service, speed delivery, lower prices, enhance quality, broaden selection, or provide some other positive benefit.

Format: [*See Appendix A:* Fig. A-1. Simple format for letters and memos.] Typed/word-processed. Business or personal letterhead.

Style/Tone/Voice: Formal. Active tone or voice. [*See Part I for more on these subjects.*]

Structure: (1) Open with a direct and candid statement, (2) Explain implications, (3) Detail current situation and what's been planned for the future, (4) Thank reader for business/support, (5) Promise to keep in touch, (6) Tell them who to contact if they need help/information.

Handy Phrases: Consequence of economic pressures; We will be merging with; Ask for your understanding and cooperation; If you could use assistance, please contact; As soon as we know more; Will keep everyone informed.

See also: *Part V:* Announcements; *Part VII:* Letters Announcing New Locations

Dear Valued Customer:

After 18 years of serving the book-buying community, I am retiring. It is my pleasure to announce all customer accounts and records will be merged with *Research Books Inc.* in Madison, Connecticut. RBI is an excellent and very "user friendly" publication supplier, and I am confident that all your needs for a responsive and flexible service agent will be satisfied.

RBI has agreed to merge with us as of October 1, 2003. Research Books Inc. has been in business for 15 years, and like Barton, is woman-owned.

All of the employees here at Barton have conferred with RBI personnel to assure a smooth transition. After retirement I will remain in regular contact with RBI to help make sure your needs are met.

The Barton staff will fill orders we receive through September 30, and during October through mid-November you can continue to reach us at our 800 numbers.

Orders placed after September 30th should be sent directly to the staff at RBI (please see the contact numbers on the following page). Orders placed through the Barton Web site will automatically be handled by RBI. Barton will transfer standing orders and backordered items to RBI over the next few weeks.

While I look forward to my retirement, I will miss working for the many wonderful customers I have been fortunate to serve.

All of us at Barton Business Services Inc. have enjoyed the relationships we have built with our customers over the years.

What a pleasure it has been to work with and for you!

Sincerely,

Patricia W. Sprecher
President

Tips for Writing Merger Announcements

- Notify the reader that your company has merged with another firm. Say whether you bought them or they bought you.

- Give the reason for the merger, if relevant and positive to the reader. Are you joining forces to consolidate operations or take advantage of economies of scale? Are there cost savings to be achieved that will be passed on to customers in the form of lower prices? Are you retiring?

- Tell what the major changes are in locations, contact information (phone numbers, e-mail addresses), personnel, product availability, pricing, and procedures.

- Thank the customer for their past business and tell them the new organization looks forward to serving them even better.

CLOSING, LIQUIDATION, AND/OR BANKRUPTCY ANNOUNCEMENTS

There is no way to put a positive spin on these situations. The best way to write this letter is to be succinct, addressing the key issues that directly impact the reader. There will be several subtypes of letters for this situation, each one addressing a particular audience (e.g., employees, creditors, investors, vendors, customers, and the general public).

In situations that involve government agencies such as the Securities and Exchange Commission (SEC), which have specific requirements of notification, it is advisable to consult with an attorney before composing and mailing your letter.

Format: [*See Appendix A:* Fig. A-1. Simple format for letters and memos.] Typed/word-processed. Business or personal letterhead.

Style/Tone/Voice: Formal. Active tone or voice. [See Part I for more on these subjects.]

Structure: (1) Explain situation — if there's any good news, state it up front, (2) Express regret, concern, and appreciation, (3) Detail any financial impact, (4) Close on a positive note of appreciation.

Handy Phrases: I am writing to inform you; We will continue; We appreciate your support; This move is in the best interest; This action is designed to enable us to continue our normal business operations; Continue operating in a "business as usual" manner; We value you as a supplier and appreciate your continued support.

See also: *Part V:* Announcements.

Notice to all xxxxx. Equityholders:

On April 25, 2003, the United States Bankruptcy Court for the Southern District of xxx entered an order (the "Court Order") approving certain notice procedures relating to the sale and/or transfer of xxxx. common stock and preferred stock. If you directly or indirectly own at least, or intend to acquire additional shares so that you would so own at least, four and three-quarters percent (4.75%) of any class of xxxxxx. common stock and/or preferred stock (or if you intend to sell shares of such stock to a person who would own at least four and three-quarters per-cent (4.75%) of any such class), we strongly urge you to review the attached Court Order and Notice, which, among other things, describe and set forth procedures that must be followed prior to certain sales and purchases of xxxx stock.

For additional information, you may leave a detailed message at (xxx) xxx-xxxx, option 7.

As in these examples, be sure to include all of the necessary details. If applicable include any court filings that you are required to disclose.

Dear Valued Supplier,

I am writing to inform you about an important step being taken by CBAC, Inc. In order to con-tinue with normal operations while the Company takes steps to improve its business and capi-tal structure. On October 1, 2003, CBAC, Inc. and certain of its subsidiaries filed voluntary petitions for reorganization under Chapter 11 of the U.S. Bankruptcy Code in the U.S. Bank-ruptcy Court for the Northern District of Anytown, USA.

This action is designed to allow us to continue our normal business operations as CBAC, Inc. takes the time to restructure its financial obligations and takes steps toward a stronger future.

Let me explain what today's action means for your company:

CBAC, Inc. is continuing to conduct business as usual. All our facilities are open for business and serving our customers.

CBAC, Inc. is providing its customers with our full range of goods and services, just as we always do, so we don't expect any reduction in our orders with you or any of our other suppliers.

The Bankruptcy Code prohibits the Company from paying any obligations to its creditors that arose prior to October 1, 2003, unless specifically approved by the Court. These obligations, referred to as prepetition claims, are subject to the completion of the bankruptcy proceeding, and will be settled in accordance with the terms of a Chapter 11 plan of reorganization.

However, under the guidelines of Chapter 11, the Company's vendors are afforded "adminis-trative" status for all shipments received by CBAC, Inc. subsequent to the Chapter 11 filing. As a result, these shipments will be paid for in the ordinary course of business.

We believe it is in the best interests of both our companies to continue to do business on the same terms and conditions we've had in the past.

To ensure that CBAC, Inc. has adequate funds to continue operating in a business-as-usual manner throughout the reorganization process, CBAC, Inc. has obtained $8 million interim cash funding and commitments for $25 million in secured debtor-in-possession financing from a group of institutions led by Doe Finance.

We have been working very hard to address the significant financial challenges faced by CBAC, Inc. While the restructuring plan we put in place last March has met with some success, CBAC, Inc. continues to be subject to many of the same financial pressures that originally led us to develop that plan. This action is the best option to allow us to continue with business as usual while we put CBAC, Inc.'s businesses on a solid financial footing for the future.

Although we cannot predict at this time exactly how long it will take to emerge from Chapter 11, we are determined to work through the process as quickly as possible and emerge as a stronger business entity. To achieve this objective, the Company needs the support of its vendors. We value you as a supplier and are committed to continuing our longstanding business relationship with you. We appreciate your support.

As always, if you have any questions, please do not hesitate to contact us. Additional information about our Chapter 11 filings is available on CBAC, Inc.'s Web site at www.CBACInc.com.

Sincerely,

As in the example below, be sure to tailor the letter to the intended recipient and provide them with the information they need to address their needs.

As we have feared for some time, the large-scale development in this part of Newark has all but destroyed our small retail market. Effective November 1, CBAC, Inc. will be closing. While this will mean a layoff for most of you, our severance package should give everyone time to find suitable work elsewhere.

We recognize that without the support and loyalty of this staff we could never have held out this long. It's been a great 20 years!

We thank you and wish you the best of success in your new positions, wherever they may be.

Tips for Writing Closing, Liquidation, and/or Bankruptcy Announcements

- In instances of bankruptcy notification, provide all of the information that is required. Check with local resources or consult your attorney to ensure that your communication meets your legal requirements.

- Be sure to address the intended recipient. Put yourself in your reader's shoes and make sure you are providing them with all of the information they will need.

- If you want the reader to react in a specific way, be clear and up front about what you want them to do.

COPYRIGHT VIOLATION NOTICE

Copyright law forbids us from using material from other sources without permission. Yet you may be attending a workshop, or reading an article, and lo and behold — you see text, visuals, or data that you created. Are you being plagiarized?

Maybe, but it might not be deliberate. There is so much information floating around, and being passed from source to source, that it's sometimes difficult to tell who owns what. The Internet in particular has made it difficult to track proper usage of intellectual property, and has made it easier to violate copyright, whether accidentally or on purpose.

Give the suspected plagiarist the benefit of the doubt. Maybe lifting your material without giving you credit is merely an oversight. Send them a letter notifying them of the problem. What you are looking for is an apology, and a promise to either give proper credit to the author, or stop using the material — or both.

Format: [*See Appendix A:* Fig. A-1. Simple format for letters and memos.] Typed/word-processed. Business or personal letterhead.

Style/Tone/Voice: Formal. Active tone or voice. [*See Part I for more on these subjects.*]

Structure: (1) State the actual violation if it has happened, include details such as location, date, usage of copyrighted material, (2) The body of the letter should either explain the action you plan to take or a warning about infringing on the copyrighted material, (3) Close by asking for an apology, monetary retribution or simply ask them to cease and desist illegal usage of material.

Handy Phrases: Any use of the materials prior to receipt of the authorization letter constitutes a violation of the copyright laws; As the copyright owner, I am writing to file a complaint; The complaint of copyright violation is based; Professional works require a great deal of study and time on the part of the creators — we deserve a return on our investment.

See also: *Part II:* Formal Information Letters.

Dear Caroline;

I attended last Thursday's QEFSG luncheon and workshop. Twice during your segment I felt you neglected to acknowledge the source of material you used and I wanted to bring this to your attention.

Master copywriter Michael Michaelson created "The All-4-1" concept. The "Four-Keyhole Door" example you used to illustrate the All-4-1 concept was a direct-mail package written by Rob Roy.

Rob has a tape called "The World's Best-Kept Secrets," which includes a great explanation of the All-4-1 — among other best practices and lots of examples. Would you like a free copy? And we're happy to have you use any material from Rob (there's lots of stuff on his Web site — with credit where it's due, of course.

Regards,

Here is another example:

Pictures on this site are all photographs I've taken myself for use on this Web site. Any use in violation of the posted guidelines constitutes copyright infringement. This creates a significant financial liability for the organization that is redistributing the images.

An established industry-standard penalty calls for triple the fair-market value for cases of unauthorized use. The use of one image on a medium- to high-traffic Web site, without prior authorization, would result in an invoice for $1,500 or more. Print use can be significantly higher. If payment is refused, it would be a mere formality to get a judgment in small claims court. Any collection costs would automatically be added to the amount of the judgment.

I have found photographs from this site used without authorization several dozen times. In some instances, such as when the use is noncommercial, I have asked the person responsible to comply with my guidelines, and they have always obliged.

When I discover commercial use, I send a demand letter for triple the market rate for their usage. If not paid within 10 days, I file suit for that amount. This has been effective in every case. Most graphics and media professionals know that the liability created by copyright violation outweighs ducking the licensing fee.

I am likely to discover unauthorized use of pictures from this site. In the above case, the Web site developer paid a settlement 5 to 10 times what I would have charged them if they licensed the photos before using them.

Because I offer very fair licensing fees (including free use in some cases), I take issue when my work is used without authorization. It is better to discuss your situation with me than assume I will not discover unauthorized use. When I do, I send a demand letter (e.g. for $1,000 to $5,000). If it's not paid, I follow with a lawsuit for that amount, based upon the violation of my copyright. Since I warn of this policy in advance, it's hard to rationalize using an image without authorization.

Tips for Writing a Notice of Copyright Violation

- Do not accuse the reader of deliberate wrongdoing. You are writing to notify them that some of the material in their presentation is from a copyrighted source. At minimum the source should be credited.

- Tell where the copyrighted material appears in their presentation or document.

- Say who the copyright owner is and where the material comes from. They may not know the original source.

- Tell them what you want done. Will being credited in future presentations of their material suffice? Or do you want something more?

- If they are using your material on their Web site without credit, and their visitors might be potential customers for your product, give them permission to continue to use it. In return you get credit with a link to your site.

VIRUS PROTECTION POLICY

When people get a computer virus from someone's e-mail, they often blame that person for their woes, whether they say so or not. And the woes can be substantial — from losing files to having to rebuild an entire PC system.

Make sure your IT department has put anti-virus protection, such as software and a firewall, in place. Get the details from them, and communicate these to vendors, suppliers, business partners, customers, and others outside the company with whom you routinely communicate with via e-mail. Include a disclaimer (see Handy Phrases, following). Even if they get a virus, they will know that you did everything in your power to prevent it, and you won't get the blame.

But, in the unhappy event that you've sent someone a virus, send them a fax as soon as you are aware of the problem. Apologize, guide them on how they can correct the problem, and let them know they can call on you and/or your IT department if they need assistance.

Format: [*See Appendix A:* Fig. A-1. Simple format for letters and memos.] Typed/word-processed. Business or personal letterhead.

Style/Tone/Voice: Formal. Active tone or voice. [*See Part I for more on these subjects.*]

Structure: (1) Open with an assurance of your concern, (2) State policies and anti-virus policies (including what you can/can't guarantee about your transmissions, (3) Educate recipients by guiding them to anti-virus sites for complete details, (4) Urge them to call if they have concerns.

Handy Phrases: Computer viruses can be transmitted via e-mail; The recipient should check this e-mail and any attachments for the presence of viruses; We'd like to inform you of a new virus that's currently circulating the Internet; These policies and procedures have been put into place to help us and our associates respond to this "Internet litter"; Although we've taken reasonable precautions to ensure no viruses are present in outbound e-mails, we cannot accept responsibility for any loss or damage arising from the use of e-mail or attachments.

See also: *Part V:* Human Resources (HR) Policies; Telephone Policy Memos; Information Technology (IT) Memos; *Part IX:* Vendor Gift Policy

TO: All clients and potential clients
FROM: Carol Harold
RE: Our anti-virus policy
LAST UPDATED: 10-13-02

1. We make every effort to ensure that files sent to our clients via e-mail or disk are virus-free — but we CANNOT guarantee it.
2. We run McAfee 3.5 VirusScan, which is the most widely used anti-virus program worldwide — 25 million people, 80 percent of the Fortune 1000, and 40,000 organizations use it.
3. According to McAfee, VirusScan technology has been shown in lab tests to detect virtually every virus. These include boot, file, multiparties, stealth, mutating, encrypted, and polymorphic viruses.
4. Because new viruses crop up all the time, we routinely upgrade our VirusScan program by downloading the latest versions from the McAfee BBS (bulletin board). We recommend that clients running VirusScan do likewise.
5. Even running the latest anti-virus software cannot guarantee a virus-free file, because new viruses are launched constantly. Clients should run the most recent version of their anti-virus software before downloading or receiving e-mail.
6. If you open a file we sent you via e-mail and it contains a virus, that does *not* mean the virus came from our end. Files sent via the Internet can pick up viruses in transit.
7. The only 100-percent foolproof protection against receiving a virus is to request that documents be faxed instead of e-mailed. You can't pick up a virus from a hard copy.
8. If you have any problems with a virus in a file we send you, please notify us immediately: 555-555-1220. If you are having a virus problem in general, we can refer you to computer consultants who may be able to help.

A memo of notification may not need to be specific about the type of protection you or your company are taking. See the memo below that outlines the general hazards of computer viruses.

Computer viruses can be transmitted via e-mail. The recipient should check this e-mail and any attachments for the presence of viruses. CBAC Company accepts no liability for any damage caused by any virus transmitted by CBAC's e-mail. E-mail transmission cannot be guaranteed to be secure or error-free as information could be intercepted, corrupted, lost, destroyed, arrive late or incomplete, or contain viruses. CBAC Company does not accept liability for any errors or omissions in the contents of this message, which arise as a result of e-mail transmission.

Warning: Although CBAC Company has taken reasonable precautions to ensure no viruses are present in their e-mail, CBAC Company cannot accept responsibility for any loss or damage arising from the use of their e-mail or attachments.

Tips for Writing an Anti-Virus Policy Memo

- Describe the major steps you have taken to make sure your computer is virus-free and does not send a virus to others.

- Show that you are using up-to-date, quality anti-virus products — and that you have good anti-virus "hygiene," updating and cleaning your system frequently.

- Point out that they may have gotten the virus in many other ways than from you. There is no way to tell, in many cases.

- Encourage them to ask their IT department for help in case of a virus, or recommend one of your computer consultants.

- Do not guarantee that every e-mail you send is virus free. You cannot ever be 100 percent sure. The only way for the person to be totally virus free is to stay unconnected — no modems, cables, Internet, or LAN connections. Not practical, of course, for modern businesspeople, so we really all have to stay at risk.

INTERNAL COMMUNICATION

In Part IV, we looked at a wide range of general business correspondence. In Part V, we focus on *internal correspondence* — e-mails, letters, and memos written to communicate with others within your organization.

On the surface, writing to others within your organization may seem a less challenging task than communicating with business partners, vendors, prospects, and customers. After all, prospects must be communicated with persuasively, or they won't buy. Customers are handled with kid gloves, less they jump to another supplier. But in theory, you can say anything you want to a colleague. After all, you both get your paychecks from the same source. You're on the same team. You are forced, by nature of your employment, to be cooperative and cordial. Or are you?

The fact is, communicating with coworkers can be just as delicate an operation as extracting money from a customer refusing to pay an invoice, or a key business partner who thinks you are taking advantage of him.

Why is this so? Several reasons:

- Organizations today are less hierarchical than a generation ago. The lines of command are not as clearly drawn. Employees see themselves more as peers than as subordinates, and act accordingly.
- Generation X and Y have less respect for "gray hairs" than Baby Boomers and Matures did when they were young. Old age and experience no longer gain instant respect. Senior employees are not taken at their word; they have to convince others that their ideas and recommendations are indeed correct.
- The pace of work in general and communication in general are faster. People are more harried, resulting in the phenomenon of "haste-based rudeness." People are less cordial and civil because they don't have time to be more thoughtful and polite. They are quick to take offense. And they have less time than ever to spend on communication.
- E-mail is less formal and more casual than letters or even memos. People write instantly, often don't check what they write, and quickly click on the Send button — increasing the potential for ineffective and offensive communication.

Businesspeople today need to slow down, just a bit — especially as far as their writing is concerned. Have you ever written an e-mail quickly and in anger, sent it, and then seconds later wish you could take it back? Then you know the importance of thinking about what you write before you write it and send it.

Many businesspeople who write internal e-mails, memos, and letters think their only or primary mission is to transmit information — to answer the question, provide the data, or give the facts. That's part of your mission, but not all of it.

Most written communications, even internal, have another objective: to persuade. That is, to convince the reader to approve your budget, grant your request, attend a meeting, cooperate with a project, contribute to a project, or to work on a team.

You have heard the old saying, "You can catch more flies with honey than with vinegar." Unfortunately, many of us give nothing but vinegar. We demand. We are brisk — too brisk, on the border of being unfriendly or rude. We assume obligation when there is none, and enthusiasm for disinterest.

The degree and type of persuasion depends on the reader and your objective. If you want to persuade senior management to spend $1 million on a new inventory system, you'll have to make your case as strongly as a trial attorney trying to clear a client of grand theft auto.

Other situations — such as convincing a team member to support your ideas, or a department manager to get you a new piece of equipment — may require a more subtle approach.

Here are a few of the persuasion techniques that are most effective in internal communications:

- Ask. Don't demand.
- Show the reader how agreeing with your idea benefits him or her, not just you.
- Be flexible. Accommodate the reader's schedule. Offer to do things at his or her convenience, not yours.
- Avoid arrogance or implying that you know it all, even if you think you do. Let the reader know you respect his or her opinion, experience, and thoughts.
- If you are turned down, be polite. Do not show anger or petulance.

FYI Internal Memos

Although e-mails are rapidly replacing the typewritten memorandum, corporate employees today still exchange large volumes of both formats.

In some instances, the entire memo can consist of the abbreviation FYI ("for your information"). For instance, let's say you get the annual report of your competitor and want your boss, Mike, to see it. You can simply attach a sticky note to it as in the following example:

> Mike,
>
> FYI.
>
> — Bill

Or, you can forward your report in an e-mail with a file attached, as long as you are writing to people who know you (virus concerns make others hesitant to open attached files from someone whom they don't know).

Using FYI lets you communicate with an economy of words, even if your message is lengthier.

> Mike,
>
> FYI, I spoke to Worldview Insurance. They will have the proposal to us next week. I'll let you know as soon as I've reviewed it, so we can determine the best option.
>
> Sincerely,
>
> Bill

Spelling Out Abbreviations

While you should generally spell out any abbreviation, some abbreviations, such as FYI, are so well known that spelling them out is unnecessary. In other cases, such as DNA, the abbreviation communicates the intended meaning, and spelling it out adds nothing to the reader's understanding. When should you just use the abbreviation and when should you give the full term? Use your judgment, but follow this rule: When in doubt, spell it out.

A good example is RAM. Almost everybody has heard of RAM, but surprisingly few people know the precise meaning. So when discussing computer memory in a memo, spell out RAM — random access memory — in its first use. Then you can abbreviate it as RAM in the remainder of the document.

Instead of using FYI, you can quickly cue the reader into the topic under discussion by using a Re: line. In a memo, a Re: line can go directly under the date in the header. "Re" (pronounced "ree" or "ray") is short for the Latin phrase *in re,* meaning "in the matter of."

TO: Tom Hernandez
FROM: Bill Jones
DATE: November 11, 2002
RE: Liability insurance

I have received the proposal from Worldview Insurance.
The premium is $15,870, which is around 40% to 50% higher than the other bids.
However, their coverage is much more comprehensive and more in line with what our attorney says we need.
Please give me a call to discuss as soon as you can.

Thanks.

[*For information about using Re: lines, see Part IV*, FYI Letters.]

Tips for Writing Memos

- Use the KISS formula ("keep it short and simple").
- Get right to the point.
- Edit ruthlessly so you can get everything on a single sheet of paper if humanly possible.

Internal Requests

Especially given the way almost everything in business today is done through teams, managers and others routinely communicate within the organization in writing.

You would think the rules of good letter writing are less important when communicating internally (within a team, department, or organization), but you'd be wrong. The same techniques of clarity, etiquette, and persuasion apply.

For instance, a common situation today is needing to make a request of a team member who is not your direct response. You are expected to manage this person's activities, yet you do not really have the authority to do so. Good communication can solve this problem by getting the other person to voluntarily comply with your request without you having to "go above his head."

MAKING AN INTERNAL REQUEST

A situation calling for persuasive and polite writing is asking someone to do something that they don't want to do, may not think they have to do, and in fact you cannot force them to do — especially if it involves money.

When such persuasion is required, written communication is most effective. It allows you to state your case in a manner that is calm and comfortable, rather than confrontational. You don't get hot under the collar if the other person doesn't immediately agree to your request. They get the time to think about it, rather than respond right away.

Format: [*See Appendix A:* Fig. A-1. Simple format for letters or memos.] Typed/ word-processed. Company letterhead.

Style/Tone/Voice: Informal or formal. Passive or active voice. [*See Part I for more on these subjects.*]

Structure: (1) Present the necessary background, (2) Spell out your request, (3) Tell the reader specifically what you want her to do and by when.

Handy Phrases: I have a favor to ask; Can you help me; I need you to; Here's the situation; Here's what we need to happen next.

See also: *Part IV:* Requests for Cooperation or Assistance.

June 28, 2004

Mr. Hiroshi Sakakawa
Manager, Sales Department
Electronics Equipment Motor Division
1-1-1 Ichikoen, Mina-ku, Tokyo, 105-xxxx Japan

Re: Charges for UL label rework on EL791

Dear Sakakawa-san,

Attached is the detailed information regarding the cost to rework the EL791 fans for our customer Computer Makers, which we discussed during my visit in May. For your reference the issue is summarized below.

Computer Makers received more than 5000 units of EL791 without the required UL symbol. The UL inspector would not allow Computer Makers to use the fans without the correct label.

Hirata-san took action to provide new drawings with correct label information, and to establish that every EL791 model ships to Computer Makers with UL labels.

We are asking your department to accept the debit for this issue. The total cost was US$1,668.66. We appreciate your strong support and understanding in this matter.

Sincerely,

Bill Johnson
Regional Sales Manager
Industrial Company

Tips for Making an Internal Request

- Say exactly what you want — and preferably, by when you want to get it.
- Explain the reason for your request.
- Give facts that help the other party see your side of it and reach the same conclusion you have.
- State your case so clearly and logically that the other person would feel he is acting irrationally *not* to comply.

AGREEING TO AN INTERNAL REQUEST

A happy time to write is when you are agreeing to a request, because you know in advance that your coworker will be happy you are doing so.

Given that you are already pleasing your colleague, you can maximize the goodwill you are earning with a letter that is positive and polite. Many people who grant requests do so grudgingly. Or they go out of their way to remind the recipient of the favor that it *is* a favor, and that they are doing it because they were pushed.

What does that accomplish? It only serves to sour the reader's disposition and negate the good feelings being created. Much better to be gracious when granting requests. This makes the recipient feel better, like you better, and more inclined to return the favor when opportunity arises.

Format: [*See Appendix A:* Fig. A-1. Simple format for letters or memos.] Typed/word-processed. Business letterhead.

Style/Tone/Voice: Informal or formal. Active voice. [*See Part I for more on these subjects.*]

Structure: (1) Give the good news that you are granting their request, (2) Say why if you feel an explanation gains you some advantage, (3) Spell out any conditions or limitations on the offer.

Handy Phrases: Good news; I have some good news for you; Sorry it took this long to get back to you.

See also: *Part II:* Letter Granting a Request; *Part IV:* Responding to Business Requests.

Hello Dan,

Sorry this took so long but you can have the $5.00 resale for this special fan. Your cost will be $4.40 each.

To achieve this, be aware that HVAC Compliance, Inc. has reduced its commission significantly. The lead-time to produce these units will be 90 to 120 days. Please let me know when you book this order.

Regards,

Brian

Tips for Agreeing to an Internal Request

- Start with the positive news. If there is any negative news, such as a condition or term that is not favorable to the other person, give this after stating the positive.

- If you have made a special effort to meet the request, be specific about what was done and what it may have cost you in time, money, and effort. This raises in the reader's mind the perceived value of what you have done for him.

- But in the second bullet point above, use a matter-of-fact tone, as if you are simply informing the reader of a situation. Do not laud it over them or cry agony or hardship.

REQUESTING A MEETING

A large portion of any corporate employee's workday is spent in meetings, and since there are usually more meetings to attend than there are hours in the day, it may take some convincing to get a person to meet with you.

Format: [*See Appendix A:* Fig. A-1. Simple format for letters or memos.] Typed/word-processed.

Style/Tone/Voice: Informal or formal. Active voice. [See Part I for more on these subjects.]

Structure: (1) State that you would like a meeting, (2) Give the agenda, objective, and reason for the meeting, (3) Ask the reader to confirm or suggest a date, time, and location.

Handy Phrases: I have a request; We need to have a meeting; When can we get together?

See also: *Part III:* Inquiring About a Job Opening; Networking Letters; *Part V:* Meetings.

First requests to attend a meeting are usually made with a phone call or a brief e-mail, the text of which follows:

> Bill:
>
> Can you meet with me Thursday at 10 a.m. to discuss our motor needs?
>
> Sincerely,
>
> Steve

If this brief request gets a positive response, you're done. But what happens when you want or need to meet with someone, and they don't get back to you?

Put your request in writing. The very fact that your second request is written rather than spoken gives it weight; the more formal communication indicates that the item is a priority with you, the need is not going to go away, and the recipient, no matter how busy or pressed, is required to reply.

> Bill,
>
> I have requested a meeting with you, and as yet have not received a response. I would like to discuss future motor business with you. Our motor requirements are growing, and we have need for an ozone-resistant motor.
>
> I will be in Tokyo on the 13th of July. On the afternoon of the 14th I would like to take the train to Osaka and meet with you on the 16th. I will be departing for Seoul on the 17th. Can you please recommend a hotel and book a room for the 15th and 16th?

Please confirm that I can meet with you on the 16th, along with hotel phone and fax numbers to Karen Overhill, at fax number 011-817-222-2222 or e-mail to sobrien@ozonemotors.com.

Kind regards,

Steve O'Brien

Tips for Requesting a Meeting

- State a clear purpose and objective for the meeting.
- Indicate how the reader will benefit by attending the meeting. Will he learn something new? Make important contacts? Sell more of his products?
- Suggest a specific location, date, and time for the meeting. That way, the reader has to say either yes or no.
- If appropriate, enclose an agenda or list of items to be discussed.

Announcements

According to the *Webster's New World Dictionary,* the verb "announce" means "to declare publicly; give notice of formally; proclaim." The key to announcement is news — you are telling others something important, new, and relevant to their interests.

CHANGE IN EMPLOYMENT STATUS ANNOUNCEMENTS

A common use of internal communications is to announce employee moves and changes   promotions, lateral moves to other divisions or positions, transfers, retirement.

The letter or memo's prime mission is to communicate simple information. But once again, more is involved.

When writing to announce a promotion, you are telling your readers about a strategic move that strengthens the organization as a whole. Say how having this person in this position will benefit the company and its customers; you never know when an employee will pass such a memo on to an outsider, such as a key account.

When writing to inform people of a termination, you have several goals. You want to spare the employee being fired further humiliation. You also want to avoid saying anything that could be used by the employee in a wrongful termination suit against the company.

When writing a retirement announcement, what to you is a routine document may become a cherished memento of a faithful employee's long career. Sincere praise goes a long way to making that person feel good about his career and the company. It also demonstrates corporate caring to other employees.

Format: [*See Appendix A:* Fig. A-1. Simple format for letters or memos.] Typed/word-processed. Business letterhead.

Style/Tone/Voice: Formal. Passive or active voice. [*See Part I for more on these subjects.*]

Structure: (1) Announce the change in personnel and employment status, (2) Name the people involved, (3) Explain how the change affects the organization.

Handy Phrases: We are pleased; Making a change; Pursue new opportunities.

See also: *Part II:* Information Letters; *Part III:* Notifying Your Present Employer That You are Taking a New Job.

TO: All Employees
FROM: Joe Garcia
SUBJECT: Frank Ueno
DATE: September 14, 2003

After spending 6 1/2 years in the United States, Frank Ueno will be returning to Japan in mid-October to take a new assignment as General Manager of Accounting in the Corporate International Business Operation Division in Osaka. I would like to take this opportunity to express my sincere appreciation for the valuable support Frank has extended to us during his stay.

Please join me in wishing Frank much success, good health, and happiness as he returns to Japan.

Here is an example of an employee joining an organization.

TO: All Employees
FROM: Bill Furman
SUBJECT: Toshi Iishi
DATE: June 22, 2003

I am pleased to announce that Mr. Toshi Iishi has joined our department as a Product Specialist directly supporting our motor sales department.

Toshi has been with the Motor Division for more than six years, working at both the Tokyo and Osaka sales offices. Toshi was recently married and will bring his new wife, Machiko, to the USA in December, after he has settled in to his new position.

Toshi will be working from our Los Angeles office, with Frank Cooper, and his contact information is:

Toshi Iishi
123 Beach Ave.
Los Angeles, CA 49120
Tel: 714-555-1234
Fax: 714-555-2345

Please begin utilizing Toshi immediately for all technical, quality, and sales support for motor products. Toshi will be preparing regular updates of the sales project log, so make sure to include him on all distribution lists for contact reports, monthly reports, factory correspondence, etc.

Please join me in welcoming Toshi to the motor department.

Regards,

The following is an example of a retirement announcement.

May 1, 2001

Industrial Company
Organization Announcement

After 25 years of service, Jim Hadley has decided to retire. Jim has held a variety of leadership positions, most recently as General Manager in our Global Telecommunications Group. His many contributions across the business are greatly appreciated.

Jim will continue to reside in the Northern California area. Please join me in thanking Jim for his dedicated service, and in wishing him and his family a full and happy retirement.

The following letter introduces a change in the company structure.

Joseph Garcia
President & CEO
Industrial Company
January 29, 2001
Organization Announcement

TO: All Employees
FROM: Joseph Garcia

As part of our continuing strategy to foster growth and to improve our ability to provide value to our customers and to our factories, we will be establishing a new Headquarters Marketing Division. The initial focus of the Division will be to analyze industrywide trends, determine market and technology shifts, and create strategic Marketing roadmaps that support our product groups and customers.

Effective February 1, Mike Jones will take the lead in creating this new Marketing function. Mike will develop a project plan and initial staffing requirements for this organization. He will continue to be located in our Los Angeles, California, office. Please note that the product marketing and management functions in each of the product groups will remain with their current organizations.

In addition to his current responsibilities, Steve Belcak will assume concurrent responsibility to lead our global sales organization. Steve will remain in the New Jersey office.

Jeff and Steve will continue to report directly to me. Please join me in wishing them continued success in these new assignments.

This last example announces a new hire and an employee transitioning into a new position.

May 27, 2002

We are pleased to announce the following changes to our Sales Team:

Effective June 1, 2002, Debbie Jones will be joining us as the Distribution Sales Manager and Emerging Accounts Sales Engineer in San Diego. Debbie comes to us with 3½ years experience in the Distribution sales arena in San Diego — having been most recently with Nickson Electronics and Whopnix Electronics prior to that. Within both companies she played a key role in Field Sales, and will be a huge asset to our organization based on her sales experience and knowledge of the San Diego marketplace, and several of our Principals already.

As soon as Debbie is "up and running," Sara Smith will be vacating her position in San Diego as the Distribution Sales Manager, to develop a new position within the company as Operations Manager. In her newly developed position, Sara will be developing a Principal Sales Data program to aid us all in our respective territories with specific product sales information pertaining to our accounts and Principals. She has had many years doing this very thing, and will be a great asset to us in this area.

Sara will also assume other responsibilities — including working with Joanna on RPMS; working with Dan on Principal Schedules, Calendars, and Principal Monthly Reports; and coordinating Trade Shows and Principal Presentations along with Doug, Mark and Rob.

Join us in welcoming Debbie and Sara into their new roles.

Sincerely,

Tips for Writing Employee Announcements

- Keep in mind your audiences: senior management, line management, support staff, the employee the announcement is about, and his or her co-workers. Will what you say offend any of them or turn them off?

- Don't say anything you would not want an outsider to learn. Internal memos sometimes get into the hands of people outside the organization.

- When appropriate, give complete contact information — name, title, location, phone number, fax, and e-mail address — for the employee. Otherwise you force your readers to contact you for that information, which wastes their time and yours.

TRAVEL NOTICES

Another area that often generates announcements is corporate travel, travel plans, travel schedules, and travel policies. Such notices are fairly routine in nature, and nothing fancy in the way of writing is required.

Just state the facts concisely and give all relevant details. If it is necessary to justify a trip, expenditure, or other travel-related decision, do so.

Format: [*See Appendix A:* Fig. A-1. Simple format for letters or memos.] Type/word-processed. Business letterhead.

Style/Tone/Voice; Informal or formal. Active voice. [*See Part I for more on these subjects.*]

Structure: (1) Remind the reader of the current travel policy, (2) State the change in policy, (3) Explain the reason for the change, (4) Give the specifics necessary to comply, (5) Say when the new policy goes into effect.

Handy Phrases: Please note; All employees; Important change; New travel policy.

See also: *Part IV:* FYI Letters; *Part V:* Announcements.

In the first example, unrest overseas is the reason for travel restrictions, and the benefit is greater safety for the reader.

George,

Given the current circumstances in China due to the NATO bombing, I believe that we should limit our visits to Taiwan only. Visits to Mainland China are potentially dangerous for American visitors at this time.

Regards,

Troy

This memo uses a bulleted list to clearly present multiple items.

ATT: Staff

Attached is a newly revised Travel and Entertainment Policy, which will be effective for travel beginning Sunday, November 2, 2004. This policy applies to all sales and service divisions and units in the United States.

Changes have been made to keep current with IRS regulations and to strengthen our vendor alliances in the agency, hotel, and airline areas. Some of the key areas that have been revised are:

- Personal and Executive Auto Mileage Allowances
- Domestic and Japan Meal Allowances Purchase Reimbursement
- E-Tickets and Prepaid Tickets
- Advance Airline Ticket Use
- Domestic and Japan Hotel Rates

Please review the complete policy for a general understanding of the policy's complete contents and the procedures and forms to be used to assure accurate and timely reimbursement for appropriate expenses. Please also distribute this information to your staff to assure that they are aware of the Travel and Entertainment Reimbursement Policy and the forms and procedures.

Please feel free to contact me if you have any questions.

Here is another example of a travel policy letter distributed to employees.

TO: Assistant General Managers and Above
FROM: Tom Hayes
DATE: March 11, 2003
RE: Travel and Entertainment Policy Mileage Allowance

Please note that the IRS has revised the personal auto mileage reimbursement allowance for all Travel and Entertainment Policy reimbursements on or after April 1, 2003. Therefore, effective with all T&E reports for the week ending April 3, 2003, the mileage allowance will be reduced to 31 cents per mile for the authorized business use of a personal auto by an employee.

Please inform your staff of this change to the T&E Policy. Should you have any questions, please feel free to contact me.

Tips for Writing Travel Notices

- Announce travel plans, methods, and restrictions sooner rather than later. People need warning if an adjustment to their schedule is required.

- If you must restrict travel or reduce a travel budget, give the reason why.

- When a policy applies to everyone in a department or area, ask the recipient to post or distribute the notice if you do not have the names and e-mail addresses or mail stops of everyone the policy affects.

TRAINING NOTICES

Although U.S. corporations spend more than $30 billion to train their employees each year, training remains a touchy subject, both to discuss and to write about.

Many businesspeople think training is a waste of time: Attending seminars and workshops takes time away from employees who are already too busy and cannot afford to be away from their desks. A decade ago, two- and three-day seminars were the norm; today, the standard is a day. People do not want give up more time than that.

Others do not want to attend training sessions, believing that they already know the subject and that the trainers have nothing to teach them. Ironically, those who are against training are often those who need it most. People who are already proficient in a topic are usually eager to improve their skills even further, while those who are mediocre are defensive and think they need no further training.

Format: [*See Appendix A:* Fig. A-1. Simple format for letters and memos.] Handwritten or typed. Personal or business letterhead.

Style/Tone/Voice: Informal or formal. Forceful tone. Active voice. [*See Part I for more on these subjects.*]

Structure: (1) Give the title of the class, (2) Say why you are holding it, (3) Tell the attendees what they will learn, (4) Instruct them on how to register and prepare for the class.

Handy Phrases: Training objectives; Learning objectives; Program modules; Hands-on workshop; Interactive program; Real-world case histories; How you will benefit.

See also: *Part IV:* Letters of Confirmation and Acknowledgment; *Part V:* Announcements.

TO: All Managers
FROM: Matt Kowalski, Chairman and CEO
DATE: October 27, 2003
SUBJECT: Mandatory XYZ 1200 Training

The purpose of this memo is to announce the mandatory XYZ 1200 General Awareness Training program for all employees working in the Chicago facility.

XYZ is an international federation promoting the development of international manufacturing, trade, and communication standards. XYZ 1200 is a series of standards that provides a framework for managing environmental impacts of an organization.

This company has committed to be a worldwide leader in the implementation of XYZ 1200 and our goal is to certify the Chicago facility by March 31, 2004. Our preliminary assessment is scheduled for January 12–13, 2004 and our certification assessment is scheduled for the week of February 21, 2004.

To ensure that every employee understands this environmental management system, the Corporate Environmental Department has instituted an XYZ 1200 General Awareness Training program. This program is a very important component of the XYZ 1200 Implementation process and is designed to prepare you for the auditor's questions.

I am, therefore, requesting that all personnel working in the Chicago facility attend one of the training sessions. You have been scheduled to attend as follows:

Date: Monday, November 15, 2003
Time: 2:00 p.m.–3:00 p.m.
Place: Main Building, 1st Floor

Please make every effort to attend the session you have been assigned to. If you have an unavoidable conflict, please contact the Training Center to reschedule.

I am confident that this training program will contribute to a successful certification audit.

Matt Kowalski
Chairman and Chief Executive Officer

Tips for Writing Training Announcements

- Describe specifically the topic of the training and what skills will be learned.
- Give the reason why you have selected this particular topic for training instead of others.

- Say how both the individual and organization can benefit through acquisition of these skills.

- Ask for a commitment to attend or send staff to attend the sessions.

- If the trainer has a track record of success, say so to build confidence that the training you have selected is worthwhile.

HUMAN RESOURCES (HR) POLICIES

HR policy affects all employees, so these memos get the widest distribution of any in the company and are the most likely to be posted in public places.

Employees are extremely sensitive about their rights, benefits, vacation, sick days, and related HR issues. Recognize this sensitivity when writing HR policy memos.

Since these HR memos represent your company's official policy, make them clear, accurate, and easy to follow. Anticipate and answer the most likely questions in your memo. Provide a name, phone number, and e-mail where the reader can get answers to her questions.

A spell-checker is only one of the methods that can be used to make sure there are no typos, misspellings, or grammar errors. But the spell-checker doesn't find everything. A manager at a Big Six accounting firm once sent out a memo, after spell checking, that referred to the company as "certified pubic accountants."

It is especially difficult to proofread a document that you have rewritten several times; your mind is tired, and your eye skips over the text without actually looking at every word. Give the memo to an assistant or colleague as a second check.

Another proofreading tip that is effective at catching typos and misspellings is to read the document backward. When you read backward, the meaning of the sentences disappears, and you are better able to focus on each word rather than the overall message.

Format: [*See Appendix A*: Fig. A-1. Simple format for letters and memos.] Type/word-processed. Company letterhead.

Style/Tone/Voice: Informal or formal. Impersonal tone. Passive or active voice. [*See Part I for more on these subjects.*]

continued

continued

Structure: (1) Identify the topic (e.g., "unscheduled personal days"), (2) Clearly state the company's official policy, (3) If appropriate, convey the reason for the policy, (4) Note any exception, and (5) Ask for compliance.

Handy Phrases: All employees; No exceptions; Our standard policy.

See also: *Part IV:* FYI Letters; *Part V:* Announcements.

TO: All Employees
FROM: Ann South, Human Resources Department
SUBJECT: Vacation/personal holiday carryover
DATE: December 21, 2003

As we approach the end of the calendar year, it is necessary to assess unused vacation and Personal/Optional days.

It is the policy of the company that all vacation time granted within a twelve (12) calendar month period beginning January 1 and ending December 31, be taken during that time. However, unused days may be carried over to the following year as specified below.

Vacation

All employees will be permitted to "carry over" any earned but unused vacation time in accordance with Nickson Electronics policy.

The maximum vacation an employee may take in a calendar year (carryover plus current year) is "capped" at 25 days. There is also a vacation earning and accrual "cap" of 25 days.

If at any time in a calendar year an employee's unused vacation (the previous year's carry over plus any earned current year's vacation) reaches 25 days, the employee will not earn or accrue any additional vacation time until all or part of the 25 days of accrued vacation are used.

Personal/Optional Days

All employees will be permitted to "carry over" any earned, but not taken, Personal/Optional Holidays in accordance with Nickson Electronics policy.

The maximum Personal/Optional Holiday benefit an employee may take in a calendar year (carryover plus current year) is "capped" at four days. There is also an earning and accrual cap of four days.

If at any time in a calendar year an employee's unused Personal/Optional Holiday benefit (the previous year's carry over plus any earned current year's benefit) reaches four days, the employee will not earn or accrue any additional Personal/Optional Holidays until all or part of the four days of accrued benefits are used.

Procedure for Carry-Over Requests

It is the responsibility of the department manager to approve carry over requests in accordance with policy guidelines and maintain accurate records in this regard. For exempt employees, this can be accomplished by maintaining an annual attendance record. Attendance record sheets for the year 2004 were recently distributed.

Nonexempt employees record absences on weekly attendance sheets, which are then maintained and updated within the time accounting system. It is recommended that department managers retain copies of all time sheets submitted to Payroll.

It is the responsibility of the Division Head to review attendance records on a quarterly, or at minimum, semi-annual basis.

If you have any questions on vacation/personal holiday policies, please feel free to contact any member of the Human Resources Department for assistance.

Tips for Writing HR Policy Memos

- In memos longer than one page or covering more than one topic, use subheads to break the text into short sections.

- In memos to be posted publicly, keep the paragraphs short to make the document more visually appealing. Also consider using a type size one or two points larger than you usually do.

- You may want to post all HR policy memos in one section on the company's Intranet or internal employees-only Web site.

TELEPHONE POLICY MEMOS

Changes in telephone systems and policies are typically communicated in a straightforward memo distributed to all personnel affected by the change.

Format: [*See Appendix A:* Fig. A-1. Simple format for letters and memos.] Type/word-processed. Company letterhead.

Style/Tone/Voice: Informal or formal. Forceful tone. Passive or active voice. [*See Part I for more on these subjects.*]

Structure: (1) List the key policies, (2) Give instructions for compliance, (3) Explain the benefits and advantages of the system.

Handy Phrases: Not applicable.

See also: *Part IV:* Instruction Letters; *Part V:* Announcements.

FROM: Fred Sikkel
DATE: 3/25/03
SUBJECT: National Cellular Phone Program

Nickson Electronics has finalized the National Cellular Phone Program with Fast Wireless Services (FWS). I have attached all necessary documents for your review.

Please issue all the attached documents to your employees who have business requirements for a cellular phone. There are different procedures for employees in Milwaukee, employees in other locations, and employees who already have a cellular phone.

Everyone should read the attached documents before submitting their order form to 2RQR Accounting for management approval. The Nickson/Fast Cellular Phone Policy is attached and I have briefly outlined it below:

- Nickson/Fast will reimburse all expenses associated with business use of the cellular phones.
- Outgoing and incoming personal calls must be highlighted and excluded from cellular phone invoices that the employee will submit for reimbursement on their expense report.
- Because of the high cost of cell phone usage, all employees are expected to use the phone for critical business needs and emergencies only.
- Incoming calls must be kept to a minimum.
- 2RQR will not reimburse employees for overseas calls unless authorization is obtained from 2RQR in writing prior to when the calls are made.
- Each manager is responsible for their staff's use of cellular phones.
- Managers must report cell phone usage for each employee in their group to accounting on a monthly basis.
- Random audits will be done by accounting to ensure that all employees adhere to the policy.

Accounting will be responsible for coordinating the Cellular Phone Program for 2RQR. 2RQR Management will approve the order form for each employee.

Fast representatives will be in Milwaukee on March 26 from 2 p.m. to 5 p.m. to answer questions and accept orders for Milwaukee employees. Please send Accounting the following documents so an order can be processed:

- Fast Wireless Services National Accounts Order Form.
- A signed Equipment Loan Agreement.
- After Receipt of the cellular phone, please fax the Acknowledgment Receipt Form to Accounting.

If there are any questions, please contact me.

Tips for Writing Telephone Policy Memos

- Remember that you are providing a service for others in your company, and in this regard, they are your customers. Treat them as such.

- Telephone policies must be flexible. Set policies, but also explain procedures for overriding them or requesting exceptions based on need. Impossible to change the setup? Think about this: If your CEO asked for something special, would you find a way to accommodate him or her? Of course.

INFORMATION TECHNOLOGY (IT) MEMOS

An unspoken, adversarial relationship often exists between IT, senior management, and end users.

Format: [*See Appendix A:* Fig. A-1. Simple format for letters and memos.] Typed/word-processed. Company letterhead.

Style/Tone/Voice: Informal or formal. Passive or active voice. [*See Part I for more on these subjects.*]

Structure: Varies depending on subject matter.

Handy Phrases: Not applicable.

See also: *Part IV:* FYI Letters; *Part V:* Announcements.

TO: System users
FROM: Mike Rizzorio, IT Team Leader

Everyone associated with the widget project has been working very hard toward the July roll-out for Nickson Electronics and Accounts Receivable. The system configuration is solid. The integration test phase went very well. However, the interfaces and monitors will require more testing before we can go live.

The interfaces and monitors are very close to completion, but we need to test them more, especially with very complex case scenarios, to ensure proper functionality post roll-out. After much discussion, the rollout schedule has been revised as follows:

- 1st week of Aug.: "Big-Bang" Accounts Receivable applications
- 1st week of Sep.: roll-out Nickson Electronics
- 1st week of Nov.: roll-out Lambbell Milkers
- 1st week of Feb.: roll-out Bicktech Consolidated

All of finance will be live in August. This will help ease the Sept. roll-out.

I am confident that this change in the implementation schedule will pay dividends in the long run.

Thank you for your understanding and continued support.

The previous example outlines a new system rollout. The example below introduces a new policy and service.

TO: Nickson Electronics members

The following service is offered to all Nickson employees:

A limited number of notebook and desktop PCs are available for use while awaiting the delivery of a new PC or the repair of an existing PC.

The loan period while awaiting delivery of a new PC for new employees shall be no more than 30 days. Requests must be in writing and approved by group management.

Additionally, the request for the new PC must accompany the loan request. A permanent e-mail address will be established, which will be maintained upon receipt of the permanent PC.

Upon receipt of the permanent PC, ISD will configure the new PC and transfer any data and mail stored on the loan PC to the new PC.

For repairs, ISD will assess the time required to service a PC. If the estimate for repairs is more than five days ISD will provide a PC. The loan period while awaiting the repair of a PC is limited to the actual time required to perform the repair.

In all cases during the loan period the group is responsible for the PC. In case of damage or loss the group must repair or replace the unit at group expense.

ISD will attempt to honor all requests. There are a limited number of machines so requests will be honored on a first-come, first-served basis. Requests should be directed to the Nickson help desk.

Tips for Writing IT Memos

- Avoid surprises. Give users plenty of advance notice for service changes, updates, and interruptions.
- Don't go into a lengthy technical explanation; just tell the readers how it affects them.
- Provide clear, specific instructions.
- Break complicated procedures into short, easy-to-follow steps.

VACATION NOTICES

Send an e-mail or letter to colleagues and customers giving advance notice of your vacation plans. You can send this notice out to important people on your list. You can also set up your e-mail to automatically send the message as a response to anyone who sends you e-mail while you are away.

Format: [*See Appendix A:* Fig. A-1. Simple format for memos.] Typed/word-processed. Personal or Business letterhead if sending letter.

Style/Tone/Voice: Informal or formal. Passive or active voice. [*See Part I for more on these subjects.*]

Structure: (1) Tell the reader the dates when you will be on vacation or away, (2) Say how often (if at all) you will be checking your voice mail and e-mail, (3) Let the reader know the best way to get in touch with you, especially in an urgent or emergency situation.

Handy Phrases: I will be checking my e-mail periodically; I will have limited access to voice mail; Please call [name of person covering for you] if you need help while I am away.

See also: *Part II:* Personal Updates; *Part IV:* FYI Letters; *Part V:* Announcements.

TO: Clients and prospects
FROM: Carolyn Zeta, assistant to Bob Miller
RE: April schedule
DATE: 3-20-2002

Bob Miller will be out of the office traveling April 21–25. He will be in touch with the office via voice mail. The office will be open during this period, and if you need anything, you can leave a voice mail for Bob at 201-444-4444, or call me directly at 201-703-8888. Let me know if you have any questions or need additional information.

Tips for Writing Vacation Notices

- Tell them when you are going on vacation and how long you will be away.
- Discuss your availability. Will you be reachable? By what means? Will you be checking voice mail and e-mail? Frequently? Or will you have limited access to your e-mail and voice mail?
- Who should the person call if they have an urgent need or question during the time you are away, if they cannot reach you?

Management Issues

Communication skill is universally recognized as an important characteristic for managers to possess. The reason is that management consists largely of getting things done through others.

The more persuasive your communication, the better the results you will get. That's why, even in the Internet age, the ability to craft a tightly written, clear letter can still be a useful tool for you.

In this section, we cover letters that deal with a wide range of management issues, from sales and account management, to IT and conflict resolution.

ACCOUNT MANAGEMENT

A key area of internal correspondence deals with the status and handling of customer accounts. Few topics are as critical as dealing with the customer. Yet unknown to the customer, there is often a massive debate going on behind the scenes about how to deal with them.

Should their credit be cut off? The credit manager says yes. The sales manager says no. Who wins the debate? Often it is the one who communicates the most persuasively verbally and in writing. Each has a big stake in the outcome. Each believes the organization will benefit if it abides by his or her view. By learning to write convincingly about account management matters, your thinking will prevail, and you will have a greater say in how the business is run.

Format: [*See Appendix A:* Fig. A-1. Simple format for letters and memos.] Typed/ word-processed. Company letterhead.

Style/Tone/Voice: Informal. Active voice. [*See Part I for more on these subjects.*]

Structure: (1) Identify the specific topic you want to discuss, (2) Make your main point, (3) Make your secondary points, (4) Support your position by giving proof, (5) Ask for action.

Handy Phrases: May I call your attention to; Let me point out: Please note; As indicated.

See also: *Part V:* Management Issues; *Part VIII:* When the Collection is in Dispute; Working Out Arrangements; Lines of Credit; *Part IX:* Letters Regarding Payment Problems.

TO: Kevin/Denise
FROM: Thomas Jefferson
SUBJECT: Lambbell Chargebacks
DATE: July 29, 2003

Attached is a summary of Lambbell chargebacks that need to be cleared up.

Freight Charges

The basic reason for all the freight chargebacks is that Lambbell requested freight collect and Nickson sent the orders freight prepaid. Nickson acknowledges that Lambbell's policy allows them to charge us a $50 processing fee and states that they will charge back Nickson for excess freight charges.

However, Lambbell must still pay for freight! They cannot simply refuse to pay any freight charges, which is what they have done in many cases. Additionally, if Lambbell "short pays" the freight bills they must provide proof of their freight rates to deduct "excess" charges.

With specific regard to airfreight from overseas, Nickson cannot send these orders freight collect. Therefore, we need to get written confirmation from Lambbell that they will pay all airfreight charges from overseas (that they have authorized), which are prepaid by Nickson. Otherwise we will not honor their request for air shipments in the future.

Product Returns

The chargebacks for product returns can be credited only after receipt of the parts by Nickson and verification of the reason for return. Please forward all product returns you currently have in-house so that we can process these ASAP.

I appreciate your doing the follow-up on the above. Please let me know if I can be of any further assistance.

The following is a letter not to a group of employees, but from one employee to another addressing one particular account.

Roger:

Yes, I have called on Lambbell recently. We have tried to sell widgets for the last several years. We have lost in competition due to performance issues in several cases.

Our 6A2 and 9P have not performed to their expectation in noise and vibration testing. We have missed some opportunities also in the past when we could not meet price competition due to our sales structure at that time.

Our last attempt was on 88 mm widgets. Neal D. was frustrated at Lambbell, as they did test our widgets, and reported that they selected another brand. They didn't want to meet with us to discuss test results further. They provided a basic test result via telephone, and became short with us when we tried a second and third time to meet after they told us no.

They do purchase from factory direct and distribution avenues both, but mostly factory direct at this one division. This division follows corporate directive to use Preferred Provider product recommendations very closely. They have told us that we can continue to call on them, but we are not an approved source, and we therefore probably cannot be seriously considered.

I have focused my efforts on the renegade divisions that will work with us, and have slowly tried to win our way back in as a Preferred Provider.

Now that I have catalogs, and some new products to discuss we will continue to attempt to penetrate this division. A lot will depend on the corporate response we get from the last failure analysis report I sent last week. Neal and Ryan have really helped coordinate with the factory for a fairly quick response. I hope it will help.

Kind regards,

John Adams

This example outlines a change in structure at an account.

Hello Larry and Bob,

Just to let you know that today, Mike Jones the Electromechanical Groups Director, along with Phil McCartney the Vice President, informed me that Andy Harmon has been appointed as the man responsible for decision-making at Nickson relative to your products.

I am meeting again with a number of personnel at Nickson this Friday and I will make a point of meeting Andy. If this information is 100% confirmed, I would then alert you and advise who else is in the "family tree" at Nickson towards setting up an appointment for Larry to visit this area shortly.

If you have any concerns at this time, please touch base with both John Adams and George Clinton in the Industrial Widgets Group to hear "first-hand" from them the results of meetings that are set up in conjunction with Nickson by Lambbell. Alternatively, please feel free to contact me immediately at the Vermont home office. (See attached.)

Sincerely,

Brian

This example is a query regarding internal policy as it regards an outside account.

Dear Scott:

John Adams at Nickson Electronics has told me that the widgets have been designed into the new product being built by his firm.

I gave them samples of models PQ12 and R6. They are using LMQ6 immediately. I am not sure if they will be purchased through Lambbell or one of the other distributors, but please keep an eye out on the point of sale reports. It will be sometime before we see the results, but at least it is beginning to happen.

Is there some other procedure I need to follow in this situation to make sure Crabgrass will get the credit? I am quite confident they will design in QRST on several boards, as I am working with quite a few engineers at Nickson. They seem to be pleased with the samples.

Every day I find more things that I have to learn, but it keeps me on my toes. I am sure you are even more swamped than I am!

Regards,

Roger

Tips for Writing Account Management Letters

- Attach any necessary background documents if you suspect the reader does not have them or cannot easily retrieve them.

- State what the problem is, the current status, your opinion, and how and why it differs from the reader's, if so.

- If you are writing to a peer or someone in another department who does not report to you, do not use your title or position as leverage unless you can really require them to comply with your recommendations. Instead, show why it is in the best interest of the reader and the organization to do so.

- If there is work, time, and effort required of the reader, offer as much assistance as you reasonably can. At minimum, promise cooperation.

SALES MANAGEMENT

In Part VII we cover writing sales letters to be read by customers and prospects. But sales correspondence also takes place internally. Much of it deals with making decisions about how to manage sales for a particular account. Other sales management correspondence deals with such topics as projections, forecasts, pending contracts, outstanding quotations, and requests for proposals.

When should these items be discussed in writing versus verbally? Both modes of communication can be used, but writing may be preferred in the following situations:

- The situation is complex rather than simple and straightforward.
- The reader is not familiar with the problem and needs to be brought up to date on the status of the account.
- The decision concerning sales management is going to be decided through group consensus rather than by an individual.
- The topic is touchy, sensitive, controversial, or at least the source of dispute.
- The decision is major — for instance, an important policy concerning a key account.

- You are being held accountable for the results of a decision, and you want to document your position in case you are questioned later on.

Format: [See Appendix A: Fig. A-1. Simple format for letters and memos.] Typed/word-processed. Company letterhead.

Style/Tone/Voice: Informal or formal. Passive or active voice. [*See Part I for more on these subjects.*]

Structure: (1) State the topic under discussion, (2) Give the background, (3) State your conclusion or opinion, (4) Support your judgment with a clear, accurate interpretation of the sales figures and what they mean.

Handy Phrases: Year to date; Versus the previous year; As the figures indicate; Meet forecasts; Exceed projections.

See also: *Part IV:* Requests for Information; *Part V:* Reports in Memo Format.

Hi Bob:

I called Bicktech to get an idea of their business prospects for FY 2003. We have enclosed two documents, one with a forecast by part number and also a graph that details the current situation at Bicktech.

After reviewing these documents you will notice two things: (1) Bicktech's current inventory is very high and (2) they are only forecasting about $750K in purchases for FY 2003. Both of these items are tied together and, as you can guess, Bicktech is in an inventory reduction mode as evidenced by the low forecast and also current order bookings. They have based the forecast on the following assumptions:

- Current inventory is $682K — a 1.4 turns ratio. The target turns ratio is 1.8 turns.
- 2002 sales at Bicktech cost for 11 months is $875K this is up 7.8% from the same time in 2001 of $811K.
- For 2003 Bicktech is forecasting sales at their cost of $956K — this is an annualized number based on November sales and a modest growth factor.

I hope this information helps you with your budgeting process. Please give me a call if there are questions on this material or if we can help in any way.

Best regards,

Phil

Tips for Writing Sales Management Memos

- Include facts, figures, and numbers that prove your case. Do not expect the reader to do the work of looking up the details for you.

- Interpret the data. What do the figures mean concerning sales revenue for this account?

- Even when providing data only, do not hesitate to give an informed opinion or conclusion. Even if the reader didn't ask for it, having you do some of the thinking for them is a time savings they may appreciate.

HANDLING A DISSATISFIED CUSTOMER

A specialized case of sales and account management is handling the dissatisfied or angry customer (Part VI provides correspondence you can use to communicate directly with the customer). As part of your job, you may have to discuss customer service issues from time to time with other departments of your company. Within an internal communication, you can be firmer and more direct than you might be if you were communicating about the same topic with the customer.

Format: [*See Appendix A:* Fig. A-1. Simple format for letters and memos.] Typed/word-processed. Company letterhead.

Style/Tone/Voice: Informal or formal. Passive or active voice. [*See Part I for more on these subjects.*]

Structure: (1) Identify the customer, (2) Explain the problem, (3) Spell out the course of action you want to take, (4) Be clear about what should be communicated to the customer and what should be kept confidential.

Handy Phrases: Sensitive situation; Handle with care; For your eyes only; Delicate situation.

See also: *Part II:* Letters that Require Special Handling; *Part VI:* Sensitive Customer Correspondence.

FROM: George Mustard
SENT: Monday, April 27, 2003, 11:09
TO: Martin (Personal)
SUJBECT: Orange widget

I received a call from Rich Orange on Friday. Rich is very upset with Bicktech because of a Bicktech Patent involving the orange widget. Nickson has no knowledge of this patent.

Rich stated that this Bicktech patent was "deliberate tampering" with Orange's licensing program. He is concerned that this patent will have a detrimental effect on his licensing business.

Mr. Orange stated that he was withdrawing his offer to provide new samples of an improved widget. He will give these samples to our competitors. He said, "What we are not entitled to by contract, we will be the last to get."

Mr. Orange threatened to begin promoting our competitors' products over Bicktech. He claims he has "Published Prior Art" that will make the Bicktech patent invalid, but this will have to be done through the legal system. Until then he stated that he will do anything he can to "cost us money."

Before Nickson can reply to Mr. Orange we need to know what is the nature of the patent. Can you provide us some information to help us understand why Rich Orange is so angry with Bicktech? Any information you can provide will be helpful.

Tips for Writing Internal Memos about Customer Service

- You must sometimes say rough things about a company or individual, but keep it on a professional level. Never insult them or attack them personally. You never know what may get back to them.
- Engage the reader in working with you to understand and solve the problem.
- If you already know what you want to do, spell it out, convince him that it is the right approach, and ask for his help, cooperation, or approval.

WEB SITE AND OTHER INFORMATION TECHNOLOGY (IT) ISSUES

A problem created by the rise of the Internet is management of the corporate Web site. In many cases, frustration arises from the fact that many people in the organization have a stake and want a say on the Web site content — but only one, the Webmaster, is physically capable of making these changes. This is different than in the offline world, where if a sales manager wants to create a sales sheet, he can do it on his PC and print out the new copy at his desk.

Another frustration with managing Web content is the time delay. An individual who has a Web site and knows HTML or Front Page can change his Web site literally in a minute. In a corporation, only the Webmaster has access to the site code. And the bureaucratic approval process can result in a time lag of weeks or months between when a product manager says to change a spec on a page and when the change is actually made.

The key thing to keep in mind when dealing with the Web or any IT (Information Technology) issues is the historically adversarial relationship between IT and nontechies.

IT people in general, and that includes Web personnel, sometimes view users as ignoramuses and pests with unrealistic expectations and deadlines, who don't appreciate the effort or skill involved to carry out their requests.

You can go a long way toward building a good relationship with your Webmaster and other IT staff simply by asking instead of demanding, being polite instead of curt, and acknowledging the effort and importance of their work.

If you are a techie, be patient when explaining your work to nontechies, especially when discussing delays or reasons why something cannot be done when they want or the way they want. Many nontechies have no patience for technical issues, and get turned off by even the slightest hint of jargon or techno-talk.

Explain things in plain English, and don't get aggravated if they don't get it the first time. It helps if you think of the user as a customer you want to make sure is happy, rather than a thorn in your side.

Users (nontechies) are often impatient with technology and are uncooperative with technical professionals, whom they sometimes refer to derogatorily as "computer geeks" behind their backs. When writing to a user, an IT professional can sometimes gain cooperation on something important to the system (but seemingly trivial to the user) by explaining the importance of the issue or task.

Format: [*See Appendix A:* Fig. A-1. Simple format for letters and memos.] Typed/ word-processed. Company letterhead.

Style/Tone/Voice: Informal or formal. Passive or active voice. [*See Part I for more on these subjects.*]

Structure: (1) Identify the item being discussed (e.g., "user access to the inventory control system"), (2) Give necessary background, (3) Explain the proposed actions or changes, (4) Ask for any action required on the part of the reader.

Handy Phrases: We request your cooperation, understanding, patience; Necessary steps.

See also: *Part IV:* Communicating Business Information; *Part V:* FYI Internal Memos.

Wendy:

Based on your notice, I asked my Web people to see if they could correct this problem. As of today they have added the address: www.Lambbell.com to the alias list and it will now be accepted by our server as an appropriate link to our Web site.

Please try to access the site using the " / " address and confirm by return that you can access the site. Based on your confirmation I will not have to revise all 10K catalogs in our inventory!

Regards,

Jeff

Despite users' wishes to the contrary, IT success often requires collaboration and cooperation between the users and the systems professionals. The letter below informs the users that the work was done but emphasizes the responsibilities they have to make the project work.

Dick and George:

Our team spent the entire day today at our location working on clearing Import errors, which we are of course happy to do.

However, I wanted to bring to your attention that the users should already be aware of their responsibility to review the Import error report as Janice points out below.

Until the admin staff clears these Import errors, billing cannot take place. (The errors are primarily method of shipment, overshipments, and model mismatches between the PO and Invoices). Some errors are from mistakes on the original orders, which were assigned to the wrong warehouse number.

Some of these errors have been amplified by the other problems, which I called to your attention last week, such as missing confirmations and part number changes.

I wanted you both to be aware of this situation so that you would have a perspective based upon the real cause of the billing delays.

If you have any questions, please give me a call.

Connie

Tips for Writing about Web and Other IT Issues

- Use short paragraphs, generous margins and line spacing, and headers where needed. Make the document look appealing and reader-friendly. Dense blocks of text turn off readers, especially when the subject is technical in nature.

- Make sure what you request in your letter is what you really want. Changing your mind after the work is done wastes time and money, and irritates the IT people who have to redo the work.

- Give a firm deadline for completion of the work. Avoid phrases such as "as soon as possible" or "at your earliest convenience." Specify a date and even a time. Tasks without a firm deadline are always done last.

- When in doubt, explain technical terms and spell out acronyms the first time you use them, unless you are 100 percent certain that 100 percent of your readers already know them.

CONGRATULATIONS TO AN INDIVIDUAL OR A TEAM

Don't get the idea from this part of the book that all business communications are difficult and unpleasant. Sure, there are many problems in business; life's full of them. But there are also many happy occasions that can be written about, too.

One of the more pleasurable writing tasks is congratulating a team or individual for a job well done, whether it's beating a quota or winning an industry award.

Format: [*See Appendix A:* Fig. A-1. Simple format for letters and memos.] Typed/ Word-processed. Company letterhead.

Style/Tone/Voice: Informal or formal. Active voice. [*See Part I for more on these subjects.*]

Structure: (1) Thank the reader in the first sentence, (2) Elaborate in the body of the letter briefly; do not go on and on, (3) Thank them again, (4) Lay the groundwork for future collaboration or cooperation.

Handy Phrases: Thanks; Thanks for your help; I appreciate; I'm grateful; I'm much obliged.

See also: *Part II:* Letters That Strengthen Relationships

Some congratulatory letters are distributed en masse to the entire organization or a group within the organization (e.g., department heads).

> TO: All Group Heads
> FROM: Randy Newman
> SUBJECT: First Half Results
> DATE: October 7, 2001
>
> Thank you all for a very successful first half. For the first time in recent memory not only did we achieve the plan on a consolidated basis, but every group achieved their business plan. It is a great way to start the second half.
>
> Thanks again to you and all your staff for all the hard work and effort. I very much appreciate it.
>
> Sincerely,
>
>
> Randy

The second example is a letter of congratulations written to an individual.

> Dear Tom:
>
> Thanks for the quick and unscheduled tour of the Lambbell lab for Bicktech.
>
> I never realized how impressive the work you are doing on the Milker project is, or how fascinating.
>
> Would you be willing to have Corporate Communications do a short video on the lab and your project?
>
> You have a great way of explaining things, so I'm hoping we can include a short Q & A interview with you about the technology on this tape.
>
> Sincerely,
>
>
> Jon Smith

Tips for Writing Letters of Congratulations

- Be sure to include everyone who deserves it. Leaving someone out who should be cited can be upsetting and offensive to that person.
- Do not make praise conditional (e.g., "of course, the good market had a lot to do with our success").
- Have an upbeat, enthusiastic tone.
- A congratulations memo says "thank you" for your great effort to date . . . and also "please" help our organization do even better now.

OFFERING ADVICE

Offering advice can be a surprisingly delicate situation. Some people welcome advice and feedback; others take it as a personal offense.

Also, think about why you are giving advice and the manner in which it is presented. Are you volunteering help because you truly want to help — or are you showing off how smart you are?

Is the advice given in a friendly, helpful, cordial manner? Or are you trying to bully the person into doing things your way, or subtly demonstrate that you're smarter and know more?

Properly given, advice can greatly help the other person and achieve everyone's business objectives. Wrongly given, advice can demean the other person, erode his self-esteem, or offend him in such a way that he avoids doing anything you say, simply because of the way you say it.

Which of these options do you prefer?

Format: [*See Appendix A:* Fig. A-1. Simple format for letters and memos.] Typed/word-processed. Company letterhead.

Style/Tone/Voice: Informal or formal. Active voice. [*See Part I for more on these subjects.*]

Structure: (1) If you are giving the advice in response to the reader's request, say so, (2) State the nature of your advice (i.e., is it a suggestion or an order?), (3) Give the advice and explain it clearly, (4) Say what the next step is (e.g., you want the reader to call you to discuss your suggestions).

Handy Phrases: Have you considered; Here's how it works; The way it works; One option to consider.

See also: *Part II:* Giving Advice.

FROM: George Washington
SENT: Thursday, February 08, 2001 10:38 a.m.
TO: Tom Jefferson
SUBJECT: Checking out Lambbell Milkers

Tom, here's a technique we've used successfully in the past to check out whether a particular publication is reaching our customers and prospects. I'm thinking specifically of Lambbell Milkers because they are not audited and there is no real definition of their subscribers.

Here's what we can do. We can give the publisher a list of your top prospects and customers. Just the company names and locations of the individuals we want to reach — no individual names.

We ask the publisher to give us their subscription list for those locations. Then, we can check the names on their list with your own, and/or your reps, and the contact list to see if the people you talk to are on the publisher's list.

If so, you know the magazine is reaching your market. If not, we can chase down their list to see whether the people on that list should be on our list. In other words, perhaps there are others in those companies we should be talking to. Or, we can try again with another list under the rare possibility of a coincidence.

If neither of those pans out, we might want to consider not advertising in the magazine because it does not serve our market. I'm not sure Lambbell Milkers will agree to this, but it is a legitimate exercise, and they should be glad to get our feedback at the conclusion.

All this will cost us nothing except a bit of your time to put the list together. Think about it. I have the same questions about this publication that you have, and this may be a way to settle it.

Tips for Giving Advice in a Memo

- Be wary of giving unsolicited advice to peers or colleagues. Reserve unsolicited advice for: bosses who expect you to make recommendations; customers you are helping achieve a better result; suppliers who serve you as their customer; and subordinates who are by nature of their position mandated to listen to you.

- If you criticize, praise first. Instead of saying what is wrong or what you don't like, first say what is right and what you did like. Then discuss the parts that need improvement. Even if you are really unhappy or think the person is doing everything wrong, you can always find at least one thing that can be praised.

- Give specific advice only, not general criticism. "I don't think this will work" is weak. Much better is to say, "Here's one thing we can try."

RESOLVING DISPUTES AND DISAGREEMENTS

It is human nature to disagree. Not only do humans have different experiences, attitudes, and points of view. But there is also an innate need to prove we are right and others are wrong — not a particularly admirable characteristic, and not always productive.

Arguments are often best settled by sitting around a conference table. But in today's business world — with multinational corporations; regional offices spanning multiple time zones; and a highly mobile "road warrior" population — getting the group together in person, let alone for a conference call, isn't always possible.

You may therefore have to deal with problems through written correspondence. The most effective alternative is e-mail for time-sensitive matters; interoffice memos for nonurgent issues.

Format: [*See Appendix A:* Fig. A-1. Simple format for letters and memos.] Typed/word-processed. Business letterhead.

Style/Tone/Voice: Informal or formal. Active or passive voice. [*See Part I for more on these subjects.*]

Structure: (1) State the problem, (2) Outline the solution, (3) Explain your reasoning, (4) Ask for agreement, approval, or action.

Handy Phrases: I'm sure you can agree; A reasonable solution; Agree to disagree; Meet in the middle.

See also: *Part IV:* Tough Situations.

In the letter below, a customer has not received parts it ordered from a motor manufacturer. The freight forwarder says the parts were delivered but does not have documentation to prove it.

Herbert, sales manager for the manufacturer, has suggested a solution: that the freight company pay for the loss, since they are responsible. But to preserve the vendor relationship, he has not firmly closed the door on negotiation.

Sam Blevins
Controller
Lambbell

Dear Sam:

The Lambbell Industrial Milker Department (LIMD) has resolved the issue of the lost widget FQ13 product to our satisfaction.

The customer claims that they never received the product. Slow-Ship, the shipping company, has been unable or unwilling to provide proof of delivery.

Based upon the attached e-mail from Jimmy Smith at Slow-Ship stating that, "Since it was a mis-arrangement by Slow-Ship, we have to bear the responsibility," we are asking them to send us $14,280 to cover the cost of the missing parts. I assume they are insured for such losses, but that is not really our problem.

Slow-Ship may object. They say they are authorized under our blanket purchase order to them to leave shipments without proof if no one is there to sign, and there is some ambiguity in the

PO wording. Jimmy's superiors may request a compromise, with each of us sharing a portion of the cost of the lost units.

We will review any proposal sent by Slow-Ship and make our decision regarding the proposal at the time of receipt. While we value them as a supplier, I am not sure they acted responsibly in this instance, the PO notwithstanding.

Regards,

Herbert Moover
Regional Sales Manager
Lambbell Industrial Milker Department

Tips for Writing Problem Resolution E-mails and Memos

- Do not assume you have reached closure on the problem. You may think the matter is closed, but the reader may want to discuss it further. Indicate that you are open to additional discussion.

- Write with the objective of finding a mutually agreeable solution. Do not make the mistake of focusing on responsibility and who is to blame.

- If you are giving up something to the other party, and don't have to, don't but it in their faces. But do let them know what you have done. Put a dollar value on it, if one can be assigned.

WARNING AN EMPLOYEE

What if the employee you hire today is not living up to your expectations 6 or 12 months from now?

The issue of disciplining, reprimanding, and terminating a nonperforming employee involves psychology, management, motivation, and employment law. We cannot begin to cover the ins and outs of this subject here. But one tip we can give: When you need to warn an employee about subpar job performance, always do it in writing, and keep a copy of each warning letter in the employee's file. Without this paper trail, a terminated employee may be able to retaliate with a lawsuit for wrongful termination — and win a judgment against your firm.

Format: [*See Appendix A:* Fig. A-1. Simple format for letters or memos.] Typed/word-processed. Company letterhead.

Style/Tone/Voice: Formal. Passive or active voice. [*See Part I for more on these subjects.*]

Structure: (1) Introduce the document as a formal warning, (2) Specify the problem (e.g., tardiness, absenteeism, use of alcohol in the workplace), (3) Say exactly what changes you expect the employee to make — and by when, (4) Spell out the consequences for failure to comply, (5) Offer to help the employee improve conduct or performance, if you can.

Handy Phrases: Unsatisfactory conduct; Continual violations; Not up to the standards of the company; Unacceptable; Subpar.

See also: *Part II:* Motivation; *Part IV:* Tough Situations.

Herman,

We are meeting to review deficiencies that continue in your performance as Account Manager. These deficiencies remain serious in that they have an impact on your overall contribution in meeting the sales targets set for the Distribution business.

During your performance appraisal on April 21, 2003, we discussed these performance deficiencies and noted that corrective action would need to be taken. To this end, we have outlined your Accountabilities and Objectives in the attached Performance Improvement Plan (PIP).

You are being placed on formal written notice that you are not meeting the performance standards relevant to your position.

It is management's belief that you are capable of achieving the accountabilities and objectives of the Account Manager II position, but your performance to date has been unacceptable and must improve substantially and immediately. Continued substandard performance will result in action up to and including termination of your employment.

The PIP, however, is not a final goal. Performance must be sustained so that you can maintain and increase your contribution to the department and its business objectives.

Both Bicktech and Personnel Management are committed to your success and remain ready to help you in any way possible. I will make myself available to assist you in this process and you are encouraged to call upon any of us whenever you have a concern or a question.

Cedric Jones
Business Unit Manager

Tips for Writing a Warning

- Be specific about your dissatisfaction.
- Compare actual performance with stated objectives.
- Give strategies and suggestions for improvement, as well as a deadline.

Meetings

Life is filled with meetings, and there are two important documents that can make them more productive and valuable. The premeeting agenda is distributed to participants before the meeting to structure the event and keep everyone on track. The agenda provides a written record of what was said and accomplished, and is distributed to attendees shortly after the meeting has taken place.

PREMEETING AGENDAS

When people complain that they spend too much of their time in long, boring, unproductive meetings, it's difficult to argue. But a premeeting agenda can help make a lot of those meetings more productive, better organized, and shorter. A premeeting agenda can help organize the meeting, keep everyone on track, and ensure that objectives are accomplished.

The degree of specificity in your agenda is a matter of personal preference. For a group where everyone knows one another, is familiar with the background, and works well together, a loosely structured agenda can get things going without limiting ideas or creativity.

On the other hand, if the participants don't know each other well, or are not up to speed on the project or topic, a tightly structured agenda may be just the thing to keep everyone informed, interested, and enthusiastic.

Format: [*See Appendix A:* Fig. A-1. Simple format for letters or memos.] Typed/word-processed. Company letterhead.

Style/Tone/Voice: Formal. Passive or active voice. [*See Part I for more on these subjects.*]

Structure: (1) Explain the purpose of the memo (to present an agenda), (2) Name the meeting, (3) Announce the time, date, and location, (4) Break the meeting into modules with topics, goals, and length, (5) Explain that the agenda can be used to plan for the meeting, (6) Instruct the participants to adhere to the agenda during the meeting.

Handy Phrases: The following agenda; Our upcoming meeting.

See also: *Part IV:* Post-Meeting Follow-Up Letter; *Part V:* Requesting a Meeting.

Here are two examples of premeeting agendas. The first is a one-page agenda for a local church group:

Board of Deacons Monthly Meeting, October 2003

1. Opening prayer
2. Acceptance of previous minutes
3. Treasurer's report
4. Bill payments authorized
5. Old business
   - Roofing fund
   - Organ repair
6. New business
   - New teacher's helper for the Sunday School
   - Choir robes
7. Closing prayer

The next is the agenda for the kick-off meeting on a new project:

TO: Task force members
FROM: Tina Ramirez
DATE: March 14, 2001
SUBJECT: Agenda for March 18 meeting

The purpose of this memo is to let you know the agenda for our first task force meeting, which is scheduled for next Tuesday at 9:30 a.m. in the third-floor conference room. The vice president for human resources asked me to write up an agenda based on the directions she gave us last week.

Since we will be trying to formulate some firm recommendations about new staffing needs, this outline can help prepare us to accomplish as much as possible on Tuesday morning. Below are the major agenda items, along with time and decision goals.

Develop criteria for creating new staff jobs.

GOAL — Devise a formula for deciding how positions will be allocated
TIME — 30 minutes

Identify areas for new staff positions.

GOAL — Choose those areas that best fit criteria
TIME — 40 minutes

Select task force members to write report to vice president.

GOAL — Pick best author for each section of report
TIME — 10 minutes

Schedule date for next meeting. Other business.

GOAL — Allow sufficient time for drafting report
TIME — 10 minutes

Having the agenda ahead of time should give everyone the chance to think about issues beforehand. Also, a plan for the meeting may help us handle business more efficiently and keep us from going off on tangents.

Please call me at extension 523 if you have comments or questions. See you all on Tuesday morning.

Tips for Writing Meeting Agendas

- The agenda for a meeting should fit on one side of a sheet of paper. Keep it simple. Do not make it overdetailed.
- Distribute the agenda so it is received at least 48 hours before the meeting.
- Bring enough copies to the meeting to hand out to every attendee in case they do not bring the agenda with them.
- Use a bullet or column format for the agenda. Avoid paragraphs of text. Make it scannable.

MEETING MINUTES

Once taking, writing up, and distributing minutes of meetings was common practice. Today, probably because we feel so inundated with reading material, the practice has abated.

So, while taking and distributing meeting minutes may be optional, we recommend it — for several reasons:

- One advantage of knowing that minutes will be distributed after the meeting is that it frees attendees from taking detailed notes, and allows them to concentrate in the discussion more fully.
- Have you ever mentioned something important that was discussed in a meeting only to be told by the other person, "I don't remember that." Minutes provide a record to refresh her memory.
- Meeting minutes also prevent disputes and settle arguments. By going back to the written minutes, you can determine what was said and agreed upon.

Minutes are written in a simple memo style format. When multiple topics are discussed in one meeting, organize the minutes by topic using bold subheads.

Format: [*See Appendix A:* Fig. A-1. Simple format for letters or memos.] Typed/word-processed. Business letterhead.

Style/Tone/Voice: Informal or formal. Passive or active voice. [*See Part I for more on these subjects.*]

Structure: (1) Recap the time, date, and place of the meeting, (2) State its main topic or objective, (3) Present the main points of action and discussion.

Handy Phrases: At our last meeting; Corrections to the minutes; Minutes are approved as read; At this meeting; During the meeting; Attendance this meeting; We have a quorum; We are ready to conduct business; Meeting began at _ _: _ _; Meeting adjourned at _ _: _ _.

See also: *Part IV:* Disseminating Technical Information; *Part V:* Reports in Memo Format.

Sewanee Tire Exchange
Store Managers Meeting

Minutes of the Store Managers Meeting, April 23, 2001

Chairman Radcliffe called the meeting to order at 7:30 p.m. in the Conference Room at the Wayside Inn, Middletown.

The minutes of the March 19 regular meeting and the March 26 special meeting were accepted.

Mr. Radcliffe presented Ms. Vulcan, new manager of the Mayfield store.

Reports

A report prepared by the Blimp Rubber Company on the long-range effects of the current labor unrest was read and discussed. One strong recommendation was for each store manager to increase his stock of capable casings.

Mr. Kennard reported briefly on the outcome of the trial methods used in the Harmon Mall store to keep customers out of the service area. A customer waiting area with magazines, a coffee table, and chairs in the corridor works if customers are politely asked to wait there. Signs are ignored.

Tips for Improving Sales and Service

Mr. Radcliffe asked each store manager to share with the group any tips for improving sales and service. A summary of these suggestions follows:

- Managers should spend half of their time outside the store promoting sales, calling on commercial accounts, talking tires to everyone they meet. Managers should be at least as aggressive as insurance salesmen.
- While tires are being changed, have a serviceman check the battery. A recent check at the Martindale store showed one battery out of six to be close to failure. Since beginning the practice, the Martindale store shows a 23 percent increase in accessory product sales.
- Instruct store personnel to push trade-ins. Many customers, especially those with comfortable incomes, are not interested in getting the last mile out of a tire. They prefer the

feeling of security that comes with a set of new tires. Sound tires traded in this way can be resold to less-affluent customers who should be encouraged to replace their hazardous bald tires. Make all drivers tire-safety conscious.

Chairman's Announcements

Customers who neglect to take the 2 percent discount should be reminded to do so. Store managers must continue to carry the credit on all accounts and cannot divert the discounts to any other purpose.

Mr. Radcliffe asked all store managers to check the employment records of all tire men they hire, making sure all months for the past five years are accounted for. He cited the case of an employee who was discharged by the Mayfield store for stealing tools and hired at the Reese Corner store the same afternoon.

Assignments

Ms. Vulcan agreed to find a guest speaker for the August Awards Dinner. She will work with Mr. Dayton who is in charge of the Awards Dinner program. Both will report to the committee at the June meeting.

The meeting was adjourned at 9:05 p.m.

The following persons attended: G. Babbitt, C. Dalchon, T. Dayton, L. Kennard, P. Lorge, T. Radcliffe, A. Todd, E. Tredd, S. Vulcan.

The following managers did not attend: D. Parelli, H. Whitewall

Respectfully submitted,

Edgar Tredd, Secretary

If only one topic was discussed, these points can simply be numbered or bulleted.

Department Meeting Update: Meeting Minutes
July 18, 2002, 2:30 – 5:15 p.m.

Action Items

- Each director/manager to give Joe the date/time they will review the new Policy and Procedures manual with their staff.
- JT to distribute updated Strategic Planning Calendar.
- Each director/manager to review revised budget distributed by Bob at 7/18 meeting and meet with Bob to discuss changes/discrepancies.
- AP will arrange for Erik to attend Bicktech's December Financial Management Workshop.
- JT, SU, and RD to discuss current time spent assisting peer groups and will consider instituting either charging hourly rates or procurement of donations in exchange for staff time spent.
- Bob to distribute new chart of accounting codes. (Expenses have been collapsed so that there are fewer codes.)
- All invoices must be approved by department directors.

Other Items

- Dates set for Department Meetings for remainder of year: September 4, October 9, October 24, November 25, December 23. Each meeting will run from 10:30 a.m.–12:00 noon.
- Next meeting scheduled for Monday, August 5, from 9:30–11:00 a.m.
- Imperative for staff to stick to May budget projections.
- Possibility for Bill Herrott to conduct a major consulting project on behalf of CBAC for Bicktech.
- Search is under way for a Director of Marketing.

Attendance

- Susan Roarman
- Joe Thompson
- Andy Pasta
- Bob Pagliacci
- Dawn Lostlotto
- Suzanne Underhill
- Robyn Dorf
- Red Smithson

Tips for Writing Meeting Minutes

- Events can be listed chronologically or in order of importance.
- Key points can be highlighted in boldface, italics, or with a border.
- The distribution list should be in alphabetical order.
- Don't try to edit or write the minutes while you are at the meeting taking notes. Write down everything during the meeting. Later, type your notes and edit the list, eliminating anything trivial and/or unimportant.

Reports in Memo Format

A report is an account that is prepared, presented, or delivered. Long reports are usually written in the format of formal, multipage documents bound in some sort of cover.

Another option for reports is to make them orally, in a workplace presentation or in a speech at a meeting or convention. With the advent of PowerPoint, most oral reports have accompanying slides, which are often distributed to listeners as hard copy.

When the report is brief, it may be written in the conventional memo format shown in the Appendix. Reporting an event or other information as a memo is an informal approach that saves the reader time and doesn't weigh her down with unnecessary detail.

As a rule of thumb, if your report can be written in three pages or less, use a memo format. When the report is five pages or more, use a formal report format, put it in a binder, and send it with a short cover memo or letter of transmittal [*see Part IV*].

STATUS REPORTS

Status reports and progress reports are two variations of the same theme. Status reports deal with the conditions of things, whether it's a factory, a computer system, or an accounting audit. A progress report, as its name implies, updates the reader on movement toward a specific goal, e.g., expanding the factory or upgrading the computer system.

Most managers have to write status reports, either on a regular basis or sporadically. But they do it often enough that it makes sense to find a way to do it more efficiently and productively. Here's how:

Spend some time on your next report developing a format that is neat, clean, clear and easy to read. Then simply copy that memo into a template file on your PC. For future status reports, you can use the same template, just filling in the specifics each time.

Format: [*See Appendix A:* Fig. A-1. Simple format for letters or memos.] Typed/word-process. Business letterhead.

Style/Tone/Voice: Informal or formal. Active voice. [*See Part I for more on these subjects.*]

Structure: (1) Identify the topic of the memo, (2) State that this is a status report or update, (3) Present a clear report of the status, (4) End with conclusions, suggestions, or recommendations.

Handy Phrases: Update; Status; Bring you up to date; Most recent.

See also: *Part IV:* FYI Letters; *Part V:* FYI Internal Memos; Reports in Memo Format.

TO: Distribution
FROM: Bill
RE: Annual Sales Goal Status Update
DATE: May 7, 2003

Congratulations! We are on target to achieve $48M in sales for FY2003, right on budget. This is a 20% increase over FY2002 results of $40M.

2003 Fiscal Year Results

As mentioned the final numbers for 2003 will be:

'03FY Budget ... $48.0 million

'03FY Actual ... $48.3 million

2004 Fiscal Year Budget

The IMMD budget for '04FY has been set at $56.7 million (18% increase). We have done away with the regional budgets and established product group budgets. These will be forwarded to all of you next week.

This budget is a significant increase over last year's sales. We have an incredible challenge since some of the budgeted customers are not currently doing business with us. Others have never had sales of this magnitude with us before.

News Flash

I am pleased to announce that we have hired a new Sales Engineer to work in the Smith Valley office. Barry Munster comes to us from Lambbell Milkers, a milking machine manufacturing services firm. Barry has a BSEE degree from the University of Wisconsin and an MBA from the University of Colorado. He has over 20 years' experience in the electronics field.

Open Order Reports / Backlog

To meet our stated goal of "Customer First" we need to be more responsive to our customers' needs, anticipate their requests, and take action on their behalf. We will look into using the _____ system for all of our customers and reply back by April/end.

Audit/General Housekeeping

The customer files are in need of a little organization and a sensible filing system. To date this has not been a priority, but it really is necessary to be able to easily access information relevant to our customer's current projects and programs.

A memo was circulated advising all account managers of the new filing system requirements and a "hard target" date of April 30th was set for completion of the file clean-up. It is of the utmost importance that this project be completed on time.

Tips for Writing Status Reports

- Use subheads to break the key topics into short sections.
- List the sections in order of importance, from most important to least.
- Use short sentences and paragraphs.
- When giving the background or history of a particular topic, use chronological order so your reader can see what happened first, next, and so on.

PROGRESS REPORTS

A progress report updates supervisors, clients, or team members on the status of a specific project. Like a meeting agenda [*see* Meeting Agendas *earlier in this part*], a progress report is best written in a linear, sequential, and scannable format — meaning you can skim it and get the gist of the message without reading the memo in its entirety. You can use a two-column format, table, or numbered or bulleted list.

Format: [See Appendix A: Fig. A-1. Simple format for letters or memos.]Typed/ word-processed. Business letterhead.

Style/Tone/Voice: Informal or formal. Passive or active voice. Past tense. [*See Part I for more on these subjects.*]

Structure: (1) Identify the project or item under discussion, (2) Summarize the progress, (3) Outline the remaining steps and what still needs to be done.

Handy Phrases: So far; Bring you up to date; Keep you current with; Outline the current status; Our progress; What we've done so far.

See also: *Part IV:* Post-Meeting Follow-Up Letter; *Part V:* Reports in Memo Format.

DATE: May 24, 2005
TO: John Smith
FROM: Hal Lewis
SUBJECT: PTSC IMPLEMENTATION

This is what the Project Team has done so far to start up the new Public Telephone Service Center (PTSC):

Site:	Arranged to convert 2nd floor of former Bloomington Central Office for PTSC use.
	Hired WeWorkQuick Contractors. Work started 5/20; completion expected 12/20.
	Placed telecommunications equipment order with Installation Department.
	STILL NEEDED: Decision from Real Estate VP regarding expansion of existing parking lot to accommodate new employee and customer volume.

Staff & Training:	Posted 14 Public Telephone Service Rep job vacancies (10 filled so far).
	Requested Transfer Training to train Reps in PT rates and service options.
	Sent Manager requisition to Personnel Planning Committee. Hope to promote a Field Assistant Manager into this position.
Computer Systems:	Submitted job requests to Software Development to modify affected systems (Customer Records, Billing, Installation Scheduling, Maintenance).
	Issued request for bid on new interactive terminals for service reps.
Methods & Procedures:	Wrote up new flow for work between PTSC and Installation. Both departments have accepted new procedure.
	Arranged for Training to include specific, updated "customer contact" scripts in transfer material.
Customers:	Requested directory to include PTSC's "800" number in next phone book and in all books thereafter.
	Asked Public Relations to design bulletin about new "800" number.

Tips for Writing Progress Reports

- Separate into two sections what was done versus what still has to be done.
- Include all important activities (e.g., "Put in a nonsmoking section") but do not weigh down the report with trivia (e.g., "Chose red ashtrays"). Use your judgment.
- Use a good document management or filing system to store progress reports. Periodic progress reports for a given project may be kept in a three-ring binder. Give the progress reports their own tabbed section. One purpose of progress reports is to prove that an action was taken, so if questioned easy document retrieval is critical.

TRIP REPORTS

Yet another routine document that is best written in scannable form is a trip report.

Do not tell everything that happened during the trip. Only include the highlights relevant to the objective and the business. Separate what was done on the trip from what follow up is required as a result of the trip.

Format: [*See Appendix A:* Fig. A-1. Simple format for memos.] Type/word-processed. Company letterhead.

Style/Tone/Voice: Formal. Active voice. [*See Part I for more on these subjects.*]

Structure: (1) Say where you went, when, and for what purpose, (2) Give the relevant highlights, (3) Close with any conclusions, recommendations, or suggestions that came out of the trip.

Handy Phrases: Recently we visited; Our recent trip; A productive visit.

See also: *Part IV:* FYI Letters; *Part V:* FYI Internal Memos; Reports in Memo Format.

TO: President, Lambbell Milkers
FROM: Business Development Consultants
SUBJECT: Switzerland Trip, August 5 through 27, 2004
SUMMARY: My staff and I obtained Swiss government approval for a new plant. We inspected and inventoried three potential plant sites (Basel, Bern, and Zug) and compiled a preliminary list of candidates for Managing Directors.

Meeting 1: August 8 and 9, **Basel**. With Swiss Minister for International Trade and his cabinet.

Accomplished:

Presented proposal and our portion of financing package.

Fielded questions from Minister and his cabinet.

Received and evaluated Swiss portion of financing package.

Written approval came through when we were in Bern!

Now we must:

Send formal acceptance.

Apply for Swiss licenses.

Submit expatriate list to Swiss Security.

Get funding approved by Board of Directors.

Also important:

Our formal acceptance must be accompanied by the traditional "greeting" and gift from our CEO to the Minister and his family (draft enclosed).

Meeting 2:   August 15 and 16, **Basel**. With Manager of Site 1 Physical Plant.

Accomplished:

Toured entire plant.

Obtained detailed specifications and drawings.

Inspected and inventoried existing equipment.

Now we must:

Have Plant Engineers evaluate the Basel site.

List and cost out any necessary capital improvements.

Meeting 3: August 17 and 18, **Bern.** With Assistant Managing Director, Site 2.

Accomplished:

Toured, obtained drawings, inspected and catalogued inventory.

Obtained local appraisal of property's value.

Now we must:

Have Plant Engineering evaluate the site.

Cost out necessary site improvements.

Meeting 4: August 23 and 24, **Zug.** With Deputy Production Manager, Site 3.

Accomplished:

Completed plant tour, inspection, inventory as at other sites.

Received Deputy PM's recommendations regarding appointment of new Managing Director (he recommends himself).

Now we must:

Have Plant Engineering evaluate the site.

Cost out necessary capital improvements.

Thank Deputy PM for his help and respond to his request for consideration as Managing Director.

My staff and I met frequently at our hotels when we were not meeting with the Swiss.

One of the products of our private sessions is the attached preliminary list of 15 Managing Director candidates. During our visits, we spoke at length with over 40 managers, foremen, and superintendents and found the listed people to be the most qualified (see attachment).

Tips for Writing Trip Reports

- State the locations visited, date of your visit, as well as whom you saw (e.g., customers, prospects, consultants, plant managers).

- Put an executive summary at the beginning of the memo. In a few sentences, state the purpose of the trip and the major accomplishments or activities.

- Keep good notes during the trip of what you did. Put the date and location on each set of notes. This makes it much easier to write the progress report, and eliminates the need to reconstruct the trip mentally or rely on memory for details, such as who was at a particular meeting.

CHANGE ORDERS

In contracting, a "change order" is a written document confirming that a change was requested in a contract or work order after the work has begun. Similarly, things change in business and life all the time. In life, we can mostly just roll with the punches. But in business, we often have to document changes in writing in order to avoid confusion and ensure consensus. Also, such memos provide a "paper audit trail" in case a dispute arises later over who told whom to do what.

You may find having to write "CYA" ("cover your 'backside'") memos distasteful. But the fact is, in corporate life some documents are written as much for "the file" as they are for the recipient. You may think everyone on your team is on the same page right now. They may think so, too. But people are quick to point fingers and lay blame when a problem arises, and senior management wants to know who is responsible. Having a document enables you to state the facts and back them up with proof.

Format: [*See Appendix A:* Fig. A-1. Simple format for letters or memos.] Type/word-processed. Business letterhead.

Style/Tone/Voice: Informal or formal. Active voice. [*See Part I for more on these subjects.*]

Structure: (1) Reference the original order, (2) Specify the change, (3) Give the reason for the change, (4) Provide instructions for compliance.

Handy Phrases: There has been a change; This memo is to alert you to; Such and such has been changed.

See also: *Part VI:* Change Order; *Part VIII:* Change of Terms

Sue and Diane,

The customer has requested a change to Contract #1621. We must comply with this immediately to keep the project on schedule and ensure that we receive payments promptly.

From now on, all online documents must be processed through the "change and approval" workflow system in the customer's CMS (Content Management System) software. Documents must be signed off on by a minimum of one Approver before prior to posting.

There is a legal issue involving the approval of content, with potential violations for information not vetted through this procedure. If the customer is fined or even cited, they may deduct the cost from our overall project fee.

For this reason, we must follow the CMS process on every module. No exceptions. If you feel this will compromise your ability to meet scheduled milestones, please notify me right away.

For a short tutorial on how to use the CMS if you are not already familiar with it, call Roger Johnson at 888-806-8888.

Thanks,

Christine

Tips for Writing Change Orders

- State what the original plan or agreement was.
- State what the change is.
- Be clear about who is responsible for approving the change, and who is responsible for carrying it out.
- If there are penalties for delay or failure, spell them out.

PART VI

CUSTOMER SERVICE CORRESPONDENCE

Customer service is often cited as the most important element of business success. And the need to write clear, friendly letters to customers is not limited to people with the words "customer service" in their title. As speaker Brian Tracy points out, "We are all in customer service — at least part of the time."

Effective client communication starts with the realization that communication is not a separate activity from rendering service; communication is a *component* of how you render service. In essence, the saying, "It's not what you say, it's what you do that counts" is inaccurate: It's what you say *and* do that counts.

Ways of expressing yourself — your phrasing of sentences, tone, style, and word choice — can sometimes make the difference between pleasing a client and annoying a client; but most communications are tied to a related action. So, while communicating with clients in the right way is extremely important, it is not a substitute for taking appropriate client-centered actions to ensure client satisfaction. It's better to do a good thing for a client and not express it well than to do a terrible thing to a client and try to cover it up with sweet talk.

Options for Communicating with Your Customers

There are many different options for communicating with clients at various times: phone, in-person visits, letter, fax. Choosing which to use is largely a matter of common sense, but if you are uncertain, consider the advantages and disadvantages of each method:

- **Drop-in visit**

  Advantages: Spontaneous acts add warmth to relationships. In-person visits remind client of your existence and value.

  Disadvantages: Clients may resent unscheduled interruption in their day.

- **Scheduled visit**

  Advantages: Client appreciates your going out of your way to see him/her even though there is no immediate ongoing assignment.

  Disadvantages: Clients may feel you view them as secondary in importance (because you only see them when in town for other purposes).

- **Phone call**

  Advantages: Easiest, least time-consuming method of keeping in frequent contact with client.

  Disadvantages: Client may not like interruption of "trivial" or nonessential communication.

- **Fax**
  Advantages: Allows you to communicate with client instantly and in writing, without two-way communication. Ideal for situations where you want to give client time to consider your message before replying, or where you want to give client information to review in advance of a phone discussion.
  Disadvantages: Client may perceive fax as impersonal or as a way to avoid direct contact with him/her.
- **Letter**
  Advantages: Customer does not feel pressured to respond. In an electronic age, letters convey greater warmth than other media.
  Disadvantages: Mass mailing of a customer service letter to your entire database may be a large and expensive undertaking. Postal mail is slow.

This part provides model letters addressing a wide range of customer service situations. Most are written for you to use as a vendor communicating with your customer. Others, where noted, are for you, as a customer to communicate with your vendors. Following the sample letters are additional tips for effective customer service communication, which are applicable to letters and e-mails as well as verbal communication.

Relationship-Building Letters

Relationship-building letters stand out in the world of letters — there's nothing negative about them. You're not refusing a request, selling a product, apologizing for a delayed shipment, or asking for payment for an overdue bill. Your focus is on giving the customer something nice — a warm welcome, a free gift, added benefits.

WELCOME LETTERS

A "welcome letter" is a friendly introductory greeting sent to someone who is a first-time customer and has just bought your product or service.

Format: [*See Appendix A:* Fig. A-1. Simple format for letters and memos.] Handwritten or typed/word-processed. Business letterhead.

Style/Tone/Voice: Can be either informal or formal. Active tone or voice. [*See Part I for more on these subjects.*]

Structure: (1) Welcome new client/customer, (2) Express your gratitude or thanks for their business, (3) Say how you will strive to meet their needs and expectations, (4) If applicable, highlight a benefit or service, (5) Invite questions.

Handy Phrases: We appreciate your business; Are pleased that you chose; Thank you for opening an account with; We welcome you as a new customer of; I have enclosed some information about; If you have any questions; Will meet your needs; Always happy to be of service; Hope to work with you again soon; Thank you for choosing us; Call if you have questions about our products or services.

See also: *Part IV:* Business Greetings.

Dear Jim:

Thank you for signing up for Ontime Banking Basic. The enclosed information will help you get started, including:

- Ontime Banking Basic Quick Start Guide — step-by-step instructions for setting up and using your service
- Customer Agreement for Second Union Online — terms and conditions for banking online with Second Union

By signing up for free Ontime Banking Basic, you've joined the thousands of other Second Union customers who appreciate how technology can simplify your busy life. Ontime Banking Basic can help you control your small business finances, *when* and *where you* want and at no monthly service charge!

If you have any questions please call us at 1-800-541-1234. Online Customer Service Representatives are available 24 hours a day, 7 days a week to help you.

Again, we welcome you to Ontime Banking Basic and thank you for banking with Second Union!

Sincerely,

Bill Mead

The next letter thanks the reader for subscribing to a magazine. Note how it points out some of the highlights of the publication.

Dear Wayne:

Thank you for your order and welcome to *Monroe Management Review*'s select community of readers.

Your first issue should arrive shortly. We hope that you enjoy it, and that you find substantive ideas inside.

In each quarterly issue of *Monroe Management Review*, you'll discover innovative and practical business strategies that will challenge your thinking and help you maximize your business performance.

When your issue arrives and you've had a chance to see how useful MMR can be, please join us as a regular subscriber by returning this invoice with your payment.

We look forward to hearing from you.

Laurie Penn

Circulation Director

P.S. Your first issue is on its way. Please take a moment now to look over the enclosed form, and check that we've entered your name and address correctly to ensure delivery.

Tips for Writing Welcome Letters

- Thank the reader for his order and welcome him as a new customer.
- Restate the benefits of the product to prevent "buyer's remorse" and make the customer feel good about his purchase.
- Give any necessary instructions for using the product or service to maximum advantage.

FREE GIFTS

One of the most pleasurable occasions for writing to customers is to send or offer them a free gift.

Obviously you are giving the free gift to build goodwill and a relationship that will result in increased customer loyalty and greater lifetime customer value (e.g., the customer will buy more from you and remain a customer longer). You get the best leverage from gift-giving with a cover letter that thanks the customer for being a good client, while saying, "Please give us your future business."

Format: [*See Appendix A:* Fig. A-1. Simple format for letters and memos.] Handwritten or typed/word-processed. Business letterhead.

Style/Tone/Voice: Can be either informal or formal. Active tone or voice. [*See Part I for more on these subjects.*]

Structure: (1) Thank customer for their business and loyalty, (2) State reason for giving the gift, (3) Say what the gift is, (4) Close with a repeated "thank you" and wishes for a continued successful relationship.

Handy Phrases: We are enclosing one of our; Please accept our gift to you; I hope you will enjoy this; A little something to thank you for your business; It's always a pleasure to serve you; We are forwarding a little gift to you; Thank you for your business; Thank you for your recent orders.

See also: *Part IV:* Giving a Business Gift.

Happy summer! Just a note to say "thank you" for shopping at Amir's Fresh Fruits and Produce. As a token of our appreciation, we've enclosed a coupon for a free small basket of peaches. Bring the coupon with you next time you stop in to redeem your free basket of fragrant, juicy peaches. We look forward to seeing you.

Thanks again for being a loyal Amir's shopper!

The following letter is more specific in its description of the business relationship and history. Notice how including these details makes the letter more personal.

Dear Mary:

Happy Anniversary! We wanted to send a note of thanks for being a customer of Pampered Pooch Pet-Sitting Service (it's been five years now). You're a valued client and we've enjoyed taking care of Hudson — he's one of the family.

We thought Hudson would enjoy these homemade dog biscuits. They're made with all fresh ingredients, including peanut butter — Hudson's favorite!

We also wanted to let you know about a new service we're offering — about pet photography. The attached brochure explains the service in more detail.

Thanks again for letting us watch Hudson for you when you're away. We look forward to many more years of the same!

Tips for Writing Free Gift Letters

- Briefly describe the gift in a manner that highlights its value and utility.
- Say they are getting this free gift because they are a preferred customer and you value your relationship with them.
- If they have to request the gift, give them instructions for doing so.
- Make it clear that the gift is free and there are no strings attached.

FREE VALUE-ADDED PROGRAMS

Sometimes the gift is not an item but a service or program. The cover letter explains the program, its benefits, and why you are giving it to the customer.

Sometimes you can remind the customer subtly of the value of your gift and then ask for their continued business in return. Other times, you can be more direct about what you want the customer to do (e.g., the second letter below encourages the readers to use a certain airline).

Format: [*See Appendix A:* Fig. A-1. Simple format for letters and memos.] Typed/word-processed, business letterhead.

Style/Tone/Voice: Can be either informal or formal; use active tone or voice. [*See Part I for more on these subjects.*]

Structure: (1) Thank reader for their business, (2) Welcome them to the value-added program, (3) Give details about the program, (4) Explain how to take best advantage of the program, (5) Close with a wish to provide continued good services.

Handy Phrases: Proud to announce; Our services will now include; You will be available to; Now are available at all; You are entitled; Your continued business is important to us.

See also: *Part IV* Cordial Contacts; *Part VII:* Loyalty Program Letters.

Welcome to the Executive Floor of the Paducah Hotel. We thank you indeed for choosing to stay with us. Our aim is to make this a home away from home so please be assured that you will be well taken care of.

As V.I.P. resident of this prestigious floor, you are entitled to the following privileges.

Complimentary use of the Club Room located on the 21st floor. These lounges give you an excellent opportunity to meet other residents. It is open from 6.30 a.m. to 11.00 p.m.

- Complimentary breakfast, which is served from 6.30 a.m. to 10.00 a.m.
- Pre-lunch cocktails from 12.00 p.m. to 1.00 p.m.
- Predinner cocktails from 6.30 p.m. to 8.00 p.m.
- Personal service from our well-trained Butlers. (Complimentary pressing of one suit.)
- Exclusive check-in and check-out on the 21st Floor.
- No-stop check-out service.
- . . . And many more.

Should you require any assistance or information, please do not hesitate to contact me or the team of Butlers at Extension 8-9998 or 8-9999.

My team and I will do our utmost to ensure that you enjoy a pleasant and memorable stay with us.

Yours Sincerely

Louisa Naidu Executive Floor Manager

The next letter is a free membership upgrade awarded to one of the recipient's service suppliers:

Dear Mr. Woods,

I am delighted to welcome you as a member of the exclusive Platinum program through February, 2005. We are extending this complimentary membership to you in recognition of your valued association with Speedyflight.

The elite status you've been awarded is accompanied by an array of exclusive privileges designed to recognize and reward your loyalty to Speedyflight. Upgrades, bonus miles, and personalized service are just a few of the benefits we're pleased to be able to offer to you. The entire program is explained in your enclosed welcome kit.

Your kit also contains your personalized membership card, which identifies you as one of Speedyflight's elite members and entitles you to all the rewards you deserve.

The pocket guide is included as a handy place to store your card, and a quick reference to your benefits. Also, you'll find upgrades and luggage tags, which we hope you'll enjoy with our compliments.

Let me remind you that the mileage you accrue during calendar year 2004 on Speedyflight and our Global Alliance partner, Ontime Airways, will count toward elite tier status, bonus miles, and upgrades. So the more you fly Speedyflight and Ontime Airways, the greater the benefits of your elite level membership.

Your continued loyalty is very important to us. We hope you will select Speedyflight as your preferred carrier.

Sincerely,

W. Thomas Long
Executive Vice President Marketing

Tips for Writing Value-Added Program Letters

- Explain each of the elements of the program, so the customer understands all the benefits he is entitled to receive.

- Say how long the program will last and give milestones or a schedule of planned events (e.g., there will be an annual holiday party, or monthly Web seminars).

- State the program objectives and the benefits for participants.

SERVICE LEVEL UPGRADES

Another pleasurable customer service letter to write is notifying customers that you are upgrading them — that is, giving them a higher level of service, better discounts, more service options, faster delivery, or whatever.

Format: [*See Appendix A:* Fig. A-1. Simple format for letters and memos.] Typed/word-processed, business letterhead.

Style/Tone/Voice: Informal/formal, active tone or voice. [*See Part I for more on these subjects.*]

Structure: (1) Open with a warm and friendly greeting, (2) Describe briefly your current relationship, (3) Let the reader know what change in service you will now be offering, (4) Let the reader know why you are offering them this service, that they are the valued customer, (5) Outline the specific benefits that they will get from this enhanced service and who they can contact if they have any questions.

Handy Phrases: It is our pleasure to inform you; We are delighted; Welcome; We hope you enjoy; Benefits include; We hope you choose; An excellent program now available.

See also: *Part VII:* Letters Offering A Free Trial; Loyalty Program Letters.

Dear Mr. Black,

With today's volatile market, you may be looking for more from your financial services provider, and we at Liberty are prepared to deliver it.

While we continue to provide you with comprehensive investing support through our online, phone, and Investor Center services, I would like to introduce you to a program that offers you an even deeper level of insight and assistance — Liberty Preferred Services.

Designed to recognize and reward customers with substantial assets with us. Liberty Preferred Services is complimentary when your eligible household assets at Liberty reach $100,000. The program offers many benefits, including:

- Investment Planning Consultations — tailored to your specific needs at key investment planning stages as you accumulate and manage your wealth.
- Silver-Level Pricing — with online trades starting as low as $14.95, compared to our bronze-level pricing with online trades of $29.92.

Preferred Services also offers enhanced customer service, featuring a special phone number with priority call routing to our more experienced Liberty representatives, exclusive publications written specifically for Preferred customers, and more.

To give you a sample of the additional support you would receive as a Preferred Services client, we would like to offer you a free Investment Planning Consultation by calling 800-444-6666. A Liberty Representative will review your portfolio and identify valuable strategies for you to consider. We hope that this experience will encourage you to consider consolidating your assets at Liberty.

As always, thank you for your business.

Sincerely,

Raymond Marx
President

Here's another example of a service-upgrade letter:

Dear Ms. Ross:

In appreciation of your recent stays with Staymore Suites, it is with pleasure that I welcome you to Staymore Suites Gold Level, the elite level of our frequent guest program. Enclosed is your new Gold membership card, which entitles you to the Gold level's many privileges at nearly 400 participating Staymore Suites in 50 countries around the world.

Among the benefits your Gold membership brings are:

- A room upgrade whenever available at check-in
- 4 p.m. late check out
- 3 ClubMilesT (2 base ClubMiles plus a 50% bonus) for every eligible US dollar (or equivalent) spent
- Benefit Certificates worth hundreds of dollars

The enclosed Program Guide provides you with complete information about the exclusive benefits of your new Gold membership. For any additional information or for award redemption, please call the Award Center nearest you (see listings on page 14).

We invite you to stay with us soon to take full advantage of the privileges and recognition that are yours as a member of Staymore Suites Gold Level.

Sincerely,

David Becker
Senior Vice President
Director, Marketing & Strategic Planning

Tips for Writing Service Level Upgrade Letters

- Tell them the reason why they qualify and why you are upgrading them to a new service level.
- Give a value-added name to the service level (e.g., "Priority Members Plus").
- List the benefits and features of the upgraded service level.
- Say what they must do to accept your offer and get the benefits of upgrading.

HOLIDAY SEASON THANK-YOUS TO VALUED CUSTOMERS

Instead of sending a greeting card, some businesses send thank-you letters to customers during the holidays. They feel it adds a more personal touch while allowing them to customize a message that helps cement the customer relationship and generate more feelings of goodwill.

As for format, you can write a straightforward letter, as in the first sample that follows. Or you can be a bit more creative in content and format, as in the second model letter.

Format: [*See Appendix A:* Fig. A-1. Simple format for letters and memos.] Handwritten or typed, Personal letterhead or Business letterhead

Style/Tone/Voice: Can be either informal or formal. Active tone or voice. [*See Part I for more on these subjects.*]

Structure: (1) Open with a warm greeting appropriate to the holiday, (2) Talk briefly about your experiences and business with the customer over the preceding year, (3) You may also make note of the year to come and how you see your relationship progressing over the next year, (4) Close with a reiteration of warm greetings for the appropriate holiday.

Handy Phrases: Wishing you a joyous holiday season; As we ring in the New Year; Enjoy this Thanksgiving break; Our best wishes for; We appreciate your business this past year; We hope next year will be even better; Wish you an enjoyable holiday.

See also: *Part II:* Thank-You Letters; *Part IV:* Cordial Contacts.

[Date]

[Addressee]

Dear [Name]:

As the Christmas season approaches, there is always so much activity and personal business to attend to that it is easy to forget to thank our valued customers, like you, for their orders.

So, before I forget, thank you, and may this holiday season bring to you and your family all of the joy and happiness that you deserve.

Very truly yours,

Marc White

Here's a well-written example of a gracious holiday letter.

Dear Roger:

As a copywriter, I make my living with words, so I choose them carefully.

With the year drawing to a close, I like to reflect on the preceding 12 months. When I look back, there's one special word that bears repeating.

Thank you.

Thank you . . .

> . . . for entrusting your assignment to me.
> . . . for placing your faith in my abilities and judgment.
> . . .for being judicious with your revisions.
> . . . for teaching me valuable lessons you acquired through your own experience.
> . . . for compensating me without complaint.
> . . . for writing or speaking about my services with elegance and generosity.
> . . . for your devoted patronage that permits me to practice the craft I love in the style I like.
> . . . for being a partner, not a taskmaster.

May you find health and prosperity throughout the seasons!

Warmest regards,

Robert Lee

Tips for Writing Holiday Season Thank-You Letters

- Acknowledge that this is a holiday greeting letter.
- Thank your customers for the business they gave you.
- Say you look forward to continuing the relationship in the New Year.
- Wish them a happy holiday.

YEAR-END ROUND-UP

Public companies send their shareholders annual reports each year, detailing the various activities of the business. The Securities and Exchange Commission (SEC) requires them to do so.

A privately held firm is not required to do an annual report. But it's a good idea to write to your customers, vendors, prospects, and other "stakeholders" at annual report time (typically in January) once a year anyway. Doing so gives you a chance to show off your achievements and remind folks of why it's to their advantage to be associated with your firm.

There is no need to print a fancy four-color annual report for this purpose — or any type of brochure, for that matter. A simple, old-fashioned letter will do just fine.

Format: [*See Appendix A:* Fig. A-1. Simple format for letters and memos.] Typed/word-processed, business letterhead.

Style/Tone/Voice: Formal, but keep free of jargon and business cliches; use, active tone or voice. [*See Part I for more on these subjects.*]

Structure: (1) Express thanks, (2) Provide information about year's highlights (and lowlights), (3) Point out any new information about your company, product, and service, (4) Explain how you plan to keep readers informed, (5) Close with warm thanks and a positive note about continued association.

Handy Phrases: Have positioned ourselves; Have enjoyed steady; We've enclosed more detailed information; You'll continue to receive quarterly meeting reports, proxies, and economic projections; We'll keep you informed about; Thanks for your support; We look forward to continued success.

See also: *Part IV:* FYI Letters; *Part V:* Reports in Memo Format.

Dear Robert:

As MoneyDirect LLC approaches the completion of our third year, I am exceptionally gratified to share with you the tremendous good fortune to which you have contributed. Consider:

- We have grown from 32 associates in February 2000 to 70 today.
- We have more than doubled our first-year commission revenue to the low eight-figures.
- MoneyBase, our proprietary cooperative database, serves all or most of the prospecting needs for more than 80 world-class B2B mailers. Plus, MoneyBase is gaining favor as beneficial environment from which to mail customers!
- We have become a leading B2B and publishing list manager (over 300 properties) and have built a respected and fast-growing e-mail brokerage and management franchise. We will book a low seven figure net profit for FY 2004.
- Our new business pipeline is brimming with exciting opportunities.
- We continue 100% member-financed and debt-free.

We have you and many other loyal and supportive clients and friends to thank for this success. Be assured going forward that all of us at MoneyDirect are 100% committed to the never ending process of improving your result and saving you money and time. That has been the purpose of our enterprise since day one . . . and thus shall it always be!

As you might expect, our rapid growth is dictating office expansion. Our Chicago branch has doubled to six associates, necessitating their August move to state-of-the-art offices in the Research Park in Dallas. And our Stamford, CT, headquarters will be moving next month to greatly expanded offices at 333 West Avenue in Buffalo, NY. The custom renovated space is in the old Kit Foods HQ situated on a bucolic campus of 15 acres a mile south of downtown Buffalo. The benefits abound:

- A 10-year, below-market, fixed rate lease (recession can have its benefits).
- 50% more space — 19,300 square feet — gives us room for continued growth.
- A shorter, less-stressful commute for 80% of our HQ based associates.
- A better location for recruiting experienced NYC-area list professionals.

We'll keep you posted as to our move-in timing and contact changes. But the overarching mission of this letter is, once again, to say " Thank You" for allowing us to serve as your strategic list and database marketing partner. In the years and decades ahead, rest assured, your early confidence and trust in us will always be remembered.

Yours very truly,

Ralph Bridges
For the Members and Associates

Tips for Writing the Year-end Round-up Letter

- Thank the recipient for being a customer (or employee, or vendor, or whatever) of your firm.
- Highlight the firm's major accomplishments for the year — new products introduced, sales records, new accounts, expanded production capabilities, hiring of a new CEO, and so on.
- Talk honestly about any problems that exist, what is being done to solve them, and when you expect them to be resolved.

CORDIAL CONTACT LETTERS

In today's modern business jargon, communicating with the customer is called "touching" the customer. "Keep-in-touch" letters, also known as cordial contact letters, were once a popular form of postal business correspondence. Now, more and more of these customer contacts or "touches" are made via e-mail instead of postal mail. The reasons are cost of delivery (virtually zero once you have a database with your customer's e-mail addresses) and speed of delivery (instant versus days or weeks).

Format: [*See Appendix A:* Fig. A-1. Simple format for letters and memos.] Handwritten or typed, business letterhead

Style/Tone/Voice: Can be either informal or formal, use active tone or voice. [*See Part I for more on these subjects.*]

Structure: (1) State appreciation, (2) Expand on opening, (3) Suggest future business with a special deal, discount, or information about a new product — if possible give a "freebie" or premium.

Handy Phrases: Express our appreciation for; It is a pleasure to deal with; On behalf of; We are glad we found you; We greatly appreciate your; Please accept our heartfelt thanks for; For many years to come; We look forward to.

See also: *Part IV:* Business Greetings.

Dear Online Friend,

My favorite time of year is here — grilling season! Since you have requested to receive special information from Lincoln Steaks, I want to share my secret for grilling perfect steaks with you.

Our Foolproof Steak Cooking Chart will allow you to grill perfect steaks every time. You'll be the hit of every barbecue! To view this chart, go to: www.lincolnsteaks.com

Tips:

- To cook perfect steaks every time, check out our Foolproof Steak Cooking Chart.
- Filet Mignons will take 30 seconds to 1 minute less time than shown in chart.
- The cooking times in the chart are for fully thawed steaks.
- All times are approximate.

Sincerely,

Sam Shultz, Owner
Lincoln Steaks

P.S. Take advantage of our Buy 1, Get 1 FREE offer! Now order 6 (5oz.) Top Sirloins and get 6 more for FREE! This offer is only available through this email. Order today!

If you feel you have received this message in error or you wish to be removed from our list, please go to:

www.lincolnsteaks.mo.net/m/u/lin/o.asp

Here's another letter by the same company. I'm showing both to illustrate how easy it is to keep in touch with customers while keeping the correspondence fresh by making a simple change (in this case the fun freebie changes from grilling instructions to a recipe).

Subject: Great Grilling Recipe from Lincoln Steaks!

Dear Online Friend,

Lincoln Steaks wants to help you make great meals at a moment's notice.

Good food — and time spent sharing it with people you love — is one of life's greatest pleasures. So today, I want to share a delicious pork chop recipe with you!

- Thaw 6 Boneless Pork Chops

Combine
- 1 cup orange juice
- 1/3 cup soy sauce
- 1/4 cup olive oil
- 2 tsp. dried, crushed rosemary
- 2 diced green onions

Marinate chops for 1½ hours in the refrigerator. Broil or grill over medium heat for approximately 7 minutes per side. Makes enough for 6 chops.

Enjoy!

Sincerely

Sam Shultz
Lincoln Steaks

P.S. Right now you can enjoy 12 (4 oz) Boneless Pork Chops for only $29.00 or any of our great monthly specials and we'll also send 6 Burgers or a Computer Game FREE to each shipping address!

Go to:

www.lincolnsteaks.com/freegame

If you feel you have received this message in error or you wish to be removed from the list, you can unsubscribe by going to: www.lincolnsteaks.mo.net/m/u/lin/o.asp

Tips for Writing Customer Contact Letters

- Include some useful, how-to, nonpromotional content — recipes, application tips, and maintenance instructions — in the letter. E-mail especially is a medium where readers expect useful information in exchange for taking the time and trouble to open and read your message.
- Don't just say "Hi." Ask for business. Offer the customer a special deal or discount on a hot product they've been wanting.
- Write in a friendly, update, conversational style. Remember, this is a "cordial" contact. So be cordial!

CUSTOMER REACTIVATION LETTERS

When customers go without making a purchase for more than a year, send them a letter to get them to start giving you orders again.

Format: [*See Appendix A:* Fig. A-1. Simple format for letters and memos.] Handwritten or typed, business letterhead

Style/Tone/Voice: Can be either informal or formal. Active tone or voice. [*See Part I for more on these subjects.*]

Structure: (1) Express appreciation for past business, (2) Explain why you're writing (i.e., to regain them as a customer and to find out why they haven't been doing business with you), (3) If applicable, describe any new products or services that may be of interest to the customer, (4) Indicate that you would appreciate the opportunity to win their business back, (5) Offer to solve any problems that may have caused them to stop doing business with you, (6) Close with a firm desire to continue the relationship

Handy Phrases: Have always appreciated your business; You've been an excellent customer; We have missed you lately; Love to know what caused you to stop ordering from us; Have we inadvertently done something; We sincerely want to know; Could you please answer and return the enclosed questionnaire; Let's bring each other up to date; I'd enjoy hearing from you again; Enclosed is a proposal outlining; I have enclosed our new catalog.

See also: *Part VII:* Letters to Lure Back Clients.

[Datc]

[Addressee]

Dear [Name]:

It has been so long since we had the opportunity to serve you that we have begun to wonder if, perhaps, we have offended you in some way in the past. If this is the case, we would greatly appreciate knowing what happened. In fact, if you have any grievance with our firm, please call so that we might discuss the problem.

We have introduced many innovations into our product line since the last order you placed with the firm. If the reason we haven't heard from you has nothing to do with a complaint, we would appreciate the opportunity to show you these innovations.

We look forward to hearing from you and we hope we have a chance to renew our relationship.

Very truly yours,

Tips for Writing Customer Reactivation Letters

- Remind them that they had previously been a customer.
- Ask why they are no longer buying.
- Offer to solve any problems that are preventing them from giving you further orders.

Routine Customer Correspondence

Routine letters to customers are an important part of your ongoing relationship with each customer. They act as friendly reminders of your existence and they help customers ensure they're either properly stocked with your product or that it's time for them to schedule your service. Make the most of these letters by adding warmth and as much personal touch as possible.

"TIME TO REORDER" LETTER

There are a number of products — envelopes, vitamin supplements, computer supplies, and calendars — which must be reordered periodically.

You should send a letter reminding them that it is time to reorder. This is important, since for many of these products, the bulk of the profits are made on the repeat sales or reorders, rather than the initial sale.

Format: [*See Appendix A:* Fig. A-1. Simple format for letters and memos.] Typed/word-processed, business letterhead.

Style/Tone/Voice: Can be either informal or formal, use active tone or voice. [*See Part I for more on these subjects.*]

Structure: (1) Open with a gentle reminder that it's time to think about your product/service, (2) Remind reader about the benefits of using your product/service, (3) Give the details of how to order, (4) Close with good wishes for a continued relationship.

Handy Phrases: It's that time again; The new year is fast approaching; Don't chance running out of; Maintenance will ensure that; Call us today to schedule; Use the enclosed form.

See also: *Part VII:* Types of Sales Letters.

Dear Greg,

Last Chance for Guaranteed Delivery Before 2004!

In case you haven't yet reordered your Planner Pal, the 2004 year is fast approaching!

Don't miss this **LAST CHANCE** to reorder your Planner Pal with *guaranteed delivery* before 2004. We must receive your order by December 9th.

Remember — in this busy, high-pressure world we live in, your Planner Pal offers welcome relief. It works like a funnel to help you set your priorities. You work smarter, get more done. In addition, your Planner Pal helps you:

- Balance everything you do — in your professional and personal life.
- Use time more effectively and to your advantage.
- Set goals for yourself and keep them.

Online Shopping and Ordering Available!

So keep a good thing coming! Order online anytime via our secure Web site at www.plannerpal.com or just return the enclosed order form with your payment by mail or fax. You can also call us TOLL FREE at (800) 315-7000.

Thank you for you continued business.

Sincerely,

Bill Cross

P.S. I know that letters can cross in the mail, so if you have already reordered, thank you!

Here is an example of a reorder letter for office supplies that are used daily.

Dear Carolyn Mayes,

Thank you for your order back in July of the products listed below. We appreciate having you as a customer. This is just a reminder to check your supply of those products, in the event you are running low.

It is easy to keep supplies current. Simply verify the information below, make changes in quantity if necessary, even add new products. Just mail or fax this form to us, with your updated imprint samples, at (800) 555-5123 or call toll-free at (800) 275-4000 and leave the rest to us.

As always, you are protected by our 100% Satisfaction Guarantee . . . no strings attached. So, check your supply now . . . and thanks for your confidence in Business Papers.

Sincerely,

Nancy B. Small
Marketing Director

P.S. We've recently added many new products like stationery, shipping and memo pads, and updated many more, so now you'll find more business bargains than ever before.

Tips for Writing "Time to Reorder" Letters

- Remind them that it is time to reorder — either their supply is running low, or their current product will be made obsolete by the new edition or version.

- Resell them on the benefits of the product. It is easy for the reader to do nothing and not reorder. You must convince him that he should continue to use the product.

- Give either a specific deadline by which the reader must reorder, or an incentive (such as an early bird discount) for reordering promptly.

ORDER ACKNOWLEDGEMENT

Order acknowledgments are a routine sort of customer service correspondence.

Format: [*See Appendix A:* Fig. A-1. Simple format for letters and memos. Typed/word-processed, business letterhead.

Style/Tone/Voice: Informal or formal, passive/active tone or voice. [*See Part I for more on these subjects.*]

Structure: (1) Acknowledge order, (2) Give necessary details (expected delivery dates, confirmation numbers), (3) Thank customer for the order and for choosing your company, (4) Explain how they can contact you if they have questions about their order, (5) Entice reader to order again (perhaps with information about new product/service or with a discount).

Handy Phrases: Are sending your; You can expect to receive; Our normal turnaround time is; Thanks again for your business; It's always a pleasure to; We are glad you have; Thank you for thinking of us; We hope you will be delighted with; We value your business; Feel free to call — our customer service number is; Remember that we also offer; We will be happy to assist you.

See also: *Part VII:* After-Sale Letters.

[Date]

[Addressee]

Dear [Name]:

We are in receipt of your order as contained in the attached purchase order form.

We confirm acceptance on said order subject only to the following exceptions: [Describe]

On exceptions noted, we shall assume you agree to same unless objection is received within ten days of receipt of this notice.

Thanks you for your patronage.

Yours very truly,

Tips for Writing Order Acknowledgments

- Thank the customer for his order.
- Confirm the terms and conditions.
- Enclose relevant documents such as a purchase order or bill of lading.

NOTIFICATION OF SHIPPING DELAY

A less-pleasant customer service letter to write is when you have to tell a customer that his shipment is going to be delayed.

Format: [*See Appendix A:* Fig. A-1. Simple format for letters and memos.] Typed/word-processed, business letterhead.

Style/Tone/Voice: Informal/formal, passive/active tone or voice. [*See Part I for more on these subjects.*]

Structure: (1) Specify which items are going to be late and how late they will be, (2) Apologize and give the reason for the delay, (3) Give them the option of waiting for the merchandise or canceling the order and getting a refund, (4) Offer a small gift to compensate them for the trouble, such as a certificate good for 10% off on their next order.

Handy Phrases: Please accept our apologies for the delay; I apologize that your shipment will be delayed; We are experiencing delay in filling orders; Our shipping department discovered that your shipment was sent to; Because of high demand; Called our driver and instructed him to; We'll make every effort; We've sent your order by express mail; Apologize for any inconvenience; Do our best to prevent a repeat of; Our sincere thanks for giving us the opportunity to.

See also: *Part VIII:* Shipment Held Up for Payment.

Dear [Name]:

Thank you for your order. At this time we cannot fill your order due to an unexpected shipment delay from our overseas suppliers.

We will hold your order for arrival of the merchandise, and ship shortly thereafter. Unfortunately, we cannot provide you with a specific shipping date at this time.

Thank you for your patience in this matter. If you decide you cannot wait, just mail back the enclosed card or call us toll-free at 800-888-8888. We will cancel your order and immediately refund your money.

Sincerely,

Tips for Writing a Notification of Shipping Delay Letter

- Send a note as soon as you are aware of the problem.
- Don't place blame.
- Make the letter sincere and succinct.
- Explain how you plan to follow up to make sure the issue gets resolved.

Change Order

When a customer asks for a change after the contract has been signed, it is a mistake to only verbally agree to this change. You should also get it in writing.

Why? When the customer is pressed by an urgent need, he will say anything to get you to solve his problem. After the crisis is passed and the service is performed and billed, the customer may say he doesn't remember the change. Then you are in the uncomfortable and unproductive situation of arguing with the customer about the bill, and his delight at your having helped him is negated by his distaste for the billing argument.

The solution? When a customer requests even a minor change, put it in writing. Put every request for changes in writing. That way, you have a paper trail that documents the authorization you received to perform the extra service and get paid for it.

Format: [*See Appendix A:* Fig. A-1. Simple format for letters and memos.] Typed/word-processed, business letterhead.

Style/Tone/Voice: Can be either informal or formal. Active tone or voice. [*See Part I for more on these subjects.*]

Structure: (1) State change, (2) Explain how change will happen (e.g., you will send new parts and customer can throw old parts away), (3) Ask reader to confirm that the change order you stated is correct.

Handy Phrases: We received your request; We're pleased to be able to; As we discussed; The attached addendum outlines; The information below reflects; Your cooperation in changing; Please indicate your approval; Let us know if this is.

See also: *Part V:* Change Orders; *Part VIII:* Change of Terms.

Here is a template you can adapt for a change order.

[client name]

[title]
[company]
[address]
[city, state, zip]

CHANGE NOTIFICATION AND AUTHORIZATION

Dear Customer

As you requested [in our meeting of . . .], we are preparing to make the following changes to

[name of project]:

[summarize changes here, preferably in a numerical list]

Although we have attempted to minimize the impact of these changes wherever possible [through such measures as . . .], they will nonetheless increase the total of our proposal of [date] [which I have revised and attached] by $0,000.

[The breakdown of the increase is . . .]

[The good news is that we do not anticipate that these changes will affect the schedule.]

or

[The schedule will also be delayed by an estimated...days. See the revised schedule attached.]

We will, of course, continue to try to reduce the impact of these changes as the project goes forward.

Please indicate your approval and return this letter to me as quickly as possible so we can avoid any delays that might further affect price or scheduling. It would not be appropriate to continue work without your agreement.

If you wish to discuss the impact of these changes with me, please call.

Thanks again for the privilege of working with [name of client firm]. We're looking forward to producing a world-class [type of project] for you.

Sincerely,

Name, Title

Changes approved: _____ Date: _____

Tips for Writing Change Orders

- Specify (a) the nature of the change, (b) the cost, (c) the deadline date.
- Get the customer to sign and return one copy of the change order. Do not proceed without this written authorization.
- Invite the customer to call if he has any questions or wants to discuss any aspect of the change requested, the cost, or the new deadline.

PREMEETING AGENDA LETTER

The premeeting agenda letter is one that should be sent prior to every major meeting with a customer or client, but seldom is.

When there is a problem, status meeting, or sales opportunity, salespeople and account managers sometimes have to work very hard to secure a meeting because of the customer's busy schedule. Often there are numerous items to discuss, and only a short time to discuss them.

Without a premeeting agenda, the meeting is disorganized, and the customer cannot adequately prepare to discuss the issues you want to cover. By sending a letter in advance with the suggested agenda, you can make the meeting more efficient, save the customer time, and enable them to get maximum benefit from the time spent with you.

Format: [*See Appendix A:* Fig. A-1. Simple format for letters and memos.] Typed/word-processed, business letterhead.

Style/Tone/Voice: Can be either formal or informal, passive/active tone or voice. [*See Part I for more on these subjects.*]

Structure: (1) Review logistics of meeting (date/time), (2) List agenda items (make each item a bullet that's clear, concise, and brief), (3) Explain what is expected of the reader as a meeting participant, (4) Confirm that the reader has received the agenda.

Handy Phrases: We are meeting to formulate a marketing plan; There will be a board meeting to discuss new inductees; Below are the topics we will cover; Attached is the meeting agenda; Please be prepared to talk about your ideas; Be prepared to report about; I'll be in touch to make sure you've receive this agenda; Please call if you have questions or concerns.

See also: *Part IV* Post-Meeting Follow-Up Letter; *Part V:* Pre-Meeting Agendas.

Ms. I. M. Important
Project Manager
My Most Important Customer, Inc.
700 Apple Street
York, PA 17700

Dear Ms. Important:

This letter outlines what we propose to accomplish at our upcoming consultation visit with your team. I have listed below some of our goals and expectations. We appreciate your willingness to talk with us about your business, your customers, and what you need from us in order to remain a successful company.

Rather than have one long grinding meeting, we propose to conduct a series of brief consultation meetings with a array of people who come in contact with our products as they make their way through your business to become part of your products, Furthermore, we tend to learn more when we can talk to people when they're in the environment where they do what they do. For example, we like to go the warehouse to talk to the warehouse manager, and go to the shop floor to talk to the end users.

Therefore, we try to prepare carefully, so as not to waste your time. This letter is one of the steps we take in the planning process.

The main goals of consultations are to:

- Understand the steps your company goes through to order, receive, deliver to the shop floor, consume, pay for, and dispose of our products.
- Understand the service levels expected from the end users.
- Understand how our products help or hurt you meet your customer's needs.
- Listen, listen, listen — particularly to areas where we're falling short, or where you have future needs that we may not be able to serve, unless we change something.

We need your help in preparation for the consultation. In general, we need the following:

- A basic map of your site, a list of required personal protective equipment, on-site conference room or empty office with phone for the duration of our site visit, and any safety orientation required by your company.
- List of contacts in the plant, accounts payable, major users MIS, purchasing, warehouse, quality control, etc. We will set up brief meetings with key personnel during the visit.
- At least one hour with your business team to discuss your customer's future needs.
- A "go-to" person to serve as a day host, and answer any basic questions we may have.
- An initial tour of the facility, led by a person(s) familiar with all the major use points on site.

We try to make consultations as enjoyable for our customers as they are for us. For this reason we strive to complete the entire visit in just half a day — or less. We send a small team of people that will split into smaller groups once they arrive. Most of our meetings with individuals will be less than an hour, and most of what we do is listen and ask questions. No prework is required on their part.

I will contact you by phone two weeks before the visit to firm up the details, and answer any questions you may have. Once again, thank you for providing this exciting opportunity to understand how we can improve our ability to help you serve your customers.

Sincerely,

Brian Hill
Industrial Company Marketing Manager

Tips for Writing Premeeting Agenda Letters

- Give the objectives of the meetings. What are the goals you propose to accomplish?
- Propose an item-by-item agenda.
- Tell what materials you need and what preparation the customer should make.

RENEWAL LETTERS

When a customer buys a product or service on a subscription or contract basis, renewal notices are sent to get them to continue getting the product or using the service when the current subscription or contract expires.

Format: [*See Appendix A:* Fig. A-1. Simple format for letters and memos.] Typed/word-processed, business letterhead.

Style/Tone/Voice: Can be either informal or formal. Use active tone or voice. [*See Part I for more on these subjects.*]

Structure: (1) Explain why you're writing and invite customer to renew, (2) State the benefits and any special offers, (3) Review the highlights of your product/service, (4) Encourage reader to take advantage of the offer to renew.

Handy Phrases: Thanks for ordering; It's time to renew; Renew now to take advantage of our special offer; This is a one-time offer; Lock in at our lowest rates; To ensure uninterrupted service; Send the attached reply card today so that you don't miss an issue; Call today to schedule.

See also: *Part VII:* Letters to Lure Back Clients.

Dear Ben Cooper:

Soon now, **your *Home* subscription will end**. Of course, our Circulation people <u>could</u> send you a series of renewal reminders, but I think <u>you deserve better:</u>

So I invite you to unclutter your mailbox (and your life) by making this **<u>the last renewal notice</u>** we send you.

Just tear off and return the above form. Then we'll charge your credit card for 26 more issues of *Home*.

It's a wonderfully easy way to make sure that . . .

> You keep receiving *Home* at <u>less than HALF</u> the store price!

> Your mailbox stays blissfully <u>free of renewal notices!</u>

> You have <u>no checks to write</u> or other payments to mail!

> You <u>don't</u> risk a missed issue!

Why, once you experience this "easy-as-falling-off-a-log" ·renewal technique, you'll wonder why you ever did it the "old-fashioned" way. So, won't you please return the above form today?

There's simply no easier way to keep your *Home* coming!

Dana Doyle,
Editor

Tips for Writing a Renewal Letter

- Tell the reader that his subscription, contract, service, or automatic monthly delivery is about to expire.
- Ask the person to renew. Restate the key benefits of the product.
- Remind him that prompt renewal will ensure uninterrupted delivery or service. For instance, if he is renewing a monthly shipment of vitamin supplements, not renewing promptly may mean he doesn't get his supplement on time next month.

RENEWAL NOTICE, FINAL

Rarely do marketers send a single renewal letter. Most find that it is more profitable to send a series of three, four, even five renewal letters or more.

Each letter in the series brings in additional renewal orders. You keep sending renewal notices until finally the profit from the renewals is less than the cost of sending the notices. At that point, the renewal efforts become unprofitable, and you are done: Further notices would only pull even less response.

The tone and content of the renewal notices change depending on where you are in the series. The first renewal notices are reminders that, for the most part, assume the customer wants the product or service. You are just reminding them to take a simple action so they keep getting it.

If the customer does not reply to the early renewal letters, either they were too busy, or they are not entirely sure they want to continue getting the product or service. These letters make more of an effort to "resell" the customer on the product benefits and show how life would be worse without it.

The final letters have an increased sense of urgency. The messages that work best here include "your subscription is about to expire" and "if you don't act now, your service will cease."

Format: [*See Appendix A:* Fig. A-1. Simple format for letters and memos.] Typed/word-processed, business letterhead.

Style/Tone/Voice: Can be informal or formal. Active tone or voice. [*See Part I for more on these subjects.*]

Structure: (1) Title the letter "Final Notice," (2) Offer a final courtesy to reactivate membership/subscription/account, (3) Explain if there is a penalty (e.g., rates will go up), (4) Urge reader to act now, (5) State that this will be the final notice and that no other offers will be sent, (6) Express wish to have a continued relationship.

Handy Phrases: We'd like to extend our offer; We hope you'll take advantage; Reactivate your account *now;* Take a moment to mail in your reply card now for uninterrupted service; No further renewals will be sent; Your name will be deleted from our active files; This is your last issue; We're sorry to see you go.

See also: *Part VII:* Letters to Lure Back Clients; *Part IX:* Second Request for Compliance.

Dear Milly Mackri:

This is it. The end. Your very last issues of *Business Scoop Weekly* are on their way to you, which means our unique business-to-business coverage, great scoops, and inside information that will make you bigger profits and higher market share will soon be *gone*.

Unless, of course, you return the enclosed renewal savings form right away.

As always *Business Scoop Weekly* is <u>guaranteed</u> to inform, inspire, and educate you like no other publication in print!

There is a revolution taking place in the way companies conduct their business to-business marketing. For many people this is a time of tremendous confusion. But for the informed professional marketer . . . this is a time of unparalleled opportunity. And the only mission of *Business Scoop Weekly* is to provide you with the intelligence you need to understand and implement these powerful new e-marketing capabilities.

Don't lose touch with the best business information there is to offer! <u>Take this opportunity to renew your subscription</u>.

You have nothing to lose . . . except for your subscription to *Business Scoop Weekly*. Renew <u>now</u>.

Sincerely,

Janice Schultz
Subscription Manager

PS: Make sure you don't miss an issue — renew your subscription today!

Tips for Writing the Final Renewal Notice

- Let the reader know that their service is about to expire.
- Stress the need for urgent action. Unless they reply today, they will not get the product.
- Often the price for renewing is less than the list price for new customers. Tell the reader that if his subscription expires and he decides he wants to keep getting the product later on, he will pay the full list price and not be entitled to the special low renewal rate you are offering him today.

"POINTS ABOUT TO EXPIRE" LETTER

Many marketers use "loyalty programs" (e.g., frequent flier miles) to reward customers who spend a lot of money with them.

Often these programs award points based on size of purchase. The more the customer spends, the more points she gets, and the bigger her reward or prize.

In many cases, loyalty programs are either temporary, or put a time limit on when points must be redeemed. One way to get customers to spend more is to remind them that their bonus points are about to expire and encourage them to come in, shop, and use the points.

Format: [*See Appendix A:* Fig. A-1. Simple format for letters and memos.] Typed/word-processed, business letterhead.

Style/Tone/Voice: Can be informal or formal. Active tone or voice. [*See Part I for more on these subjects.*]

Structure: (1) Notify the reader of the impending loss of points, (2) Briefly restate the major benefits of the program, (3) Explain how participants can redeem or retain their points, (4) Specify exact date on which points will expire if action is not taken.

Handy Phrases: Don't let your points expire; We do not want you to lose your points; We hope you will continue; To continue without interruption; We haven't heard from you; Your points will expire soon, Just a reminder; You won't want to miss out on; This notice is your last reminder; In order to stay active in the program you must.

See also: *Part VII:* Loyalty Program Letters; Discount Offers.

We've Missed You and Time is Running Out!

We do not want you to lose your Best of Bob's points that have accumulated over the past year. This notice is your last reminder that in order to stay active in the program you must make a purchase using your Best of Bob's card by the final date printed on the coupon below. This will ensure that you continue to receive future mailings regarding discounts, store event days, a birthday gift, and much more.

So don't let your points expire! Visit your nearest Bob's Store and use this coupon along with your Best of Bob's card to continue enjoying all the benefits we have to offer.

If you have lost or misplaced your card or have any questions about your account, please call Customer Service at 1-866-333-BOBS.

Best of Bob's is a trademark of Bob's Stores.

Tips for Writing Loyalty Points Expiration Letters

- Tell the reader that he has unused bonus points he can redeem for discounts, gifts, or valuable prizes. Show how many points he has accumulated.

- Explain the action he has to take to either use these points or prevent their loss. Give a deadline.

- Remind him that he is getting these points because he is a loyal customer and you want to show your appreciation for his business.

LETTERS OF INSTRUCTION

No matter how well you write them, most people do not like written instructions and find them boring. So when you must give customer instructions in a letter, your main goals are to be as clear and concise as possible.

Format: [*See Appendix A:* Fig. A-1. Simple format for letters and memos.] Typed/word-processed, business letterhead.

Style/Tone/Voice: Can be informal or formal. Active tone or voice. [*See Part I for more on these subjects.*]

Structure: (1) If appropriate, identify the issue that has made the directive necessary, (2) State or explain the existing or new procedure, (3) Close by expressing appreciation and reiterating the importance of the information you have conveyed. Offer to respond to questions and problems.

continued

continued

Handy Phrases: Because of the; Due to the increase in; Have a new procedure; Seems to be some confusion; The proper procedure for; Do the following; Implementation date will be; Must be accompanied by; Must be signed by; Must be arranged through; Pay careful attention to; Proper procedure for; Please remember to; The following procedure; Will require all; Appreciate your cooperation; For further information; If you have any problems with; If you have any questions about; If you need any; Thank you for; Will be subject to.

See also: *Part IV:* Instruction Letters.

You Must Replace Your Profit Sharing Plan Documents by the End of the Year.

Dear Employer:

Due to tax law changes, your Union Securities Prototype Profit Sharing Plan documents are obsolete and must be replaced. Using the enclosed Restatement guide, here are the steps you must take by the end of the year:

1. Determine which new Adoption Agreement you'll need to restate your plan by using the Plan Selection portion of the Restatement guide.
2. Complete the new Adoption Agreement you've selected using the Adoption Agreement Instructions to answer any questions you may have concerning the document. Make sure you review it with your tax or legal advisor.
3. Sign the Adoption Agreement and place it in your permanent Plan files. **Do not send it to Union Securities.** (Please refer to **Trustee Signature**, below.)
4. Complete the Prototype Plan Election Form for the Adoption Agreement you have chosen. **Send it to your Union Securities Financial Advisor listed below.**
5. If employees also participate in your plan, furnish each employee with a copy of the Summary Plan Description, updated General Information Sheet, and Summary of Material Modifications.

Timing. Failure to comply may lead to immediate taxation of plan assets, loss of deductions, and loss of future rollover opportunities. **Don't let this mailing get buried in your paperwork.** Discuss the restatement with your tax or legal advisor **right away.** You should complete the restatement process and mail your signed Prototype Plan Election Form to us by the end of the year.

We hope you'll take the time to review the enclosed materials and see for yourself how manageable the restatement process can be. We appreciate your business and stand ready to provide any further assistance you may require.

Very truly yours,

Tips for Writing Letters of Instruction

- Keep sentences and paragraphs short.
- Use bold headings, bullets, and numbered lists to break the instructions into bite-size, easy-to-follow steps.
- Write in the imperative voice (e.g., "Complete the form," not "The form should be completed").
- "Test-drive" the letter. Give it to your assistant, child, or spouse and see if they can follow the instructions. If not, rewrite.

CUSTOMER SATISFACTION SURVEYS

There are two major benefits to surveying your customers.

First, it shows them that you care about them and genuinely want them to be happy and satisfied.

Second, it brings you vital feedback on what customers think of you — what they like, don't like, want more of, and want you to improve. By making these changes, you can take their satisfaction to a whole new level.

Format: [*See Appendix A:* Fig. A-1. Simple format for letters and memos.] Typed/word-processed, business letterhead.

Style/Tone/Voice: Can be informal or formal. Active tone or voice. [*See Part I for more on these subjects.*]

Structure: (1) Explain your need, mentioning your reader's qualification to help, (2) Indicate what benefit the reader will receive by responding, (3) Express appreciation for the reader's cooperation. Indicate the date by which you need a response. Enclose a stamped, self-addressed envelope for return of the survey or questionnaire.

Handy Phrases: All responses will be kept confidential; May we ask a favor of you; Would appreciate your input; Give us your opinions concerning; In view of your experience in; Collecting data about; Complete a short questionnaire; Evaluate and improve our; In order for us to provide; Will help us in our planning; Help us to improve our service; Improve our procedure; Plan to modify our; Will prove to be of significant value to; Take just a minute or two; Circle the answers; Mark the appropriate box; In the accompanying envelope; Return it to us by; A free copy of; As many responses as possible; Expect to publish the results; Results of this study will be; Will share the results with; Appreciate your assistance; Could we have your completed survey by; Have enclosed a postage-paid envelope; Hope to complete our report by; Hope to receive your response by; Input is very important to us; Look forward to receiving your; Our deadline is; Please return the completed; Will be doubly appreciative if you can; Self-addressed, stamped envelope.

See also: *Part IV:* Request to Participate in a Survey; *Part VII:* Surveys or Questionnaires.

TO: Clients
FROM: Doug Jennings
RE: Performance evaluation

Dear Valued Client:

Would you please take a minute to complete and return this brief questionnaire to me? (Doing so is optional, of course.) It would help me serve you better — and ensure that you get the level of quality and service you want on every job. Thanks!

1. How would you rate the quality of the final draft of the copy I wrote for you?

   ❏ Excellent ❏ Very good ❏ Good ❏ Fair ❏ Poor

2. What overall rating would you give my copywriting services?

   ❏ Excellent ❏ Very good ❏ Good ❏ Fair ❏ Poor

3. How would you rate the value received compared with the fee you paid?

   ❏ Excellent ❏ Very good ❏ Good ❏ Fair ❏ Poor

4. What did you like best about my service?_____

5. What would you like to see improved?_____

Your name
(optional):_____

Company_____

Please return this form to:

Doug Jennings
222 E. Western Avenue
Seattle, WA

Tips for Writing Customer Surveys

- Say "please." You are asking the busy customer to take time out of his schedule to do you a favor. A good opening line for surveys is: "Would you do me a favor?"

- Tell them that the purpose of the survey is to learn what they think of your company, product, and service so you can better meet their needs.

- Keep the survey to one page if possible, two pages at the most.

- Ask questions that the reader can answer off the top of his head without checking his records or doing any other work. If it is work, customers won't do it.

- You may want to offer a small incentive for completing the survey, such as a discount on their next purchase or a free gift.

Sensitive Customer Correspondence

Correspondence that deals with requests for refunds, returns, or credit; resolving problems and disputes; and handling pricing, payment, and collection issues is often difficult to write, but such letters are necessary.

When responding to sensitive customer issues you must remember to keep the correspondence professional and free from emotion and personal opinion. These letters should be models of fairness and tact, and rejections or refusals of any nature should be done politely. Any explanations must be straightforward, definite, and reasonable. Adjustment letters must use positive language — positive from the complainer's point of view.

In some cases the customer is clearly incorrect and it will be difficult not to state that directly in your response, but remain calm and polite in your response. Give convincing reasons for your position and, when possible, offer some help or an alternative. End on a friendly note.

RESOLVING PROBLEMS

Although problems are not always resolved in the customer's favor, it's important to discuss them in a friendly, positive manner. The customer is not always right — sometimes they are wrong. But, since they *are* the customer, their opinions must be treated with respect; their complaints listened to; and their feelings acknowledged.

Format: [*See Appendix A:* Fig. A-1. Simple format for letters and memos.] Typed/word-processed, business letterhead.

Style/Tone/Voice: Use formal, active tone or voice. [*See Part I for more on these subjects.*]

Structure: (1) Identify the issue that is being addressed, (2) Tell what action has been taken, (3) State or explain the resolution, (3) Close by expressing appreciation and reiterating the importance of the information you have conveyed — offer to respond to questions and problems, (4) End with a goodwill-building statement.

Handy Phrases: Because we value you as our customer; Because you have been a faithful customer for many years; Thank you for taking the time to explain; Want your continued loyalty; Didn't meet with your approval; Regret the problem you reported concerning our; Usual procedure for claims of this sort; Have discussed your description of the problem with; Not due to defects in material or workmanship; As our local service representative pointed out; Have examined the items you returned; Investigated the issue; Please read the instruction manual carefully; Repair department has discovered that; While we can find no evidence of the flaws you mentioned; As the instruction manual accompanying your product states; Stand behind our respective services and employees; Because we think there might have been some misunderstanding; Will ship you a replacement; Apologize for the inconvenience this situation caused you; Hope that these actions will be satisfactory to you; Let me know if I can be of further assistance; Let me know if there is anything else we need to address; Please write me or call our toll-free, 24-hour number.

See also: *Part V:* Handling a Dissatisfied Customer.

May 6, 2003

Attn: Brian Heath
Motor Powor
105 W. Allisonville Road
Portland, Or.

Ref: Bricktown Corp. Request
Subject: ED4W

Dear Brian,

In response to the request from Bricktown regarding motor life expectancy and performance at 84 degrees Celsius, please note below the feedback from our Engineering Department.

Our motor product line (including the ED4W model) is designed to operate in the *commercial* temperature range (0–70 deg. C) per the specifications. We guarantee our fans within this temperature range only.

The temperature range that Bricktown is inquiring about (84 deg. C) is approaching the maximum *industrial* temperature range, which is -40 to +85 deg. C. Based on this fact, we would recommend that Bricktown consider using an industrial grade fan for their application. Unfortunately, we do not manufacture industrial or military grade fans.

Please feel free to contact me if you should have any questions or require any additional information.

Sincerely,

Michele Piper
Account Manager

Tips for Writing Problem-Resolution Letters

- Do not show any sense of smugness in pointing out that the customer is wrong and you are right. It's not about who is right or wrong — it's about keeping the customer as a customer.

- Restate the facts as they are, correcting any wrong information or misunderstanding along the way.

- Suggest possible solutions to problems, including attractive alternatives to what the customer asked for but you are unwilling or unable to provide.

- If you can't comply with a request, give the reason why.

- Invite the customer to call you to discuss any issue further.

INVENTORY ADJUSTMENT

The handling of inventory can have significant financial impact on the customer's business, so the situation of inventory adjustment or credit must be handled with sensitivity.

Format: [*See Appendix A:* Fig. A-1. Simple format for letters and memos.] Typed/word-processed, business letterhead.

Style/Tone/Voice: Use formal, active tone or voice. [*See Part I for more on these subjects.*]

Structure: (1) Identify the issue that is being addressed, (2) Tell what action has been taken, (3) State or explain the resolution, (4) Close by expressing appreciation and reiterating the importance of the information you have conveyed — offer to respond to questions and problems, (5) End with a goodwill-building statement.

Handy Phrases: Because we value you as our customer; Because you have been a faithful customer for many years; Thank you for taking the time to explain; Want your continued loyalty; Usual procedure for claims of this sort; Have discussed your description of the problem with; As our local service representative pointed out; Have examined the items you returned; Investigated the issue; As the agreement states; Hope that these actions will be satisfactory to you; Let me know if I can be of further assistance; Let me know if there is anything else we need to address; Please write me or call our toll-free, 24-hour number.

See also: *Part VIII:* Lines of Credit.

October 22, 2002

Bill Power
Electric Corp.
400 Ore Ave.
Aspen, CO

Thank you for your letter dated October 4, 2002. Mr. Johnson has forwarded your letter to me requesting that we provide consideration to your inventory situation.

As per the official Distributor contract, Merit Tech has the option to repurchase from Electric all or any part of Electric's inventory of Merit Tech products existing on the effective date of termination.

After careful consideration, Merit Tech offers to accept the following parts/quantities from Electric's current inventory. In keeping with Merit Tech's standard distribution policy, we will not accept returns of open cases, nonstandard parts, or obsolete inventory.

Part Number	Unit Price	Quantity	Extended Cost
XX12H	4.25	500	
XX12U	4.25	200	
XX24H	4.50	200	
XX8M	4.25	500	
XX9U	4.25	1,000	
XX9BX	5.25	100	
XX4F	6.30	300	
XX4U	6.30	150	

Total Returns

All returns will be credited at the Merit Tech current selling price noted above. Freight costs for the returned product are Electric's sole cost and expense. Merit Tech retains the right to offset any monies payable to Electric against any monies owed to Merit Tech by Electric. An RMA will be issued to Electric, under separate cover, which will contain all shipping instructions for the return.

Bill Smith
Business Unit Manager
Merit Tech Company

Tips for Writing Inventory Adjustment Notices

- Give an accurate item-by-item account in the letter or an attached report.
- Say what you are willing to do with the inventory situation.
- Spell out any charges, credits, or penalties involved.

DENIAL OF REQUEST FOR ADDITIONAL DISCOUNT

Not every customer communication is good news for the customer. Reason: Customers often make requests that are not reasonable. When you are denying a request for credit or other pricing considerations, do so in writing.

Format: [*See Appendix A:* Fig. A-1. Simple format for letters and memos.] Typed/word-processed, business letterhead.

Style/Tone/Voice: Typically written in a formal, active tone or voice. [*See Part I for more on these subjects.*]

Structure: (1) Acknowledge the customer's issue and show that you understand his or her point of view, (2) Explain the facts and the reasoning that led to your decision, and then state your decision, (3) Suggest appropriate action to resolve the customer's difficulty, (4) Close with a positive statement expressing goodwill and the assurance that you value the customer's business.

Handy Phrases: Fully appreciate your patience and desire to work with us; Have completed a thorough investigation of the situation; Have received your request for; Not difficult to understand your comments regarding; Our representatives have completed their review of your; Received your letter asking us to investigate; Thank you for bringing your problem to our attention; Although there is the temptation to make an exception; Because the terms of our agreement were not met; Cannot show partiality to one customer; Completed a thorough investigation of the situation; Have no legally acceptable way to provide you with; Must decline to offer the discount; Our laboratory analysis and that of an outside expert indicated; Please note in the first paragraph of the contract letter; Would simply not be fair to others involved; Help you implement any of the alternatives outlined above; Hope you can understand why we cannot; If there are other circumstances of which we are unaware; Let us know what other actions you would like us to take; Possible preventative measures for future; Could adversely affect good relations with our customers; Hope this is helpful; Hope we can continue to serve you in the future; Look forward to your giving us another opportunity to serve you; Thank you for giving us an opportunity to explain our position; Value you as a customer; Want to continue to serve you in the future; Wish you the best in resolving this matter.

See also: *Part VII;* Discount Offers; *Part VIII:* Lines of Credit; *Part X:* Purchasing Policy Letter.

Dear John:

This letter is in response to your inquiry regarding our flexibility in the discount rate we offer for early settlement of accounts.

Our established discount is 2% of the total invoiced amount when payment is received within 10 days of delivery. This figure is not one that has been arbitrarily chosen, but is based on cost, overhead and profit. To increase this discount rate for all of our accounts would seriously jeopardize our company. To increase the rate for an individual account would be both unfair and unethical. We believe that you will find that the 2% discount rate we offer our customers is standard in the industry.

We consider you to be a most valued customer and hope that you can appreciate our position in the matter. If we are able to accommodate you in any way that is within our company policy, we will be most happy to do so.

Very truly yours,

Tips for Denying a Request for Better Terms or Pricing

- State your current credit or pricing policy.
- Give the reason why you cannot make an exception to it.
- Ask for their understanding and pledge to help them in any other way you can.

RETURNING MERCHANDISE

As a consumer or business customer, you may want to return unsatisfactory merchandise to the manufacturer or seller. Here is a model letter you can adapt for that purpose. Most businesses are eager to satisfy their customers and will respond to a complaint letter. There is no need to be challenging, so use a congenial tone. The problem is a mutual one. If you do not receive satisfaction, consider taking more serious action.

Format: [*See Appendix A:* Fig. A-1. Simple format for letters and memos.] Can be handwritten, but typed is best. Can be on personal or business letterhead

Style/Tone/Voice: Use either an informal or formal, active tone or voice. [*See Part I for more on these subjects.*]

Structure: (1) State all the relevant facts concerning the situation, (2) Include photocopies of purchase orders, contracts, or invoices that will validate your claim, (3) Include a specific request regarding how you feel the situation should be rectified, (4) Close the letter on a positive note, expressing confidence that the reader will do what is necessary to rectify the situation.

Handy Phrases: Are most dissatisfied; Arrived in unsatisfactory condition; Did not work; Expected everything to be; Had been damaged; Have never before experienced this; Need to inform you; Nonrefundable policy surely does not include; Not in working order; Was not included; Were distressed to discover when we opened the boxes; Accompanying this letter are; Am sending photocopies of; Clearly demonstrates that; Feel we are justified in; Has been documented; Have sent a copy of the entire file; The accompanying documents to substantiate my claim; Am returning the defective; Credit my account with; Entitled to a replacement; Expect more careful handling; If you could rectify this situation; Kindly issue us a full refund; Situation seems to merit a; Situation warrants immediate action; Specifically request that; Arrive at a satisfactory solution; Do what is necessary; For giving this matter your consideration; Have always been satisfied with; Hope to hear from you; Trust that you will; Will be mutually beneficial.

See also: *Part II:* Letters that Require Special Handling; *Part IX:* Letters Expressing Dissatisfaction.

Dear G. Smith,

On August 19, 2002, I purchased a widget at Widget Store, 111 Main Street, Big City. On August 20, I returned the widget to your customer service department because it was missing Part #32 and could not be assembled. Your customer service representative ordered the missing part from your warehouse, telling me it would arrive within ten days.

Two months later, it has not arrived. I contacted your customer service department on August 30, September 15, October 1, and October 20. On each of those occasions, your customer service representative assured me that the missing part was en route from your warehouse.

Today, I asked that my money be refunded since I am unable to use the widget without the missing part. Your customer service representative told me that it is not store policy to refund my money because I opened the package and partially assembled the widget.

I am writing you to request that my money be refunded in full. I cannot use the widget without the part that is missing.

I can be reached at the address given above, or by telephone at [your number].

Yours truly,

Tips for Returning Unsatisfactory Goods

- Tell where you bought the product, what you bought, when, and what you paid for it.
- Say why the product is unsatisfactory and why you believe you should be able to return it.
- Say whether you want an exchange, credit, or refund.

REFUSING A REQUEST FOR REFUND

As a business manager, you will have customers asking you for refunds or adjustments that they are not entitled to under the terms of the purchase, or that you cannot provide.

Format: [*See Appendix A:* Fig. A-1. Simple format for letters and memos.] Typed/word-processed, business letterhead.

Style/Tone/Voice: Formal, active tone or voice. [*See Part I for more on these subjects.*]

Structure: (1) Acknowledge the customer's issue and show that you understand his or her point of view, (2) Explain the facts and the reasoning that led to your decision, and then state your decision, (3) Suggest appropriate action to resolve the customer's difficulty, (4) Close with a positive statement expressing goodwill and the assurance that you value the customer's business.

Handy Phrases: Have completed a thorough investigation of the situation; Not difficult to understand your comments regarding; Our representatives have completed their review of your; Received your letter asking us to investigate; Thank you for bringing your problem to our attention; Although there is the temptation to make an exception; Because the terms of our agreement were not met; Cannot show partiality to one customer; Completed a thorough investigation of the situation; Have no legally acceptable way to provide you with; Must decline to offer; Our laboratory analysis and that of an outside expert indicated; Please note in the first paragraph of the contract letter; Found the error not to be with our organization; Make sure the warranty terms are clearly understood; Not covered under the warranty; Warning label states; Hope you can understand why we cannot; Possible preventative measures for future; Could adversely affect good relations with our customers; Hope we can continue to serve you in the future; Look forward to your giving us another opportunity to serve you; Thank you for giving us an opportunity to explain our position; Value you as a customer; Want to continue to serve you in the future.

continued

continued

See also: *Part II:* Refusing a Request; *Part IV:* Refusing Business Requests; *Part V:* Handling a Dissatisfied Customer; *Part VII:* Turning Down a Request for Credit; Credit Adjustments.

John Jones
11 Apple Acre Road
Tomatillo, OR 06101

Dear John,

I've done all I can to retrieve your $5000.00 investment in the oil and gas limited partnership you purchased in 1980. I'm sorry to say, there is nothing else to do to recoup your money.

Despite the risk, and as disappointing as this is, your original attraction to the partnership was the outstanding tax advantages it could provide. In fact, it did just that. During the first three years of the partnership, you realized 50% of your original investment in tax savings. Over the next three years, a combination of cash flow and depreciation recovered another 60% of your original purchase. In total, you have received 110% of your investment in the form of tax write-offs and cash flow.

We couldn't have predicted the nature of the tax overhauls or the poor performance in the oil field that have made this investment unfortunate.

However, you were level-headed about the original investment. Although no loss is a good loss, the loss represents just 1% of your total assets. It will in no way affect the success of the rest of your portfolio.

John, if I can answer any other questions for you regarding the partnership, or if I can be of service in any other way, please call.

Sincerely,

Marty Richer

Tips for Writing Letters Refusing Refund Requests

- Do not beat around the bush. Tell them that you cannot grant their request for refund or credit.
- Tell the reader the reason why they are not going to get the refund they think they are entitled to.

- Say what you can and are willing to do for them instead (e.g., you can't refund the product, but you will give them another product at a discount or free).

"WE NEED TO HEAR FROM YOU" LETTER

Often when businesses need to contact their customers, a phone call is the simplest and easiest method. If they have the customer's e-mail address, that's also a fast, convenient choice.

But what happens when it's imperative that the customer contacts you, but they do not return your calls or answer your e-mails? Send a letter. Getting a request on letterhead in the mail somehow carries more weight, and can elicit the response you need where other media fail.

Keep in mind that you are likely to get the information you need if you make your request very specific. Although it is not necessary to explain your reason for requesting information, you may get a more helpful response if you do.

Format: [*See Appendix A:* Fig. A-1. Simple format for letters and memos.] Typed/word-processed, business letterhead.

Style/Tone/Voice: Can be informal or formal, passive tone or voice. [*See Part I for more on these subjects.*]

Structure: (1) Tell the reader exactly what information you need and ask him or her to send it, (2) Explain why you need the information, (3) Thank the reader.

Handy Phrases: Additional information about; Any information you can provide; Hope that you can send me; Please furnish me with; Some references on; Am processing your paperwork; Fill in some background on; In order to process your; Matter is rather urgent, as; Need this information in order to; Received your application for; This information is vital to; Am grateful for your assistance; Thank you for supplying us with this information; Would appreciate your kind cooperation; Your timely response; Your prompt attention.

See also: *Part IV:* Requests for Information; *Part VIII:* When the Account is in Collections; *Part IX:* Letters Requesting Information.

Policy Number: 1519156

Dear: Insured

UPFRONT Associates has been contracted by Motorist Club of America Insurance Company to contact you concerning the status of your automobile insurance policy and to verify information pertinent to the proper rating of your policy.

We were either unable to obtain your telephone number or unsuccessful after several attempts to reach you by phone. It is important that we reach you and ask that you contact our office within the next three days. Please call our office toll free at 1-800-423-9999 and ask for the Auto Department when you call.

Failure to respond to this letter may result in a change in the rate classification on your policy. This change may cause your automobile insurance premiums to increase.

Thank you for your cooperation.

Tips for Requesting a Customer to Contact You

- Mention that you tried to contact them previously but were unsuccessful.
- Tell the reader why it is essential that he contact you right away.
- Provide a toll-free number or a regular phone number and encourage the reader to call right away.

CONTRACT TERMINATION LETTER

When you decide you want to get out of a contract or agreement, and it is legally possible for you to do so, you must notify the other party in writing, especially if you are the vendor rather than the customer. A letter rejecting or terminating a business relationship should clearly inform the reader of your decision, but it should not blame or antagonize the reader.

Format: [*See Appendix A:* Fig. A-1. Simple format for letters and memos.] Typed/word-processed, business letterhead.

Style/Tone/Voice: Use a formal, active tone or voice. [*See Part I for more on these subjects.*]

Structure: (1) Begin with a positive remark where appropriate, (2) Briefly explain your reasons for rejecting or terminating the business relationship, (3) End with a positive remark.

Phrases: A long history of cooperation; Had a long and mutually profitable relationship; Have evaluated your proposal and must respectfully decline; Need more references than you can provide at this time; Recent price hike has required us to find another vendor for; Simply cannot continue because; Think it is best if we; Think that you will agree on the sticky issues of; Appreciate your interest in discussing the matter with us; Best wishes in all your efforts; Feel our association with your company has been; Please be assured that we have your best interests; Wish you every success in the future.

See also: *Part IX:* Termination of Contract and/or Agreement.

Hello, Diane

I regret to inform you that I must withdraw from the VIP Meetings and Convention brochure project effective today.

Since June 2001, I have taken the initiative to keep your project on track and ensure you were happy with my service. It has been almost a year since the last version was written. I understand that unforeseen events have hindered the project's progress, but I do not want to continue being put off for weeks and months at a time. I do not do business like this.

The half-down fee you already paid covers the writing of the copy. However, usage rights are granted only when the original fee is paid in full. If you would like to use any of the copy in the future, please pay the amount on the enclosed invoice. Once full payment is received and deposited, the copy will be yours to use and rework as you like, even by another copywriter. Unfortunately, I do not know any copywriters in your area to refer to you.

If you choose not to use any of the copy (you indicated you wanted to take a different direction with the brochure anyway), please sign the enclosed Agreement To Forego Copy Usage Rights; you will not have to pay the above fee. Simply send it at your earliest convenience to the address below or fax it to 1-888-888-8888 (eFax).

I regret that this has not worked out. I wish you good luck with your business, Diane.

Sincerely,

Stevie Raymond

Tips for Writing a Letter to Cancel a Contract

- Deliver the news in the first paragraph: You are terminating the agreement. Reference the agreement by name, project, date, or purchase order number.

- Explain why you are canceling.

- Express your regret, but do not invite discussion. Your decision is final.

FEE DISPUTE

At times, customers haggle over fees and refuse to pay bills.

For you as a vendor, this issue may be too emotional to discuss over the phone. Phone call discussions of this nature also tend to irritate customers. The best way to resolve a dispute or disagreement concerning an invoice is usually in a letter.

Clearly state the problem and explain what you want the reader to do about it. If the problem remains unresolved, you may wish to state clearly in a later letter what action you will take, but only if you are prepared to follow through.

Format: [See Appendix A: Fig. A-1. Simple format for letters and memos.] Typed/word-processed, business letterhead.

Style/Tone/Voice: Can be informal or formal, active tone or voice. [*See Part I for more on these subjects.*]

Structure: (1) Identify the disagreement and give evidence for your argument, (2) Clearly state the outcome you desire — if appropriate state what action you are prepared to take to ensure a just outcome, (3) End by expressing your confidence in reaching a mutually agreeable solution.

Handy Phrases: According to my records; Have enclosed a copy of; Have no recollection of; Seems to be an error in the terms of our contract; A prompt correction; A written explanation; As we discussed over the telephone; Correct this oversight; Issue a revised; Kindly check your records; Reimburse my account for; Send written acknowledgment; Trust that it will not be necessary to; A simple clerical error; Appears to be a misunderstanding; Can sort this error out quite easily to our mutual satisfaction; Resuming our mutually beneficial relationship; Would appreciate your immediate attention to this matter.

See also: *Part VIII:* When the Collection is in Dispute; *Part IX:* Vendor Payment Terms.

John,

I've given a lot of thought to our conversation last week and I'm not comfortable with how we left it (i.e., you're not going to pay me for the second proofreading of your Web site but rather you want to barter your copywriting services).

While I agree that I should have confirmed that I would charge you for the second proofing I am stunned that you think I would give you 4½ hours of my time as a "favor." John, that is time I could have spent doing a project for a paying client!

I am asking to get paid for my work. I've made your Web site much more professional than it was before I proofed it. There were dozens of typos and mistakes on 99% of the pages. If you get one new client because they are impressed with your professionalism — then you have me to thank. And that client will pay you a lot more than $157.50.

I look forward to hearing from you.

Regards,

Tips for Resolving a Disagreement about Payment

- Specify the contract, product, or service for which you want to be paid, and the amount of payment you believe the customer owes you.
- Reinforce the value of the products or services provided. If possible, demonstrate that the value the customer received is far in excess of the small payment you are owed.
- Show understanding of their position without agreeing to it. Refuse it without venom but decidedly. Then ask to be paid.
- Avoid accusations and threats, particularly in a first letter.

DAMAGED FREIGHT

Customers who have been eagerly waiting for delivery can become unreasonably irked when the merchandise arrives in damaged condition. Recognize their mood when you respond to their complaint. Include an apology with a promise of compensation or restitution. A sincere apology can go a long way to winning back a disgruntled customer.

Format: [*See Appendix A:* Fig. A-1. Simple format for letters and memos.] Typed/word-processed, business letterhead.

Style/Tone/Voice: Use a formal, active tone or voice. [*See Part I for more on these subjects.*]

Structure: (1) Apologize for the reader's inconvenience. Explain (without excusing) the problem, (2) Point out that this is an exceptional circumstance and that your firm values quality, (3) State the action(s) that will be taken to remedy the situation, and, if appropriate, offer compensation or restitution, (4) End on a positive note.

Handy Phrases: Apologize that your model arrived damaged; Assure you that despite our best effort; Determined that the damage occurred during shipment; Regret the inconvenience; Sorry that the merchandise arrived damaged; Take pride in the quality of; Will do our best to satisfy you; Customer satisfaction is our first priority; Ensure that our merchandise reaches our buyers in perfect condition; Have generally had success in delivering; Have rarely received complaints; Most of the feedback from our customers indicates that this is the first time that; Unpredictable events sometimes occur; A replacement is on its way to; Corrective action will be taken; In-store credit equal to the value of your original purchase has been issued; Please accept the enclosed check as compensation; Please call to make arrangements for us to pick up the defective; Prefer a refund or a replacement for; Will take action to remedy the situation; Apologize for your inconvenience; Are committed to making it right for you; Thank you for allowing us to rectify; Want our customers to be satisfied.

See also: *Part II:* Letter of Apology; *Part V:* Handling a Dissatisfied Customer; *Part VII:* Discount Offers.

Dear Mrs. Holt:

I have just received your March 24 letter about the damaged shipment you received through Green Light Freight and regret the inconvenience that it has caused you.

From your account of the problem, I am quite sure that your request for the $240 adjustment on the damage to the two crates of Valjean Crystal stemware will be granted. A certain amount of breakage of this sort does unavoidably occur in cross-country shipping; I am sorry that it was your company that had to be the one to suffer the delay.

I must remind you to keep the damaged crates in the same condition in which you received them until one of our representatives can inspect them. That inspection should take place within two weeks.

If all is in order, as it sounds to be in your letter, you can expect the full reimbursement within two weeks after our representative's inspection. I hope this unfortunate accident will not keep you from having merchandise shipped by Green Light Freight in the future.

Sincerely,

David F. Miller, Customer Relations
Green Light Freight Co., Inc.

Tips for Responding to Customers Who Complain about Damaged Freight

- Acknowledge receipt of the complaint.
- Tell the customer you are going to take care of the problem and say how and by when.
- Emphasize any instructions or precautions they must follow. Warn them about conditions that would penalize them (e.g., they used the product but want reimbursement for the full shipment).
- Write this letter as soon as possible after the incident.

RATE INCREASE

Especially in today's weak economy, rate increases are almost always unwelcome news to the customer. At the same time, customers are also businesspeople. They know costs go up, fees increase, and vendors have to make a fair profit. Because this letter delivers unwelcome news, you should soften the blow by explaining how the change is justified and by showing appreciation for the customer's understanding. Be sure to express how important customer satisfaction is to you.

Format: [*See Appendix A:* Fig. A-1. Simple format for letters and memos.] Typed/word-processed, business letterhead.

Style/Tone/Voice: Use a formal, active tone or voice. [*See Part I for more on these subjects.*]

Structure: (1) Announce the price increase, but try to soften the blow to the customer, (2) Express goodwill and appreciation.

continued

continued

Handy Phrases: Advance notice of a modest rate increase; Additional operating expenses have forced us to; Along with the increased price of; Are always reluctant to raise prices; Prices will increase effective immediately; Have found it necessary to adjust; In order to continue to provide the best service possible; Due to the increased price of raw materials; Keep prices as low as possible; May be more increases in near future; To put this increase in perspective; Appreciate your continuing patronage; Have been a loyal customer; Is a pleasure to serve; You trust you will agree that; Value you as a customer.

See also: *Part VIII:* Change of Terms.

Dear Consumer:

Please accept this letter as notification of a modest 3.5% rate adjustment, effective May 1. The adjustment is a result of increased costs of raw materials as noted in the Consumer Price Index (CPI) over the last 12 months.

Fortunately, our recent efforts to upgrade our facilities and our utilization of improved technologies have enabled us to keep the rate increase below the 8.7% CPI average. We anticipate no additional rate adjustments for the next full year.

Should you have any questions regarding our services, please contact our office at 555-5555 and our customer service representatives will be happy to help you. Thank you for understanding that this price increase means that we can continue to maintain the superior standard of our products and services for the coming year.

Sincerely,

Tips for Notifying Customers of Rate Increases

- Provide the new rates and state the date they go into effect.
- If external factors beyond your control are the reason for the rate increase (e.g., raw material prices rising), explain what these factors are.
- If you are raising rates because you are providing more value and benefits, say what these are.

REQUEST FOR PAYMENT

Even when invoices are not in dispute, customers often don't pay them promptly.

Experience shows that the longer a bill goes unpaid, the less likely you are to collect. Therefore, many vendors send letters to customers who buy on credit urging them to pay promptly, before the account becomes past due.

Format: [*See Appendix A:* Fig. A-1. Simple format for letters and memos.] Typed/word-processed, business letterhead.

Style/Tone/Voice: Use a formal, active tone or voice. [*See Part I for more on these subjects.*]

Structure: (1) Remind the customer that payment is past due and state the amount owed, (2) Ask the customer to send payment, (3) Note that the customer may have already sent payment and thank him or her accordingly.

Handy Phrases: A review of your account; According to our records your account is overdue; Are delinquent on your March 15 payment; Did you forget?; Just a reminder that we have not received payment; Have you overlooked a payment?; Seems that you have forgotten; Thought you might appreciate this friendly reminder; Your account is now past due; Appreciate your early remittance; If you haven't already done so please send us a check; We are sure you want to protect your credit rating; Will appreciate prompt payment by; If you have already remitted payment please disregard this notice; If your check has crossed this letter in the mail please disregard this notice; Please accept our thanks; Would appreciate your immediate attention to this matter; Expect to receive a payment by.

See also: *Part VIII:* Billing Letters; When the Account is in Collections.

Dear Arthur Long,

Thank you for your recent order of this *Natural Life* video series. Your satisfaction with your video series is very important to us.

This is to remind you that we have not yet received your payment for the video(s) you ordered. Please mail the attached invoice with your payment. Thank you for your prompt response. If you have any questions, please contact one of our customer service associates at 1-800-627-5000.

Thank you for your support and anticipated response.

Natural Life Television

PS: If you have already sent your payment, please disregard this notice. Thank you.

Tips for Writing a Request for Payment Notice

- Thank the customer for the order.
- Remind them that although you shipped the product, they have not paid for it.
- Do not threaten collection, dun, or imply in any way that they are negligent; remember, the account is *not* past due. Just ask them to pay promptly, and thank them for doing so.

Tips for Effective Client Communication

This section provides additional suggestions for communicating with clients in a client-centered way — that is, in a way that suits them rather than annoys them, and also encourages effective two-way communication in which they feel you are listening as well as talking. The result is communication that helps resolve important issues and leaves clients feeling good about you and positive about their relationship with your firm.

PRIORITIZE BY CLIENT NEED, NOT YOUR NEED.

Do what the client wants to do, not what you want to do. Work on what is important to the client, not what is important to you. Talk about what the client wants to talk about, not what you want to talk about.

Too many consultants, freelancers, and service providers in all areas focus on their own agenda when dealing with clients. For example, if you constantly ask your clients what else you can do for them and what other projects you can help them with, you may think you are coming across as being helpful, but it is obvious to your clients that you are trying to get more business from them.

This is not a bad thing in itself, except you end up focusing so much on projects you'd like to do for the client that your clients may think that you is not paying careful enough attention to current projects. A case in point is that of Harry, a graphic designer. "Harry is always asking what our plans are and what pieces we will be producing," one of Harry's corporate clients complains. "Frankly, I wish he'd worry less about what's coming and show more interest in what we're paying him to do now."

Our tendency is to focus on future business, profitable projects, and ongoing selling of the accounts. Another tendency is to put the most effort into those projects that we find most interesting or challenging and give less attention to client work we think is routine, boring, or less important.

The client, however, wants to feel that you place his or her interests, needs, concerns, and goals *above* your own. This means giving your best on every job, not just the high-visibility assignments. It means finding out what the client needs and expects and then filling those needs and meeting those expectations.

In communication, we are inclined to talk and write about what excites and motivates us; we are usually more interested in ourselves than in the other person. If you don't believe this, pay attention to your conversation with your spouse or significant other when you come home from a busy day of work. Each of you is "bursting" with a flood of information and stories you want to convey to the other. You want to get it all out while it's fresh in your mind, so your focus is on your agenda — what you want to discuss — and you want the first opportunity to yak.

In a service business, however, part of your service is acting as counselor, advisor, friend, confidant, therapist, father-confessor, or parent to your clients. They want to be able to transmit their wishes, concerns, problems, and information to you quickly and efficiently, without interruption, and then have you respond and address each issue in a problem-solving or supportive manner.

When you write about what you want, instead of writing with care and concern for what is best for the client, you step out of the "listening" role that is a large part of what your client pays you for. The client becomes unhappy and impatient, even annoyed. Not what you want.

Find out what is on the client's mind, and address those issues first. Then get to your agenda. The client will not be satisfied until he attends to his most pressing concerns first. In his mind, yours can wait. And since he's the one paying the bills, he's probably right.

MAKE SURE ONE PROBLEM IS FULLY RESOLVED BEFORE DISCUSSING THE NEXT ISSUE.

A big mistake many service providers make is not to give their full attention to the topic at hand. Because we're busy people, and our minds work faster than our mouths, we tend to jump ahead and think about items B, C, and D while we're still on the phone discussing item A with the client.

Have you ever tried to conduct a phone conversation with someone while you were, unknown to them, doing something else, like sending a fax, typing a letter, or proofreading a report? If you have, you know it doesn't work. You invariably lose your train of thought, or drift out of the conversation, or answer in incomplete "ums" and uhs." The person you are having the conversation with will sense this, realize you are not paying attention, and become annoyed.

Motivational speaker Dr. Rob Gilbert gives this advice: "Do what you're doing while you're doing it." What he means is that you should focus on one item at a time, handle it with your full attention and to the best of your abilities, resolve it or take it as far as you can go, and then — and only then — move on to the next item on the schedule or agenda.

A basic mistake in business communication is to attempt to handle too many issues or items in a single letter, e-mail, or conversation. People can take in only so much at one time. If you attempt to cover too many things in a single communication, you lose your listener or reader.

Consider this rule of thumb: Each client communication should ideally deal with only one major topic. A letter or report should have only one major subject, and a phone conversation should cover one concern or issue. If there are multiple items to discuss, you can cover them briefly at the tail end of your conversation, and then schedule another meeting or phone conference to handle each of the items.

Sometimes, when handling multiple projects for a client, or complex projects with many parts and components, you are forced to cover more than one item in your letter, report, or call. That's okay, but be careful you don't overload your communication and confuse the client or take the focus away from what's really important.

Ideally, a letter, report, or phone call should have one major topic that takes 90 percent of the space or time, with the other 10 percent devoted to covering two or three other items in brief.

If needed, a meeting, letter, or memo can cover two, three, four, even five items. More than that, though, and your reader gets bored or confused. Better to say, "This is about issue A; we'll cover B, C, and D in a separate communication/report."

What's the maximum number of items the human mind can deal with at one time? A scientific test was conducted to measure it. The researchers used slide projectors to flash dots of light against a black background. The dots were bright and appeared for only a fraction of a second; the subjects of the experiment (students) were then asked how many dots they thought had been projected.

The result? The average person could answer correctly when seven or fewer dots were projected. When there were more than seven points of light, the subjects could not accurately say how many dots had been flashed. The conclusion: The maximum number of items the human mind can handle at any one time is seven.

Is this true? It's not a universally accepted scientific fact, but it seems about right. So don't overload the client. Focus your written communication on one thing at a time. Discuss it thoroughly. Give it your full attention by making sure your writing is clear, concise, and conversational. When the client is satisfied with the resolution or conclusion, move ahead to the next topic.

KEEP YOUR COMMUNICATION BRIEF.

Clients value service providers who keep communication short and to the point, yet that's difficult to achieve. It's easier to ramble on and let the reader sort it all out. But part of your job is to save the client time by being an effective communicator.

People in service businesses tend to be talkers, because the service business is essentially a "people business." Most photographers can talk for hours about the finer points of their trade, as can landscapers, architects, engineers, graphic designers, and others in similar trades.

While the client values the information you provide, clients today want to get it concisely, quickly, in a compact format. Your communications should be concise. This means no wasted words, no unnecessary detours and sidetracks. Write what you need to write, tell the client only what they want and need to know — and no more. Today's clients want the bottom line, not the fine details. They simply do not have the patience or time.

According to Dr. Gilbert, you should not swamp your clients with excess information or details, but should give them just what they ask for or what is essential for them to know. Reason? When you present more information than you have to, you risk saying something that the client will find disagreeable, wrong, or annoying.

To paraphrase Dr. Gilbert: Most businesspeople worry too much about always writing the right thing. The important thing is not to worry about writing the right thing, but to avoid writing the wrong thing. And the less you write, the less chance there is of saying that wrong thing.

There is no rule of thumb for how long to make your communication; let the client's patterns guide you. Some clients like to get their information in written form, and want everything in a detailed memo or report before discussing it over the phone or in person. Others won't read a letter longer than a page or an e-mail longer than a paragraph or two. [*See Part I for more on the discussion of length.*]

SHOW EMPATHY AND UNDERSTANDING.

Your clients want to believe that you truly, genuinely care about them. Perhaps you do. Then again, you may, like some service providers, dislike your clients and only want their money.

You will be better off and happier if you do like and care about your clients. But you don't have to — what's important is that you consistently *act as if you* care about and like your clients, regardless of how you feel. Clients are extremely sensitive to your "attitude" and how you come across to them. In the past, clients would take a fair amount of abuse, even scorn from vendors, because good vendors were hard to find. Clients felt they had to be "nice" to you, for fear you would cut them off from service or dump them from your client list.

In the Age of the Customer, things have changed. Clients no longer have to take guff from vendors; the supply of vendors in many cases outweighs demand, and clients are firmly in control of the client/vendor relationship.

This means clients can be choosier about vendors, and they are. For example, if you are uncaring and inconsiderate, the client doesn't have to put up with it anymore: They can simply go elsewhere.

You want to "bond" with the client, or more important, you want the client to "bond" with you. To accomplish this, you must care about the client, or at least behave as if you do.

Customer care takes several forms. It means empathizing with the client and their problems. It means listening even when you're not getting paid to. It means caring more about serving the client and meeting their needs than about collecting your bill or taking more money out of the client's pocket. It means helping and supporting your client in any way you can, not just in the way you were hired for.

Clients often vent frustration and anger to service providers, and in many cases you may not agree with what they say. It is not necessary for you always to agree with the client; this would be phony. You merely have to demonstrate understanding and empathy. You want to communicate to the client that you are listening, you hear what they are saying, and you can sympathize with their situation.

Have you ever hired a babysitter? If you have, you know you want to feel as if the sitter really cares about and likes your children. If the sitter acts caring and loving, that's all that matters — it's not important that she'd rather be out on a date and is watching your kids only for the money.

It's the same with you and your clients. Act as if you like and care about your clients, and your clients will like and care about you. If you are understanding, kind, and sympathetic, that's all that matters — it's not important that you'd rather be golfing and are doing the client's taxes or painting their garage only for the money.

BE ENTHUSIASTIC.

Clients are naturally enthusiastic about what you are doing for them or at least about the end result of what you are doing. For example, a homeowner who is adding a large addition to a house is probably ecstatic about doing so and is excited about how it will transform the house, improve the family's standard of living, and give the family more space. It's the only addition they're doing to their home, and so, during construction, it becomes the focus of their life.

As the contractor, the addition is just another job, one of many you have this month or this year. So you can approach it in one of two ways. You can treat it as "just another job," which to you, it is. Or you can *act as if* it's as thrilling and exciting to you as to the homeowner.

Doing the latter will enhance your client's satisfaction with you and your contracting firm. Yes, the most important aspect of rendering your service is to do a good job — in this case, to build a nice room. But almost as important is how the client *feels* about what you've done, and sharing in her enthusiasm will make her feel more pleased and happy about your work and the decision to have hired you.

KEEP ARGUMENTS AND DISAGREEMENTS WITH CLIENTS TO A MINIMUM.

Do not give the client a hard time. Don't be a prima donna or difficult in any way. Always communicate that you are working with the client to achieve what they want, not what you think is best.

The service provider rarely profits from arguing or disagreeing with the client. You've heard the saying, "The client is always right." Unless what the client wants risks failure of the project or job, that's true. And really, it's true even if doing it the client's way will result in a less-than-perfect job.

Remember, the judging of the end result of most services is on subjective criteria. You may think your opinion should count for more because, after all, you are the expert, and expertise is what the client is buying from you.

But the client's opinion counts more, because it is the client's money you are spending — and ultimately, they must be happy with what they are buying from you. You earn your fee and repeat business by *pleasing clients,* not by being right. Vendors who feel they are right all the time and must constantly prove it to their clients are usually going broke.

Does this mean you should be a mouse and never have an opinion? No. The client is paying you for advice, and so you should give it, freely and honestly. But then respond in a cooperative and pleasant manner if the client disagrees and wants to do things another way.

When should you fight — and when should you back off? David Ogilvy, founder of Ogilvy & Mather advertising agency, compares dealing with clients in a service business to a game of chess: "Fight for the king and queen; don't argue over the pawns," he advises.

In other words, if you must argue (and therefore engage in conflict) with a client, do so only when it's critical to the project's success. Fight over major issues only — those that really make a difference in the end result.

Do not quibble and quarrel over every minor point or argue every time a client wants to change a word or delete a comma. If you do, clients will quickly become frustrated and feel that you are too argumentative and difficult to work with.

Although client conflicts invariably create tension, the tension can be temporary and even beneficial rather than long-lasting and harmful, as long as you follow these simple steps:

WARN CLIENTS IN ADVANCE THAT A DISAGREEMENT IS COMING.

A disagreement will not offend or annoy the clients nearly as much when they expect it and know it's coming.

So if you're going to disagree with a client, don't jump in with your argument right away with an abrupt "You're wrong — and here's why."

Instead, use a warm-up sentence in your letter or e-mail to let the client know the two of you are going to have a short, friendly discussion about the matter. Say something like, "We understand what you are saying, but on this one point we are in slight disagreement, and I'd like to give you another option to consider." This says to the client, in effect: "We're about to have a small conflict, but I respect you and I'm doing it to serve you, not to give you a hard time, okay?" By preparing the client in advance, your disagreement comes as less of a surprise, and they are better able to handle it.

AGREE TO DISAGREE.

Not only should you tell the client you are about to disagree with him, but you should also seek permission to do so. You might say in e-mail, "Can we spend five minutes later today discussing the pros and cons of redesigning the widget as you've drawn it, or keeping the twin manifold, as I've suggested?"

If the client says "yes," you proceed knowing they'll at least be somewhat receptive — after all, they agreed to let you plead your case.

If the client says no, you should probably accept their argument and move on — they've told you they want it their way, and don't want to discuss it.

ASSURE THE CLIENT THAT THE ARGUMENT IS NOT PERSONAL OR PERVASIVE.

Like you, clients do not enjoy conflict. For one thing, they don't have the time for it. For another, they are afraid that if they argue with you and you lose or get angry, it will adversely affect your relationship and the quality of the work you are doing for them.

Assure them that this is not so. One consultant uses this line very effectively: "We are about to discuss something of major importance to your company. These are important issues, so it's only natural that we will get emotional about them and have a discussion that is passionate, probably heated. It's okay to argue — that's what will help us get the best result." By saying this, he makes the client feel comfortable about the discussion, and it becomes productive rather than awkward.

LET THEM KNOW YOU ARE DOING THIS FOR THEIR OWN BENEFIT.

If clients resist discussing something you think is important, let them know that you are bringing it up for their benefit, not yours.

For example, if the client acts annoyed that you would dare disagree with him, or indicates you are being uncooperative, say, "Paul, I know it seems like I'm arguing with you. But in addition to my service, you are paying for advice on how to do this best. I am bringing this up for your benefit, because I think doing it this way would be better for you. You know, I don't like arguing with clients, because it gets people like you mad at me. From my point of view, the easiest thing would be for me to shut up and not bring this up. But from your point of view, you at least want me to let you know if a design change may hurt the final product, right?" These kinds of messages are fine to send via e-mail — with a follow-up phone call. It gives your customer a chance to digest the information before you speak.

Clients will be much more receptive to your arguments when they perceive that you are making the argument because you are genuinely looking out for their best interests, rather than fighting because of your ego or pride.

ASSURE THEM THEY ARE THE FINAL JUDGE.

The client also will be much less bothered by a heated discussion or disagreement if she is assured in advance that, no matter what is said, she is the final decisionmaker and you will happily and cooperatively abide by that decision.

Explain your role to the client in this way: "I know we disagree on this. You pay me for advice, so I feel obligated to let you know my opinion on this. But my job is to make suggestions and recommendations only, not decisions. The final decision is yours, and we will do it the way you feel is best."

The client already knows in advance that she can win any argument at any time simply by insisting, but when she hears that you know it too, she relaxes and feels more inclined to at least listen to you. After all, what could it hurt?

SAY WHAT IS GOOD BEFORE YOU SAY WHAT IS BAD.

Aside from arguing with the client, the worst thing you can do is to criticize them — to say that something they did or like or bought is bad or wrong or inferior.

But during the working relationship, there will be times when criticizing the client or telling them something is wrong becomes necessary to performing your task. To do this in a way that is most palatable to the client involves this simple principle: *Praise before you criticize.*

Whenever you have something bad to say, say something good first. Always find one positive aspect, point it out, and praise it. People react negatively when you totally shoot down whatever they've done. People can handle criticism when they feel that they were basically right and that you are only offering to improve upon what they did or thought.

And when you do get to the bad part, state the negatives in the gentlest, most positive manner possible. Do it in a way that is constructive, not in a way that is mean or hurts feelings. Remember, profitable relationships with clients occur when the client feels pleased, happy, helped, and supported by you and your service. Being right all the time may give you a temporary satisfaction, but it turns clients off and takes money out of your pocket.

IF THE CONVERSATION IS NEGATIVE, FOLLOW UP QUICKLY WITH A POSITIVE E-MAIL OR FAX.

The fax and e-mail have given service providers a marvelous tool for enhancing client communication and satisfaction. Here's why.

Previously, if you had a bad encounter with a client in person or over the phone, you would leave the encounter on a negative note. The client would be dissatisfied, unhappy, or angry. You would be nervous and fearful that you had done something wrong and that you would lose their business.

Typically, as you drove home, or sat at your desk, ways you could have handled the situation better would begin to occur to you. You'd wish you could go back in time and do the meeting again, using these ideas, but of course, you couldn't.

You would think about calling the client back, but you didn't. Perhaps you were afraid, or perhaps you judged, rightly so, that a phone conversation would precipitate another confrontation and only make things worse. So the phone was out.

What to do? You could write a letter and mail it, but by the time the client received your letter, the negative encounter has done its damage, and your letter won't help; at worst, it may even remind them of that day and make them experience their anger and frustration all over again.

E-mail has solved this problem. With e-mail, you now have an instant way of recontacting the client after a negative encounter in a dignified, professional, well-thought-out, nonconfrontational way. I say "nonconfrontational" because with an e-mail or fax, unlike a phone call, the client does not have to respond on the spot. Nor are you exposed to more of the client's wrath. Instead, the client can receive your e-mail, and then read and consider it at his or her leisure. [*See Part X for more about e-mail and conflict resolution.*]

If their response is still negative, at least you've taken your shot at making it better, and the client doesn't have to tell you to your face that it didn't work. If the response is positive, you'll know it next time you talk with the client from their mood and tone of voice.

While the ability to "think on your feet" is usually lauded as a critical factor to business success, the fact is none of us thinks on our feet as well as we'd like to; we think only as well and as quickly as we can. Most often, the best ideas and solutions occur after the incident, not during.

Well, with e-mail, you can immediately communicate these superior solutions and problem-solving ideas to their clients as they occur to you and *while the need to resolve the problem is still fresh in the client's mind.* You can send the e-mail within minutes of a negative conversation or as soon as you return from a less-than-successful meeting.

A caveat: As we mention in Part X, "Reply Wisely," we do recommend that you wait before hitting "Send" — on either a fax or an e-mail. Give your response some time to breathe, show it to colleagues, read it aloud — then review it again before sending it. It's too easy to write a badly worded message and send it off into cyberspace, further damaging your relationship. Be careful about wording, tone, and message. For your e-mail or fax to right the relationship, it must be impervious to any negative interpretation.

The e-mail gives you a "second chance" to set right what went wrong earlier in the day. The instant nature of the communication is what makes it work. Even an overnight letter or express package will take 12 to 24 hours to reach your client; an e-mail can be there in 30 seconds or less.

FOLLOW UP IN A FEW DAYS TO ENSURE SATISFACTION OR RESOLVE UNRESOLVED ISSUES.

Unless your instincts tell you to do otherwise, it is usually best to resolve conflicts or problems with clients rather than let them fester. When a problem between you and the client is unresolved, you risk having it cloud your dealings or cause the client to become unhappier and unhappier as time goes on.

Send your letter, fax, or proposal. Wait a day or so. Take your cues from the client's mood. If the client is friendly and relaxed, you know he is eager to "make up" with you, resolve the problem, and move on to more productive issues.

On the other hand, if the client is stiff, unfriendly, or distant, you know you have a problem. What to do? You need to get the client to acknowledge it directly and head on.

You simply cannot go forward with a client who starts out in a foul mood or unreceptive state, because he is likely to stay there unless moved, by your skilled conversation, into a better mood or a more receptive state. Remember, the key to successful client communication is not what you say to the client but rather how they receive it. In a negative mood, the client will be unreceptive. You have to correct the mood and get "good reception" before you can communicate effectively with your client.

DO NOT ALLOW YOURSELF TO BE TREATED IN A DISMISSIVE OR INFERIOR MANNER.

While today is the Age of the Customer, and you may have to kowtow to clients a bit more than in years past, this does not mean you need to put up with abusive, rude, inconsiderate, or unprofessional behavior.

Most clients are reasonable people, but some are not. Do not allow a difficult or unreasonable client to bully you. Should you be respectful? Of course. Should you follow orders? Yes. Should you let other people treat you badly or make you feel bad about yourself? Definitely not!

Consultant Howard Shenson said that for a client/service provider relationship to be effective, the relationship must be one of equals, of peers. While that sounds good, I'm not sure it's accurate and viable anymore.

In today's marketplace, the clients are in the driver's seat, and clearly, they know it. No matter how good you are, no matter how big your reputation, the client controls the dollars and therefore controls you.

You exist to serve the client. Therefore the client/service provider relationship is more boss/employee than peer/peer. Vendors who think otherwise are, for the most part, fooling themselves.

However, just as employees have a right to expect human decency from their employers, we service providers have a right to expect the same level of decent treatment from clients.

How do you know if a client is treating you badly? Dealing with them will create anxiety, fear, and nervousness in you. You'll find yourself avoiding contact with them. You'll spend time fretting over thoughts like, "I wonder what I did to get Betty mad today" or "I haven't heard from Mark; he must have really hated the work again." Finally, when coping with this client keeps you up at night, affects your appetite, and gives you stomachaches or migraines, you know things have reached a critical level.

At this point, you try to change client behavior by bringing up the subject of their behavior with them, preferably in an e-mail. This naturally will be a confrontational conversation, but you should strive to do it in a constructive and positive way. For example:

> "Joann, I really like working for you, but there are some things in our working relationship that make me uncomfortable and affect what I do for you. I'd like to spend a few minutes discussing them to let you know the story and see what we can do about it. When would be a good time?"

In many cases, clients do not realize that their behavior has been abusive or makes you feel uncomfortable or unhappy, and when you tell them, they say, "Oh, sorry" — and stop. In some cases, the client may become indignant; if this is the case, let them fume, and see if you can resolve it later. Or they may deny that they are treating you poorly and refuse to acknowledge your feelings or the conditions of the relationship.

Keep in mind that when a client treats you badly, it's not you — it's them. Do you think the client has just singled you out? No. More than likely, they treat *everyone* this way. So don't let it bother you; *they're* the one with the problem, not you.

If their behavior does not change, you have one of two choices: You can continue in the relationship and accept the abuse or aggravation, or you can put an end to the relationship and move on to better, happier, more productive relationships with other clients.

Are you staying in a bad relationship with a client because of you need the money? In today's economy, many do. But understand that you don't *have* to stay in that relationship; no one is forcing you — it's your choice.

If you lost the client tomorrow because he went bankrupt (something over which you have no control and could happen at any time with any client), you would survive, and your family would not starve. Therefore, if a bad, ongoing relationship with a client continues to drain your enthusiasm and self-esteem, it is ultimately not the client's fault. It's yours, for not putting a stop to it, which is something that is within your power to do and do immediately.

ASK CLIENTS TO TELL YOU HOW YOU ARE DOING.

Ed Koch, former mayor of New York City, made famous the phrase, "How am I doing?" Whenever he was on the streets, or in a public forum, he would ask people in the city for their opinion of his performance as mayor — "How'm I doing?" You also should constantly be asking your clients how you are doing. This is the only way to determine whether they are satisfied.

Just because a client is not complaining doesn't mean he or she is totally satisfied with your service. Many clients who have some level of dissatisfaction won't tell you *unless you ask them.* In fact, some may take your *not* asking them as a sign of your lack of attention to client service.

Packaged goods manufacturers discovered this principle when they began putting 800 numbers on boxes and can labels. Suddenly, manufacturers who had received very few complaints about their products were getting phone calls by the hundreds.

Apparently, many consumers did have problems with these products, but they just didn't bother to complain. Perhaps they were too busy, or it just wasn't that important to them.

But with the toll-free number (and now the Web site URL) right there on the cereal box, it suddenly became easy to let the manufacturer know that his crunchies didn't stay crunchy in milk, or that the surprise toy was broken.

An effective, nonthreatening method of understanding clients' opinions of you and your company is to send out a cordial letter with a reply element. Clients can choose to reply anonymously and you get the added benefit of seeing responses from a variety of clients.

Is this bad? Many service providers do not ask their clients whether the clients are satisfied, and one of the main reasons is they are afraid to find out the truth! It's like someone who has a lump in his neck but doesn't go to the doctor for fear of being told he has cancer. This person has convinced himself that if he ignores the problem, it will go away or turn out to be nothing. But of course, we know that isn't so. It's the same with you and your clients. You may think that if you don't hear any complaints, everything will be okay and nothing is wrong. You may feel that asking clients, "Is everything all right with our service?" will cause the client to *think* of problems so they can answer you meaningfully, thereby generating complaints that would not have otherwise existed.

The truth is, however, that communicating with customers to assess their satisfaction with your service is a positive act. The dissatisfaction is there anyway. When you don't know about it, you can't fix it, and it can become more serious as time goes on. When you ask what's wrong, and the client tells you, you can do something about it to repair the damage and get the relationship back on track.

COMMUNICATE TO SHOW APPRECIATION, NOT JUST TO COMPLAIN.

When the only time the client hears from you is when you send an e-mail to discuss an ongoing project or to sell them on something new, how do you think that makes them feel?

Our tendency is to contact the client only when we want or need something, or when it is necessary to transact business or attend to a task we are performing on the client's behalf. While this may be efficient, it does not show the client any level of consideration above the ordinary. Therefore, you should take time out to contact different clients to say "hello" or to let them know how much you appreciate their business.

When was the last time you got a letter from a department store, plumber, doctor, lawyer, electrician, or accountant that said, "No special reason for this letter, other than to say thanks for your continued business, and I value you as a client"? It's rare, very rare. Therefore, here's an opportunity for you to stand out from your competition and strengthen your relationship with your clients.

As mentioned earlier, this type of communication was actually quite popular years ago, and many businesspeople sent thank-you and "cordial contact" notes to their clients and customers on a regular basis. As the world became more hurried, this polite, almost quaint practice diminished and virtually disappeared. But that means it will be even more effective today, because no one else is doing it.

There are many ways to make contact: e-mail, fax, letter, handwritten note, and a sticky note attached to an interesting article. It doesn't have to be slick or formal. In fact, the more personal it looks, the more effective it will be.

Another method is to write several cordial contact letters that are mailed periodically to your client list. If you serve a smaller number of clients, a personally typed or short, handwritten note is a nice touch.

BE POLITE.

Because of the increased pressure and stress in our society, many people have a short fuse today, with tempers quick to flare. If you don't believe this, take your car on the highway, get in the middle lane, and drive at or slightly below the speed limit. People will flash their lights, swerve around you in their rush to get ahead, and otherwise communicate to you their annoyance with your slow driving.

People have gotten ruder, not more polite, over the past decade or so. Do you agree? Do you feel the stores you patronize, the service providers you hire, are nicer or nastier than in the 1990s? And when a clerk or serviceperson is rude to you, how does it make you feel about giving that store or company more of your business?

Because politeness is vanishing, you can gain an enormous competitive edge over the competition *simply by being polite at all times.* "Be nicer to people," advises marketing consultant Bruce E. Davids. "I guarantee, if you don't give me the kind of attention I desire, you won't have my repeat business. People remember the niceties."

This strategy of "be polite" sounds simple in theory, but it can be difficult in practice, for two reasons. First, although many service providers are "people people," some of us are not. We went into our profession because we love our craft, be it photography, design, computer programming, or whatever. And we went into business to make money and be our own boss.

Neither of these necessitates a love of people, and many service providers have said, "I'd love this business — if it weren't for the clients." So if caring about and being nice to people does not come naturally to you, it's a habit and skill you will have to develop.

Second, even those of us who are inclined to be nice have bad days. And when a client initiates contact with us in the middle of one of those bad days, our control over our veneer of politeness becomes thin. For example, to find out that your child has just flunked out of college, and then try to deal successfully two minutes later with a phone call from a client who's yelling at you because he didn't get your Federal Express package, takes enormous self-control. The tendency is to get angry and explode. And since we're only human, there will be times when this happens, much to our regret.

A simple strategy for preventing this is to not be accessible to clients during periods where you are overly busy, annoyed, pressured, or for some other reason in a foul mood. If you have a secretary or assistant, have that person pick up the phone and take a message; otherwise put on the answering machine. Or switch on your voice mail. And don't answer e-mail if you are in a foul mood. Wait until you cool off.

When you have someone or something else take a message, this gives you time to calm down and prepare for the call, no matter how annoying or bad it may be. By calling back, you initiate the contact when you are in control of your emotions, which prevents slips of protocol and lapses in appropriate professional behavior.

There are some days, of course, when no amount of preparation will put you in the right mood. At these times, it's better not to return the call, fax, or e-mail, if you can avoid it. Perhaps your assistant can say you're out of town and will return the call tomorrow. Or you can send a fax or e-mail saying you are in a seminar or meeting but will get back to them the next day.

Just as rudeness can quickly cause a client to be angry or unhappy, politeness, provided it is sincere and not faked, is a valuable asset in client communication.

How do you ensure politeness? One technique sales trainers teach is to "put a smile in your voice." We've learned from the sales pros that when the phone rings, you pause, put a big smile on your face, and then, still smiling, pick up the phone. I know this smiling idea sounds ridiculous, but it works. As one psychologist explained to me, the physical act of smiling does something biologically or psychologically which makes it *impossible* for us not to feel better and in a lighter mood, not matter how harried or upset we are.

Don't believe it? You're probably frowning or expressionless right now. Okay, smile. Big smile. Do you feel the difference as the corners of your mouth move up? Try smiling as you're writing your message. Sound silly — yes, but guess what? It truly works!

IF YOU ARE DOING THE CLIENT A FAVOR, OR DOING A GOOD JOB, LET THEM KNOW IT.

Let's face it. In today's world, you have to toot your own horn. Clients are not as appreciative of all the extras and favors you give them as they should be.

You do a good job for your clients because that's what makes them give you repeat business and referrals (not to mention payment for your invoice); you do extras and favors because you want the client to consider you for future projects.

But sometimes clients don't realize what a wonderful job you've done, or that you've given them more than their money's worth. So you have to communicate to them the value of what you have provided and the level of service they are getting.

You don't want to come right out and say, "Look at what a good job we are doing," because it sounds self-serving. You don't want to say, "I hope you appreciate all the extras we are giving you," because it sounds as if you are trying to make the client feel guilty. You need to be more subtle.

One excellent method of letting the client know, in a subtle way, that you have given some extras or "freebies," is the "courtesy discount" invoice. Here's how it works:

Let's say you do a small extra task for a client, at his request, and you decide not to charge him but rather to do it as a freebie so the client will be happy and delighted.

You should do the work and not charge, but you should *send the client an invoice for it* anyway. This invoice should show the dollar amount that you would normally charge for the service, and the fact that you are giving it free. Below is a model courtesy discount invoice you can copy and adapt to your purposes.

Sample Courtesy Discount Invoice

INVOICE FOR SERVICES   Date

TO: *Client name, address*

FROM: *Your name, address*

FOR: *Service you rendered*

    Service fee $100

    Less: 100% courtesy discount   -$100

Total $ 0

AMOUNT DUE: *NO CHARGE*

THANK YOU!

This invoice can also be used when you do something not for free but for a reduced rate. For instance, if you charge the client only $50 but would normally charge $100, the courtesy discount would be 50 percent off. But you should only remind them of the reduced rate if you have let them know up front that they are getting a special price — this is something that can be written into your e-mail, PDF, or faxed agreement.

This invoice requires no response or payment, but it serves two purposes. First, it reminds the client of what you did for them. (They may not even be aware of what you did or that it is something you normally charge for.)

Second, it creates a higher perceived value of the service rendered. If you spent an hour repairing the client's cracked foundation while painting the home exterior, he might take it for granted. If your invoice shows this free service as having a normal charge of $150, then the client sees you have given him something worth $150 at no charge. He'll appreciate it more and remember it longer.

Notify Clients Early about Any Problem that Arises

Clients hate surprises, if they're bad surprises. So if you are going to miss a deadline, or not provide something you promised to provide, or the paper stock or molding the client wanted is not available, tell them as early on in the process as you can.

This isn't necessarily as soon as you know there's a potential problem — that may be too early, since with some legwork, the problem can possibly be resolved, but problem notification should occur as soon as you are reasonably certain that you will be unable to meet all or part of your original commitment to the client.

The tendency is to delay notifying clients or not tell them at all, since we are quite rightly anxious about the clients' response to the bad news. But from the clients' point of view, they'd rather find out sooner than later. With enough advance notice, the damage of any problem can be minimized. It's only when clients find out about the problem at the 11th hour that maximum damage to the relationship occurs.

As with all order or project changes, the problem should be stated or reiterated in writing.

AVOID TABOO TOPICS.

Some of us keep our distance from clients, operating professionally but in a detached manner. Others have warmer relationships. And some service providers actually become close personal friends with their clients.

The advantage of forming a closer personal relationship is that it bonds you to the client more closely than if the relationship is strictly professional. The disadvantage is that when you feel the client is a friend as well as a colleague, you tend to talk too loosely. As a result, you increase the risk of saying something that will offend or anger the client.

As a rule, it's better not to write too much. In any event, there are certain topics that you should *never* discuss with any client:

- Sex
- Religion
- Politics

These are sensitive and emotionally charged issues and should therefore be avoided. You should also not express strong opinions about nonbusiness-related subjects, since the client may have the opposite opinion, and the difference in opinion can serve to distance you from the client.

Note: A letter or e-mail states the facts more permanently than a conversation. They can be read and reread — and offend the reader increasingly more each time.

In general, avoid negative comments. For instance, when dealing with a Florida client by e-mail, don't complain how humid it is and that you hate the hot weather; in Florida, it's always hot, and therefore your comment is critical of the client's chosen lifestyle and residence. Of course, if a client says he likes pizza, and you love pizza, by all means talk about that mutual interest, share your tips on making pizza at home, or where the best pizza joints are, and so forth.

As a rule, avoid telling jokes or ribald stories. Gentle, self-effacing humor? Fine. But yuk-yuk punch line jokes? No. Why not? The problem with humor is that it's highly subjective: What is funny to one person may be offensive to another. So don't be a clown.

PLAN FREQUENT, REGULAR COMMUNICATION WITH YOUR CLIENTS.

How frequently should you contact the clients you work with? It depends on the ongoing nature of your work with them, your relationship, your type of business. Obviously a public relations firm on monthly retainer communicates with its clients much more frequently than does a contractor who performs an occasional job for the client every year or so.

As a rule of thumb, however, you should probably keep in touch with the client *more often than you think, and more than you do now.* If you think about a client and say, "Gee, I haven't heard from them in a while," you should send that client a cordial contact now. Your instinct was probably correct.

Here's another tip. Do your clients interrupt you at work with calls and ask you "How's it going?" If they do, it's because they need to hear from you more than they do. This need to hear from you may not be required to do the actual work, but it's important from a client service point of view: They want to be reassured that you are forging ahead and making progress on their work, and this is their way of letting you know that a periodic "progress report" via letter, e-mail, or fax would be welcome.

So take their cue. Don't wait to get a "How's it going?" call. Contact them regularly to create/maintain a real relationship.

BE AVAILABLE FOR INSTANT ACCESS.

The rule of instant access is simple: The client should be able to deliver a message to you at your office 24 hours a day, 7 days a week, 52 weeks a year. This doesn't mean you have to be sitting at your phone or computer night and day but that your business should always able to receive and respond to messages.

Why is this important? Because the client is busy, and part of your role is to shift the burden from the client's shoulders to yours. And that includes communication. If the client calls your office but no one answers, or sends an e-mail and doesn't get a response back, that forces them to post a note to remind them to try you later. That's extra work, and it's annoying. The client would much prefer it if she could leave a short message and have you get back to *her*. This puts the burden on your shoulders — where it should be.

New wireless technologies, like the Blackberry, allow you to retrieve and respond to e-mails and (and voice mail messages) while you're away from your desk.

Another thing clients find extremely annoying is to call you and get a busy signal. If you have only a single line, ask your telephone company about the "call waiting" feature that lets you take two calls simultaneously on your line instead of just one. This cuts way down the probability of any client getting a busy signal.

Even better is the new electronic voice mail offered by the telephone companies in many states: If you are on the line, the second incoming call is automatically routed to a voice mail box that takes the message. Again, a busy signal is avoided.

Maintain a Dedicated Fax Line

Business clients prefer a fax machine that is switched on and ready to receive around the clock with a dedicated (separate) phone number for fax calls.

Some businesses, to save the cost of a second phone line, have phone and fax on the same line. When you call to send a fax, a person picks up. They tell you to hang up and call back. In the interim, they switch on their fax so you will get a fax signal when you reconnect with them.

This is wrong, and don't you do it! Provide your clients with a dedicated fax line they can call to send you a fax at any time of the day or night. Why should the client have to make and pay for two phone calls because you're too cheap to install another line? It's a pain for them, unprofessional for you. Also, it makes you look cheap and small time. [*For more on faxes and faxing, see Part X.*]

One other way service providers cement their relationship with their clients is giving out their cell phone number (and in some cases, when appropriate, a home telephone number). It impresses clients when you say, "You know, I want you to feel free to call me any time if you have a question or problem or need to discuss a project. Here is my mobile telephone number." This conveys to the client the impression that you value his business success above your personal life.

Check your e-mail often — twice daily at a minimum, and preferably every hour when at work. Carry your cell phone (and a personal digital assistant if possible) so you can keep in touch when you are out of the office or on the road.

RESPOND TO CLIENTS PROMPTLY.

Another simple rule: When a client calls and you are not in, get back to them promptly. How quickly must you return calls? Again, it depends on your client base, your business, your industry, and the nature of your work.

A problem with landscaping, for example, is not as urgent as a problem with a kidney dialysis machine, so quickness of response is less urgent. Every service provider has a somewhat different philosophy on how accessible they want to make themselves to clients and how promptly they return phone calls.

One successful consultant set up an auto-responder e-mail message that promises a return answer within 48 hours, but gives the name and number of an assistant to call if the need is urgent. A local printer, also successful, wears a beeper, has a car phone, and promises instant return of a call at any time of the day or night — something his competitors do not do. A successful ad agency executive I know has a telephone *and* a fax machine in his car.

Two rules of thumb for how quickly you must return customer contacts. First, by the client's tone of voice and the content of the message, you can usually assess whether it is routine or urgent. If it's routine, it can probably hold overnight until the next business day; if it's urgent, be sure to get back to the customer on the same business day, preferably within three to four hours or sooner.

Second, it's especially important for you to be accessible, reachable, and available and return e-mails, faxes, and calls promptly if you are a subcontractor and your client is hiring you to perform a service that he in turn must deliver to his client; for example, a computer programmer who is writing part of a larger system as a subcontractor to a large systems development firm producing a new application for a major client.

In most situations, the clients expect prompt answers to questions and requests and will be displeased and uncomfortable if you are never available and don't get in touch in a timely manner. When the client contacts you, you should as a rule always respond within three to four hours (half a business day) or less.

PART VII

SALES AND MARKETING LETTERS

In letter writing, there is a fine line between "sales" letters and "marketing" letters.

The technical definition says that selling is one-to-one communication from a salesperson to an individual prospect or customer. Marketing is mass communication, where the identical text of one single prewritten letter may be sent to hundreds or even thousands of prospects or customers simultaneously.

In practice, the distinction is less clear. With modern advances in database technology, prewritten letters can be personalized and customized, coming very close to the old-fashioned "one-on-one" communication of a salesperson sitting down and writing a customer about an important matter.

In tone and content, marketing writers strive to make their marketing or "direct mail" letters virtually indistinguishable from personally written letters. The reason is that mass communication makes people feel they are being "sold" as names on a list or files in a database; they prefer to be treated as individuals. So you should strive to make sure that your correspondence does not begin with "Dear Professional" or "Dear Homeowner," but rather uses the names, titles, etc., of your target audience.

As you read through this chapter, note the most important elements common to all good sales and marketing letters:

- They speak to the reader in a "you-to-me," personal tone.
- They are warm, conversational, and friendly — not a "corporate communication" from on high.
- They start with the prospect, not the product. The minds of your customers are tuned in to radio station "WIIFM" — "What's In It For Me?" Your customers care about their needs, wants, concerns, fears, desires — not your product, your company, or your service.
- They all have a specific call to action. The reader is told what to do next, and why (what's in it for him).

Types of Sales Letters

We all receive many sales letters and e-mail marketing messages every day. With the glut of messages, you'd think every sales letter and e-mail would get thrown away or deleted without a second glance. But that is not the case.

It's a matter of return on investment. If you send 100 letters at a cost of 60 cents a letter, the mailing costs $60. Say 99% of the recipients do not respond. Seems wasteful, right? After all, you've just poured $59.40 down the drain.

But wait a minute. Your product costs $60. So even if just one person responds and buys one unit, you have reached "break even" — the cost of the mailing equals the gross sales generated.

Now suppose you can write a stronger letter that pulls not 1% but 2% response. Now you are generating $120 in sales for every $60 spent in the mail. You have created a direct-mail "machine" that turns $1 into $2 every time you use it.

ALL-PURPOSE SALES LETTERS

Almost everyone has better things to do than read your sales letter. They will only respond when there is something real and tangible in it for them. The following sales letters provide some examples of good writing techniques and can be used as templates for your specific product or service.

Note that the letters are formatted for skimmers and scanners. They get straight to the point by establishing the reader's need for your services and use short, active sentences that are easy to read and remember. They don't just make an offer, they ask the readers to take action, and urge your readers to take action right away.

And they all use a P.S. in the letter to repeat the offer, ask for the order, or offer a discount. After your headline, P.S. will be the most widely read element in your letter.

Format: [*See Appendix A:* Fig. A-1. Simple format for letters and memos.] Typed/word-processed. Business or personal letterhead.

Style/Tone/Voice: Can be either informal or formal, active tone or voice. [*See Part I for more on these subjects.*]

Structure: (1) Begin with an attention-getting sentence that introduces the product or service, (2) Explain how your product or service differs from other similar products or services, (3) Invite the reader to respond.

Handy Phrases: A truly remarkable value; Can now cut your bill drastically; Have you ever wished that; Will be thrilled to learn that; All at a price that; At no additional cost; Can guarantee that; Can save your company; Gives you better performance than; Includes these convenient features; Independent research shows that; Industry authorities confirm that; Is totally revolutionary; Our name is synonymous with quality; This amazing value includes a free sample; Act now, and we'll throw in a; Call our toll-free number; No obligation whatsoever; Special promotional offer; To find out about our new; Will show you how much you can save; Would love to hear from you.

See also: *Part VI:* Relationship-Building Letters.

Bob Lemming
Accounts Receivable Manager
XYZ Corporation

Dear Bob,

Are Past Due Accounts Costing You Too Much Time and Money?

Many companies have discovered that in-house collections are costing more than the delinquent accounts are worth. In fact, many find that their collection departments are actually losing money.

To manage this situation and improve their return on the investment, many companies have engaged the services of Crack Knuckles Corporation to support their organization in the collection of delinquent accounts. Our professional and experienced collection agents can handle every detail of your collections and recover more money at lower cost.

And that's our guarantee, because collections are our business. During our 30 years in the collection business, we have developed and refined a system that is unmatched in producing noteworthy results.

What's more, there is no fee for our services. We simply take a percentage of what we collect. If we don't collect, we aren't paid!

Please review our extensive customer list and feel free to contact them to ask about our efficiency and results. Their satisfaction is a better endorsement than we could ever give.

We have a special introductory offer for you. Try us out for three months at 50% off our regular rate. To receive this special price, you must mail in the enclosed card within two weeks. After October 31, this special offer will no longer be available.

Act today. We look forward to helping you collect more of the money that is owed you.

Sincerely,

Stanley Martin
President

P.S. Our customers realize an average 40% increase over their own collection efforts in the first 30 days! We can do the same for you!

Sales letters are used to market products and services to both businesses and consumers. In the above example, the letter generates a lead for collection services. The letter below produces direct sales for high-speed Internet access.

Dear Charles:

Imagine how convenient and simple it would be to get everything you need to communicate the way you want — including a blink-of-an-eye DSL Internet connection — all from one place. Now you can. Introducing the Blinky DSL Package. Sign up today and you'll be talking, e-mailing, surfing, downloading, speed dialing, all while saving $120 a year. Here's how it works.

Get the power of high-speed Blinky DSL and save $120 with this exclusive offer.

With high-speed Blinky DSL, you'll get everything done in a flash. Like downloading vacation photos, or sending huge files to work in a fraction of the time it takes with dial-up. And since you can connect in an instant, there's no more waiting around to get online. Plus, you won't have to log off to make or receive calls or faxes — you can do it all at the same time on your existing phone line. How's that for convenience?

So sign up now and you can get a Blinky DSL Package for as low as $39.95 — that's a savings of $10 a month ($120 a year). It's just another way you'll save when you get it all together with the Blinky DSL Package. Of course, applicable taxes and surcharges apply,

Make one simple call to Supercharge your Internet experience.

So get it all together with the Blinky DSL Package and start saving time and money today. To see for yourself how the savings really add up call 1-800-000-0000 today and one of our knowledgeable representatives will be glad to help you.

Sincerely,

Rebecca Smith
Vice President, Consumer Marketing

P.S. If this package isn't right for you, just give us a call and we'll be happy to find one that fits your needs. Call us today at 1-800-000-0000 (Mon. - Fri., 8am-6pm).

Should the letter be logical or emotional? Should you appeal to the reader on an intellectual level, or a personal one?

Conventional wisdom says that people buy based on emotion, and then rationalize their purchase decision based on logic. Probably true, but certainly some situations lend themselves toward more of an emotional appeal, such as a dating service for singles or long-term care insurance for an adult who does not want to financially drain his family when he can no longer live independently.

Dear Debra,

Let's face it, the conventional ways of meeting someone special isn't working. With the divorce rate as high as it is, this tells us as a society that we are not meeting people who we are compatible with. If you are tired of having your intelligence insulted by all the *games* associated with finding someone special, then you need to explore Special Someone.

At Special Someone we are the pioneers of the singles industry. We have created the most exciting, most advanced, and safest way for singles to meet someone special.

If you're not happy with your current single situation sit back and answer the following questions that apply to you:

Yes *or* No

- Have you dated someone who gave you the IMPRESSION they were everything that you ever wanted and you found out six months or a year later that they weren't even close?
- When you see someone that you are attracted to, does your conscience take over and make you ponder: Are they single? Are they looking for a relationship? Are they compatible with me? and so on and so on, and you never approach that person because you don't have the answers to these questions.
- Are you frustrated with not having a place to go to meet people who are also looking for a long-term relationship?
- Have you ever tried one of those online dating services and all you have accomplished is chatting or when you finally met someone you found out they were nowhere close to what they represented themselves to be?
- Have you ever joined a matchmaking or lunch date service that said they will introduce you to the "Right One" and you found out later you could have done much better on your own?
- Do you work a lot of hours and don't have the time to look for someone special but would like someone special in your life?

If you have found yourself in any of these situations, then it is time to explore Special Someone. We have a saying at Special Someone, "We do all of the work and you get to have all the fun." At Special Someone we take the frustration out of finding someone special. So, if you would like to meet someone special, fill out the 90-second profile and send it back in the postage-paid envelope. Special Someone will share with you how fun and easy it can be to find that special person.

Sincerely,

Jacqueline Salinger
Membership Committee

P.S. Remember, no matter how hard you are looking to meet the right person, that person wants just as much to meet you. We can bring the two of you together.

The dating service letter talks to the reader on a personal level. The following insurance letter does too. But note how it uses facts and statistics to make its argument more credible.

"People need to prepare before it's too late," says the American Society on Aging.

Dear Mr. & Mrs. Walters,

As Americans take better care of their health, they are increasing their projected longevity. Unfortunately, as people age, they are more likely to suffer from chronic illnesses such as strokes or Alzheimer's. Statistically, Americans over the age of 65 face a 40% risk of entering a nursing home for long-term care services.

What is Long-Term Care (LTC)?

Long-term care includes a wide range of medical and support services for people with a chronic, degenerative condition (e.g. Parkinson's, stroke, etc.), a prolonged illness (cancer), or cognitive disorder (Alzheimer's).

Long-term care is not necessarily medical care but rather "custodial care." Custodial care involves providing an individual assistance with Activities of Daily Living (ADL) or supervision of someone who is cognitively impaired. Long-term care can be provided in many settings including nursing homes, your own home, assisted living facilities, and adult day care.

What is Long-Term Care Insurance?

The federal government has neither the intent nor the resources to fund a national long-term care program. Currently, the primary public funding source for long-term care is Medicaid. However, in order to qualify for Medicaid support you must meet specific financial criteria — criteria so onerous that you will be forced to deplete all of your life savings on the private cost of long-term care before you are eligible for Medicaid assistance.

Individuals looking to help protect themselves against the costs of long-term care must look to the private market, and this is where we believe we can help you — by offering an insurance plan that will help protect your finances, your freedom, and your dignity when the time comes to seek long term care. . .

Our long-term care insurance policies can help pay the costs of long-term care for you or your spouse, protecting you against an unaffordable catastrophic event.

And you'll feel secure knowing that this protection is provided by Burlington Assurance Company. Our company pioneered the development of long-term care insurance and is widely recognized as an industry leader.

Just complete the accompanying FREE Information Request and mail it to us in the enclosed, postage-paid business-reply envelope. Complete details about the benefits, cost, limitations, and exclusions of this valuable long-term care insurance policy will be provided by a long-term care representative. There is absolutely no cost or obligation for this service.

Sincerely,

Rick Tompkins
President

P.S. Don't let the high costs of long-term care diminish your retirement assets, your freedom, and your dignity. Once again, this valuable information will be provided to you at no cost or obligation.

Tips for Writing Sales Letters

- Start with the prospect, not the product. Talk about the prospect and what is important to her — her needs, fears, concerns, desires, goals, and dreams.

- Stress the benefits of your product — what it will do to make the reader's life better. Show how the various features enable the product or service to deliver these benefits.

- End the letter with a call to action. Ask the reader to call or write for more information or to place an order.

MAIL ORDER SALES

A mail-order letter is one that sells a product or service directly from the mailing. It typically consists of a sales letter, an order form, a business reply envelope, and possibly some other enclosures such as a brochure, circular, or flier.

Unlike the lead-generating letter, which offers more information or a meeting, the mail order letter must do the entire selling job: gain attention, present the product benefits, answer questions, overcome objections, ask for the order, and collect the payment. This is the reason why mail-order letters are typically two to four pages, with many running eight pages, and a few even longer.

Format: [*See Appendix A:* Fig. A-1. Simple format for letters and memos.] Typed/word-processed. Business or personal letterhead.

Style/Tone/Voice: Can be either informal or formal, active tone or voice. [*See Part I for more on these subjects.*]

Structure: (1) Introduce your product or service with a statement that will catch the reader's attention, (2) Make a special offer (if applicable), (3) Passionately highlight the benefits of your service or product, (4) Urge the reader to order your product and be sure to explain *how* to order it.

continued

continued

Handy Phrases: Announcing the; Making it easier and quicker for you; Finally! Here's your chance to; The easiest to use, most powerful; The perfect way to cause your sales to skyrocket; Upgrade now at this low price; We proudly introduce the quickest, most convenient way to; Just do it! If you love sports, here's your invitation to purchase; We're offering a perfect opportunity you won't want to miss; Look inside the accompanying catalog for all your favorite; You will be amazed at how much you can save with; Save up to 30% on your current; Buy direct and save.

See also: *Part VI:* "Time to Reorder" Letter.

Smart new ways to cost-effectively control pollution and run your plant cleaner.

Dear Colleague:

It's the world's most perfect pollution control technology.

Zero capital investment. Zero operating costs. And 100% emission control efficiency.

Unfortunately, it doesn't exist.

But . . . scientists and engineers are working daily to develop better, cheaper, and more efficient pollution-abatement technology.

You'll find these advances — first — in *In the Know* . . . the American Institute of Chemical Engineers' quarterly journal dedicated to pollution control in process industries.

When you complete and return the enclosed Free Issue Certificate, I'll send you the next issue of *In the Know* — absolutely free — along with a special bonus gift I'll describe in a minute.

In the Know — The official AIChE magazine of pollution prevention and environmental management.

Since 1982, thousands of engineers, plant managers, regulatory officers, and other process professionals have relied on *In the Know* for practical, easy-to-implement solutions that ensure environmental compliance — while reducing operating and capital costs.

In each quarterly issue, you get clear, plant-tested guidance on a wide range of topics critical to effective environmental management, including:

Filtration . . . biological treatment of wastewater . . . absorption technologies . . . soil remediation . . . regulatory compliance . . . solid and hazardous waste management . . . wet and dry scrubbing techniques . . . pollution prevention . . . waste reduction and recycling . . . handling VOCs . . . incineration . . . oxidation . . . catalytic recovery processes . . . and more.

Answers to industry's increasingly difficult environmental challenges.

You care what pollution control costs. But unfortunately, regulatory agencies often seem not to.

For instance, the EPA recently ordered 19 companies to clean up the contaminated San Gabriel Valley aquifer. Estimates for total remediation cost range from $150 to $200 million, and construction of treatment plants must be completed within two years.

And in the western outskirts of Denver, Colorado, the U.S government is undertaking a costly program to make Rocky Flats — one of the world's most toxic nuclear bomb factories — safe for civilian activity. The cleanup effort includes recovery of 1,100 pounds of plutonium lost in ducts, drums, and industrial glove boxes.

Special FREE bonus issue on life cycle assessment.

In *In the Know*, you find out how to meet EPA demands . . . at a cost that *won't* put you out of business.

Respond within 15 days, and you get a special FREE gift, our bonus issue on life cycle assessment (LCA). See the enclosed flier for details.

A 100% risk-free offer.

As an engineer, you're skilled in assessing risks. So you can see that this special offer is absolutely risk free.

That's because, if you are not 100% delighted with *In the Know,* you may cancel within 90 days for a full and prompt refund of every penny you paid — no questions asked.

And whatever you decide, you get to keep the free sample issue *and* bonus issue on LCA. That's our way of saying "thanks" for giving *In the Know* a try!

So please take a minute now to complete and mail the enclosed Request Certificate today. But I urge you to hurry. We've allocated only a limited number of copies of *Life Cycle Assessment* to give away as part of this special offer. And once our supply is exhausted, it will not be reprinted.

Sincerely,

Hae Jatton, Associate Publisher, AIChE

P.S. Is the phone more convenient? For immediate delivery of your free issue of *In the Know* and your FREE *Life Cycle Assessment* Report, call toll-free 800-555-5555 now.

The magazine offering above is a subscription-based product that appeals to a narrow technical audience, but can be sent to both current and prospective customers. The following fitness video letter has a much wider target audience, but is generally a one-shot sales offer.

Learn how the Jill Lyon Aerobics Workout
can help you look better FAST . . .

Dear Julie:

As a fellow fitness enthusiast I thought you would be interested in learning about a new aerobics exercise program. It's called the Jill Lyon Aerobics Workout Program and I want to tell you all about it — and a special price offer I'm making to a select few friends.

Jill Lyon Aerobics Workout is a powerful total body-conditioning program designed to help you lose weight, develop long, lean muscles, and reshape your entire body . . . **FAST!** This home-based workout leaves you refreshed and alert. Aerobics is the perfect exercise for everyone — young or old, fit or flabby, male or female.

Jill Lyon is one of the most sought-after trainers in Hollywood. On these aerobics videos, she teaches you a special combination of controlled movements that are guaranteed to shape and sculpt long, lean muscles. And, best of all, you'll enjoy every minute of it!

Find out for yourself why so many celebrities are using and enjoying Jill Lyon Aerobics Workout. Without a doubt, this is one of the most effective workouts ever created!

The Jill Lyon Aerobics Program Includes:

- **Basics Step-By-Step Video (30 Min):** This workout consists of several basic exercises that are the foundation for high-intensity aerobic movements. Jill breaks down the exercises step by step. With the easy-to-follow instructions, it's the next best thing to having a personal trainer right in the room with you.
- **20-Minute Workout Video:** A fast, fun, no-nonsense program designed to sculpt your body in just 20 minutes a day!
- **Accelerated Aerobics Video (50 Min):** This workout will get you over the workout "plateau" like no other video. This advanced workout is a more intense, total body workout that's designed to get you results quickly.
- **Bonus #1 — 10/10 Meal Plan:** This plan will help you lose weight quickly, sensibly, and without starving yourself. It's a great way to speed up weight loss while on the Jill Lyon Aerobics program.
- **Bonus #2 — Exercise Journal:** Track your progress with this daily motivational system that's customized to your needs.

Thousands of people around the world have already used the Jill Lyon Aerobics Workout to get and stay in shape. There's a reason it's become so popular so fast — IT WORKS! If you want to look and feel significantly better in only a few weeks, you owe it to yourself to try the Jill Lyon Aerobics program!

Your Satisfaction Is Guaranteed!

If, after trying Jill's workout, you aren't completely satisfied, you can return the videos for a full refund. No questions asked. The bonus gifts are yours to keep.

Order NOW online at www.JillLyon.com or complete the enclosed order form to receive your exercise program right away.

Thank you,

Veronica Beldon
Vice President

P.S. Take advantage of our Limited Time Offer for **33% savings** on your order. You can deduct one payment of $19.95 from the regular price of three $19.95 payments. Remember, you'll look and feel better in only a few short weeks. Order today!

Three easy payments of $19.95

NOW ONLY

Two easy payments of $19.95

Tips for Writing Mail-Order Letters

- Give the reader a reason to order now instead of later — a discount, free bonus gift, or other extra incentive for quick response.
- Have a money-back guarantee. If the buyer does not like the product, allow him to return it within 30 or 60 days for a full refund.
- Add a P.S. that stresses a key selling point. This may be a point already covered in the letter or an entirely new thought.

CATALOG LETTERS

Some catalog marketers print text in letter format (single spaced, in a box, against a white background) on either the inside front cover or the first page of the catalog.

The disadvantage is that the letter takes valuable space that could be used to sell a product. The advantage is that you can use the letter to effectively sell "intangibles" such as company reputation, brand, product quality, or service.

Should you have a letter or not in your catalog? This is a question you cannot answer by debate; you simply have to test it.

Format: [*See Appendix A:* Fig. A-1. Simple format for letters and memos.] Typed/word-processed. Business or personal letterhead.

Style/Tone/Voice: Can be either informal or formal, active tone or voice. [*See Part I for more on these subjects.*]

continued

continued

Structure: (1) Start the letter with short sales pitch describing the products or services featured in the catalog, (2) Entice the reader to look through your catalog by pointing out specific features or unique resources available in the catalog (e.g., market data, cross-reference information, application instructions, etc.), (3) Explain how to order.

Handy Phrases: Best quality you can buy at the lowest cost possible; Decided to bring the selections right to your front door; Guarantee that our handmade products are crafted from the finest materials available; Guaranteed to please you and the many friends on your gift list; Here are our latest fall fashions in all their splendor; Hundreds of your fellow executives reviewed our; Rated among the most durable and practical in the nation; Did not want you to miss out on this important information; Here it is! The catalog you have been waiting for; Our old standbys, proven best-sellers like; This month's catalog gives an even wider selection than usual; Will find an unbeatable selection in; All orders over $50 are shipped free; Call our representatives at our toll-free number during; Don't miss out on this limited offer; Turn to page 91 and fill out the order form; When you decide what you want to order.

See also: *Part VI:* Relationship-Building Letters.

Dear Direct Marketer,

Experts agree. The single most important action you can take to ensure the success of your next direct-mail campaign is to choose the right list.

Every one of the 100+ lists in our catalog has received John Turner's "seal of quality." The Turner seal of quality is only given to names from recent and highly responsive lists of magazine subscribers, responders to opt-in email campaigns, catalog customers, and trade show and seminar attendees. No lists of dubious quality ever make it into our catalog or get our quality seal.

If you test our managed files, you too will discover why so many prestigious mailers use our managed lists over and over again. Because they work! Whether you need to generate sales leads, sell products, circulate your catalog, attract seminar attendees, or build your subscriber or customer base, John Turner's lists can work for you.

Start your next direct-mail campaign with John Turner's easy-to-use catalog. You'll find insightful list descriptions, national and state counts, reasonable list prices, and simple instructions on how to order. John Turner Inc., is one of the oldest and largest direct marketing firms in the country. With over 45 years of experience, our list recommendations produce superior results. That's why 90 percent of our orders are repeat business from existing clients.

John Turner's highly trained representatives care about your business and are eager to help you achieve direct marketing success. For free list recommendations and current counts on lists that can boost response on your next mailing, call toll-free 800-555-5555 today.

We welcome the opportunity to be of service.

Very truly yours,

Justin Lansbury
President

P.S. If you have recent and highly responsive lists of magazine subscribers, opt-in e-mail responders, catalog customers, or trade show and seminar attendees who you'd like to have professionally managed, give us a call. We'd like to make your list a John Turner list!

Tips for Writing Catalog Letters

- Tell the reader how the catalog is a valuable tool for their business or shopping aid (for consumers).
- Highlight your best-selling products or special offers.
- Have the letter signed by the company owner or president or, if a business catalog, the VP of catalog marketing.

SALES-BUILDING LETTERS

A "sales-building" letter is a mailing that does not attempt to sell a product, but rather, generates revenue by encouraging the customer to use more of a product or service. An example of this in TV advertising is the commercials for baking soda that encouraged consumers to buy two boxes instead of one — one for baking, and another to open in the refrigerator to get rid of odors.

Format: [*See Appendix A:* Fig. A-1. Simple format for letters and memos.] Typed/word-processed. Business or personal letterhead.

Style/Tone/Voice: Can use either informal or formal, active tone or voice. [*See Part I for more on these subjects.*]

Structure: (1) Thank the reader for past business and solicit them to order/use the product or service in the future, (2) Remind the reader of the benefits of the product or service and suggest complementary uses to stimulate additional sales, (3) If you wish, offer an added incentive to motivate the reader to reorder your product or service, (4) Express anticipation for doing more business with the customer.

Handy Phrases: Are one of our most valued customers; As a longtime user of our; Let you know before anyone else; Loyal customers like you; Like to have the opinions of our most valued clients; Sending our valued customers advance notice of; Special offer to our best customers; Want to thank you for your; Want you to know how much we appreciate; Great opportunity to stock up on; Have already experienced our quality; Hope you will again choose our; The quality hasn't changed; As a preferred customer you are eligible for free shipping; As an added bonus; Take advantage of our special sale on; Discount applies to your next purchase; Free gift just for coming in; Preferred customer rates; Special pricing for repeat buyers; Fill out the attached form and; Just come into the store and; Note that the offer ends on; Appreciate the opportunity to; Have valued our past association; It's always a pleasure to; Look forward to hearing from; Thank you for your; We appreciate your continued.

See also: *Part VI:* Relationship-Building Letters; *Part VII:* After-Sale Letters.

Dear Lewis,

Here's a deal you'll have to see to believe!

Save 25% on your next 12 video rentals and receive a bonus 13th rental free! This offer is exclusive to our best customers at On the Corner Video.

To take advantage of this incredible offer, simply fill out the enclosed registration form and return it to us by (date). Or you can sign up the next time you rent a video from us.

But hurry! This offer is only good until November 28.

We look forward to seeing you!

Neil Barber
Manager

Tips for Writing Sales-Building Letters

- Remind the customer that they own a supply of the product or subscribe to the service. Remind them of its benefits — the reasons why they purchased it in the first place.
- If they are underusing the product or service, or not using it at all, encourage them to start using it so they get their money's worth. If they don't use it, the money they paid will have been wasted.

- Give them an added incentive to use more of the product or service. For instance, if they have bought face creams, let them know about a study that says it is best to treat your face twice a day instead of once a day.

TRADE-IN OFFER LETTERS

Giving the customer a discount on a new or upgraded model in exchange for trade-in of the old model works not only for auto dealerships, but also for a wide variety of businesses.

Its appeal is threefold. First, there is a cost savings. Second, the chance to get value out of old, obsolete equipment is appealing. Third, the idea of a trade-in communicates the message that the new product is so much better than the old, there's no sense hanging on to your old model.

Format: [*See Appendix A:* Fig. A-1. Simple format for letters and memos.] Typed/word-processed. Business or personal letterhead.

Style/Tone/Voice: Depending on the customer the style can be informal or formal, active tone or voice. [*See Part I for more on these subjects.*]

Structure: (1) Open by announcing the trade-in offer, (2) Introduce the product or service you are selling to the customer, stressing its benefits to the customer, (3) Identify the competing or outdated products that the offer replaces, (4) Instruct the customer on how to proceed with the order, (5) Explicitly state the conditions of the offer (e.g., credit amount, qualifying products, offer expiration date, shipping instructions, etc.), (6) If appropriate, offer added incentives for the customer (e.g., free shipping).

Handy Phrases: The offer we are prepared to make you; Special savings we want to pass on to qualified; Best quality you can buy; Easier to use than ever before; Guarantee your satisfaction; Includes an even more powerful; Making superb quality affordable; Of particular importance to you; Will be pleased with our new; You can enjoy all the benefits of; You can save even more on your; And the shipping is free; As an added bonus; Come take advantage of this very special trade-in offer; Note that the offer is

continued

continued

good only through; Supplies are limited; The offer expires on; Are sure you will be pleased with; Can save hundreds of dollars on; Mail us your proof of purchase; Offer is only to a select group of customers; Time is running out for you to save on; Your chance to take advantage of our mail-in cash rebate offer; Engineered for dependability; Is fun and easy to use; More advanced features; More powerful and sensitive; If you order within the next week we will; Is good only while supplies last; Start enjoying your savings today; The best time to buy is right now; When they're gone, they're gone; The first 200 customers will receive.

See also: *Part VI:* Service Level Upgrades; *Part VII:* Discount Offers.

Fuller Software Competitive Trade-in Offer

Dear Tracy Anders,

Fuller is offering a 30% discount off the retail price of LinNet to all customers who wish to trade in their licenses of competing FullNET connectivity software products. This trade-in discount cannot exceed the original price of the product being traded in (as shown on the invoice).

Products covered by this policy include: NetPrint 3.0, SoftNet, and ProNetNT. Other systems may be covered; ask your Fuller sales representative if you have another package that you think should qualify.

To grant this discount, we must receive a copy of the original invoice for the product that you're trading in, along with your order for LinNet. Within 30 days after your Fuller purchase, we must receive:

- The complete trade-in product (with all media, manuals, and documentation)
- Any and all licensing information and material

Please send your trade-in package to:

Fuller LinNet Trade-In Offer
12345 Ninth Street
Burbank, CA 12345

The above items must be received within 30 days, or your Fuller purchase will be reinvoiced at the full retail price.

The bottom line: You get 30% savings immediately and our advanced new software that will make you more productive for years to come. So take advantage of this exceptional offer today.

But there's only one catch. This special trade-in offer expires June 30. So you've got to act now. After that, it's too late.

Call Fuller toll-free 800-000-0000 today, or fax back to us the enclosed Trade-Up Certificate and we'll place your order without delay.

Sincerely,

Candace Michaels
President, Fuller Software

P.S. You can learn more about the new LinNet Software at our upcoming May 22–25 Conference. Click on www.website.com for details.

Disclaimer: This trade-in discount cannot exceed the original price of the product being traded in (as shown on the trade-in invoice). Please call Fuller for details regarding discounts on trade-ins of multiple 100+ user licenses. Trade-In Policy is subject to change without notice. All brand, company, or product names are trademarks, registered trademarks, or service marks of their respective holders.

Tips for Writing Trade-in Offer Letters

- If you are offering a trade-in in an industry where it is not common practice, warm up the customer to the idea of a trade-in by referencing a trade-in with which he or she is familiar, such as trading in your old car for a new one.
- Announce the new model. When will it be available? What are its major advantages over the old model?
- Encourage the customer to contact you to find out the trade-in value of their old model, even if they are not sure whether they want to buy the new model.

LETTERS OFFERING A PRODUCT GIVEAWAY

Another common and effective sales strategy is a product giveaway. In return for agreeing to buy one product, the customer gets a second (less-expensive) product at a deep discount or for free. Ideally, the two products are complementary or at least related. Example: Buy our vacuum cleaner and get the hose attachment free.

Format: [*See Appendix A:* Fig. A-1. Simple format for letters and memos.] Typed/word-processed. Business or personal letterhead.

Style/Tone/Voice: Typically uses informal, active tone or voice. [*See Part I for more on these subjects.*]

continued

continued

Structure: (1) Thank the customer for past business, or offer a welcome to a prospective customer as applicable, (2) The letter should be succinct and friendly, briefly mentioning the benefits of your principal product or service, (3) Close with a repeated thank you or another positive statement.

Handy Phrases: Come to our store this week and receive; For one week we can give you deep discounts on all; We are celebrating our anniversary; Offer is only to a select group of customers; Your chance to take advantage of; Are actually taking a loss on these; As a preferred customer you are eligible for; Bring in this letter and save; Buy one at the regular price and get one of equal or lesser value free; Free gift just for coming in; Free month's trial; Great prices and free installation; Marked down our entire inventory; No obligation to buy anything further; Receive a free gift with the purchase of any; Special coupon for further savings; Great opportunity to stock up on; Guarantee your satisfaction; Arrive early for the best selection; Come in today for your free; Don't miss this unbeatable offer; If you order within the next week we will; Is good only while supplies last; Start enjoying your savings today; The best time to buy is right now; The first 200 customers will receive; Supplies are limited; This offer ends on.

See also: *Part VI:* Free Gifts.

Dear Ms. Murphy,

Great news! As one of our most valued customers we wanted to let you know before anyone else that next month, on January 25, Maxwell fine cosmetics will extend a special offer to our best customers.

Buy $15 worth of your favorite cosmetics and you will receive a handy carrying case, our newest lipstick in Mulberry-Rose, lip liner in Rose-Mauve, and our famous age-defying moisturizing cream. Don't be left out! Mark your calendar now. This unique offer is available for one day only.

As a longtime user of Maxwell cosmetics, you are no doubt aware of their hypoallergenic ingredients and color that stays true. But did you know they are made of only the finest natural ingredients, which makes them gentle to your skin and environmentally friendly? And Maxwell never tests its products on animals.

To take advantage of this fantastic offer simply bring this letter with you on January 25 to the nearest fine department store. Redeem it for your special gift with a $15 Maxwell cosmetic purchase.

Here's looking at you!

Emma Lewis
President, Corporate Promotions

P.S. Don't forget it's for one day only, January 25. We look forward to seeing you then.

Tips for Writing a Product Giveaway Letter

- Sell the customer on the benefits of the primary product you are offering. Then offer the gift or discount with a statement like, "And if you act now, you get . . . "

- Select as the bonus a product or service that is easily understood. You do not want to have to explain the bonus in detail, because this would take the focus off the main product you are selling.

- Set a definite time limit on the offer with a firm expiration date.

LETTERS OFFERING A FREE TRIAL

Many marketers — but especially software publishers, direct marketers, online service firms, and telephone companies — offer a free trial as an inducement to try their product or service.

It works this way: You ask the customer to sign up for the service or accept delivery of the product on a no-risk trial basis. You then start the service or ship the product.

If they are not satisfied, they may return the product or cancel the service within a specified time period, typically 30 days. Customers who return the product or cancel the service get a full refund of the entire purchase price or service fee paid.

Format: [*See Appendix A:* Fig. A-1. Simple format for letters and memos.] Typed/word-processed. Business or personal letterhead.

Style/Tone/Voice: Can be either informal or formal, active tone or voice. [*See Part I for more on these subjects.*]

Structure: (1) Detail when, where, and how the reader can benefit from your offer, (2) Announce what the specifics of your offer are, such as the exact term of service, or what action the reader needs to take, (3) Sell the product or service that the trial offer promotes, (4) Invite the reader to respond immediately, or offer to contact the customer yourself.

Handy Phrases: Now is the best time to take advantage of; Offer is only to a select group of customers; This week only we can offer you; We are celebrating our; We want you to try us out; Would like to invite you to our; Your chance to take advantage of; As a preferred customer you are eligible for; Free month's trial; No obligation to buy anything further; Take advantage of this very special; Can arrange delivery right now; Don't

continued

continued

have to wait another day for your; Experience the pleasure of; Guarantee your satisfaction; Simple to operate; You too can enjoy the; Call immediately for; Call now to set up an; Don't miss this unbeatable offer; Fill out attached form and mail it in today; Now is the time to learn more about; Offer is good only through the end of; Send today for your; This offer ends on; The coupon expires on; Will call you in a few days to.

See also: *Part VI:* Free Value-Added Programs.

FROM: The UpNRunning Level I Support Team
RE: Get rid of pesky computer problems — permanently

Dear Ms. Edwards,

You can't afford to have your business disrupted because of pesky PC problems, can you? If not, click on [link] right now to sign up for a FREE 30-day trial of UpNRunning.

UpNRunning, the Web's premiere online PC support service, can help you:

- Eliminate PC repair headaches.
- Recover lost or damaged files.
- Minimize downtime.
- Keep your business's computer running at peak performance.
- Easily install new upgrades and enhancements.
- Fix crashes, freezes, memory run-out, and other common PC problems.

Unlimited live tech support for your PC over the Internet

UpNRunning can help you get your PC problems resolved quickly, easily, and professionally 24 hours a day, 7 days a week. No more waiting for a repair person to show up (late as usual). No more big repair bills from costly PC service firms.

Best of all, you get a big discount as a new member if you sign up for our risk-free 30-day trial now. The cost is unbelievably low . . . less than 14 cents a day!

To get your 30-day free trial, click on [link] today. Spend your time running your business using your PC — not running after your computer dealer to fix it.

John Smith, Consumer Rep.

P.S. Accept our risk-free 30-day trial offer at [link] now and you can download a free copy of "UpNRunning Firewall" . . . a nifty little program that gives you many of the anti-virus and security features found in expensive corporate firewalls.

We respect your online time and privacy, and pledge not to abuse this medium. If you prefer not to receive further e-mails from us of this type, please reply to this e-mail and type "Remove" in the subject line.

Tips for Writing Letters That Offer a Free Trial

- If the free trial is unusual in your industry or a big incentive to a skeptical or hesitant buyer, stress it up front in the letter — even on the outer envelope.

- Say that buyers are protected by your money-back guarantee. You ensure their total satisfaction or they pay nothing.

- Explain that they may cancel at any time during the trial period, and if they do, they get a refund and have no further obligation of commitment of any kind.

FREE BOOKLET OFFER

If you have a really strong sales brochure with a lot of appeal to the consumer, you can send a letter offering the brochure free to prospects, with no strings attached. Even better is to offer something that appears to be informational in nature rather than a sales piece, such as free booklets, pamphlets, white papers, or special reports.

Format: [*See Appendix A:* Fig. A-1. Simple format for letters and memos.] Typed/ word-processed. Business or personal letterhead.

Style/Tone/Voice: The offer can use either informal or formal, active tone or voice. [*See Part I for more on these subjects.*]

Structure: (1) Open the letter by describing the material being offered and inviting the reader to order it, (2) Ask the prospective customer to take an active role in discovering what you offer, (3) Using a very light sales pitch, share the products or services you offer that relate to the subject material featured in the booklet, pamphlet, white paper, or special report, (4) Explain how to order the booklet, pamphlet, white paper, or special report.

Handy Phrases: Firm supplies products and programs that are designed for; Gave a great presentation on the newest; Have just presented a seminar on the subject of; Did not want you to miss out on this important information; A brochure that shows the types of programs that; Hope you will review it and discuss the material with; Please take some time to read; Report presents techniques and therapeutic methods; Offering you this pamphlet that explains our services in; The brochure features; Will give you the opportunity to review; Call our representatives at our toll-free number; Fill out the order blank and send it in today; Mail it to us in the envelope provided.

See also: *Part VI:* Relationship-Building Letters; *Part VII:* Generating Leads.

Free Booklet About Osteoporosis

Dear Ms. Stevens,

Get a better understanding about this often silent threat to your health, and promote ongoing communication between you and your doctor or health-care professional. This **FREE** booklet shows you how.

You'll learn: What happens after menopause. Why your risk for osteoporosis increases. What you can do to help protect yourself. How lifestyle changes can affect your health. And what topics to discuss with your doctor. Request your **FREE** copy today!

It's A FACT:

- Osteoporosis doesn't have to be a natural part of aging. It's a disease that can be prevented.
- Each year, there will be more osteoporotic fractures in women than strokes, heart attacks, and breast cancers combined.
- Up to half of women over age 50 will break a bone due to osteoporosis in their lifetime.
- Women may lose up to $\frac{1}{3}$ of the bone mass in their spines in the first six years after menopause.
- Spinal fractures can lead to loss of height or stooped posture, often referred to as "Dowager's hump."
- In women aged 45-69, spinal fractures outnumber hip fractures by an average 3 to 1.

The **FREE** booklet also comes with a $10 rebate offer for filling your NewDrug® prescription, the #1 doctor-prescribed brand of its kind.

Order today! Take action to help protect your bones by calling 800-000-0000. Or order online at www.NewPharm.com/.

Sincerely,

Dr. Judith Bailey
Director, Clinical Research

NewPharm respects your privacy, and so we will use your personal and medical facts in the way that you tell us below. NewPharm will only share your information with companies that are acting on NewPharm's behalf. We will never sell your name.

NewDrug® Prevents and Treats Osteoporosis in Women Past Menopause

Tips for Writing Letters Offering Free Booklets, White Papers, or Special Reports

- Sell the free booklet or white paper — not the product or service.

- Let the reader know they will learn something useful when they send for and read the booklet, regardless of whether they buy the product.

- Avoid mentioning that you are selling the product, if possible. Make it appear as if you are offering a free and valuable service, not trying to generate a sales lead.

NEW SERVICE LETTERS

Sales letters can be used to announce new products and new services, as well as upgrades to existing products and services. People are always interested in what is new.

Format: [*See Appendix A:* Fig. A-1. Simple format for letters and memos.] Typed/word-processed. Business or personal letterhead.

Style/Tone/Voice: Use informal or formal, active tone or voice. [*See Part I for more on these subjects.*]

Structure: (1) Introduce your product or service with an enthusiastic statement, (2) State when the product or service will be available and highlight the main benefits to the reader (you can mention availability in step #1 as well), (3) Close by explaining how to get more information or purchase your product or service.

Handy Phrases: A new concept in; A welcome innovation; Are now able to offer; Are pleased to let you know of our; Awarded the exclusive distribution of; Eager to introduce; In response to customer requests; Is now expanding to; Our services will now include; Proud to announce; Remarkable new achievement; Will wonder how you ever did without our; 24-hour availability; Built around the sophisticated; Cutting-edge technology; Have been completely redesigned; Independent tests have shown; Known throughout the industry for; Make your life easier by; New ergonomic design; Peace of mind; Quality and durability; Specially designed to help you; State-of-the-art design; Using the latest technology; Are available at all; Attend our demonstration on; Bring this letter in for; For a copy of our brochure call; For a free sample call; For more information; For the name of your nearest supplier; If you would like more information; May schedule an appointment by; Special discount for.

See also: *Part VI:* Relationship-Building Letters.

Introducing New Mesmerize™ Multi-Purpose Stain Remover!

Dear Mildred,

Finally, a stain remover that removes stains! You've tried all the other brands — that promise but don't deliver. Now try Mesmerize™ Multi-Purpose Stain Remover, the stain remover that actually works.

Mesmerize™ Multi-Purpose Stain Remover combines amazing stain eliminating abilities with the power of oxygen to help you remove stubborn stains — wherever you need it!

Because Spills Can Strike At Any Time

You will understand how it got its name the first time you easily wipe away day-old spaghetti sauce from your light green upholstery. Nothing is tougher on stains, and nothing works faster.

- Removes wine, tea, juice, coffee, and more!
- For laundry, carpets, and other household surfaces.
- Chlorine bleach–free.

Now available in a convenient spray! No mixing, no mess! Just apply directly onto your stain and let Mesmerize™ stain remover do the rest!

Ask your grocer for Mesmerize™ or call 800-000-0000.

Sincerely,

Samuel Clemons
Director, Laundry Products

Tips for Writing New Product or Service Announcements

- Introduce the product or service. Say it is new. Give the major benefit.
- Give the cost. If it is free, stress that. Tell them they are getting this valuable service free because they are a preferred customer.
- Encourage the customer to use the service or order the product right away. Give them a reason to act now instead of later.

CROSS-SELLING

"Cross-selling" means selling one of your products or services to a customer who has already purchased one of your other products or services.

The logic is that someone who knows you because they bought product A from you is more likely to buy your product B from you — because they already know and trust you — than they are to buy product B from another company with whom they don't have a relationship.

That's the theory, and — it works! Cross-selling letters sent to existing files typically generate two to five times as many orders as letters offering the same product sent to a rented mailing list.

Format: [*See Appendix A:* Fig. A-1. Simple format for letters and memos.] Typed/word-processed. Business or personal letterhead.

Style/Tone/Voice: May use either an informal or formal, active tone or voice. [*See Part I for more on these subjects.*]

Structure: (1) Thank the reader for past business and invite them to order/use the product or service in the future, (2) Explain to the reader the benefits of the alternate products or services, (3) If appropriate, offer an added incentive to motivate the reader to order the additional product or service, (4) Express anticipation for doing more business with the customer.

Handy Phrases: Are one of our most valued customers; As a longtime user of our; Let you know before anyone else; Loyal customers like you; Like to have the opinions of our most valued clients; Sending our valued customers advance notice of; Special offer to our best customers; Want to thank you for your; Want you to know how much we appreciate; Great opportunity to stock up on; Have already experienced our quality; Hope you will again choose our; The quality hasn't changed; As a preferred customer you are eligible for free shipping; As an added bonus; Take advantage of our special sale on; Discount applies to your next purchase; Free gift just for coming in; Preferred customer rates; Special pricing for repeat buyers; Fill out the attached form and; Just come into the store and; Note that the offer ends on; Appreciate the opportunity to; Have valued our past association; It's always a pleasure to; Look forward to hearing from; Thank you for your; We appreciate your continued.

See also: *Part VI* "Time to Reorder" Letter; *Part VII:* After-Sale Letters.

Dear Sondra,

In time for the fall season we are offering our most valued customers an exceptional opportunity to save on one of our most popular labels — the Giavanna clothing line. In looking over our records I noted that you have never ordered apparel from this design house. Perhaps you were unaware that we carry the line. Well, we want to give you a chance to become acquainted with it.

I think you will be impressed with Giavanna's exclusive cotton/polyester blend — it feels like superior quality soft wool but at a fraction of the price. For a limited time, you can purchase a faux wool sweater that is virtually impossible to tell from the real thing at a 25% reduction.

Go ahead, take advantage of the opportunity. You won't be disappointed! Fill out the enclosed order form and we will rush your sweaters to you. We are pleased that you have chosen Infinite Creations for your clothing needs and look forward to serving you in the future.

Sincerely,

Margaret Smith
Sales Manager

P.S. This offer is for a limited time only, you must order by October 30 to take advantage of this incredible discount.

Tips for Writing Cross-Selling Letters

- Lead by reminding the customer that he *is* in fact a customer — and that therefore you have proven your ability to help him.
- Say you want to help him more by offering another product you know will be right for him.
- Name the product. Give a brief description of its major benefits.
- Give instructions for ordering or requesting further details.

Selling by Invitation

Selling by invitation refers to the indirect selling of a product or service in the course of an intermediary venue. The letter doesn't so much sell the product or service as much as provide intrigue to pique the interest of the reader.

The letter will ask for a face-to-face meeting, in various forums, to sell your product or service. When extending the invitation, hint at what your product or service can do for the reader, but leave the details out. An excellent way to interest the reader is to ask a leading question or a series of questions pertaining to what you offer.

Because you are not depending solely on this letter to sell your product or service, you can make a softer sales pitch than you would in other sale letters.

Trade Show Invitations

Some selling can be done remotely by letter or e-mail, with little or no contact between the buyer and the seller.

But in many situations, both business-to-business and business-to-consumer, getting "face time" with the prospect can greatly increase your chances of closing the sale.

But many people don't enjoy being focal point of a direct sales pitch or the intense atmosphere inherent in sales meetings or presentations. So contact can be accomplished through venues that are ostensibly educational and informative rather than sales-oriented.

One of these is trade shows. Although trade show sponsors (typically industry organizations) invite people in the industry to the event, exhibitors planning to sell at the show should send their own invitations to customers and prospects in their database. Doing so increases the odds that an important prospect or key customer will attend.

Format: [*See Appendix A:* Fig. A-1. Simple format for letters and memos.] Typed/word-processed. Business or personal letterhead.

Style/Tone/Voice: You would typically use a formal, active tone or voice. [*See Part I for more on these subjects.*]

Structure: (1) Spark the reader's interest and, if applicable, remind the reader of any previous personal contact or of any referrals, (2) Extend an invitation while offering the reader an incentive to attend. Make the customer want to know more about your product or service by omitting the finer points of your speech, (3) Provide specifics relating to the event, such as the date, time, and location, (4) Express anticipation of the reader's acceptance.

Handy Phrases: Appreciated the interest you showed in; Are once again presenting; Enjoyed meeting you at; Enjoyed our brief conversation; Opportunity to meet you; Suggested that I get in touch with you; Understand that you are considering; Keep reading to find out; Meet your present and future needs; Might be interested in our latest model; Offer a free consultation; Share the latest developments in; Would like to show you; Come to a demonstration as our guest; Demonstration will be held; Discuss your specific needs; Face-to-face meeting; Hope you will join us; Just 15 minutes of your time; Let me know if you are interested; Make time in your schedule for; No obligation on your part; Please indicate whether you are likely to attend; Several points I would like to explain; To explain what it is we offer; Welcome the opportunity to; Will call to set up a meeting; Will call you in a few days.

See also: *Part II:* Invitations to Events; *Part IV:* Invitations; *Part V:* Meetings.

Dear Janice,

It was a pleasure speaking with you on the telephone last week. As I mentioned, I am especially eager to introduce you to a new product that will make mealtimes much more enjoyable. If you have ever been hungry, but haven't had the time to fix something; or if you have ever been discouraged by the clean up that follows (and who hasn't), you won't want to miss this new product.

I will be demonstrating our revolutionary new system at the Cooking Appliance Trade Show in Boston on Saturday, June 5, and hope you can join us. If this time is inconvenient, please call me, toll free, at 800-000-0000 and we will work out another schedule. I hope to see you soon.

Sincerely,

Martin Day
Sales Manager

P.S. You can register now for the Boston Cooking Appliance Trade Show (June 3-5).

Tips for Writing Trade Show Invitations

- Enclose at least two tickets that give the customer free entry into the exhibit hall. Imprint the tickets provided by the trade show company with your company name and booth number.
- Studies show that a major reason for trade show attendance is to find out what's new in a particular industry or technology. If you are introducing a new product or system at the show, say so.
- Consider an added incentive, such as the chance to win a prize by entering a drawing at the booth. One company, for instance, routinely includes a designer cufflink (with its the company logo) in the trade show invitation. You get the other cufflink in the set when you attend the show and visit the company's booth.

SPEECH INVITATIONS

Whenever you or someone from your company speaks at an event, it's an excellent marketing opportunity.

Do not assume your customers and prospects will learn about your speech from materials sent by the sponsoring organization. Maximize attendance at your speech by sending your own letter of invitation.

Format: [*See Appendix A:* Fig. A-1. Simple format for letters and memos.] Typed/word-processed. Business or personal letterhead.

Style/Tone/Voice: May use an informal or formal, active tone or voice. [*See Part I for more on these subjects.*]

Structure: (1) Remind the reader of any previous personal contact or of any referrals, update them on your background and qualifications to give the speech, (2) Inform the reader of the details of the event (e.g., the International Beauty Show), date, time, place, attire, etc., (3) Make your sales pitch by providing the reader with the topic and a general outline of the speech, but don't provide excessive detail — you want to create a desire in the customer to know more about your product or service, (4) Ask the reader to attend.

Handy Phrases: Appreciated the interest you showed in; Am once again presenting; Enjoyed meeting you at; Enjoyed our brief conversation; Opportunity to meet you; Meet your present and future needs; Might be interested in the latest information on; Offer a free consultation; Share the latest developments in; Would like to explain to you; Come to the lecture as our guest; Discuss your specific needs; Hope you will join us; Let me know if you are interested; Make time in your schedule for; No obligation on your part; Please indicate whether you are likely to attend; Several points I would like to explain; Welcome the opportunity to; Will call you in a few days.

See also: *Part II:* Invitations to Events; *Part IV:* Invitations; *Part V:* Meetings.

Dear Mr. Holcomb,

I hope you'll join me at the 15th Annual Florida Flower Show, February 19–22, 2003, at the Boynton Resort. When you and I met last year I had just started a formal garden and promised to update you on its progress. Well, that happens to be the topic of this year's keynote address.

Be prepared to hear from other top-notch speakers who can help you best develop your gardening skills by utilizing the finest domestic and international flora! Plus, you will learn how to make the best use of the latest tools available to maximize your efforts.

As previously mentioned, I'll be giving the keynote address on formal gardens. Additionally, I will give a talk on pest control and another on the importation of Asian flora. The Show is also an excellent opportunity for you to get to know my fellow advisors like John Doss, Louis Nell, and Mark Somers. Plus, you won't want to miss the panel on meditation gardens.

FREE tickets to this year's Florida Flower Show are available by calling 800-000-0000, by visiting www.petalshow.com, or by mailing the Registration Form below. After registering you'll receive a packet with detailed information on all the speakers' topics, as well as information to help you make your hotel reservations.

I look forward to seeing you in Florida!

Sincerely,

Michael Troph
Author, *The Plant Dictionary*

P.S. Tickets for the Show will go quickly — reserve yours today so you don't miss out!

Tips for Writing an Invitation to a Speech

- Say who the speaker is, the topic, the date, and the location.
- Tell the reader what he has to do to reserve a seat. Give all contact information.
- Most venues have a finite amount of space, so attendance is limited. Therefore, urge the reader to take quick action to ensure that he gets a seat.

REQUESTING TO SPEAK AT A MEETING OR EVENT

Public speaking is an effective way to promote your company, your career, or your product or service. There are thousands of groups eager to find speakers for their lunch or dinner meetings. But because they don't know you, your desire to speak, or the topics you want to speak on, they're not calling you.

You can remedy this with a simple "pitch letter" to the meeting or program chairperson.

Briefly describe your presentation — and your qualifications for giving the talk. You do not need to say why you want to give the talk; the reader already knows you want to reach his group with your message.

In closing, be specific. Say you want to speak before the group and ask for the opportunity to do so.

Format: [*See Appendix A:* Fig. A-1. Simple format for letters and memos.] Typed/word-processed. Business or personal letterhead.

Style/Tone/Voice: Can be either informal or formal. Passive or active tone or voice. [*See Part I for more on these subjects.*]

Structure: (1) Assuming your topic is relevant and of interest to the group, your letter lead should have a hook opening that grabs the reader's attention, (2) Next, you want to briefly describe your presentation — and your qualifications for giving the talk. You do not need to say why you want to give the talk; the reader already knows you want to reach his group with your message, (3) In closing, be specific: Say you want to speak before the group and ask for the opportunity to do so.

Handy Phrases: We've talked many times about; I think your members would enjoy; I have worked in the field of [name field] for [time frame]; Would a 60-minute talk on this topic be of interest to your group?

See also: *Part IX:* Invitation to Exhibit.

Ms. Jane Smiley
Program Director
Women in Engineering
Big City, U.S.A.

Dear Ms. Smiley:

Did you know that, according to a recent survey in *Engineering Today,* the ability to write clearly and concisely can mean $100,000 extra in earnings over the lifetime of an engineer's career?

For this reason, I think your members might enjoy a presentation I have given to several business organizations around town, "10 Ways to Improve Your Technical Writing."

As the director of Plain Language, Inc., a company that specializes in technical documentation, I have worked with hundreds of engineers to help them improve their writing. My presentation highlights the 10 most common writing mistakes engineers make, and gives strategies for self-improvement.

Does this sound like the type of presentation that might fit well into your winter program schedule? I'd be delighted to speak before your group. Please phone or write so we can set a date.

Regards,

Blake Garibaldi, Director
Plain Language, Inc.

Tips for Requesting to Speak at Meetings

- Realize that local clubs usually do not pay speakers and you will be expected to speak for free. Out-of-town groups should pay your travel and lodging expenses. Don't mention this in your letter, but bring it up once they express interest in having you talk.

- The groups know that the reason you are speaking for free is to promote yourself, your company, or your product. Although it is understood, it is a point of slight discomfort for the meeting planner, so do not bring it up in your letter. They won't either.

- Even though you are speaking to promote something, the group expects a valuable, informative talk, not a commercial. Again, don't bring this up in your letter, but know that it is expected. The best way to show that you are going to deliver a valuable talk is to list some of the ideas your audience will learn.

- Although you are not getting paid, you can sometimes get other compensation, such as free ads in the club's newsletter or a mailing list of members. Do not hint that you want such compensation when you write; wait until they express interest, and then bring it up.

CONFERENCE INVITATIONS

A conference invitation is similar to a speech invitation. The difference is that the speech invitation is sent by the speaker to ensure that attendees attend his specific talk. A conference invitation is sent by the conference sponsor to get people to register for the entire event. (Conference registrations are the product being sold by the conference sponsor.)

Format: [*See Appendix A:* Fig. A-1. Simple format for letters and memos.] Typed/ word-processed. Business or personal letterhead.

Style/Tone/Voice: An informal or formal, active tone or voice should be used. [*See Part I for more on these subjects.*]

Structure: (1) Spark the reader's interest and, if applicable, remind the reader of any previous personal contact or of any referrals, (2) Extend an invitation while offering the reader an incentive to attend. Make the customer want to know more about your product or service by omitting the finer points of your speech, (3) Provide specifics relating to the event, such as the date, time, and location, (4) Express anticipation of the reader's acceptance.

Handy Phrases: Appreciated the interest you showed in; Are once again presenting; Enjoyed meeting you at; Enjoyed our brief conversation; Opportunity to meet you; Suggested that I get in touch with you; Understand that you are considering; Keep reading to find out; Meet your present and future needs; Might be interested in our latest model; Offer a free consultation; Share the latest developments in; Would like to show you; Come to a demonstration as our guest; Demonstration will be held; Discuss your specific needs; Face-to-face meeting; Hope you will join us; Just 15 minutes of your time; Let me know if you are interested; Make time in your schedule for; No obligation on your part; Please indicate whether you are likely to attend; Several points I would like to explain; To explain what it is we offer; Welcome the opportunity to; Will call to set up a meeting; Will call you in a few days.

See also: *Part II:* Invitations to Events; *Part IV:* Invitations; *Part V:* Meetings; Training Notices.

Can your prepress staff pass this test?

October 20, 1995

Dear Ms. Ratchett:

Can you (and your staff) perform all of the following WRITE! word-processor functions?

1. Insert a text box as the first text box in chain.   ___Yes ___No
2. Use math in every dialog box and palette.   ___Yes ___No

3. Grab through object to select hidden items.	___Yes	___No
4. Build coupon-box lines quickly with Space/Align.	___Yes	___No
5. Revert to the last Autosave.	___Yes	___No
6. Create hanging subheads in text margins.	___Yes	___No
7. Copy a master page from one document to another.	___Yes	___No

If you're like the average WRITE! word processor user, you probably answered NO to at least some of these functions. If you'd like to improve your abilities by learning more about this popular and powerful software program, we invite you to attend a workshop that will help you learn these and many more tips and tidbits that will speed up your production and increase your productivity.

A special WRITE! Workshop is being offered at the November 9–11 "Crossing the Digital Divide" conference sponsored by APL and JIT. The workshop will be taught by David Latner, author of *The WRITE! Book*, the reference guide recommended by WRITE!'s Technical Support Staff. Among the topics being covered in this workshop include document navigation, essential utilities, text chain tricks, and keystrokes for common tasks.

Please join us at this informative workshop on Saturday, November 11, from 9:00 a.m. – 12:00 noon at the Marriott In Chicago, Illinois. The workshop fee is $50 for APL members/$100 for nonmembers. (See page 8 of the enclosed brochure for details; see page 10 to register.)

We look forward to seeing you in Chicago! If you have questions or would like additional information, please call me at 800-000-0000 (ext. 1344).

Sincerely,

Robert E. Crowe
Meetings Manager

The preceding conference invitation used as its hook the mastering of a specific product and the intricacies of its use. The following invitation is for an informational conference and is designed to sell specific business knowledge.

Dear Ms. Nikols:

This year's conference, Menu for the Mind, promises to deliver the principles and techniques used by proven industry leaders to give your company the ideas, experiences, and motivation that you will put to use in hundreds of productive and profitable ways back home.

We encourage you to take full advantage of the unique atmosphere of the Management Conference. We hope you'll attend the general sessions to hear the top names that have been highlighted in all our brochures. And, we know that the breakout sessions will put you in touch with great ideas for systems and savings that will be well worth the cost of this trip to Tampa. And we also want you to take advantage of the opportunity to meet and develop relationships with the finest group of printers, business leaders, and consultants in our industry.

Each day of the conference contains a full schedule of educational, as well as social, events. Enjoy the brilliance of some of the finest minds around, but we also hope you take the time to enjoy the brilliance of the beautiful surroundings with old friends and new acquaintances.

If you decide to attend please let our staff know if we can make your stay more enjoyable. If you need Information, assistance, or answers to any questions, please visit our registration desk, which will be open throughout the conference.

Here's hoping you will join us.

Sincerely,

Timothy Ryan
Director
Center for Continuing Education

Save $25.00 off the registration fee. See details below.

Tips for Writing Conference Invitations

- Offer an "Early Bird" discount of 10% or more if they register before a certain date.

- There are many conferences in every industry. Make the case for why yours is a "must-attend" event. Highlight special sessions, new features, and famous speakers.

- Either in the letter or in a separate enclosure (e.g., a conference brochure), be sure to cover these important topics: the theme or topic of the conference; the title, contents, and speakers for each session; who should attend; what they will learn; how they will benefit.

- Don't forget the nitty-gritty details: hotel, dates, hours, how to make reservations, payment, and cancellation policy.

SEMINAR INVITATIONS

Seminars are another common marketing tool. When the purpose of the seminar is to sell people a product or service (e.g., timeshares, baby furniture, computer software, financial services), the event is usually brief (one to three hours) and free. The goal is to make money from product or service sales, not the seminar itself.

Another situation you may face is inviting people to a seminar for which you want to charge a tuition fee. Paid seminars sell information, rather than a physical product or service and primarily make money from the seminar registrations, although, of course, any tangential sales are welcome (e.g., from consulting assignments or product sales.)

Format: [*See Appendix A:* Fig. A-1. Simple format for letters and memos.] Typed/word-processed. Business or personal letterhead.

Style/Tone/Voice: Can be either informal or formal, active tone or voice. [*See Part I for more on these subjects.*]

Structure: (1) Spark the reader's interest and, if applicable, remind the reader of any previous personal contact or of any referrals, (2) Extend an invitation while offering the reader an incentive to attend — make the customer want to know more about your product or service by omitting the finer points of your speech, (3) Provide specifics relating to the event, such as the date, time, and location, (4) Express anticipation of the reader's acceptance.

Handy Phrases: Appreciated the interest you showed in; Are once again presenting; Enjoyed meeting you at; Enjoyed our brief conversation; Opportunity to meet you; Suggested that I get in touch with you; Understand that you are considering; Keep reading to find out; Meet your present and future needs; Might be interested in our latest model; Offer a free consultation; Share the latest developments in; Would like to show you; Come to a demonstration as our guest; Demonstration will be held; Discuss your specific needs; Face-to-face meeting; Hope you will join us; Just 15 minutes of your time; Let me know if you are interested; Make time in your schedule for; No obligation on your part; Please indicate whether you are likely to attend; Several points I would like to explain; To explain what it is we offer; Welcome the opportunity to; Will call to set up a meeting; Will call you in a few days

See also: *Part II:* Invitations to Events; *Part IV:* Invitations; *Part V:* Meetings.

Below is an example of a free seminar that provides free investment advice. The advice is designed to be a thinly veiled sales pitch for the trading and investment services offered by the seminar sponsor.

August 5, 2002

Mr. Charles Wilkers
162 President Ave
Waterford, NJ 12345

Dear Mr. Wilkers:

Quality and diversification have always been the cornerstone of a secure investment portfolio. Safeguarding your assets is always significantly important and maximizing the return on your investments should be particularly important.

Over the past <u>four decades</u>, MENTOR has developed three simple investments that include: 1) High Yielding Liquid Cash Investments; 2) Specific Marketable Securities; and 3) Local Income-Producing Real Estate.

Most people have an understanding of cash and marketable securities; very few people, however, have a good understanding of the values of a real estate investment. We have specialized in providing income-producing real estate investments for our clients over the past <u>40 years</u>. Over the years, we have found income-producing real estate investments, specifically local apartment buildings, to be a valuable part of our clients' investment portfolio. It provides a number of great benefits including, <u>tax-free income additional reduction of income taxes and tax-free-capital gains from appreciation and mortgage amortization</u>. Benefits can be even greater for senior citizens. Recently, real estate values have increased dramatically and there are no indications that this will not continue. At the same time the general stock market has lost considerable ground. What better time to diversify your portfolio and take advantage of this wonderful opportunity than now?

Having over <u>40 years</u> of experience in investments and taxation, my firm is in a perfect position to work with you on investing a portion of your assets in an income-producing real estate investment. I have often said that if I had to pick only one asset to invest in it would be real estate. I consider it to be the finest investment and yet the least understood. <u>It is possible to receive 20% or more as returns on investments. How? Come and find out!</u>

To discuss this in more detail, I will be conducting a <u>free investment seminar</u>, as indicated below, which will more thoroughly describe how these investments work

As we do not charge for consultations, you may want to take advantage of this opportunity to discuss your particular financial situation with us and please note that you are in no way obligated to make any commitments. Thank you so much for your time and attention: I look forward to meeting with you at the seminar or in my office to create opportunities and solve problems.

Sincerely,

Fred Dryer, President

This letter is a special invitation to join us at a <u>FREE</u> seminar to be held at the <u>Marriott Hotel in Park Ridge, NJ on Thursday. August 15th at 7:00 P.M.</u> If you are interested in attending this seminar, future ones, or coming in to the office for a free consultation, please call Constance Well at 555-555-5555 to register as soon as possible, so we can reserve you a seat.

Below is an example of a fee-based seminar that provides professional training in management techniques. The product is the knowledge that is being taught in the seminar.

Dear Bernard,

No doubt you have heard or read how Seven Pillars is reemerging as a popular management technique. Its growing popularity is spawning variations in techniques, exaggerated claims, and a legion of new consultants. For this reason, the Center for Continuing Development at Anderson College is pleased to sponsor *Seven Pillars Basics, a* one-day executive briefing that will help you evaluate how (and if) your organization can benefit from the Seven Pillars approach.

A true expert on the subject, Frank Black, will facilitate our briefing. Mr. Black was one of the original architects of Seven Pillars when it all started at GenCont in the 1980s. He has led Seven Pillars implementations at numerous Fortune 500 companies; Seven Pillars has been a remarkable change agent for these companies and, with Frank's leadership, they have achieved over $1 billion in documented savings to date.

At *Seven Pillars Basics,* you will learn how to:

- Determine when and where Seven Pillars is an appropriate tactical approach for your organization
- Establish leadership and organizational prerequisites for Seven Pillars success
- Sustain the longterm operational and strategic gains Seven Pillars can produce

This one-day executive briefing will be held on October 31st in New Brunswick, NJ, and November 1st in Bergon County, NJ, from 9:00 a.m. to 4:30 p.m. The fee is $595 per person, including lunch and all workshop materials. Groups of three or more qualify for a discounted price of $495 per person. To register call 555-555-5555 or you may fax the attached registration form to 555-555-5000.

I hope you will join us as we explore how Seven Pillars can help you and your organization achieve your business goals.

Sincerely,

Richard Baldwin
Executive Director — Continuing Education & Distance Learning

Tips for Writing Seminar Invitations

- State the topic and why it is important for the reader to be up to date in it.
- Give a detailed description, preferably in bullet form, of the topics to be covered (this is often done in an accompanying brochure or flier).
- Establish your credentials for being the seminar leader. Describe the accomplishments and background of your seminar presenter. Name prestigious companies who have already attended the seminar, and include testimonials from them.
- For a free seminar, notify the reader that seating is limited, so they must call and reserve a space.
- In a fee-based seminar, advise the reader of any degree or certificate that they will receive upon successful completion of the course.

BOOT CAMP INVITATIONS

A boot camp is an intensive, long-format seminar on a specialized topic. Boot camps are typically (but not always) multiday events featuring half a dozen or so expert speakers. The attendees who pay are usually highly motivated with a strong interest in the topic.

The topics are typically related to business success, wealth, or self-improvement. Attendees pay a hefty tuition fee, usually out of their own pocket rather than a corporate expense account, since the event is usually aimed at personal gain rather than benefiting an employer.

Format: [*See Appendix A:* Fig. A-1. Simple format for letters and memos.] Typed/word-processed. Business or personal letterhead.

Style/Tone/Voice: Can be informal or formal, use active tone or voice. [*See Part I for more on these subjects.*]

Structure: (1) Kindle the reader's interest and, if applicable, remind the reader of any previous personal contact or of any referrals, (2) Extend an invitation while offering the reader an incentive to attend. Make the customer want to know more about your product or service by omitting the finer points of the seminar, (3) Provide specifics relating to the event, such as the date, time, and location, (4) Express anticipation of the reader's acceptance.

Handy Phrases: Appreciated the interest you showed in; Are once again presenting; Enjoyed meeting you at; Enjoyed our brief conversation; Opportunity to meet you; Suggested that I get in touch with you; Understand that you are considering; Keep reading to find out; Meet your present and future needs; Might be interested in our latest model; Offer a free consultation; Share the latest developments in; Would like to show you; Come to a demonstration as our guest; Demonstration will be held; Discuss your specific needs; Face-to-face meeting; Hope you will join us; Just 15 minutes of your time; Let me know if you are interested; Make time in your schedule for; No obligation on your part; Please indicate whether you are likely to attend; Several points I would like to explain; To explain what it is we offer; Welcome the opportunity to; Will call to set up a meeting; Will call you in a few days.

See also: *Part II:* Invitations to Events; *Part IV:* Invitations; *Part V:* Meetings.

Dear Lauren:

It's here. The 2003 Kick-off-the-New-Year Experience. Prepare to take home fresh business-boosting insights. Brand new strategies. An unforgettable happening. Plus a review of proven ways that work.

Get your body to Paducah January 2, 2003. Be part of a memorable adventure.

Only at this January adventure do I let myself fully out, eyeball-to-eyeball with you. Here's where you harvest ideas I've been refining for months.

The enclosed information tells you exactly what you get. What it doesn't tell you is the positive delight you feel with your experience.

Attend with confidence that you're to receive transcendent value. And you alone are the judge of the take-home value you receive. You get a better-than-money-back guarantee six months to use the new strategies. Then, all your tuition back, 100% of the tuition fee, if you don't perceive value-plus when you do what I say.

Have you been at previous January Boot Camp experiences? If so, your Registration Application gets you in at 50% off. If not, know that you not only get superb value now, when you return in January 2003, you invest less and get even more. You meet old friends and make new ones. You have lots of time to rekindle friendships with your fellow Boot Campers.

Space is limited. Last year we actually sold out. Please send in your Reservation Application today. You get the early bird reduced fee for registering by 1 November 2002.

Get an unforgettable start on the new millennium. Reserve your space while you still can. Do it now. Right now!

Kindest regards,

Burt Dubin

P.S. In the first segment I show you how to produce more powerful programs that thrill and satisfy your audiences while delighting clients who engage you. This alone is worth 100 times the tuition fee for Boot Camp VI.

Let nothing stand in your way. Do whatever it takes. Get a second mortgage. Sell the car. Hock your kids.

Tips for Writing Invitations to Boot Camps

- Be ultraenthusiastic. These are high-energy events, and you must create high enthusiasm in the readers to convince them to attend.
- Give success stories of others who attended past boot camps and achieved outstanding results.
- Show the benefits. These must be big, life-changing benefits — financial independence, happy family, great relationships. If the readers do not believe you can help them get these benefits, they will not give thousands of dollars and several days of their time to attend your event.

AUDIO CONFERENCE INVITATIONS

Because people are so busy today, but also because of the increasing inconvenience of air travel in our post-9/11 age, alternatives to in-person, live seminars have emerged. The most popular is the teleseminar or audio conference, in which attendees dial into a special number to hear the presentation on the phone.

Format: [*See Appendix A:* Fig. A-1. Simple format for letters and memos.] Typed/word-processed. Business or personal letterhead.

Style/Tone/Voice: Can be informal or formal, use active tone or voice. [*See Part I for more on these subjects.*]

Structure: (1) Open with a brief statement of the reason for the conference, (2) Discuss what the conference will cover and why people should attend, (3) Reveal who will be involved in the discussion and whether or not there will be the opportunity for Q&A, (4) Offer the details of the conference, (5) Close with a reiteration of the invitation to participate.

Handy Phrases: From the privacy and comfort of your own office; No need to hassle with travel arrangements and expenses; Cutting-edge format; Post-millennium technology; Opportunity to access conference yet never leave your office; Listen in as; You'll be able to pose questions.

See also: *Part II:* Invitations to Events; *Part IV:* Invitations; *Part V:* Meetings.

Dear Member,

Our community is growing and changing every day. Each week new permit requests, business license applications, and exemption requests come before the city council. Exercise your rights as a concerned community member and join us for an audio conference on February 3rd.

Listen as three experts on community development discuss positive neighborhood growth. Ask questions as they review their experiences in reversing the negative trends of the Langley Street Neighborhood and its emergence as the premier example of revitalization in the city.

This conference will cover channeling volunteer activities, organizing participation in zoning decisions, and incorporating neighborhood associations. Don't miss the opportunity to participate in this lively discussion. You'll hear how the panelists built their success story and then will be given the opportunity to ask questions that will help us tailor the future of this neighborhood.

Please join these three local experts.

- Jennifer Smithe, Ph.D., Chair, Institute for Development Strategies, State University. Dr. Smith was instrumental in supporting and guiding the Langley Street Neighborhood through his knowledge and experience of government relations and public affairs.

- John Block, President Langley Street Neighborhood Association. Mr. Block has been involved in this neighborhood development project for over 15 years. He was one of the original members of the informal neighborhood committee that evolved into the current neighborhood association.
- Jane Street, J.D., is an attorney with Local Law Offices. She lives in the Langley Street Neighborhood and worked on the committee to draft the local covenants and create the formal neighborhood association.

Date: February 3rd

Time: Noon

Cost: Free

Place: Your home or office

Join us for this free conference. We hope that you'll be able to take this lunch break to learn more about the community job of revitalizing a valued neighborhood.

Sincerely,

Director of Neighborhood Improvement Club

Tips for Writing Letters Inviting Prospects to Teleseminars

- Create a sense of excitement about the topic, the speaker, and the event. Make it seem important and exclusive.
- Offer a bonus gift for registering early.
- Point out that they can attend the teleseminar without leaving their home or office. Stress the convenience and savings in time and travel costs.

WEBCAST INVITATIONS

Another type of seminar that does not require travel or face-to-face meeting between the attendees and the speaker is the online seminar, commonly known as a Webcast or Webinar.

As with a teleseminar, participants dial into a special number to listen to the audio portion via telephone. But in addition, they can view the speaker's PowerPoint presentation online by going to a special URL (Web address).

Format: [*See Appendix A:* Fig. A-1. Simple format for letters and memos.] Typed/word-processed. Business or personal letterhead.

Style/Tone/Voice: Can be informal or formal, use active tone or voice. [*See Part I for more on these subjects.*]

Structure: (1) Open with a brief statement of the reason for the Webcast, (2) Discuss what the conference will cover and why people should attend, (3) Reveal who will be involved in the discussion and whether or not there will be the opportunity for Q&A, (4) Offer the details of the conference, (5) Close with a reiteration of the invitation to participate.

Handy Phrases: From the privacy and comfort of your own office; No need to hassle with travel arrangements and expenses; Cutting-edge format; Post-millennium technology: Opportunity to access conference yet never leave your office.

See also: *Part II:* Invitations to Events; *Part IV:* Invitations; *Part V:* Meetings.

You're invited to attend a FREE Enduro Audio/Web Seminar . . .

"Implementing a Collaborative Extranet to Enhance Customer Satisfaction and Increase Sales"

Space on this Audio/Web Seminar is limited. To register online, visit www.website.com/seminar. Or fax the enclosed Registration Form today.

Dear Mr. Mitchell:

Your company employs hundreds, maybe thousands, of professionals working toward a common goal: creating satisfied customers.

Unfortunately, with so many people spread out over so many places, working together to achieve this goal isn't always so easy.

That's the problem Keckler, Inc. faced when they hired Enduro Technology to help them implement a "Collaborative WebWorking."

The objective: to get salespeople, product managers, marketing departments, customer service personnel, technical staff, product designers, and thousands of other employees at 27 different Keckler operating companies in the U.S. to communicate and collaborate more efficiently — so they can serve customers better and faster.

Is a "Collaborative WebWorking" a cost-effective solution to your own customer service, communication, and sales and marketing challenges? Now you can find out — without leaving your desk — by participating in our FREE 1-hour Web/Audio Seminar ...

"Implementing a Collaborative Extranet to Enhance Customer Satisfaction and Increase Sales"

This informative 60-minute session reveals the strategies Keckler used to design, build, and implement its new enterprise WebWorking for improved sales, marketing, and customer service collaboration and teamwork. You'll also discover new ways WebWorking technology can help improve business results in your own organization (see enclosed flier for details).

The seminar is free, but registration is on a first-come, first-served basis. To register online visit www.website.com/seminar. Or fill in the enclosed form and fax it to 555-555-5000. Participation is limited, so reply today while space is still available! Note that you will need both a phone line and a separate internet connection to participate.

Sincerely,

Kris Barrow, President

P.S. Since 1989, Enduro Technology has helped numerous clients improve productivity, communication, and sales using Internet technology. To register for our new Audio/Web Seminar . . . or for more information on Enduro Technology's Internet consulting services . . . call 555-555-5555 today.

Tips for Writing Letters Inviting Prospects to Attend a Webcast

- Explain that they need both a phone and a computer with an Internet connection to participate. The phone must be on a line separate from the modem.
- Give them an incentive to register now instead of later (e.g., space is limited, free bonus gift).
- Tell what will be covered in the presentation and what they will learn by attending.

Generating Leads

Some letters do not sell a product directly, but generate a lead. A lead is someone who has seen your marketing message and has contacted you because they are interested in your service or product. Like the samples below, the best lead-generating letters have a strong call to action (e.g., "call today for a free brochure," "complete the enclosed questionnaire for a free sample of a skin care product that matches your skin type").

Salespeople follow up the lead to close a sale for a product or service — usually a bigger-ticket item than can be sold directly by mail order.

The same math works, but you must factor in conversion of leads to sales.

Say your letter generates a 1 percent response — 10 inquiries for every 1,000 letters mailed. The cost of mailing is $600 per thousand.

Of the ten inquiries you generate, two become customers, buying a $2,000 product. You therefore make $4,000 in sales for a direct-mail cost of $600.

SURVEYS OR QUESTIONNAIRES

Sending prospects or customers a survey or questionnaire is a time-tested "soft sell" approach to marketing. Instead of asking for the order or inquiry directly, you send out a needs assessment in the guise of a survey. Everyone who answers is a lead; those respondents whose answers indicate a need for your product or service are qualified leads (e.g., you know right off the bat that they are a good prospect).

Format: [*See Appendix A:* Fig. A-1. Simple format for letters and memos.] Typed/word-processed. Business or personal letterhead.

Style/Tone/Voice: Can be informal or formal, use active tone or voice. [*See Part I for more on these subjects.*]

Structure: (1) Open with an attention-getting statement or question, (2) Identify the reader's need or problem, (3) Explain how their response will help you help them reach their goals, (3a) If possible, entice them with a free gift, such as a discount or a special report, (4) Tell the reader what to do next.

Handy Phrases: Thank you for taking time; Thank you for agreeing to participate; Enclosed is; No postage is necessary; Fax your reply; Please accept the enclosed token; Reply now to receive a free.

See also: *Part IV:* Request to Participate in a Survey; *Part VI:* Customer Satisfaction Survey.

Dear Desktop Conference Attendee:

Never mind "a penny for your thoughts" how about $25.00?? We've been reviewing and using your suggestions and comments to plan the 2005 Desktop Conference. However, we're interested to learn how your needs may have changed in the last six months. What challenges have cropped up, what equipment problems do you face, what knowledge would help you succeed this year? In order to help us help you achieve your goals, please fill out and fax back the attached one-page mini-survey by TUESDAY, APRIL 18 AT 3:00 P.M. (EST) to 555-555-5000.

To show our appreciation, we will deduct $25.00 from your conference registration fee. Your completed, faxed survey will automatically qualify you for this deduction. We thank you, as always, for your time and support, and look forward to seeing you at the 2005 HCGT Desktop Conference, November 9–10, at the Marriott O' Hare in Chicago, Illinois.

Please call me at 555-555-5000 (ext. 1234) if you have questions.

Sincerely,

Dena Kimble
Meetings Manager

Here is the survey that goes with the above cover letter.

Desktop Issues Survey

Please fax to Greta Cravens at 555-555-5000

Please complete and return by Tuesday, April 16.

Here are the ten most-requested desktop education topics. Please number them in order of importance to you, with 1 being most important. Please add specific issues about topics, if appropriate. (For example, if you choose "Troubleshooting," you might write in "Adobe Photo-shop," for Training and Education, or you might write "training customer service reps," or "customer education programs for preflighting.")

- Training and Education ___
- Database Management ___
- Preflighting ___
- Troubleshooting (i.e., software programs) ___
- New Technologies ___
- Sales/Marketing ___
- Production/Scheduling ___
- Estimating/Desktop Hourly Rates ___
- Printing Guidelines ___
- The Internet ___

What other desktop issues are you interested in learning more about?

_____

_____

Your Name/Title:

_____

Company: _____

Phone: _____ Email: _____

Tips for Writing Surveys and Questionnaires

- Keep the survey or questionnaire short and simple. Ideally questions should fit on one side of a sheet of paper.

- Provide a response mechanism — e.g., allow the recipient to fax back the completed survey, or include a business-reply envelope he can use to return the questionnaire by mail.

- Give her an incentive to fill out the survey. Market research surveys for consumer products often include a dollar bill tucked away inside. A favorite phrase is, "I know this dollar bill does not compensate you for your time, but it may brighten the day of a child you know" (although many people keep the buck for themselves).

LIFT NOTES

A "lift note" is a small, second letter enclosed in an envelope to accompany the main sales letter. It is called a "lift note" because it can lift, or increase, the response (i.e., number of leads) to the mailing through its inclusion in the envelope.

The first lift note ever written began, "Frankly, I'm puzzled why you won't take us up on our offer," and most of them are some variation of that theme. Another common headline for lift notes is, "Read this only if you are *not* interested in [name of product, service, or offer]." Celebrity and third-party endorsements are also very effective.

The lift note works by catching the uninterested reader before he tosses your mailing aside. It gains attention by acknowledging the lack of interest. It then attempts to create greater interest by restating one or more benefits.

Format: [*See Appendix A:* Fig. A-1. Simple format for letters and memos.] Typed/word-processed. Business or personal letterhead.

Style/Tone/Voice: Can be either informal or formal. Active tone or voice. [*See Part I for more on these subjects.*]

Structure: (1) Open with a strong call to attention, (2) State reason to order/use product or service, (3) Highlight offer, guarantee or deadline if applicable, (4) Restate call to action.

Handy Phrases: Open only if you decide not to subscribe; Here's an extra reason to order now; A note from the Executive Director; My personal guarantee; A personal note from; This offer will not be repeated again this year; Here are three good reasons to respond today.

See also: *Part VI:* Relationship-Building Letters; *Part VII:* Types of Sales Letters.

A Personal Note from Homemaker Susie Smiley

"Having yellow or stained teeth is embarrassing. You're self-conscious; you smile with your mouth closed or with your hand over your mouth. You look like you're hiding something and you are! By the time I was 25, I had a ten-cup-a-day coffee habit and my teeth were — let's face it — just not pretty. And I didn't have the big bucks that my dentist required for his professional teeth-whitening services. Other over-the-counter products were basically ineffective or lasted just a short time. Then a neighbor introduced me to Blitz Your Teeth White. Within hours, after my initial application I noticed an immediate change in my tooth color. After two weeks, I had the white teeth I'd always dreamed of — and I've kept it that way for a year now with Blitz Your Teeth White's once-a-week maintenance schedule. Now I no longer smile with my mouth closed. I can show off my pearly whites for the whole world to see!

Sincerely,

Susie Smiley

Tips for Writing Lift Notes

- Fold the lift note to insert into the envelope. Print a message on the outer flap of the folded letter along these lines: "Read this only if you are *not* interested in _____."

- Express either surprise or dismay that they are not interested. Appear to be upset — not because you will lose a sale, but because they are passing up an opportunity that is really good for them.

- Give reasons why they should reconsider their impulse to pass up your offer. These can be reasons already stated in the main letter, or preferably, additional benefits they will get when they buy.

LEAD-GENERATING LETTERS

Lead-generating letters seek to generate an inquiry from a qualified prospect. The goal is to get the prospect to stand up, raise his hand, and say, "Yes, I might be interested.

Format: [*See Appendix A:* Fig. A-1. Simple format for letters and memos.] Typed/word-processed. Business or personal letterhead.

Style/Tone/Voice: Can be either informal or formal. Active tone or voice. [*See Part I for more on these subjects.*]

Structure: (1) Identify and empathize with the reader's problem, (2) Position your product or service as the solution, (3) Describe details (benefits/features), (4) Close with a strong call to action.

Handy Phrases: We are eager to offer you; Do you know how to; Thank you for your; I am enclosing a; We can save you more than; Detailed in the enclosed brochure; We specialize in; Would like to show you; Address any concerns you may have; Promise you'll be delighted; Glad to arrange an on-site demonstration; If you need any further information; Just fill out the order form.

See also: *Part IV:* Cordial Contacts; Business Requests.

Tell me more." No money changes hands at this point, and the prospect is not obligated to buy. He is "just looking" — possibly interested, but not committed.

Letters remain one of the most effective methods of generating leads for products. Letters selling products usually include a teaser on an outer envelope, a one-to two-page letter, an insert such as a small brochure and some kind of reply element (e.g., a return postcard). E-mails have also found great success in selling products. E-mails that elicit a high response rate usually contain a link to something free — like a free downloadable report or a trial version of a software product.

FROM: "The Milestones Professional Team" <sales@email.com>
TO: email@email.com
SUBJECT: Download Milestones Professional Now!

Dear Warren Major,

Are you a project manager? Do you find project management software to be more trouble than it's worth? Are you looking for a truly EASY way to schedule and track your projects? You need Milestones Professional!

Click this Web link and a free trial copy is yours: http://www.kidasa.com/.

Milestones Professional is designed for engineers, managers, and ANYONE who needs to schedule and track projects. It's by far the easiest project-scheduling tool on the market today. Milestones Professional offers a simple "click and drag" solution, which will let you put together brilliant, presentation-ready schedules, timeliness, and Gantt charts in minutes.

How will it benefit you?

- Drastically reduce your scheduling time.
- Easily communicate and sell your project's objectives.
- Effortlessly track and monitor your project's progress.
- Win more customer and coworker recognition.

Important:

The software is not a watered-down version of Milestones Professional. You'll try the actual, fully functioning version of software that's used by demanding managers, team leaders, planners, and administrators every single day.

Here's a key code, which you can use to unlock the software through May 1999: 007-063067-VDO30

A personal note: I know you get a lot of e-mail. I just want to personally assure you that Milestones Professional is worth the trouble. If you regularly schedule and manage projects, Milestones Professional can make your life easier. All I ask is for a chance to prove it. www.kidasa.com/miles.

Sincerely,

Sue Butler, President
KIDASA Software, Inc.

Letters are also effective at generating sales leads for a variety of services. Often the goal is to get the prospect to call and request a meeting with your sales rep or agent.

Dear [Name]:

"It's hard to find good mailing lists," a client told me the other day. "I've searched and searched, but our market is so specialized, no one really knows it."

Do you have that same problem? If so, please complete and mail the enclosed reply card for information on a service that can help.

Mailing Lists To Go can help you find *just the right list* for your next business-to-business direct mail, e-mail, or telemarketing campaign.

Why spend countless hours searching for mailing lists? Let MLTG do the list research for you. Our services are FREE! You pay us only when you rent names from the lists we recommend to you. There's no cost or obligation to get list recommendations from us. If you decide not to rent the lists we recommend, you pay us nothing.

With our extensive knowledge of business-to-business, we can find lists other brokers don't even know about. For example, when WBJ, Inc. Software gave us the "impossible" task of finding users of an old programming language, DBQ, we located the distributor of the replacement language. Turns out they still owned the customer list of DBQ, the long-defunct marketer of DBQ 5.0 and were willing to rent that list to WBJ, Inc. Problem solved.

And, when you *do* rent lists from us, we don't mark up those lists one penny. List brokers are like travel agents. We make our money from a small commission we get from the seller (the list owner), not the buyer (you). You pay the exact same price as if you rented the list from its owner directly. There's *no charge whatsover* for our list research and brokerage services!

For more information on our list consulting services . . . or list recommendations on an upcoming direct-mail campaign . . . call us toll-free at **800-555-5555.** Or complete and mail the enclosed reply card today. Remember, our list research services are free. And there's no obligation of any kind. You can't lose!

Sincerely,

Gail Richards, President

P.S. If you need recommendations on other aspects of your direct-mail program — such as mailing formats (e.g., postcards versus sales letters), structuring offers for lead-generation, testing, tracking and analyzing results, database modeling — we can help with that, too! For immediate feedback and list recommendations, you can fax your mailing piece — finished or in rough layout or manuscript — to 555-555-5555. We'll keep it confidential, of course.

Outlining tangible results that the prospect can expect is a great way to generate a response.

Dear Phillip:

Recently, I designed and implemented a writing program for 12 supervisors at Mutual of Michigan. Among the many skills they learned was how to edit the "fat" out of their letters, memos, and reports.

We figured out that if each of the 12 trainees cut just one paragraph out of each of their communications, MOM would save 2,400 paragraphs per year. Because each paragraph takes an average of 20 minutes to write, edit, type, read, and understand, MOM would save 800 work hours a year.

As corporate time costs about $60 per hour, the savings could amount to as much as $50,000 in the first year. And that's a conservative figure.

Why? Because extra dividends are paid in an employee's greater confidence, improved productivity, and sharper communication skills, as well as in a better corporate image.

Next year, these same 12 people will again save their company $50,000 in wasted words, effort, and time and it won't cost MOM another penny. And, if MOM trains another 12 people, they'd probably save an additional $50,000 a year . . . every year.

Insurance companies such as MOM (and First Rate Insurance), for whom I designed a similar program, must feel I'm doing something right — they've invited me back to help train new groups of employees.

Before you begin your search for a training program, please call me to set up a meeting to learn more about how our communications programs can benefit you — and save you thousands of wasted work hours. And take a moment to review the free enclosed brochure. If you'd like more information about how improved writing can make your company more productive, just fill out the enclosed card and mail it. Or call me today at 555-555-5555 or e-mail me at email@email.com. There's no cost to talk to us. And no obligation of any kind.

Gary Cummings, Ph.D.
Director, Say It Right!

Tips for Writing Lead-Generating Letters

- Lead with the prospect and his problem. Then position your product as the solution.

- Describe the product briefly, including the top three or four benefits.

- Assure the prospect that there is no obligation to buy, and no sales pressure.

- Have both a "hard" offer (call to arrange a meeting or appointment) and a "soft" offer (send me a free brochure). Prospects with an immediate need will take you up on the hard offer. Those with a future or possible need will opt for the soft offer.

- Stress the value of the prospect meeting with you even if they do not buy from you (e.g., they get a price quote that gives them the idea of how expensive something will be, or they get your ideas or recommendations on how to approach a project). Say something like, "Even if you don't buy from us, you'll get at least one good idea for doing ____. And it won't cost you a dime."

- Give them several response options. Most common are a business-reply card they can mail back, and a phone number to call. Other response options include fax, e-mail, and going to a specific URL on the Web.

Inquiry-Fulfillment Letters

An "inquiry-fulfillment letter" is sent to prospects who have requested more information on your product or service. It is usually a cover letter mailed with the marketing collaterals (e.g., sales fliers, brochures, and other material) you use to sell your product/service and should include an order form or other call to action.

INQUIRY-FULFILLMENT LETTERS WITH LITERATURE ENCLOSED

The most common marketing method of inquiry-fulfillment is to send the prospect the brochures and other sales literature she has requested, accompanied by a cover letter. According to www.pen.com, studies show that when promotional products or advertising specialty items are used as part of the direct-mail package, response rates increase between 12 and 13 percent. Products can include brochures, forms, posters, premiums, banners, training manuals, labels, and catalogs.

Format: [*See Appendix A:* Fig. A-1. Simple format for letters and memos.] Typed/word-processed. Business or personal letterhead.

Style/Tone/Voice: Can be either informal or formal. Active tone or voice. [*See Part I for more on these subjects.*]

Structure: (1) Thank the prospect for responding, (2) Highlight key points in the material you enclose with your letter (rather than trying to write a summary about the material), (3) Tell the reader what to do next.

Handy Phrases: Here is; As you requested; To schedule an appointment; Call now for your free; Don't miss this special offer; Don't miss this opportunity to; To find out how; To take advantage of this now.

See also: *Part IV:* Communicating Business Information; Business Requests.

August 12, 2002

Ms. Amy Lomer
123 Main Street
Philadelphia, PA

Dear Ms. Lomer,

Thank you for your inquiry concerning swimming pools and spas. Cryder Pools is a 27-year-old, financially strong company and the only source you'll need for all your swimming dreams. With over 100,000 in-ground pools and spas in our experience base, Cryder is a strong contender in the backyard pool market.

As you requested, enclosed is our signature brochure that highlights our exciting pool and spa designs. Included with the brochure is a CD-ROM that graphically illustrates design ideas, special features, and how the pool-installation process occurs. As you look through this information, make notes on which designs and features appeal to you and think about how you will use your new pool. For example, pools can be focused around your family, recreation, exercise, entertainment, or as part of an overall landscaping plan.

After you have had a chance to review the enclosed brochure, you will receive a call from one of our design consultants to discuss how we can make your backyard dream come true. If you wish to contact us directly, feel free to call us at 800-555-5555 or through our Web site (www.website.com).

With over 100,000 pools built all across the U.S., we know the importance of customer satisfaction. We look forward to providing you and your family with a wonderful Cryder Pool. Come join the family; we are *"Where You'll Find Fun in Your Own Backyard."*

Karen Wilson
Chairman & Chief Executive Officer

Tips for Writing Inquiry-Fulfillment Letters Accompanying Enclosed Sales Literature

- Thank the prospect for their interest in your product or service.
- Briefly describe what you have sent them. Give the highlights of the contents, especially useful how-to content, reference material, and product benefits.
- Suggest a tangible next step to take if the prospect has any interest in the product (e.g., a demonstration in their home or office).

INQUIRY-FULFILLMENT LETTERS WITH PRODUCT ENCLOSED

In some cases, an inquiry may be fulfilled by sending the actual product for a free trial, or by sending a demo or evaluation copy. Magazines often fulfill inquiries with a sample magazine and a trial subscription (usually for three months). Software manufacturers often give demo disks with limited capabilities or with a time-restraint (e.g., WinZip lets you try the product 25 times, and then you are supposed to purchase the product). Keep in mind that by law, unsolicited merchandise is the recipient's to keep.

Format: [*See Appendix A:* Fig. A-1. Simple format for letters and memos.] Typed/word-processed. Business or personal letterhead.

Style/Tone/Voice: Can be either informal or formal. Active tone or voice. [*See Part I for more on these subjects.*]

continued

continued

Structure: (1) Thank the reader for requesting information, (2) Explain what the enclosed literature covers, (3) Highlight the enclosed product — either offer tips on usage or highlight benefits, (4) Close with an offer to discuss your product or service by phone or in person, (5) Include a call for action.

Handy Phrases: Thanks for requesting; Thanks for asking about; The enclosed sample; To schedule an appointment; Hope you enjoy the enclosed; We promise you'll be delighted; There is no charge.

See also: *Part IV:* Communicating Business Information.

Ms. D. Lee
Director of Operations
Kinser Air Terminal
PO Box 123
Fargo, ND 12345

Enclosed, Ms. Lee. . .

. . . is the information which you requested on our GateProgram software license.

I am pleased to enclose a "first customer" GateProgram software license and payment plan for Kinser.

Included in this license are our software warranty, maintenance, and extended warranty agreements.

There's no other product of its kind on the market today that has proven to be as effective in the managing of gate operations of a major airline. The installation, training process, and guidelines of support will allow Kinser to perform without the purchase of an additional site license.

If the package is agreeable, please call me to discuss setting up your contract.

Sincerely,

Monte Robbins
Manager, Software Marketing

Tips for Writing Inquiry-Fulfillment Letters Accompanying a Product or Product Sample

- Explain what it is you have sent them and why.

- Tell them what to do with it (e.g., sign a licensing agreement, put it in their CD-ROM drive and click "Run").

- Stress the quick benefits they get when they buy and start using the product immediately.

INQUIRY-FULFILLMENT, LONG-FORM

Although inquiry-fulfillment letters are traditionally short, a longer letter can sometimes work well. This is especially true if you are not sending a brochure; in that case, the letter must do most of the selling job.

Format: [*See Appendix A:* Fig. A-1. Simple format for letters and memos.] Typed/word-processed. Business or personal letterhead.

Style/Tone/Voice: Can be either informal or formal. Active tone or voice. [*See Part I for more on these subjects.*]

Structure: (1) Thank the prospect for responding, (2) Highlight key points in the material you enclose with your letter, (3) Anticipate and answer most common objections, (4) Tell the reader what to do next.

Handy Phrases: Here is; As you requested; To schedule an appointment; Call now for your free; Don't miss this special offer; Don't miss this opportunity to; To find out how; To take advantage of this now; Thanks for requesting; Thanks for asking about; The enclosed sample; Hope you enjoy the enclosed; We promise you'll be delighted; There is no charge.

See also: *Part IV:* Communicating Business Information; *Part IX:* Purchasing Policy Letter.

Memphis Mineral Corp.
P.O. Box 123
Valencia, Pa. 12345
555-555-5555

Mr. L. Manor, Proj. Engr.
Kensington, Inc.
133 Third Ave.
New York, NY 10021

Subject: Palletizing Information

Dear Mr. Manor,

Thanks for your interest in our Pelletizers. Literature is enclosed that will give you a pretty good idea of the simplicity of our equipment and the rugged, trouble-free construction.

The key question, of course, is the cost for equipment to handle the volume required at your plant. Since the capacity of our Pelletizers will vary slightly with the particulates involved, we'll be glad to take a look at a random 5-gallon sample of your material. We'll evaluate it and get back to you with our equipment recommendation. If you will note with your sample the size pellets you prefer and the volume you wish to handle, we can give you an estimate of the cost involved.

From this point on we can do an exploratory palletizing test, a full day's test run, or we will rent you a production machine with an option to purchase. You can see for yourself how efficiently it works and how easy it is to use. Of course the equipment can be purchased outright too.

Thanks again for your interest. We'll be happy to answer any questions for you. Simply phone or write.

Very truly yours,

Memphis Mineral Corporation
Phil Harold
Vice President, Sales

Tips for Writing Long-Form Inquiry-Fulfillment Letters

- Lead by thanking the prospect for their interest in your product or service.
- Anticipate and answer the major questions and objections the prospect is likely to have.
- Do not let data, pictures, tables, or other information interrupt the flow of the letter. Consider making these enclosures on separate sheets.

LEAD INQUIRY-FULFILLMENT FOLLOW-UPS

You send the inquiry fulfillment and wait for the prospect to respond. But it often doesn't work that way. Why? People are busy; they have too many other items competing for their attention, and don't have time to read sales materials. Unless the need is urgent, they are likely to set your material aside, lose it, or throw it away. In fact, according to a study by Thomas Publishing, 80 percent of business sales are made on the fifth follow-up, but most marketers follow up three times or less.

To maximize conversion of leads to sales, you must create and send a series of follow-up letters to leads who received your product literature but have not taken further action.

Format: [*See Appendix A:* Fig. A-1. Simple format for letters and memos.] Typed/word-processed. Business or personal letterhead.

Style/Tone/Voice: Can be informal or formal. Active tone or voice. [*See Part I for more on these subjects.*]

Structure: (1) Mention the material that was already sent, (2) Make a statement about how your product/service can benefit the reader, (3) Entice the reader to act now, (4) Make an offer to resend material if it hasn't been received/seen by reader.

Handy Phrases: Recently we sent you; We can help you; If you didn't receive the information, or if you need additional material; The next step; As you can see; We'd love to help you; I hope you'll feel it worthwhile; You risk nothing; To encourage you to give us a try; We've enclosed a coupon for.

See also: *Part IV:* Communicating Business Information; Post-Meeting Follow-Up Letter.

Dear Jack:

Not everyone gets a second chance in life.

Some time ago, you asked for your free Writing Aptitude Test to find out if you could write for children and teenagers. The test must have come at a busy time for you — or perhaps it never reached you. Whatever the reason, we have not received it.

Here's your second chance to put your talent to work. Enclosed is another aptitude test. Why not sit down and take it right now? Don't worry about doing something "fancy." Writing is fun. Just relax and write naturally.

When you finish, fold your test in half and mail it back in the enclosed envelope. We'll have it reviewed and let you know by mail as quickly as possible whether or not we feel you are qualified for admission.

Please understand, though, this is not one of those "everybody passes" tests. There are several reasons why we must discourage those without apparent talent.

First, if we did otherwise, we'd risk losing our talented instructors. Each is a published writer or editor, and, we've agreed to assign only qualified students. Second, we've promised you'll have a manuscript suitable for submission to a publisher when you finish the course. Returning a satisfactory test will show us that you're ready to commit yourself to becoming a writer.

Returning the test to us places you under no obligation, but, if you qualify and then choose to enroll, we'll spare no effort in helping you build a new career for fun and perhaps even profit.

So now it is really up to you. We can review your test most promptly if we have it before October 9th.

Sincerely,

C. Judith Brunstad
Director of Admissions

P.S. This is your second chance. Don't let it slip away.

Below is the second follow-up letter from Cryder Pools. See how they vary the letter from their initial contact to the reader (see earlier "Inquiry-Fulfillment Letters with Literature Enclosed").

November 8, 2002

Dear Ms. Lomer:

We have an exciting limited-time opportunity for you and your family!

You previously contacted us about building a Cryder pool . . . but decided to wait. Well, don't wait any longer — we are giving you a great reason to buy your pool now, and start enjoying every summer just a few steps from your back door.

Cryder Pools has created a special program for families that plan to build their pool in the spring of 2003. Imagine! Here's a chance to guarantee our current pricing and be sure that your family will enjoy your beautiful backyard oasis when summer arrives.

And, best of all, you'll save thousands of dollars.

If you place a fully refundable deposit of $500. 00 before December 31, 2002, you will receive our low 2002 pricing and we will schedule the construction of your pool for an early completion. You can't lose . . . remember, your deposit is fully refundable.

If next summer is as hot as this past one was, your decision to build with us will prove to be a very smart one. Not only will you be swimming sooner, but also you'll be saving money . . . a great combination!

Interested? Don't wait any longer! Take advantage of this unbeatable offer now. Call me at 1-800-555-5555 for your opportunity to get America's finest swimming pool at the lowest possible price from the most-trusted name in swimming: Cryder Pools!

Sincerely,

Rob Philmore
Design Consultant

P.S. Remember that a fully refundable deposit guarantees your family our present low prices. So act now . . . it's a decision your family will thank you for.

Tips for Writing Inquiry Follow-up Letters

- Ask whether they received your material. Offer to send it again if they did not.
- Restate the benefits of the product and what it can do for them.
- Say how they will miss out or lose by not having your product or service (e.g., if you are selling central air conditioning, they will swelter through another hot summer if they do not act now).
- Give the reader a reason to act now (e.g., a special offer, temporary price reduction, free installation, etc.). Put a time limit on this special offer.

After-Sale Letters

After-sale letters share a similarity with cordial contacts in that their main goal is to build a feeling of trust and goodwill. Use these letters to make sure postsale activities go smoothly and to ensure that you remain on your customers' A list. In addition to confirming sales, two common after-sale letters are (1) follow-ups to ensure customer satisfaction and (2) ongoing letters promoting customer loyalty programs.

SALES AGREEMENTS

Once the customer has agreed to buy, you should confirm the order in writing. The confirmation may be a simple letter of agreement or a more formal contract.

Format: [*See Appendix A:* Fig. A-1. Simple format for letters and memos.] Typed/word-processed. Business or personal letterhead.

Style/Tone/Voice: Can be informal or formal. Active tone or voice. [*See Part I for more on these subjects.*]

Structure: (1) Thank the customer for the order, (2) Confirm details such as amount and price, (3) If necessary, amend or confirm any details, (4) End with an expression of goodwill.

Handy Phrases: As we discussed; We received your order for; This is to confirm that as you requested; There has been a slight delay in; Due to exceptionally high demand; Please expect delivery in; We will be happy to; Are sure you will be pleased with; At no extra charge; Will be glad to hear; We'd be delighted to answer any questions you may have; We appreciate your order; Call our customer service line at; Thank you again for.

See also: *Part IX:* Letters Regarding Bids, Contracts, and Agreements.

Dear Mrs. Stringer,

Thank you for your May 15 telephone order for various beads and beading tools. Delivery of our catalog items generally takes less than a week. Larger orders such as yours may take two to three weeks because some of the beads you selected are custom-made in Canada. We are pleased to notify you, however, that your large order qualifies you for our new 20% bulk discount, applied to all orders over $200. (As you will see on the accompanying invoice, we have already deducted your discount from the total price of your order.)

Your order number is xxx-xxxxx. We are shipping [give details] to [address]. The total purchase price, including shipping, is $xx.xx.

Please take a moment to look over these details. If you have any changes or questions, please call us at 800-555-5555.

Bobbie Cunningham,
Customer Service Rep.
Baubles and Bobbleheads

Tips for Writing Sales Agreements

- Give a specific and accurate decision of the work to be performed and the products to be delivered.
- Cover all the main points: price, payment schedule, guarantees of satisfaction.

- Anticipate and discuss common problem situations (e.g., what happens if a contractor misses the deadline for project completion because of bad weather, material shortages, or other circumstances beyond his control?).

AFTER-SALE FOLLOW-UP LETTERS

You would think that once the customer had bought, there would be no need to send him a sales letter. But you should anyway. Why?

The customer may suffer "buyer's remorse" immediately following the purchase. He has just spent money — maybe a lot of money (to him, anyway). He hasn't started using your product and enjoying its benefits — he doesn't see a result yet. And so if you don't reassure him that he made a wise decision, he may change his mind, return the product (or cancel the service), and ask for his money back.

By sending an "after-sale follow-up" letter, you can *resell* the customer on the product, making him happy with his decision and therefore less likely to stop the service or request a refund. Also, the more comfortable he is with his purchase decision, the more satisfied he will be, and the more likely to purchase other products from you and recommend you to others.

Format: [*See Appendix A:* Fig. A-1. Simple format for letters and memos.] Typed/word-processed. Business or personal letterhead.

Style/Tone/Voice: Can be informal or formal, use active tone or voice. [*See Part I for more on these subjects.*]

Structure: (1) Thank reader for purchasing your product or service, (2) Restate how the product/service will benefit the reader, (3) Offer further assistance or remind reader of special discounts or upcoming sales, (4) If applicable, mention other products/services they may be interested in, (5) Express desire to serve reader and for continued business.

Handy Phrases: We appreciate your business; Express our sincere appreciation for; We welcome you as a new; Thanks for your order; We are sure that you are enjoying your; Have already noticed the difference with your; Will be pleased with your results; Please call our toll-free number; Enclosed you will find a special discount on repeat orders; Enclosed is our latest catalog; We will send you a notice of special offers; To a long and enjoyable business relationship; Continue to rely on our service; We will be happy to serve you.

See also: *Part VI:* Relationship-Building Letters; "Time to Reorder" Letter.

Dear Mr. Hamilton,

We are pleased that you have chosen Snuggle Futons and More for your furniture purchase. We hope you are enjoying the convenience, quality, and affordability of your new futon. Isn't it nice to have a piece of furniture that is actually two pieces in one? Even in limited space, you can offer your out-of-town guests a comfortable place to sleep.

We remind you of the special offer with your new futon. The throw pillows that we ordered in beautiful colors to accent your futon have arrived. These pillows are yours as a gift from us. Drop in any time this month to pick them up.

And, were you aware that we also sell coffee tables? A new shipment in many beautiful colors and elegant styles has just arrived. Come see the selection. We would like to help you find the perfect table to match your futon.

Sincerely,

Andrea Schlesinger,
Customer Rep.

Tips for Writing After-Sale Follow-up Letters

- Thank the customer for buying from you.
- Reinforce the benefits of the product to assure him he has made a wise purchase.
- Add a small (and unexpected) bonus or gift as an extra token of your appreciation.

LOYALTY PROGRAM LETTERS

A "loyalty program" rewards customers with prizes — merchandise, travel incentives, discounts — in return for doing business with you. The more they spend, the more and better prizes they qualify for. The most visible example of a loyalty program is the frequent-flyer programs offered by airlines, which award benefits (free travel, free upgrades to first class) based on number of miles flown by the customer.

Format: [*See Appendix A:* Fig. A-1. Simple format for letters and memos.] There are lots of formats for loyalty programs, including invitation packages, program welcome kits, promotional mailings, certificate packages, program statements, members-only Web sites, and e-mail messages.

Style/Tone/Voice: Can be informal or formal, use active tone or voice. [*See Part I for more on these subjects.*]

Structure: (1) Welcome reader to the program, (2) Explain program benefits, (3) Refer, if applicable, to enclosed literature for more information, (3a) Explain how to use enclosed literature and what pieces should be kept on file for handy reference, (4) Explain any restrictions, (5) Close with a statement thanking them for continued business.

Handy Phrases: Welcome to a new level of distinction; Welcome to the special benefits and privileges; Your status is designed; Through the year, you'll enjoy; There are just a few; It is a pleasure; To show our appreciation; In addition, we've arranged to have two additional upgrades; I'm pleased to share some important news about our loyalty program.

See also: *Part VI:* Relationship-Building Letters.

Dear Ms. Edna Smythe,

Delicious Chocolate Factory created its loyalty program to reward those who frequent our locations most often. With every purchase, your card will be swiped for your opportunity at winning one of our great instant-win prizes. You have a chance to win gift boxes, discounts on future purchases, gift certificates, and much more. Every fourth card swiped is guaranteed to be a winner.

In addition to instant-win prizes you will earn one point for every dollar that you spend. These points are redeemable for gift certificates. We have a customer card for everyone! To join, simply fill out the online application form.

Points can be redeemed as follows:

- $10 gift certificate at 125 points
- $25 gift certificate at 250 points
- $250 gift certificate at 2,000 points

The Delicious Chocolate Factory Customer Card Program is valid at participating U.S. locations only.

Thank you for your continued patronage!

Lilly Lonke, President
Delicious Chocolate Factory

Tips for Loyalty Program Letters

- Base the awarding of prizes or incentives on money spent — amount of service used or dollar value of products purchased. The more you spend, the better the prize.

- If you use a bonus points system, fill their account with 500 or 1,000 free bonus points at the start, just for participating in the program. Reason: The customer will then spend to accumulate enough points to win a prize, since he is unwilling to let the points you have given him go to waste.

- Describe the prizes. Enclose a separate folder or brochure with the pictures of the prizes — product shots if you are offering merchandise, destination photos for travel incentives.

LETTERS TO LURE BACK CLIENTS

What turns clients off? How often have you said to yourself, "That's funny, but Joe Smith hasn't bought from us this year. I wonder what's happened?"

The reason is that Smith has probably gone elsewhere. But the fact that a client has stopped buying from you does not necessarily mean that he cannot be induced to buy again. A small percentage of these "lost sheep" may even wander back on their own initiative. But a far greater percentage needs just a little encouragement.

That encouragement may simply be asking, in a letter, "We've missed you; where have you been?" It takes only a postage stamp and a little time to ask that question. The payoff in revived business makes the effort worth many times the cost of sending out the mail. And you'll be surprised at how easily you can get some of those lost clients back.

Some sales experts say that a company spends ten times as much to land a new client as to regain an old one. If that seems a bit large, at least it must be conceded that the cost of getting back the old customer is considerably less than searching for a replacement.

A new prospect is merely a stranger to your company. She knows nothing of your product, service, you, or your organization. She may have been buying a long time from a competitor and has no reason for wanting to buy elsewhere. It takes hard, intensive effort to get her first order.

Now the old client knows all about your business, its capabilities, and convenient services. Three-fourths of your usual sales pitch is unnecessary in his case. What remains may involve adjusting a complaint, or simply giving him the attention that was lacking when he drifted away.

Of course, the inactive buyer likes to be noticed and probably will *never* return if you remain aloof. Not to be asked to buy again is damaging to one's ego. Why should a customer go back to a place where he has not been missed?

But suppose, for example, that *you* were the inactive client of a travel agency. How would you react to this letter below from your former agent?

Format: [*See Appendix A:* Fig. A-1. Simple format for letters and memos.] Typed/word-processed. Business or personal letterhead.

Style/Tone/Voice: Can be informal or formal. Active tone or voice. [*See Part I for more on these subjects.*]

Structure: (1) Express appreciation for past business, (2) State reason for writing and explain that you want to find out why the reader no longer uses your product/service (if you are aware of a problem, explain that you want to correct it), (3) Invite customer to reply, (4) Highlight new offerings or detail something the reader may not have known about.

Handy Phrases: We appreciate your past business; It has been some time since we've worked with you; Have always appreciated your business; Value you as a client; Anything about our product or service; Are worried that we may be losing your; Have we inadvertently done something; I hope nothing serious has happened; We would welcome an opportunity to; Would appreciate if you could answer and return the enclosed questionnaire; Love to bring each other up to date; Call you next week to discuss; Hope to hear from you soon; Will make this issue a top priority; Would like your opinion so that we can improve; We are proud to announce that; Brand-new organization; Ready to serve you; Our company offers; I think you'll be impressed with our; Open the door to a new relationship; Take a fresh look at our; Would very much like to welcome you back.

See also: *Part VI:* Relationship-Building Letters.

Dear Mr. Browne:

Back in the early days of this travel agency, I learned a very valuable lesson.

In those days we depended more on footwork — and less on headwork! Well, here's what happened.

One day I was traveling through the territory with one of our agents and we called on an old-time client who had suddenly stopped booking. After exchanging the usual greeting I asked him why we weren't receiving any more of his travel business. Here's his reply:

"There's really no reason at all. I just happened to give my travel business to another travel agent who had been calling on me for a long time — a nice lady and I wanted to give her a break!

> "You folks have never made any effort to resell me, so I concluded you no longer were interested in my business. Never even got a letter from you asking why I quit and so I've been going along with this other agency."
>
> Well, we ARE interested in your business.
>
> And to prove it, we're writing to ask you why we haven't been booking any of your travel business. We don't want to make the same mistake we made years ago. We want you to know that your account is really valued and that we'd like to keep it. If there's anything we can do to restore our relationship, we'd appreciate it a lot if you would let us know.
>
> Will you? Thanks!
>
> Sincerely yours,

That letter was used with considerable success by a travel agency in Chicago. The approach is simple — *"We appreciate your business . . . why have you stopped buying?"*

The story made the letter longer but it was a good one and helped to convey the agency's sentiments. Here are three additional examples (also from the travel field) that are shorter:

> Dear Ms. Bailey:
>
> Do you realize that it has been all of six months since you and Hotel Frisco got together?
>
> We enjoyed having you with us. When will you be back? We miss you.
>
> Watchfully yours,

This example is also short and alludes to the longterm relationship the client and business have enjoyed.

> Dear Mrs. Tomkins:
>
> Just a short note to let you know that we have missed your coming in for your yearly three-week vacation.
>
> Anything wrong? If so, tell us, because you know we want to please you in every way possible.
>
> Won't you come in? Or better still, phone — the number is 800-555-5555. Thank you.

This example is a little bit more generic; it doesn't discuss the specific history of the client. It does, however, ask for a very concrete step to be taken in response and facilitates that step by providing the format (fill in the blank), and the means (self-addressed stamped envelope) of providing that response.

Dear Mr. Roberts:

Can you spare me two minutes? One minute to read this — and one minute to say: "We haven't booked any travel business with you because: _____ "

Please fill in your answer and return this sheet to us in the enclosed stamped envelope.

This won't obligate you in the least and we'll surely thank you for your two minutes — and your courtesy.

Yours in anticipation,

The light, humorous touch can help you get the inactive client back in the fold again. Such a letter certainly would be read and go a long way toward re-establishing a favorable image.

Some sales letters simply express appreciation of past business and say the customer has been missed; some ask casually what is wrong; some assume a grievance and lavishly promise to make things right.

Dear Former Client:

Have you heard the saying, "Old friends are like the ticking of a clock?" You get so used to hearing the tick that you rarely notice it until it stops.

We get used to doing business with old customers, too — so much so, that now and then we assume that everything is running along smoothly and we sometimes fail to express our appreciation as often as we should.

And then, suddenly the clock stops and we find that an old customer has stopped buying.

That's the position in which we find ourselves with you — your company stopped doing business with us.

We are wondering if you would tell us frankly just what the trouble has been — whether there is something we did not do that we should have done, and whether there is anything we can do NOW to get you back on our list of regular clients. If there is, we surely want to do it.

If there is anything wrong, let us see what is out of kilter. Mistakes will happen at times, of course, and if one has occurred in your case, we hope you will tell us about it. We think we can fix it up the very day we receive your reply.

Like any successful business, our progress is largely dependent on satisfied clients. That's why we want you satisfied and that's why we earnestly request you to fill in the attached postage-free business reply card.

Let's see if we can get the old clock to ticking again.

Sincerely,

Tips for Writing Letters to Bring Customers Back

- Tell your customer past business was appreciated. If the fact was not mentioned when she was buying, perhaps there should be some form of mild apology for the oversight.

- Tell her how much she has been missed. *Don't* say you noticed her absence while "going over the records." No one is really missed if the fact is called to attention by a *record*. She wants to be missed as an *individual* — not as a name on the books.

- Tell her you want to *serve* her again. That's better than asking her to *buy* again.

- Tell her you are keenly interested in knowing *why* she stopped buying. Merely asking that question is *not* an assumption of dissatisfaction; it might be for some other purely normal reason.

- Tell her about anything new and beneficial in the service or product — things that have happened since she stopped buying. Or mention some other inducement that might be interesting, such as a new product, extended warranty, special discount, or free bonus gift.

- Ask if something happened to displease her and express how eager you are to make things right.

DISCOUNT OFFERS

When you are offering a discount, say it loud and clear in your letter. Saving money is always a big appeal to your customer.

Format: [*See Appendix A:* Fig. A-1. Simple format for letters and memos.] Typed/word-processed. Business or personal letterhead.

Style/Tone/Voice: Can be either informal or formal. Active tone or voice. [*See Part I for more on these subjects.*]

Structure: (1) Thank reader for continued business, (2) Extend special offer/discount, (3) Explain offer/discount and how reader can take advantage of it, (4) Highlight a particular product/service they may wish to try or renew, (5) Close with an expression of appreciation.

Handy Phrases: We can offer you 25% off anything in our catalog; Remember the sales ends on (date); Here's a deal you can't pass up; We'd like to give you an extra; Let us know if you want to place an order; Here's a once-in-a-blue moon deal; Call our order department now; We'll throw in free shipping; This offer is too good to pass up; For details on this special offer, call our customer service department; Buy "x" now and receive an extra 15% off anything else you buy.

See also: *Part VI:* Free Value-Added Programs; Denial of Request for Additional Discount.

Thank you, Kelly Hayes!

Because you're a loyal customer, we're extending to you this exclusive special offer on our most popular Office Essentials . . . TAKE 33% OFF ANY PRODUCT IN THE ENCLOSED BROCHURE!

Now is a perfect time to review your inventory. Stock up on Envelopes, Checks, Stationery, Labels and much more. But hurry . . . this limited-time offer expires December 31, 2002!

We have included our most popular Office Essentials to make it easier for you to order the products that you need to run your business smoothly and efficiently. Don't miss our Expressions® check designs — these checks are compatible with the most popular accounting software programs including Quicken®, QuickBooks®, Peachtree®, and many more! And, they can be used in laser or inkjet printers. Use the handy order form below, or call us toll free at 800-555-5555 to ensure the quickest turnaround on the office essentials you need.

Thanks again. We appreciate your business.

Sincerely,

Frances Leonard
President

P.S. Act quickly! This special offer ends soon. Be sure to place your order by December 31, 2002 to take advantage of these incredible savings.

Tips for Writing Letters Offering Discounts

- State the discount up front in the lead of the letter — even on the outer envelope!
- If there is a reason why you are offering a discount (e.g., end-of-year clearance sale, a reward for being a good customer, a bribe to get you to become a customer), say so.
- Put a limit on the discount. Give an expiration date for the offer.

LETTERS ANNOUNCING NEW LOCATIONS

Whenever you move or open a new retail location or branch office, write to customers to let them know the news. If you are a retailer or service business, a new location may mean greater service and convenience for customers who live near it. If you are a distributor or product seller, more locations mean a bigger distribution service, and better delivery.

Even if the customer doesn't directly benefit, it's still news — and an excuse to write. Also, having more locations is an impressive feat. It reassures your customers that you are profitable and successful, and intend to be around to serve them for the long haul.

Format: [*See Appendix A:* Fig. A-1. Simple format for letters and memos.] Typed/word-processed. Business or personal letterhead.

Style/Tone/Voice: Can be informal or formal, use active tone or voice. [*See Part I for more on these subjects.*]

Structure: (1). Announce specific details of your move, including effective date and new address, (2) Give your new telephone number or fax number if those are changing, (3) Include directions, if applicable, (4) Thank customer for business received and invite reader to visit your new location.

Handy Phrases: We are excited about our move; We're now at a more convenient location; You won't need to drive across town anymore; You can call us at; I've enclosed is a map showing our new location; It's easy to find us; We are sure you will be impressed by our new; We can't wait to show you our new offices; Don't miss our grand opening; Will be much more convenient; As always, we value your patronage; Thank you for your business over the years; Our new location has ample parking.

See also: *Part IV:* FYI Letters; *Part V:* Announcements.

Dear Mr. Thomas,

We are moving! Beginning July 1, XYZ Pet Feed & Supply will be located in the new Paterson Town Center, 1600 Main Street. With double the space of our old store we will be able to carry a larger selection of products for our customers' convenience. And, you'll find ample parking — no more searching for a space! Please note our new phone number, 555-5555, for phone orders. Come during the month of July and take advantage of our great grand opening sale prices.

Hope to see you soon!

Frank Smith, XYZ Pet Feed & Supply Owner

Tips for Writing Change-of-Location Letters

- Tell the big news first: the number of new branch offices or stores, and their locations, including street addresses and directions (e.g., "conveniently located on the corner of Fifth and Main").

- Spell out the benefits to the customer of the new location (e.g., easier access, less travel time, faster delivery).

- Position the new location openings as a customer service, not a corporate expansion. You are doing it to serve the customer better, not build your empire.

Nonprofit Fundraising

Like a good sales letter, fundraising letters arouse interest in the reader and urge the reader to take action. Unlike most sales letters, letters requesting donations usually tug on the heartstrings and have emotional or human-interest appeal.

FUNDRAISING LETTERS

A fundraising letter is sent by an organization, typically nonprofit, to raise money for a worthy cause. This can range from keeping a college running, to giving comfort to children who are hungry or ill, to battling illnesses ranging from cancer to AIDS.

Format: [*See Appendix A:* Fig. A-1. Simple format for letters and memos.] Typed/word-processed. Business or personal letterhead.

Style/Tone/Voice: Can be informal or formal. Active tone or voice. [*See Part I for more on these subjects.*]

Structure: (1) Open with an attention-getting statement or question, (2) Explain the need for the donation, (3) Indicate how the reader would benefit from making a donation, (4) Explain donation process (and make the donation process easy as possible).

continued

continued

Handy Phrases: We're a nonprofit organization for the disadvantaged; For the past 20 years; To raise funds for; An urgent need for; Desperately need help; Make every penny count; Will help us to; Will all be used; For your donation; Are so grateful for caring people like you; Each small triumph; Such a huge difference to; Your past contributions helped; Donation may be tax-deductible; Is no feeling quite like; Know the joy of; Your name will be listed in our; As a token of our appreciation; For administrative and fundraising costs; Our income and expenditures; Even the smallest contribution helps; Make your pledge by phone or mail; Matching your donation; Return your donation in the; Use your credit card; Your stamp adds to your donation.

See also: *Part II:* Local Fundraising Requests; *Part IV:* Special Requests: Sponsorship, Fundraising, Donation Letters, and Grant Proposals.

Dear _____,

My name is Aja and I'm 9 years old. This is a picture of Gran and me. I love her very much.

We used to do lots of things together. We had sleepovers and I would cuddle up close to Gran. She told me the neatest stories. We made cookies together and special milkshakes that only she and I knew how to make. She taught Mommy and me many things too — like which berries were best to make jam with, how to make yummy pancakes, and the best place to have ice cream.

But, something happened to Gran. She started to get her words mixed up. She even forgot my name sometimes . . . put milk in a cupboard instead of the fridge . . . and forgot to turn off the stove. I was so scared and upset that I used to cry.

Then, Mommy and Daddy explained to me that Gran got Alzheimer's. They went to this place called the Alzheimer Society of B.C. They talked to someone there and got lots of information about this awful disease. They even got me a book to read. Mom and Dad sometimes meet in a group with other people who know someone with Alzheimer's. Now, we all know more about what Gran is going through. And, we know how we can help her too.

I'm not scared anymore. But, I hate Alzheimer's for picking on my Gran. I miss her. I miss her stories. And, I miss doing things with her. I hope they'll find a cure to make her all better soon.

You can create hope for Aja and give help to families like hers.

Alzheimer's is a disease that hits the family just as hard as the person suffering from it. Families lose their loved ones not once, but twice — first when the person stops recognizing people and eventually when he dies a slow death.

Every year, we reach over 43,000 people and their families who're affected by this devastating disease. Like Aja and her family, these people feel frightened, confused, overwhelmed, and often alone. They have nowhere else to turn except to us. We are here for them in many ways . . .

We provide them with the right information . . . support through sharing in groups or individual counseling . . . relief from their 24-hour-a-day care-giving responsibilities . . . and hope through research . . .

But, we can't do all of this without your kindness and support! Please give us your most generous donations. You're giving a gift of love and compassion for families like Aja and her Gran.

With the increasing number of people being diagnosed with Alzheimer's and related dementia, our needs are more urgent than ever. Please fill in the enclosed reply card now and return it to us with your gift. Thank you so much for caring.

Warm regards,

Anne Carswell
President
Alzheimer Society of B.C.

P.S. I've enclosed a bookmark from Aja and her Gran. You can use it to read your favorite book or give it to a friend. You'll be identified as someone concerned about people who're affected by Alzheimer's. Also, you'll help to raise awareness about this fatal disease.

Tips for Writing Fundraising Letters

- Make it personal. The reader is more moved by the account of one little boy who goes hungry, rather than the statistic, "More than 50,000 Ethiopians don't know where their next meal is coming from."

- Appeal to emotion. People inherently want to help other people. Appeal to their natural instinct to be altruistic and benevolent.

- Also show how they can personally benefit. If you are raising money for cancer research, a component is that, if you are successful, your reader can live cancer-free.

FUNDRAISING FOLLOW-UPS

Fundraisers get the bulk of their donations not from sending solicitations to strangers, but by asking past donors for even more money.

When should you follow up? Surprisingly, the best time to send a follow-up asking a donor for more money is immediately after he has given his latest donation.

Strange? It seems so. But in direct marketing, the law of "RFM" — recency, frequency, and monetary — rules. For fundraising, RFM works as follows:

- Recency — the donor who just gave is more likely to give again than a donor who has not given in a while (or at all).
- Frequency — donors who give many times during the year are more likely to give again than a donor who makes only an infrequent donation.
- Monetary — donors who gave a big sum of money in the past are more likely to give large amounts today. Donors who only gave $10 or $25 are unlikely to give $100 or more.

Format: [*See Appendix A:* Fig. A-1. Simple format for letters and memos.] Typed/word-processed. Business or personal letterhead.

Style/Tone/Voice: Can be informal or formal, use active tone or voice. [See Part I for more on these subjects.]

Structure: (1) Thank reader for past donations, (2) Give an interesting statement/statistic about what the organization has accomplished through donations, (3) Expand on need for ongoing donations, (4) Close with a request for donation.

Handy Phrases: We're so close to our goal; So many have helped; Together we can; Concerned citizens like you; For the past 20 years; To help defray the costs; Are proud to say that every dollar you donate goes toward; Your contribution will; Your donation will provide; Caring people like you; We have achieved so much; You'll have the satisfaction of; Thank you for your support; A reply envelope is enclosed for your convenience.

See also: *Part IV:* Donation Thank-You Letters.

Dear Mr. McMullen

Thank you for supporting The Salvation Army. You're certainly a generous and caring friend to people in need.

It's heartbreaking to see people hurting — especially during the holidays. They come to us poor . . . hungry . . . and alone. And the children, whose faces normally light up our holidays, have little hope and less to be joyful about.

We want to help by providing food, shelter, clothing, toys. And most of all, joy and hope. Can The Salvation Army count on your generosity again this holiday season? You do make a difference in people's lives all year 'round.

Sincerely,

Tips for Writing Fundraising Follow-ups to Donors

- Thank them for their past contributions.
- Remind them of why they donated — whom they are helping and what their money buys.
- Ask them for another donation.

PART VIII

CREDIT, COLLECTION, AND BILLING

Credit and collections is a touchy subject. If your writing is too weak and wishy-washy, you may not get all the money you are trying to collect. Sounding too tough and demanding, on the other hand, can cost you goodwill and cause some debtors to dig down even further in their refusal to honor your invoice.

When you turn down someone for credit, they are quick to take insult. "My credit record is good," they protest — whether it is or not. "Are you calling me a deadbeat?" they challenge — even though they may be.

Those same people who think credit is a God-given right in a free nation, rather than a privilege given at the discretion of businesses that take risk granting it, are surprisingly casual about paying bills. A popular consumer magazine, *Bottom Line Personal*, even promises to tell its subscribers about "bills it's OK to pay late."

One view of the situation is to conclude that the overall decay of ethics in our society includes the lack of commitment to meeting one's financial obligations; not paying back college loans is a standing joke among professional comediennes.

Another view says that in today's economy, the consumer feels more in control. It is a buyer's market, not a seller's market. Therefore, if there is even the slightest dissatisfaction with the product, many people feel no hesitation in expressing this satisfaction by not paying the bill.

In this section, we'll examine how to write letters that get favorable credit decisions and collection results for you by addressing (sometimes subtly) these feelings, emotions, and attitudes.

Billing Letters

When you allow customers to buy on credit, you send them invoices that they are supposed to pay within a set time period, typically 30 to 60 days. However, in many cases vendors are providing "90 days same as cash" payment terms, or extended billing terms of 6 to 12 months.

In all of these cases it is good business to remind your customers of their obligation, or provide an inducement (e.g., discount) to pay their bill before it is due. You can do this with a letter or series of letters called "billing letters."

A billing letter is not the same thing as a collection letter. Collection letters are sent only when the account becomes past due or delinquent. A "delinquent" account is a customer who has not paid one or more invoices within the credit terms you have extended.

The purpose of the billing letter is to persuade your customers to pay now instead of later for two key reasons: (1) to prevent delinquencies, and (2) to get your money sooner and improve cash flow.

A SINGLE BILLING LETTER

Billing letters provide an opportunity to strengthen the bond with your customer by explaining how you expect the credit relationship to be handled. The letter should create a dialogue and build additional goodwill with the reader, since you're trying to coax them into parting with their money sooner than they expected.

A billing letter is always sent before payment is due and is routinely sent out with the initial invoice.

Format: [*See Appendix A:* Fig. A-1. Simple format for letters and memos.] Typed/word-processed. Business or personal letterhead.

Style/Tone/Voice: Use an informal, active tone or voice. [*See Part I for more on these subjects.*]

Structure: (1) Express appreciation for the customer's purchase, (2) If applicable, remind or notify the customer of the discount for early payment on the product or service — be specific about the conditions for the discount as well as the discount amount, (3) Urge the customer to send the payment immediately and offer additional assistance.

Handy Phrases: Thank you for your recent order!; Thank you for requesting our services; Please remember that if we receive payment for this order within one week, you will receive a 5% discount off the regular price; You may take the discount if we receive your payment by; Remember, you will receive $25.00 off your next purchase if you return full payment by; I hope you will take advantage of this offer; We are happy to offer this discount on your payment; Please call us at 000-0000 if you have any questions; We look forward to receiving your check for the discounted amount of; Thank you in advance for your prompt payment; As always, I have enjoyed serving you. Thank you.

See also: *Part VII:* After-Sale Letters.

Dear Robert Smart,

Thank you for ordering from W&W Publications Inc. We hope the books will be a valuable resource for your upcoming projects. We have enclosed your invoice and a postage-paid return envelope for your convenience.

I want you to be aware of the 5% discount we offer for early payment. To qualify, simply be sure that your discounted payment is postmarked no later than 10 days after the date of your invoice. I hope you take advantage of this offer by sending in your payment as soon as possible.

We appreciate your business and look forward to providing more of the resources you need in the future.

Thanks again for your order.

Sincerely,

Jen Franklin,
Customer Representative

Tips for Writing a Billing Letter

- Enclose or attach an invoice listing the items purchased and the amount due.
- Thank the customer for her order.
- Urge the customer to pay the bill now, while it is still handy.
- If your terms reward the customer for prompt payment, make this the main point of your letter. (For instance, some vendors give a 2-percent discount if payment is received within ten days.)

BILLING SERIES

Some businesses send a single billing letter, finding that the most cost-effective method of speeding payment. Others send a series of letters — two, three, or four.

Which should you do? When in doubt, you can test.

If you are merely sending out an invoice and then sitting back and waiting to see whether you are paid on time, start with a single billing letter.

Does sending that billing letter increase payments? You may want to start adding billing letters after the first, creating a series of such letters.

How many billing letters is too many? When the results generated by a letter do not pay its cost, you know that letter should be eliminated from the series, and the previous effort should be your last.

In the following scenario we will send three letters to our customer. The first billing letter in a series traditionally accompanies the initial invoice. The second letter will arrive at the customer in time to take advantage of our discount policy. And the third letter will arrive just before payment is due. If you do not have a discount policy and/or your billing cycle is short, then simply skip the second billing letter and use only #1 and #3 for your series.

Billing Letter #1

This letter, the first in your series of billing letters, will accompany the initial invoice. It should outline any discount for early payment, if applicable. It should be friendly and should make the customer feel valued. This letter should also outline all the terms of payment that have been agreed to and should clearly state the final payment deadline.

Format: [*See Appendix A:* Fig. A-1. Simple format for letters and memos.] Typed/word-processed. Business or personal letterhead.

Style/Tone/Voice: Use an informal, active tone or voice. [*See Part I for more on these subjects.*]

Structure: (1) Express appreciation for the customer's purchase, (2) Remind or notify the customer of the discount for early payment on the product or service — be specific about the conditions for the discount as well as the discount amount, (3) Urge the customer to send the payment immediately and offer additional assistance.

Handy Phrases: We appreciate your order; Your order is enclosed; We hope you enjoy it; We extend a warm welcome to you as a new customer; We want to remind you that we offer a 4% discount for early payment; We urge you to take advantage of this offer; We await your payment. If it arrives within the next ten days, we will be happy to credit your account 5% of the purchase price; We are happy to offer this discount on your payment; Please call us at 000-0000 if you have any questions; Thank you in advance for your prompt payment.

See also: *Part VI:* Request for Payment; *Part VII:* After-Sale Letters.

Dear [NAME]:

There are two kinds of people on Wall Street: those who have an edge, and those who don't.

And by making the smart move of becoming a *Buying/Selling* newsletter subscriber, you've just given yourself an even bigger "leg up" on the market.

When it comes to market intelligence, news, and analysis, the 10,000 financial professionals who read *Buying/Selling* simply refuse to settle for anything but the best.

As you'll see when your first issue arrives, *Buying/Selling* delivers the insight and information you — and they — need to increase profits and control risks in today's uncertain economy.

The invoice you asked us to send you is enclosed. Would you mind giving it to your assistant for processing, while it is still in front of you?

That way, you avoid pesky billing notices — and ensure prompt delivery of your monthly *Personal Investor* with no missed issues.

Thanks,

Bernie Tate, Circulation Director

P.S. To pay by phone with a credit card, call toll-free at 800-000-0000.

Tips for Writing the First Billing Letter in a Series

- Enclose or attach the initial invoice with the letter.
- Reinforce the customer's decision to buy. Tell her why she made a good decision and how she will benefit from using your product.
- Call her attention to the invoice and ask for prompt payment.

Billing Letter #2

The second billing letter should be sent midway through the credit term, or shortly before the discount grace period will expire.

At this point the approach is to sell the customer on the benefit of paying their invoice now. Your tone should be casual and the letter should create the feeling that you are simply reminding the customer of the advantages of paying the invoice early.

The second letter is a friendly reminder to get to it now, since there is a deadline looming. You are simply providing an additional opportunity for your customer to benefit from their relationship with you.

Format: [*See Appendix A:* Fig. A-1. Simple format for letters and memos.] Typed/word-processed. Business or personal letterhead.

Style/Tone/Voice: Use an informal, active tone or voice. [*See Part I for more on these subjects.*]

continued

continued

Structure: (1) Express appreciation for the customer's purchase, (2) Remind the customer of the deadline for the early payment discount. Be specific about the conditions for the discount as well as the discount amount, (3) Call attention to the invoice and ask for prompt payment. Give them an easy way to communicate with you.

Handy Phrases: If we receive your payment within 12 days from the shipping date, we will deduct $10.00 from your next bill; We invite you to subtract 2% from your purchase amount if you send payment within seven days of the invoice date; I hope you will take advantage of this offer; If you have any questions, you can reach me at; We hope you enjoy your order; Please call us at 000-0000 if you have any questions.

See also: *Part VI:* Request for Payment*; Part VII:* After-Sale Letters.

Dear [NAME]:

We hope you are enjoying your new subscription to *Buying/Selling* newsletter, the choice of elite financial professionals like yourself for up-to-date market intelligence, news, and analysis.

I want you to remind you of the 5% discount we offer for early payment. To qualify, simply be sure that your discounted payment is postmarked no later than 10 days after the date of your invoice. I hope you take advantage of this offer by sending in your payment as soon as possible.

Why not take advantage of this generous offer by simply mailing the attached invoice to us, along with your payment, today. (A postage-paid reply envelope is provided for your convenience.) Or, to pay by phone with a credit card, call toll-free at 800-000-0000.

Sincerely,

Bernie Tate, Circulation Director

P.S. Remember, the discount is only available for a limited time.

Tips for Writing the Second Billing Letter

- Enclose a copy of the invoice.
- Give them a choice of payment options — for instance, allowing them to pay by mail or phone.
- Provide an easy way to communicate with you.

Billing Letter #3 (Final Letter of the Series)

The billing series gains urgency with the third and final letter. The third billing letter should be sent around the time the invoice is due.

You have asked the customer politely to pay the bill early and received no response. Now you can turn the pressure up a notch because the bill is due. You are still polite and cordial. But at the same time, you are clear about your position: Payment is due and you expect it promptly.

This final billing letter is a friendly reminder to get to it now. There is no cajoling, no scolding. Everything is kept on a professional level, and the customer is treated with nothing but respect.

Format: [*See Appendix A:* Fig. A-1. Simple format for letters and memos.] Typed/word-processed. Business or personal letterhead.

Style/Tone/Voice: Use an informal, active tone or voice. [*See Part I for more on these subjects.*]

Structure: (1) Express appreciation for the customer's purchase, (2) Remind the customer of the invoice due date and provide specific information on how to make payments, (3) Firmly ask the customer to send the payment immediately and offer additional assistance, (4) Note that payment may already have been sent.

Handy Phrases: We appreciate your order; Remind you that payment for this order is due on; Return full payment by; We urge you to make the payment now; I hope you will take advantage of this offer by sending in your payment within the specified time period; We await your payment; If you have any questions, you can reach me at; We hope to receive your payment shortly; We look forward to receiving your check for; Thank you in advance for your prompt payment; If you have already sent this month's payment, please disregard this notice.

See also: *Part VI:* Request for Payment; *Part VIII:* When the Account is in Collections; *Part IX:* Letters Regarding Payment Problems.

Dear [NAME]:

Your *Buying/Selling* newsletter subscription premium is now due.

To keep your newsletters coming ... and prevent your account from falling into arrears ... simply mail the attached invoice to us, along with your payment, today. (A postage-paid reply envelope is provided for your convenience.) Or, to pay by phone with a credit card, call toll-free at 800-000-0000.

Sincerely,

Bernie Tate, Circulation Director

P.S. If there is a question or problem with your subscription, please call Jane Searles, Account Manager, toll-free at 800-000-0000.

Tips for Writing the Third Billing Letter

- Enclose the invoice. By now you see that the invoice should be enclosed with every billing letter.

- Remind the reader what the invoice was for. The customer won't want to go back and look it up (she probably doesn't even have the original invoice), so the temptation to toss the whole thing and wait for your next collection effort becomes greater.

- You may want to say, "If our letters have crossed, and your payment is already in the mail to us, please disregard this notice."

When the Account Is in Collections

Collecting money is a serious matter and vital to your continued success. Depending on the business, anywhere from 10 percent to 70 percent of a company's assets are in receivables at any one time.

Unfortunately, it is becoming all too common for customers to allow their accounts to become delinquent. This requires significant time and effort on the part of the vendor to attempt to collect past-due invoices. And the principal method of collecting money is the collection letter.

Since the primary function of a collection letter is to collect money, you must be as succinct and purposeful as possible. The objective is to collect the money with the first letter. On the other hand you must retain the goodwill of your customer. So a tactful balance must be struck between the need to collect and the need to retain your customer.

The exception to the empathetic collection letter is a collection letter to a large business organization. The tone of the business-to-business (B-to-B) letter is secondary to the details of the past-due amount. This is because in a large organization a collection letter is delegated to the lowest-ranking clerk capable of searching for the bill and determining if and when it was paid. This functional approach to B-to-B collection letters does not mean that politeness and fairness can be disregarded. The main distinction is that a B-to-B collection letter must contain more technical information than is usually necessary in a personal collection letter.

The First Collection Letter

Unlike a billing series, where the first letter starts the date the invoice is sent, the collection letter or series is not sent until the 30- or 60-day credit period has past and the invoice is officially past due.

The purpose of the collection letter is to get payment in full for the money owed while retaining the buyer as a satisfied, loyal customer who will continue to buy more.

Format: [*See Appendix A:* Fig. A-1. Simple format for letters and memos.] Typed/word-processed. Business or personal letterhead.

Style/Tone/Voice: Use a formal, active tone or voice. [*See Part I for more on these subjects.*]

Structure: (1) Remind the customer that payment is past due and state the amount owed, (2) Ask the customer to send payment, (3) Acknowledge that the customer may have already sent payment and thank him or her accordingly.

Handy Phrases: Discovered that payment for your purchase is past due; Realize that this may be an oversight on your part; My records indicate that your account is ten days past due; I thought you might appreciate this friendly reminder; We appreciated receiving your order; If you have not already sent in your payment, will you please do so now?; May we remind you that your June payment is now overdue?; We want to remind you that your account is past due; Perhaps you have forgotten that your payment was due on; Our records show that you have not paid your bill for; Did you forget to send us June's payment for $500.00?; Will you please send us your payment now?; We will appreciate your attention to this oversight; If you have not sent us your payment, please do so by March 30; We need your payment in full so we can continue to serve your needs; Will you kindly send your check today?; Perhaps you have already sent your payment, but if not, we would appreciate your immediate attention to this matter; If your check is already in the mail, please accept our apology for this letter; Past payment history indicates that you are always prompt; If our current record of your delinquency is incorrect, please contact us immediately.

See also: *Part VI:* Request for Payment; *Part VIII:* When the Account is in Collections; *Part IX:* Letters Regarding Payment Problems; *Part IX:* Requests for Compliance.

Account # 8087-20
July 27, 2003

DEAR SUE SMITH

We are concerned that we have not heard from you since we sent you the selections you chose when you joined the Club.

As you know, payment is always due when you receive your selections. <u>Because we have not received payment, we have suspended your membership privileges</u>.

Don't miss out on all the benefits your membership offers you . . . the widest selection of music . . . your favorite artists . . . great discounts and more!

Please return the bottom portion of this letter with your check or money order in the enclosed envelope. Or, if you want to pay by credit card, please see the reverse side of the attached statement for details.

Send us your payment today. Paying promptly will restore your membership to good standing.

Sincerely,

Membership Services

P.S. If payment is not made within 30 days, an additional late charge of $1.50 will be added to your account (not a finance charge). Amount now due includes late charges.

For your convenience, you may now pay by using your credit card. Please see the reverse side for details.

Tips for Writing a Collection Letter

- Say how much is owed, what it is for, and that it is past due.
- Ask for immediate payment in full.
- Describe the penalties for noncompliance (e.g., late charges, suspension of service and credit).
- Tell them the benefits of compliance (e.g., service continues uninterrupted, a free gift).

COLLECTION SERIES

Professional collection agencies and in-house bill collectors do not send a single collection letter and let the matter go at that.

Decades of experience have shown that a concerted effort will pay back its cost many times over.

Letters are typically spaced one, two, or four weeks apart. The intensity and aggressiveness of the collection letter increases as the series progresses.

The last letter typically states that unless payment is made promptly, the invoice will be turned over to a collection agency or attorney. Another effective tactic is to suggest that the customer's credit rating may be damaged by nonpayment of the bill.

LETTER #1

This letter is to notify the customer that the status on their account is now in collections. You should outline the efforts you have taken thus far in securing payment from the customer. It should also clearly state the course of action you wish the customer to take.

The tone of this letter should be less cordial than that used in billing letters as discussed above. Be polite to the customer, but be firm in your wording. Be sure to explain the consequences of not complying with the letter.

Format: [*See Appendix A:* Fig. A-1. Simple format for letters and memos.] Typed/word-processed. Business or personal letterhead.

Style/Tone/Voice: Use a formal, active tone or voice. [*See Part I for more on these subjects.*]

Structure: (1) Mention any previous letters you may have written and state that you have still not received the customer's reply, (2) Remind the customer that the payment is past due, (3) Request immediate payment and tell the customer that withholding payment jeopardizes his or her credit standing, (4) Express your confidence that the reader will remit payment soon, (5) Direct the customer to respond immediately, (6) Indicate your willingness to discuss any difficulties the customer may be having with making the payment, (7) State what action you plan to take against the customer if the bill is not paid immediately.

Handy Phrases: Understand how busy you may have been; Unintentionally overlooked the payment date; This is your second notice; Your payment of $1,000 is now 30 days past due; Although we sent you a letter two weeks ago, notifying you that your account is past due, we still have not received payment; We wonder if you have forgotten that your payment is 45 days past due; Our recent review of your account reveals that your payment of $00 is overdue; We remind you that our credit terms dictate prompt monthly payments and we are still waiting for your payment; Our credit department will appreciate your prompt payment; We want to continue offering you credit. Please help us do so by mailing your payment today; We must receive your

continued

continued

payment by; Although you did not respond to my first attempt to collect payment on your account, I trust that this time you will remit payment in full; Since payment is long past due, we request immediate attention to this matter; Won't you please clear up this matter today by sending us a check for the full amount; As you know, a good credit record is a valuable asset. By withholding payment, you are in danger of seriously jeopardizing not only your credit standing with our company, but also your potential to obtain credit elsewhere. Please be aware that your delinquency will be reported to credit agencies; I am assuming that you are intending to send in your payment. Please do so immediately; Enclosed is a self-addressed envelope for your convenience; I sincerely hope you will send the money immediately so we can continue to serve you.

See also: *Part VI:* Request for Payment; *Part VIII:* When the Account is in Collections; *Part IX:* Requests for Compliance; Letters Regarding Payment Problems.

Dear Jim:

Just a reminder . . .

. . . that payment for the brochure I wrote for you (see copy of invoice attached) is now past due.

Would you please send me a check today? A self-addressed stamped reply envelope is enclosed for your convenience.

Regards,

Karen Hodge

Tips for Writing the First Collection Letter in a Series

- Enclose the invoice with this and every other letter in the series.
- Do not accuse them of wrongdoing. Assume they forgot or just haven't gotten around to paying the bill yet.
- But be clear that, even though you are understanding, you also expect the bill to be paid now.

LETTER #2

The tone of this letter should increase in urgency from your first collections letter. Again outline the history of your correspondence in this matter and note that the customer has still not complied with the terms of payment that they agreed to. Outline the action that you expect the reader to take and encourage them to contact you to discuss the terms of payment.

Format: [*See Appendix A:* Fig. A-1. Simple format for letters and memos.] Typed/word-processed. Business or personal letterhead.

Style/Tone/Voice: Use a formal, active tone or voice. [*See Part I for more on these subjects.*]

Structure: (1) Mention any previous letters you may have written and state that you have still not received the customer's reply, (2) Remind the customer that the payment is past due, (3) Request immediate payment and tell the customer that withholding payment jeopardizes his or her credit standing, (4) Express your confidence that the reader will remit payment soon, (5) Direct the customer to respond immediately, (6) Indicate your willingness to discuss any difficulties the customer may be having with making the payment, (7) State what action you plan to take against the customer if the bill is not paid immediately.

Handy Phrases: Understand how busy you may have been; Unintentionally overlooked the payment date; This is your second notice. Your payment of $1,000 is now 30 days past due; Although we sent you a letter two weeks ago, notifying you that your account is past due, we still have not received payment; We wonder if you have forgotten that your payment is 45 days past due; Our recent review of your account reveals that your payment of $00 is overdue; We remind you that our credit terms dictate prompt monthly payments and we are still waiting for your payment; Our credit department will appreciate your prompt payment; We want to continue offering you credit. Please help us do so by mailing your payment today; We must receive your payment by; Although you did not respond to my first attempt to collect payment on your account, I trust that this time you will remit payment in full; Since payment is long past due, we request immediate attention to this matter; Won't you please clear up this matter today by sending us a check for the full amount; As you know, a good credit record is a valuable asset. By withholding payment, you are in danger of seriously jeopardizing not only your credit standing with our company, but also your potential to obtain credit elsewhere. Please be aware that your delinquency will be reported to credit agencies; I am assuming that you are intending to send in your payment. Please do so immediately; Enclosed is a self-addressed envelope for your convenience; I sincerely hope you will send the money immediately so we can continue to serve you.

See also: *Part VI:* Request for Payment*; Part VIII:* When the Account is in Collections; *Part IX:* Requests for Compliance; Letters Regarding Payment Problems.

Dear Jim:

I haven't gotten payment for this invoice yet. Did you receive my original bill and follow-up letter?

If there is any problem, please let me know. Otherwise, please send me a check for the amount due within the next few days.

Thanks,

Karen Hodge

Tips for Writing the Second Collection Letter in a Series

- Ask whether they got your previous collection letter (e.g., What you are *really* asking is, "Why didn't you reply to it?").
- One reason they may not have paid, other than being too busy or forgetful, is that they are not fully satisfied with the product or service. Another may be a cash flow problem. Encourage them to share the reason for nonpayment with you.
- Ask for immediate payment politely but firmly.

LETTER #3

This letter should be firm and more urgent that the first two, but should still be polite. Like the first two letters in the series, you will want to review the history of the correspondence, outline the terms of payment, review what action you expect them to take, and encourage them to contact you to discuss the payment in question.

Format: [*See Appendix A:* Fig. A-1. Simple format for letters and memos.] Typed/word-processed. Business or personal letterhead.

Style/Tone/Voice: Use a formal, active tone or voice. [*See Part I for more on these subjects.*]

Structure: (1) Mention any previous letters you may have written and state that you have still not received the customer's reply, (2) Remind the customer that the payment is past due, (3) Request immediate payment and tell the customer that withholding payment jeopardizes his or her credit standing, (4) Express your confidence that the reader will remit payment soon, (5) Direct the customer to respond immediately, (6) Indicate your willingness to discuss any difficulties the customer may be having with making the payment, (7) State what action you plan to take against the customer if the bill is not paid immediately.

Handy Phrases: We have mailed three notices, and still have received no reply; I am disappointed that I have not yet received your payment; We strongly urge you pay the balance due immediately; Each passing day that you do not remit payment, you injure your reputation; You are creating a potentially embarrassing and difficult situation by refusing to mail your check; To avoid a negative credit report, send the above-stated amount immediately; We trust that you recognize the seriousness of your failure to pay, and that you will remit full payment immediately; Trust you are concerned about your outstanding balance and intend to remit payment promptly. Please make that intention a reality now; I will contact you on Monday to discuss your payment options. I want to resolve this situation, so please be prepared to help me understand your current financial status; Perhaps if you give me the opportunity to discuss this matter with you face to face we can come up with an alternative payment schedule that will satisfy us both; If you have any questions about the enclosed invoice, please phone me and I will be happy to answer them; Is there a reason why you have not yet sent your payment? Please call me so we can discuss this matter before I consider taking more aggressive action.

See also: *Part VI:* Request for Payment; *Part VIII:* When the Account is in Collections; *Part IX:* Requests for Compliance; Letters Regarding Payment Problems.

Dear Jim:

This is the third notice I've sent about the enclosed invoice, which is now many weeks past due.

Was there a problem with this job I don't know about? When may I expect payment?

Sincerely,

Karen Hodge

Tips for Writing the Third Collection Letter in a Series

- Your tone becomes slightly more aggressive. Your reader should get the sense, without you being rude, that you are about out of patience concerning this matter.
- If you take credit cards, consider making that a payment option. Encourage them to use your toll-free 800 number, if you have one.
- The basic message: Time is up. Pay or tell us why you think you should not pay. Silence is not an option.

LETTER #4

This, the last in our series of collection letters, is the most aggressive. It should note that you are at the end of this matter and should outline the steps you will take if you do not get an adequate response from the reader. You may want to mention possible damage to the customer's credit rating, which could result from nonpayment.

Format: [*See Appendix A:* Fig. A-1. Simple format for letters and memos.] Typed/word-processed. Business or personal letterhead.

Style/Tone/Voice: Use a formal, active tone or voice. [*See Part I for more on these subjects.*]

Structure: (1) Mention any previous letters you may have written and state that you have still not received the customer's reply, (2) Remind the customer that the payment is past due, (3) Request immediate payment and tell the customer that withholding payment jeopardizes his or her credit standing, (4) Express your confidence that the reader will remit payment soon, (5) Direct the customer to respond immediately, (6) Indicate your willingness to discuss any difficulties the customer may be having with making the payment, (7) State what action you plan to take against the customer if the bill is not paid immediately.

Handy Phrases: Agreed to send your payment without delay; Because you have failed to respond; Extremely late payment; Have ignored our requests; Have not received any response; Have sent you five notices; Previous efforts were unsuccessful; Previous letters and statement reminders; This letter is our final appeal; Were unable to resolve the matter and have no other choice but to take legal action against your firm; If we do not hear from you by; If you do not send payment; Must make full payment now to avoid further action; Plan to refer your account over to a collection agency; Pursue aggressive collection efforts; Pursue legal action; Repossession will result; Will refer the matter to our attorney; Will take the matter to court.

See also: *Part VI:* Request for Payment; *Part VIII:* When the Account is in Collections; *Part IX:* Requests for Compliance; Letters Regarding Payment Problems.

Dear Jim:

What do you think I should do?

Despite three previous notices about this invoice, it remains unpaid. I haven't heard from you, and you haven't responded to my letters.

Please remit payment within 10 days of receipt of this letter. I dislike sending you these annoying notices, nor do I like turning accounts over to my attorney for collection. But you are leaving me little choice.

Sincerely,

Karen Hodge

P.S. Please be aware that the copyright on the copy I wrote for you for this assignment does not transfer to your company until my invoice has been paid in full.

Tips for Writing the Fourth Collection Letter in a Series

- Even though you are thoroughly irritated at this point, don't show it. Be firm, but not rude or threatening.
- Remind them that this is the fourth notice.
- Tell them this is their last chance to pay before you turn the account over to an agency or attorney for collections.
- State any penalty they may suffer as a result of their inaction — for instance, they may lose their ability to order from you on credit.

PAST-DUE LETTERS

When there are many invoices past due, or when the amount is significant, or when the payment is extremely late (and the customer seems to have no intention of paying) your best bet for securing payment is to send a personal letter rather than a series of form collection letters as shown earlier.

Format: [*See Appendix A:* Fig. A-1. Simple format for letters and memos.] Typed/word-processed. Business or personal letterhead.

Style/Tone/Voice: Use either informal or formal, active tone or voice. [*See Part I for more on these subjects.*]

Structure: (1) Immediately state the letter's purpose by acknowledging the customer's difficulty in making payments, (2) If necessary, tell the customer that it is in their best interest to pay you, (3) Request payment or suggest an alternate plan or schedule for payments, (4) If appropriate, indicate your willingness to discuss any difficulties the customer may be having with making the payment.

continued

continued

Handy Phrases: We have enjoyed serving you for the past five years; You have been a valued customer; We hope you realize how much we appreciate you as our customer; We notice that you are two months behind in your payments and are wondering what the problem may be; Before letting the account become more delinquent, please let us know what the problem is. We may be able to help by offering an alternate payment plan; Thank you for your letter explaining your company's financial difficulties. It clarified the matter for us, and we will be glad to help you in any way we can; We appreciate your candor in helping us understand your difficulty in making payments at this time; Perhaps you believe that you must either make full payment or no payment at all. This is not the case. We are willing to provide a modified payment plan to protect your credit standing; We will accept partial payments until June 30, after which we will require full payments; Next week a representative from our credit department will contact you to work out a permanent payment schedule; Are you aware that we have a monthly payment plan? If you would like, I will be happy to switch your account over to this plan; Please inform us of your decision as soon as possible; This is an urgent matter that requires an immediate reply; May we expect your phone call by; We will expect your first payment under this new plan by next week.

See also: *Part VIII:* Credit Hold; Working Out Arrangements; *Part IX* Termination of Contract and/or Agreement.

DATE: October 11, 2003
RE: Past Due Account

Dear Ms. Taylor,

I am writing to you to ask for your assistance in securing payment of past-due invoices.

Cleaning Corp. has received notice from Industrial Corporation for past-due invoices in the amount of $76,260.00. The response from Cleaning has been less than satisfactory. I would like to call your attention to the following invoices, which, according to our records, are still unpaid well beyond our normal terms:

Item	Cleaning Purchase Order No.	Industrial Corporation Invoice No.	Invoice Date	Amount
1	K8283	19473-003	8-January-02	$ 2,660.00
2	K8283	17881-004	6-April-02	$ 50,040.00
3	K8283	17881-003	29-May-02	$ 5,560.00
4	K8721	20346-001	27-March-03	$ 15,400.00

Item	Cleaning Purchase Order No.	Industrial Corporation Invoice No.	Invoice Date	Amount
5	K8721	20161-004	26-March-03	$ 2,200.00
6	K8283	19699-003	26-February-03	$ 5,720.00
				$ 76,260.00

Industrial Corporation has contacted both Mary Peeler and Alan Smith regarding the above. We believe that Industrial Corporation has provided appropriate documentation to support our claims. Unfortunately, we have received neither payment nor notice of the reason for nonpayment. Therefore, I am appealing to you to assist Industrial Corporation in collecting the amount past due.

Cleaning's account with Industrial Corporation is more than twelve (12) months behind our terms of 30 days. Your past-due account does not seem to support your good reputation and I am sure it is not your intention to ignore past-due notices.

It is our policy to help our customers as much as possible because we appreciate their business. If Cleaning has any questions or disputes regarding the above, please let us know what it is so that we can help. We must hear from you to understand what the problem is.

We ask for your cooperation in paying Cleaning's past due account.

Sincerely,

Industrial Corporation

Tips for Writing Past-Due Letters

- The tone of your letter should convey the seriousness of the situation. The message: "This is an important debt and we are not going to let it go."

- Insist upon some type of immediate response — either payment or a phone call to discuss the matter.

- Make a logical argument why having the matter unresolved is bad for the debtor and unacceptable for the vendor.

"LETTERS CROSSED IN THE MAIL"

Because of delays in mail and processing, anyone who sends collections letters risks sending a dunning notice to a customer who may in fact have already paid.

Obviously there is potential to irritate or offend if you send a strongly worded collection notice to a good customer who does not owe you money. You can cover yourself in such situations with an "our letters may have crossed in the mail" letter.

Format: [*See Appendix A:* Fig. A-1. Simple format for letters and memos.] Typed/word-processed. Business or personal letterhead.

Style/Tone/Voice: Use either informal or formal, active tone or voice. [*See Part I for more on these subjects.*]

Structure: (1) Remind the customer that payment is past due and state the amount owed, (2) Ask the customer to send payment, (3) Acknowledge that the customer may have already sent payment and thank him or her accordingly.

Handy Phrases: Discovered that payment for your purchase is past due; Realize that this may be an oversight on your part; My records indicate that your account is ten days past due; I thought you might appreciate this friendly reminder; We appreciated receiving your order; If you have not already sent in your payment, will you please do so now?; May we remind you that your June payment is now overdue?; We want to remind you that your account is past due; Perhaps you have forgotten that your payment was due on; Our records show that you have not paid your bill for; Did you forget to send us June's payment for $00.00?; Will you please send us your payment now?; We will appreciate your attention to this oversight; If you have not sent us your payment, please do so by March 30; Perhaps you have already sent your payment, but if not, we would appreciate your immediate attention to this matter; If your check is already in the mail, please accept our apology for this letter; If our current record of your delinquency is incorrect, please contact us immediately.

See also: *Part VI:* Request for Payment; *Part VIII:* Working Out Arrangements.

Dear Customer,

THE ENCLOSED INVOICE MAY NOT APPLY TO YOU . . .

. . . if, within the last 2–3 weeks, you mailed a payment or returned your merchandise to us.

If so, we simply crossed in the mail and your transaction is being processed here now. There is no need to contact us; simply disregard the enclosed invoice.

We are sorry for the confusion crossed payments cause. We are constantly working to cut the time it takes us to send out statements in order to provide better service to you, our valued customer.

However, if this is not the case, please give the enclosed invoice your prompt attention.

Sincerely,

Tips for Writing an "Our Letters May Have Crossed in the Mail" Letter

- Remind them that crossed payments, while an annoyance, are unavoidable.
- Acknowledge that they may have already paid and apologize for any confusion.
- Spell out the action required on their part: no action if they have already paid, or sending money if the invoice is indeed past due.

SHIPMENT HELD UP FOR PAYMENT

A common practice, especially among "continuity marketers" (e.g., book and record clubs) is not to ship next month's selection until last month's invoice is paid.

Format: [*See Appendix A:* Fig. A-1. Simple format for letters and memos.] Typed/word-processed. Business or personal letterhead.

Style/Tone/Voice: Use a formal, active tone or voice. [*See Part I for more on these subjects.*]

Structure: (1) Acknowledge receipt of the order and explain what prevents you from filling it, (2) State directly what information or action you need from the reader, (3) Close with an expression of appreciation and assurance that you will send the order as soon as you receive the necessary information or payment.

Handy Phrases: Your order is being held because we require; We need to receive either payment or the following information before we can ship your order; Please remit a check or money order for the full amount; We apologize for the inconvenience, and will ship your order as soon as we receive; Will ship your order as soon as your check arrives; We look forward to hearing from you so that we can ship your order without further delay.

See also: *Part VI:* Notification of Shipping Delay.

Dear Book Collector:

As soon as your account is up to date, we can send you the next volume in The First Choice Library.

Each will be an exact replica of the original first edition of a great American classic.

Your library can hold some incredible treasures! The great novels of Hemingway. Fitzgerald, Faulkner. Steinbeck. Sinclair Lewis. Robert Penn Warren. Norman Mailer. Edith Wharton. Willa Cather. Mark Twain.

These works are timeless classics, and with The First Choice Library, they are brand new again. You will own them as they first appeared — the same size, same binding, same typeface. There's even an identical dust jacket with evocative art that comes from the same period when the book was written.

Ordinary editions simply reprint the great American classics — these authentic editions re-create the experience of being alive and reading them at the time they appeared. As a subscriber, you have the unique privilege of enjoying these works "in the original."

For your convenience, you may want to have your First Choice Library volumes charged to your credit card — please see the back of the enclosed statement for details, or call us toll-free at 1-800-000-0000, Monday to Friday, 8 a.m. to 6 p.m. Eastern time. One of our Customer Service representatives would be happy to assist you.

We don't want to keep your collection on hold — there's too much pleasure to be had! Please send your payment today and enclose it with the invoice in the reply envelope provided. Your next exciting volume is ready for shipment!

Sincerely,

Sharon Cross
Publishing Director

P.S. If you ever have questions about your collection or billing, please call us (again, the toll-free number is 1-800-000-0000).

Tips for Writing a "Shipment Held for Payment" Collection Letter

- Avoid negative language like "we refuse to ship" and "failure to pay." Keep everything positive.
- Create a desire to continue receiving the product. Reinforce that they want to get further items in the series.
- Then tell them that you can start shipping again as soon as the account is paid up in full.

CREDIT HOLD

Unfortunately, not every past-due situation resolves favorably. Some customers, unwilling or unable to pay, go into denial. They don't want to think about their debt, and never respond to your letters and calls despite your best efforts.

In these situations, you have little recourse but to take away the customer's access to credit with your company. But, do not eliminate the possibility of continuing business. You should still be open to accepting orders on a cash-in-advance or cash-on-delivery basis until the customer has brought their account current.

The letter should explain why the decision was made to put the account on credit hold and what the customer can do to restore credit status.

Format: [*See Appendix A:* Fig. A-1. Simple format for letters and memos.] Typed/word-processed. Business or personal letterhead.

Style/Tone/Voice: Use a formal, active tone or voice. [*See Part I for more on these subjects.*]

Structure: (1) Inform the customer that payment is past due — state when it was due and indicate the amount, (2) Inform the customer that you are canceling the credit account, (3) Offer an alternative plan for your customer to make payments and continue doing business with you, (4) Thank the customer for past business and express your good wishes for his or her future.

Handy Phrases: We found that you still owe us the $00 that you promised to pay two months ago; Your account balance of $00 has been overdue for five months; Understand how difficult a financial setback can be; Have been generous in overlooking many of your late payments; Our records indicate that you have not made any payments for 60 days; Regret that we are no longer able to do business on a credit basis; We are forced to close your credit account; Need to make other arrangements with you to pay for our services; Reconsider your payment options and cancel your credit account; Effective immediately, we must discontinue your company's credit account; Hope that you will understand that we can no longer extend credit to your company; Future dealings will have to be on a cash basis; Be happy to continue to serve you on a cash basis; Aware of your current financial situation and will be happy to work with you toward getting your account paid in full as soon as possible; Have appreciated your business in the past and hope that you will find financial success in the future; Do not want this problem to leave any bad feelings between us; We are grateful for your understanding; We have appreciated doing business with you and hope this matter will be resolved soon.

See also: *Part VI:* Request for Payment; *Part VIII:* Past Due Letters.

Dear Bill,

You may be aware that the distribution groups for Stereos and Speakers have terminated Electronics, Inc. This has resulted in slow payment for Headphone and Stereo invoices and nonpayment of Speaker invoices. Below is the present A/R situation for each group.

*Speakers   A/R Balance, $81.5K, all past due. No payment confirmation provided
*Headphones   A/R Balance, $2.4K, $1.8K past due
*Stereos   A/R Balance, $642.00 credit balance

Please note that prior to the termination, Electronics, Inc. maintained a satisfactory payment history. However, payments over the last month have been slow or nonexistent.

For instance, the last payment received for Stereo invoices was 1/13 paying invoices due 11/21, 11/25, and 12/9. Additionally, the last payment received for Headphones was 1/8, paying invoices due 11/12, 11/18, and 11/27. It is my understanding that A/P was holding back payments at the direction of management.

Given the recent payment trend, I would not recommend releasing orders on net 30-day terms. I truly believe that would result in a doubtful receivable.

If you feel differently, the credit department will prepare, but not sign, a special shipment approval for the signatures of the Stereo Group management.

Let me know if you have any questions.

Thanks,

Winston

Tips for Writing a Credit Hold Letter

- Update all parties — vendor, customer, credit departments, purchasing — on the history and status of the account.
- Since putting a customer on credit hold is a serious matter that may put your relationship with them at risk, don't do it unless the size of the debt and slowness of payment become intolerable.
- Show how much is owed and how slowly if at all the debt is being paid.
- Tell the customer the new limitations you put on their credit. This may be shorter terms (e.g., payment due upon receipt versus net 30 days), a lower credit limit, or refusal to ship more product until all or part of the past due receivables are paid.

When the Collection Is in Dispute

Since most businesses invoice their customers based on product shipment, and pay invoices based on product receipt, any mistake in shipping or receiving will generate disputes over whether or not charges are legitimate. Likewise, simple mistakes in data entry — unit pricing, part numbers and keying errors — can also lead to disputes over invoices.

These disputes must be addressed in writing because of the detailed information — shipping documents, freight bills, invoices, receiving reports, etc. — that must be provided in order to determine the validity of the charges.

Once again, it is imperative that you do not criticize, insult, or blame your customer in any way because the customer may be right! You don't want to lose a customer because you were too stubborn to consider that the mistake originated on your side of the transaction.

REFUSING TO PAY A BILL

Keep in mind that just because you send collection letters doesn't mean the customer actually owes you the money. Sometimes, there may be a dispute or even an error.

That's why your collection series should always be polite and cordial. If the person you accuse of being a deadbeat is not, the relationship with that customer is destroyed.

When on the receiving end of a collection effort for money you do not believe you owe, you will have to resolve the matter in writing.

Format: [*See Appendix A:* Fig. A-1. Simple format for letters and memos.] Typed/word-processed. Business or personal letterhead.

Style/Tone/Voice: Use a formal, active tone or voice. [*See Part I for more on these subjects.*]

Structure: (1) Identify the disagreement and give evidence for your argument, (2) Clearly state the outcome you desire. If appropriate, state what action you are prepared to take to ensure a just outcome, (3) End by expressing your confidence in reaching a mutually agreeable solution.

continued

continued

Handy Phrases: According to my records; Am not liable for; Have enclosed a copy of; Have no recollection of; Seems to be an error in; Received notification that; If I do not receive a bill with the correct charge by next month, I will report your office to the Better Business Bureau and seek legal representation to protect my credit rating; Please send me a letter acknowledging; Please contact me immediately regarding this problem; If the error is yours, please remove the charge from my account, correct my balance, and send a letter describing these corrections; Thank you for correcting this error; I trust that this time you will correct your records; It appears that this is a simple oversight; Thank you for your prompt attention to this matter.

See also: *Part II:* Letter of Complaint; *Part VI:* Fee Dispute; *Part IX:* Letters Expressing Dissatisfaction.

Dear Mr. Smith:

I am sure that you value having a good name with the investment community. I am surprised that you continue to send me payment notices, since I was offered a free trial of your newsletter.

I have repeatedly indicated that I have no interest in the *Buying/Selling* newsletter. I have repeatedly marked cancel on your invoices as your initial offer indicated. Enclosed, please find that original offer. As your offer indicates, "This will end the matter — with no cost to me."

Wouldn't [the editor] be embarrassed to learn that annoying collection letters were sent to individuals who took him at his word?

I expect this matter to end now.

Sincerely,

Kelly Jacobs

Tips for Writing a Letter Disputing a Bill

- Say why you do not owe the money.
- Back up the statement with as much proof as you can provide.
- Express your annoyance at being billed for something you did not order or did not find satisfactory.
- Tell the reader what you expect to happen (e.g., you want them to stop billing you, credit your account, replace the product, redo the service, etc.).

ACCOUNTS RECEIVABLE DISPUTES

As a vendor, you may have customers sending you letters telling you that they do not owe you money. But that doesn't mean they are always right or that you agree with them.

If you don't agree — and you want the money you believe they owe you — you must state your case in a letter. The delicate part of this operation is to convince the customer to pay without unduly offending him.

Format: [*See Appendix A:* Fig. A-1. Simple format for letters and memos.] Typed/word-processed. Business or personal letterhead.

Style/Tone/Voice: Use a formal, active tone or voice. [*See Part I for more on these subjects.*]

Structure: (1) Indicate directly the point of disagreement, (2) State your disagreement and give evidence to support your view, (3) Clearly state the outcome you desire, (4) Advise any action you will take to protect your interests, (5) End by expressing your confidence in reaching a mutually agreeable solution.

Handy Phrases: According to the lease; Have enclosed a copy of; Pursuant to your letter of; The terms of our contract; Am enclosing copies of; Contradicts the terms; Must disagree with; Our previous agreement; Prompt correction; A written explanation; Honor the agreement you made; If necessary, call me at; Kindly check your records; Trust that it will not be necessary to; Study the enclosed; Appears to be a misunderstanding; If you need any more information; Resuming our mutually beneficial; Would appreciate your attention to this matter.

See also: *Part V:* Account Management; Resolving Disputes and Disagreements; *Part VI:* Fee Disputes; Request for Payment.

Festus:

I've given a lot of thought to our conversation last week and I'm not happy with how we left it (i.e., you're not going to pay me for the second load of mulch but rather you want to barter your mowing services).

Festus, I appreciate that you want to barter but the truth is I have no need for the services you offer; I have my own mower and mow my own acreage.

I am asking to get paid for the work that I put into chipping/shredding and hauling that mulch sixty miles to your place. I expect the $212 we agreed upon.

I look forward to hearing from you.

Regards,

Lester

Tips for Writing an Accounts Receivable Dispute Resolution Letter

- Acknowledge that you received, read, and thought about the other person's ideas.
- Demonstrate why you cannot or do not want to accept their proposal.
- Prove the value of the product or service you are asking them to pay for.

Working Out Arrangements

There are unique situations that will arise in your attempts to collect past-due amounts. The following situations — partial payments, payment plans, and credit gracing — require flexibility and understanding of your customer's special circumstances. These should be options of last resort, used only when you are convinced that your customer is unable to meet the payment terms originally agreed to.

PARTIAL PAYMENTS

Let's say you are a customer who wants to pay his or her bill in full, but you do not have the cash on hand to do so.

You convince yourself that the seller would be happy with a partial payment, and so you send a small check with the invoice.

But the accountant or clerk opening the envelope sees red. The bill is for $1,000, but your check is only $100. The numbers do not match up. They think you are pulling a fast one, and fire off a threatening collections letter. Not what you want.

So when you want to make a good-faith gesture toward paying back money you don't have, don't just send a check. Enclose a letter telling the company what you are doing and why.

Format: [*See Appendix A:* Fig. A-1. Simple format for letters and memos.] Typed/word-processed. Business or personal letterhead.

Style/Tone/Voice: Use a formal, active tone or voice. [*See Part I for more on these subjects.*]

Structure: (1) Inform the reader that you wish to make only a partial payment, (2) Explain the reasons for the request, (3) Acknowledge the inconvenience the change may cause, (4) Thank the reader for their consideration.

Handy Phrases: We have experienced some minor setbacks; We wish to extend our; I would appreciate your patience; As we smooth out some rough spots; Will be unable to; Sincerely hope it will not cause a problem; I hope you will understand that this delay is unavoidable; I realize that this will not be easy, but ask for your best effort; Although the delay may cause some inconvenience now, I think in the long run; Thank you for your patience and understanding; I apologize for the inconvenience our request may cause and thank you for; Will negotiate the payment of extra expenses this may cause you to incur; Thank you in advance for your flexibility in this matter.

See also: *Part II:* Favor Requests; *Part IV:* Requests for Business Favors; *Part IX:* Warning of Delayed Payment.

Dear Mr. Rosa:

I am late paying your invoice #548 for an embarrassing reason: I find my bank account short of funds to cover the amount due in full.

So instead of ducking you, and ignoring the bills and statements you send, I want to make an effort to pay the bill in full. Can you give me the time to do it?

I have enclosed $100 as a good-faith gesture. I can, with difficulty, manage to send you another $100, every six weeks or so, until the invoice is cleared up. Please let me know if that works for you.

I hope that you will accept my suggestion. I simply do not have the funds to pay more, and I am sure you would rather help a customer maintain her good credit and standing with your store, rather than dun someone who has shopped with you for over a decade.

Sincerely,

Pamela Hess

Tips for Offering Partial Payment

- Show a sincere interest in paying everything that you owe. Don't hedge by bringing up a complaint about product or service, as if to say, "I am going to pay you, but I really shouldn't." You know you owe the money. Otherwise, you wouldn't be sending money.
- Tell what you can afford to pay. If that's your absolute limit based on your financial situation, say so.
- Remind them that you have been a good customer. The reader will be more receptive to extending a payment plan if they think that, once you are done, you will give them more business.

PAYMENT PLANS

Customers often don't realize that if they cannot pay the $1,000 they owe you today, you would be more than willing to accept a partial payment now and the rest later.

If you are not willing to do so, reconsider your position. Getting part of the money is better than getting none of the money. Also, the longer you go without receiving even a partial payment, the more likely it is that the bill will never be paid.

The solution is to work out a payment plan with the customer. The plan should require regular monthly payments for an amount both you and the customer can live with.

As long as the customer continues his monthly payments on time, you allow him to pay off according to the schedule. If he misses payments or does not make them, his account is put back into the collection process.

Format: [*See Appendix A:* Fig. A-1. Simple format for letters and memos.] Typed/word-processed. Business or personal letterhead.

Style/Tone/Voice: Can be informal or formal. Active tone or voice. [*See Part I for more on these subjects.*]

Structure: (1) Express your gratitude for the customer's business, (2) Acknowledge the customer's difficulty in making payments, (3) Suggest an alternate plan or schedule for payments, (4) Ask for a reply.

Handy Phrases: Appreciate you as our customer; Enjoy being your supplier; Extremely valuable customer; Able to help by offering; Account is delinquent; Acknowledge your difficulty; Alternate method of payment; Appreciate the situation that you are in; Before you let the account become more delinquent; Faces financial difficulties at one time or another; Revised payment schedule; Thank you for your letter explaining; Are you aware we have a monthly payment program; Be aware of additional accrued interest; Extension on your loan; Once you have cleared this financial hurdle; Require a slightly higher interest rate; Will apply partial payments; Would like to help you through this difficult time; Hope our program can; How we can resolve your outstanding balance; If you can suggest an alternative; Let us know by Friday what you have decided; Payment plan that best suits your circumstances; Take advantage of this opportunity; This is very urgent.

See also: *Part II:* Letter Granting a Request; *Part IV:* Responding to Business Requests; *Part VI:* Resolving Problems.

Dear Mr. Shore:

Since you're unable to pay back the full $1,000 you owe us at this time, we are offering you an affordable payment plan.

Just send us $50 a month for 20 months. You indicated that that the $50 is an affordable amount, and we in turn are willing to accept these monthly payments in lieu of receiving the entire $1,000 now.

A booklet of monthly payment coupons and packet of payment envelopes is enclosed. Just send one in with your $50 check on the first of each month. There will be no mark on your credit history, as long as you follow this procedure. And we are not charging interest on your account.

It is important for you to make your payment each and every month. If there is a problem, call us. Otherwise, we will presume your acceptance of this offer and expect your payment on the first.

Sincerely,

Kim Rogers

Tips for Writing a Payment Plan Offer

- State the full amount owed, the monthly payment, and the number of months (terms) of the plan.
- Assure the client that they will not be considered a "delinquent account" as long as they pay the installments on time.
- You may provide payment coupons or envelopes, but let the reader know it is his responsibility to remember to make his payments; you are not going to remind him.

CREDIT "GRACING"

Maybe you want to retain the client's goodwill; they are so important to you, that you will allow them to be slow payers. Or perhaps you are giving the benefit of the doubt to a down-in-his-luck customer who really wants to pay but can't at this time.

Whatever the reason, you have decided to give the customer a break, and either forgive the debt, reduce the debt, or extend the deadline for payment. Your letter here has two purposes: to let the customer know what you are offering, and to maximize the goodwill you attain from doing so.

Format: [*See Appendix A:* Fig. A-1. Simple format for letters and memos.] Typed/word-processed. Business or personal letterhead.

Style/Tone/Voice: Can be informal or formal. Active tone or voice. [*See Part I for more on these subjects.*]

Structure: (1) Express appreciation for the customer's business, (2) Indicate your willingness to discuss any difficulties the customer may be having with making the payment, (3) Suggest an alternate plan or schedule for payments, (4) State what action the customer must take, (5) Direct the customer to respond immediately.

Handy Phrases: I will contact you on Monday to discuss your payment options. I want to resolve this situation, so please be prepared to help me understand your current financial status; We hope you realize how much we appreciate you as our customer; We notice that you are two months behind in your payments; We may be able to help by offering an alternate payment plan; Thank you for your letter explaining your company's financial difficulties. It clarified the matter for us, and we will be glad to help you in any way we can; We appreciate your candor in helping us understand your difficulty in making payments at this time; Perhaps you believe that you must either make full payment or no payment at all. This is not the case. We are willing to provide a modified payment plan to protect your credit standing; Are willing to discount your past-due amount by 50%; Will waive any accrued interest; We will provide a grace period until June 30, after which we will accept partial payments until the debt is paid in full; Next week a representative from our credit department will contact you to work out a permanent payment schedule; Please inform us of your decision as soon as possible; This is an urgent matter that requires an immediate reply; May we expect your phone call by.

See also: *Part VIII:* Partial Payments; Payment Plans; *Part IX:* Letters Regarding Payment Problems.

Dear Mr. Hall:

Thank you for your cooperation with regard to the supplementary proceeding. Mr. Adams joins me in wishing you better fortune in the employment market.

We will make no further efforts to enforce this debt against you personally in the near future. We will waive any interest accruing from the time of your last payment, provided that, when you are able, you resume efforts to satisfy the judgment. Should you be "back on your feet" and make no effort to contact us once you are able to make payments, we will include interest in our claim.

Periodically, that is every two years or so, we may contact you for a similar appearance. We would appreciate your continued cooperation.

Very truly yours,

Raymond Fuller, Esq.

Tips for Writing a Gracing Letter

- Make clear the terms and conditions.
- Give the reason why you are making an exception to your standard credit and collection policies.
- Ask them to reciprocate and pay back your trust by complying with any requests you make.

Lines of Credit

In order to operate your business expeditiously you will have to allow your customers to purchase on credit. In large business organizations all customers must apply for a credit line by completing a credit application. The credit department will then investigate the customer's creditworthiness by bank and trade reports, or by requesting a credit report from a credit-reporting agency or from an industry credit group. A credit line will then be assigned based upon the information obtained. This is the same procedure followed when an individual is applying for a credit card or personal loan.

In a small business the owner-operator will approve credit based on wide-ranging criteria, from credit reports to personal relationships to past business dealings.

Customers are authorized to receive products and services as long as their account is current and within the line of credit. If an order is placed that brings their balance higher than the line of credit, the account must be reviewed before a decision is made to allow the sale.

The following series of letters deals with requesting credit, extending credit, denying credit, adjusting credit lines, and changing credit terms.

EXTENDING CREDIT

At times you may want to offer a line of credit to existing customers, prospects you want to do business with, or both. When extending credit or increasing the credit line of an existing customer, you are providing the customer with a value-added service, and your letter should let them know it.

When extending credit to a noncustomer, you must of course first establish who you are and why it makes good sense for them to do business with you.

Format: [*See Appendix A:* Fig. A-1. Simple format for letters and memos.] Typed/word-processed. Business or personal letterhead.

Style/Tone/Voice: Use either an informal or formal, active tone or voice. [*See Part I for more on these subjects.*]

Structure: (1) Inform the reader that the credit line has been approved, (2) Discuss the credit terms, (3) Close with an offer or pledge of service.

Handy Phrases: Thank you for your letter requesting credit; Your credit has been approved and your charge card is enclosed; I am happy to inform you that your line of credit has been approved; Congratulations! Our financial department has approved your; According to the terms set forth; Your references reported favorably, and we are delighted to approve your application for; Thank you for your patience as we checked your credit references; Your credit history is exemplary; We are pleased to offer you a $5,000 credit line; Payment terms will be; Subject to the terms of; If, after six months, you would like us to review this limit; You will receive an invoice for each order and a cumulative statement at the end of; Charge no interest on payments made within 30 days; Enclosed are our standard credit terms. Please read them carefully, sign them, and return them so that we can set up your account; If I can help you at any time, please call; Thank you for choosing us as a supplier; We look forward to a longstanding business relationship; We wish to extend our warmest welcome and hope that you will find your new account convenient.

See also: *Part VI:* Free Value-Added Programs; Service Level Upgrades; *Part VII:* Loyalty Program Letters: *Part IX* Vendor Payment Terms.

XYZ Telecommunications
22 East First Street
Anywhere, USA 00000

RE: $25,000.00 Business Credit Line Renewal
Account #:000-00000-00
LWB #: 000000

Starter Credit Association is pleased to inform you that the above line of credit has been automatically extended for an additional year because of your valued relationship and excellent payment record with the association. Except as expressly provided in this letter, all other terms and conditions of the above-referenced Line of Credit will remain in full force and effect.

As stated in your Promissory Note, at some point during this 12-month renewal period, the balance owed on the line of credit must be reduced to $100.00, or less, for 30 consecutive days.

Please return your check in the amount of $50.00 within the next 30 days for the renewal fee in the enclosed envelope to: Attention Business Credit Solutions, Post-Closing Department, Starter Credit Association, 30 South College St, Anywhere, USA 00000.

We would like to express our appreciation for your business. If you need further assistance; please do not hesitate to call me at (800) 000-0000 option 1, then option 3.

Sincerely,

Daniel Bond
Client Specialist

While the preceding example outlines a renewal of an existing service, the example below offers a new service to an existing customer.

July 29, 2002

Mr. Bill Hatter
Hatter & Co.
410 North Avenue
Anywhere, USA 00000

Dear Mr. Hatter:

As you may know, State Bank now offers equipment leasing through its wholly owned subsidiary, State-National Leasing Corp.

I am pleased to inform you that your company has been preapproved for a $100,000 Lease Line of Credit. This line is in addition to your existing credit facility with State Bank and is available to you immediately. If you require lease financing for amounts greater than the preapproved initial line, please call me.

I am enclosing a letter and brochure from State-National with more details about the leasing program.

Very truly yours,

William Bolling
Senior Vice President

Tips for Extending or Granting Credit

- Say how much credit they have and whether there are any restrictions (e.g., the credit can only be used toward the purchase of some product lines but not others).
- Tell the reader what she has to do to activate the line of credit. If no action is required, say so.
- Say why they are having their credit increased; e.g., because they are a valued customer, or they have never missed a payment, or whatever the reason.

REQUESTING CREDIT

We looked earlier at letters from companies eager to extend credit to potential and existing customers.

As a consumer or business buyer, you may want to actively request credit from vendors who currently give you either no credit, or credit too limited for the purchases you want to make.

If you want credit, simply ask for it. In today's competitive economy, companies are actively seeking new customers. Many will be glad to extend credit to you, if they know that doing so will get you to start buying from them.

Format: [*See Appendix A:* Fig. A-1. Simple format for letters and memos.] Typed/word-processed. Business or personal letterhead.

Style/Tone/Voice: Use a formal, active tone or voice. [*See Part I for more on these subjects.*]

Structure: (1) Make your request, (2) State the reason for your request, (3) Explain why you are a good credit risk and give credit references, (4) Ask for an immediate response.

Handy Phrases: I wish to open a credit account with your company to purchase; Need to make an unusually large purchase from your company and wish to set up a credit account; Have spent $00 over the past 12 months and anticipate maintaining this level of spending; Been your loyal customer for two years; Always paid for your services in cash and now wish to request a $00 credit line; We have recently expanded our business; We must purchase larger quantities; Increase in demand for our products means that we will need to purchase more; Pleased with your services and want to continue doing business with you on a regular basis, therefore, we feel it would be mutually beneficial for us to open a charge account with you; Our company is expanding rapidly and is financially secure; Enclosed are the names of three credit references who will be happy to respond to any inquiries regarding my credit history; We have held credit accounts with the following companies for the past three years; It is important that we receive your response as soon as possible. Thank you for your consideration; Thank you for your help and swift response; We will appreciate receiving your response as soon as possible; I will contact you in two weeks if I have not received your reply.

See also: *Part II:* Favor Requests; *Part IV:* Requests for Business Favors.

Vince Sanders
Sanders Printing
Anytown, USA

Dear Mr. Sanders:

We are a small ad agency — new, but growing rapidly. And as our client roster expands, so has our printing needs — and we are looking to work with a reliable, quality printer in the area. You came highly recommended.

As you know, ad agencies, especially small ones, buy and resell a lot of services — especially media and printing — on behalf of their clients. Therefore we are looking to do business with you on a net 60-day credit basis.

Our business account is #00000 at State Bank. We pride ourselves on paying our vendors on time, and I have enclosed references from three of our vendors. Feel free to call them, and let me know if you need other references.

We have an immediate brochure project that will be ready to go to press within 3 weeks. If we can pay you net 60 days, we would like to make this our first project with you.

Please let me know immediately whether you can accommodate us — we have a lot of printing jobs coming up and need a printer we can rely on. And I believe that Sanders Printing can meet that need for us.

Sincerely,

Jill Raymond
Raymond Advertising

Tips for Requesting Credit

- Establish that you are creditworthy. Give bank references, vendors, financial statements, your credit report, D&B rating of your company, and so on.
- Explain why you want or need the credit.
- Promise to be a loyal, active customer when credit is granted.

TURNING DOWN A REQUEST FOR CREDIT

What happens when someone actively applies for credit, but they are a bad credit risk?

You turn them down, but you do it in a way that retains them as a customer or potential customer.

Keep in mind that although your decision not to extend credit is based on financial or business considerations, people take it personally. Therefore credit denial must be made with a gentle hand.

Format: [*See Appendix A:* Fig. A-1. Simple format for letters and memos.] Typed/word-processed. Business or personal letterhead.

Style/Tone/Voice: Use a formal, active tone or voice. [*See Part I for more on these subjects.*]

Structure: (1) Thank the applicant for applying for credit, (2) Soften the refusal by noting any positive items in the reader's application, (3) State the reasons for refusal, followed by a brief refusal, (4) Suggest other possibilities for doing business, (5) Offer encouragement or a suggestion to reapply later.

Handy Phrases: Appreciate your application; Desire to establish credit with us; Thank you for your recent request for a line of credit with; Underwent our standard credit investigation; According to your financial statements and our credit information; Are not in a position to extend the amount of credit you desire; Based on your application and the formulas we use; Committee decided to not grant the requested line of credit; Does not conform to our company credit requirements; My unfortunate duty to inform you of your ineligibility; Not able to extend credit to you; Sorry to inform you that we cannot extend credit at this time; Considered finding a cosigner for your loan; Glad to consider any additional information you can provide; Hope you will understand our position; Am sorry we can't do more for you at this time; Available at your convenience to discuss a smaller line of credit; Hope you will apply again later; Look forward to continuing our business association; Please don't hesitate to get back in touch with us; Sincerely want you as a customer

See also: *Part II:* Refusing a Request; *Part IV:* Refusing Business Requests; *Part VI:* Sensitive Customer Correspondence.

Dear Mr. Volt:

Your decision to enter the growing television and radio repair business is good news to us at Local Electronics Distributors. In addition to sharing common interest in a rapidly advancing field, our competent salespeople look forward to supplying you with the test equipment and parts you will need to get your business going.

As you know, the financial burdens of beginning any business, particularly one as complex and changing as electronics, are substantial. We have had the experience of extending credit to new customers to help them get their business going only to find out we had done them a disservice. For in the early months the young businesses did not generate enough servicing volume to meet the demand that large credit purchases placed on them.

Let's help each other by dealing on a cash basis, at least for a few months. As a dealer, you are welcome to attend our annual show, April 14, from 7 to 9 p.m., at the Main Avenue store. In the meantime, you can count on our large in-store inventory and direct factory ordering to get the parts you need in your hands as quickly as possible.

Sincerely,

Tips for Writing Letters Refusing Credit

- Thank the prospect or customer for their interest in your company and products.
- Say that you want them as a customer, but for now, on a cash-with-order basis.
- Say that you are not able to establish a credit line with them now, and give a credible but nonoffensive reason.
- If they can do something to become creditworthy, tell them what it is. Encourage and help them to do it.

CREDIT ADJUSTMENTS

For a variety of reasons — an accounting error, late charges, special discounts, items not received — adjustments may have to be made to customer accounts from time to time.

The less time you take to make these adjustments clear to the customer, the busier you will be answering e-mails and phone calls from customers who don't understand the adjustments and want them explained.

Format: [*See Appendix A:* Fig. A-1. Simple format for letters and memos.] Typed/word-processed. Business or personal letterhead.

Style/Tone/Voice: Use either an informal or formal, active tone or voice. [*See Part I for more on these subjects.*]

Structure: (1) Explain the error, (2) Explain what you will do to remedy the problem, (3) Offer an apology.

Handy Phrases: Clerical errors occur at times; Failed to inform him that you had been given a discount; Incorrect computer entry; Our data processing department erred; Simply forgot to tell; Account is clear; Accounting department will make the correction; As you can see from the enclosed statement; Have adjusted our records to reflect; Have canceled the invoice amount; Have credited you for the amount; Have enclosed a corrected invoice; Have taken action to rectify the situation; Will apply the overcharge toward next month's bill; Will take every precaution to make certain that; Apologize for any inconvenience apologize for the error; Appreciate your business; Please accept my sincere apology; Thank you for your patience.

See also: *Part VI:* Sensitive Customer Correspondence.

Ms. Amy Adams
Anytown, USA

RE: Credit adjustment — account #306

Dear Ms. Adams,

We have credited your account at Bellinger's Department store $75 for the pair of dress shoes you returned.

I'm sorry the shoes discolored in rain, and appreciate you telling me about this defect. We have taken steps to ensure this problem will not happen in the future.

In the meantime, we have a new line of dress shoes from another manufacturer. The styles are gorgeous and the quality without peer.

These shoes naturally are more expensive — $90 to $110 a pair. But to compensate you for your inconvenience, I want you to have a pair for the $75 price of the less-expensive brand. Simply bring this letter into the store and ask for me at the shoe department.

Sincerely,

Melanie Roth

Tips for Writing Adjustment Letters

- If the adjustment is necessitated by a problem or error on your end, apologize.
- State the amount and reason for the credit.
- Use this as an opportunity to sell more of your products to the customer on credit.

CHANGE OF TERMS

As time goes on, you may be forced change the credit status of a customer, including limit and terms.

Do you have to give a reason? It depends. If the customer is likely to accept the need for changes as logical and reasonable, then give the reason for them.

On the other hand, if the customer is likely to take offense, you can give no reason or just say it is a new policy. People tend to argue less with something that is a policy rather than an individual decision:

Format: [*See Appendix A:* Fig. A-1. Simple format for letters and memos.] Typed/word-processed. Business or personal letterhead.

Style/Tone/Voice: Use a formal, active tone or voice. [*See Part I for more on these subjects.*]

Structure: (1) Explain the circumstances that require the change in terms, (2) Review the current agreement and then outline the specific changes to be made, (3) Express your desire for a mutually beneficial agreement and thank him for considering your request.

Handy Phrases: Has necessitated a; Make a temporary change in; No longer suits our needs; Am sure you understand that; Contract will expire on; Hope you will give the matter your attention; Request that we renegotiate; Under the following terms; Would like to revise the contract; Draw up an addendum; Mutually beneficial; Regret the necessity of; Satisfactory to both of us; Work out a new agreement; Would very much appreciate; Your kind cooperation.

See also: *Part VI:* Sensitive Customer Correspondence.

Edward Smart
Smart Products
Anytown, USA

Dear Mr. Smart:

As you know, production costs in the widget industry are rapidly rising, mainly due to the sky-rocketing price of raw widget powder.

While we do not want to pass all of these cost increases on to our customers, we still need, just like your business, to make a decent profit — and our margins have been steadily shrinking for a decade.

That is why we must announce that we can no longer continue to offer our traditional free shipping and handling on orders of $1,000 or more.

Effective 1/2/04, the customer is required to pay all shipping and handling charges on all widget orders, regardless of quantity or dollar amount of purchase.

However, our volume discount schedule remains in effect. And by ordering in quantity, your entire order is sent to you in one shipment, which keeps shipping & handling costs low.

We look forward to continuing to serve you, and if you have questions or want to discuss this, please give me a call.

Sincerely,

Tom Pottinger

P.S. Your quantities are large enough for you to become a Distributor, which would further lower your costs.

Tips for Announcing a Change in Credit Terms or Policies

- Notify the customer of the change well in advance of when the change goes into effect. Allow them to buy under the old terms for three to six months before the new terms kick in.
- Give the reason why you must make these changes.
- Remind the customer why you are still the best vendor for this product, even with the changing terms.

PART IX

VENDOR COMMUNICATIONS

Often we only communicate with vendors — those people whose products or services we need to run our own business or to help us in our personal lives — when we have a need. We write to them to place an order, issue a complaint, or make a payment. But by limiting our communications, we're missing an opportunity to build valuable relationships with people who can be a great help to us. Being on a vendor's 'A' list can be a plus if you have an emergency, need a price break, or want to be a person the vendor refers other business to (if applicable). Communicating with vendors may not seem like such an important topic if you don't own a business, but don't skip this chapter yet. Communicating professionally may help you get answers and better customer service from large corporations that are sometimes hard nuts to crack. Likewise, it can help establish good relationships with local vendors. Contractors and service providers are more likely to go out of their way for someone who can eloquently respond to references.

If you're like most people, you pay a lot of attention to how you communicate with customers and prospects. You pay a modest amount of attention to how you communicate with your employees. And you pay virtually no attention to how you communicate with vendors. Until recently, vendors occupied the bottom rung of the "communications totem pole." After all, they work for you. You pay them. You are the customer. And, it's a buyer's market.

It's only in the last decade, with the relatively new concepts of strategic partnerships and supply chain management, that businesspeople are paying closer attention to how they deal with and treat vendors. And that makes good business sense.

The performance of your vendors affects your own performance and ability to deliver quality products to your customers on time. By managing vendor relationships through effective communication, you can increase the value their products and services bring to your organization, while motivating them to always give their best when servicing your account.

Letters Requesting Information

Letters, faxes, and e-mails are all effective ways to keep in touch with vendors when requesting information about pricing and availability, not only because it makes good sense to do so, but because you often have to relay lots of details — including some-times complicated alpha-numerical sequences (e.g., my fax machine is a KX-FHD331 and the refill cartridge is KX-FA93). The following samples show you how to request a wholesale price list or additional information, inquire about product or service availability, and ask for quotes and estimates.

Request for Wholesale Price Lists

Let's start with a simple communication: contacting a potential vendor and asking about his prices.

Format: [*See Appendix A:* Fig. A-1. Simple format for letters and memos.] Typed/word-processed. Business or personal letterhead.

Style/Tone/Voice: Can be either informal or formal. Active tone or voice. [*See Part I for more on these subjects.*]

Structure: (1) Request information, be specific as possible about product lines or specific models, (2) Explain who you are, (3) Close with a friendly expression of a desire to work together.

Handy Phrases: We are interested in your product; Please send information; We look forward to working with you; It would be a privilege to partner with you.

See also: *Part IV:* Requests for Information; *Part VII:* Inquiry-Fulfillment Letters; *Part IX:* Letters Requesting Information.

August 20, 2003

Dear Rob:

Your advertisement in the June issue of *Groom and Bride* magazine is of great interest to us. We would like to know more about the products your firm offers and would appreciate receiving your wholesale price list and information regarding terms, ordering policy, and discounts on volume purchases.

It is our desire to offer our customers the widest selection possible of [type of product]. Since we are always interested in new products that fall within that area, we request that you send us information.

We look forward to your prompt response. Thank you.

Very truly yours,

Tips for Making Wholesale Price List Requests

- Let the vendor know where you learned about his company and products or services.

- Ask for a current price list.

- Inquire about terms and conditions. Will they let you buy on a bill-me basis or consignment? What is the return policy for unsold or unused goods?

REQUEST FOR ADDITIONAL INFORMATION

Whether they are brochures, catalogs, or data sheets, rarely does the initial inquiry fulfillment material sent by the vendor answer every conceivable question a prospect may have before making a purchase decision. Therefore you will probably request additional information or answers to your specific questions by phone, mail, or e-mail.

Format: [*See Appendix A:* Fig. A-1. Simple format for letters and memos.] Typed/word-processed. Business or personal letterhead.

Style/Tone/Voice: Can be informal or formal. Active tone or voice. [*See Part I for more on these subjects.*]

Structure: (1) Ask for the information you want. If applicable, explain how you learned about the product/service, (2) If applicable, explain why you are interested in more information, (3) Give your contact information, (4) Thank vendor and state that you look forward to receiving the additional material.

Handy Phrases: Please provide a list; catalog and pricing list; Could you please provide; I have some questions about; Need the information by; Need to make a decision by; Please notify me about; Please send it to the following address; We'd appreciate receiving; Finding out more about; Thank you for your help.

See also: *Part II:* Information Letters: Formal Information Letters and Requests; *Part IV:* Business Requests; *Part VII:* Inquiry-Fulfillment Letters; *Part IX:* Letters Requesting Information.

January 17, 2002

Dear Frank:

On December 13, we requested information on your chocolates, and your brochure was delivered to our office on December 16.

Thank you for the manner in which you expedited this information to us. You are to be commended. We do have one question regarding your new selection. What is the minimum purchase order for the truffles? I will be looking forward to your response.

Very truly yours,

Tips for Requesting Additional Information

- Tell the vendor that you previously made an inquiry and that you have some follow-up questions.
- Remind them of what they already sent you (e.g., their brochure) so they do not merely send you the same thing again.
- List the questions you want answered and the additional information you want them to provide.

REQUESTS FOR PRODUCT AVAILABILITY INFORMATION

There are lots of reasons why you may be contacting a manufacturer. You may be trying to buy directly from the manufacturer to save money or inquiring to see if a particular item is still being produced. Here are some samples to follow.

Format: [*See Appendix A:* Fig. A-1. Simple format for letters and memos.] Typed/word-processed. Business or personal letterhead.

Style/Tone/Voice: Can be informal or formal. Active tone or voice. [*See Part I for more on these subjects.*]

Structure: (1) Explain what product you are trying to locate, (1a) Give as much detail as possible (where you read/heard about it, model number, sizing), (2) Ask to be contacted regarding availability, state specific date if necessary, (3) Request ordering information, (4) Close by thanking manufacturer for their time and assistance.

Handy Phrases: I read about; I would like to replace; Do you carry; Is this product still being manufactured; Where can I find; Is there a retail outlet; Can I purchase this online; Can you give more information about.

See also: *Part IV:* Requests for Information; *Part VII:* Inquiry-Fulfillment Letters; *Part IX:* Letters Requesting Information.

June 4, 2002

Dear Irene:

My mother gave me her blender when I was married in 1999. While I have no record of a serial number, I would venture to say that she purchased it around 1984. The fact that this appliance never once failed either of us, and did not require any service whatsoever throughout all of those years of use, is one that deserves to be brought to your attention. You truly make fine kitchen equipment.

The problem is that during our recent move to Florida the movers lost my blender. After inquiring at several retail outlets as to where I could locate an older model as a replacement, I am following their suggestions that I write to you. While I know your current model has many new advantages, I would prefer to purchase one of older vintage. Can you help?

I shall be looking forward to your reply.

Very truly yours,

Tips for Requesting Product Availability Information

- Check the vendor's Web site first. Do a search of the site by product name and model number.

- If you cannot find the product online, write to the manufacturer and inquire.

- If you do not have the model name or number, give the most accurate description you can.

- The item may be an outdated mode. Let the vendor know you would be interested in purchasing their most current model if the old one has been replaced or is obsolete.

INQUIRING ABOUT SERVICES

You'll most likely find yourself requesting information on services fairly often, both professionally and personally. Requesting service information from vendors can run the gamut from gathering information on printing party invitations to requesting the fee structure from a marketing firm.

In most cases, the information you'll be looking for will be a description of services offered, a fee schedule, and/or a description of their experience in the type of work in question.

Format: [*See Appendix A:* Fig. A-1. Simple format for letters and memos.] Typed/word-processed. Business or personal letterhead.

Style/Tone/Voice: Can be informal or formal. Active tone or voice. [*See Part I for more on these subjects.*]

Structure: (1) Introduce yourself and/or your company, (2) Make a request and explain how/why you might be using the reader's service, (3) Give the reader your contact information so they can send the material, (4) Close with an expression of appreciation for their time.

Handy Phrases: We are interested in; I am working on a project for; We are considering buying; I'd appreciate information about; We need to make a decision by; Our deadline is; Enclosed is a self-addressed, stamped envelope; Please send an information kit to the following address; Any information you can give me.

See also: *Part II:* Formal Information Letters; *Part IV:* Requests for Information; *Part VII:* Inquiry-Fulfillment Letters; *Part IX:* Letters Requesting Information.

Mr. Russell Paul

Computertime, Inc.
123 Any Avenue
Anytown, CA

Dear Mr. Paul:

We recently noted in the Mill Valley News "Business Talks" column that you offer consulting services to small businesses. We have a public relations firm, and we need help interconnecting our current systems. We have three Power Mac 65s and two IBM ThinkPads.

We would like consulting help about how to network our systems, whether we need to purchase some software to port data between the two systems, and what kind of software we need to support our substantial business in presentation visuals.

Please call us and let us know your background, whether this is the type of work you do, and hourly rates.

Sincerely,

Tom Robinson,
Office Manager

Tips for Inquiring about a Service

- Let the vendor know where you learned about him and his services. Vendors like to be able to track response to their marketing efforts and know where each lead came from.
- Describe your requirement and the type of services you think you need.
- Ask the vendor whether he can help solve your problem, his experience in this area, and fee structure and rates.

REQUEST FOR PRICE QUOTE

When you make a request for a price quotation (RFQ), you ask the vendor to give you an exact price for specific goods or services, rather than send you a general price list.

A *quotation* is a firm and exact price. It carries with it an obligation to deliver the goods or services and then bill the customer the exact amount in the quotation.

Format: [*See Appendix A:* Fig. A-1. Simple format for letters and memos.] Typed/word-processed. Business or personal letterhead.

Style/Tone/Voice: Can be informal, but is usually formal. Active tone or voice. [*See Part I for more on these subjects.*]

Structure: (1) Open by stating that you are requesting a price quote, (2) Give detailed specifications (if there are lots of details, list them as bullets), (3) Give deadline for submissions, (4) Give deadline for vendor selection.

continued

continued

Handy Phrases: We are currently accepting bids for; I am soliciting price quotations on; If you are interested in bidding; Please let us know what you would charge; I've attached a list; Details are outlined in the attached spec sheet; Should include shipping and handling; We cannot accept substitutions; Please submit your bid by; Make our decision by.

See also: *Part II:* Information Letters; *Part IV:* Business Requests

April 30, 2003

Re: An Estimate

Dear Lisa;

Please quote us your firm price for the following goods:

1. Widget replacement valves
2. Widget insert (part # 65JK)

Please indicate all prices as they would be shipped under a rate that includes cost of delivery to and the loading onto a carrier at our place of business and indicate when your price quote expires.

Very truly yours,

Tips for Writing RFQ Letters

- Specify the goods or services for which you want a quotation.
- Ask the vendor to specify all terms and conditions (e.g., is there a charge for delivery and installation?).
- If you want the quotation in writing, say so.

Letters Expressing Dissatisfaction

Unfortunately, there are many times that a letter of complaint is necessary. As a customer, you are going to be dissatisfied with things you buy from time to time. Or there will be billing errors. Or you will receive the wrong item. Or you will be the recipient of shoddy service.

Complaints are best made in writing. Doing so creates a record you can refer to in case the issue is not immediately resolved to your satisfaction. It also shows that you consider the matter serious enough to warrant a letter and will not rest until it is resolved.

WRITING A LETTER OF DISSATISFACTION

We have all been in situations where there are continuous problems with the vendor during the course of a contract, and no matter how much you complain, things never get better.

If the vendor isn't "getting it," a letter expressing your dissatisfaction with their performance is in order and should be sent.

Format: [*See Appendix A:* Fig. A-1. Simple format for letters and memos.] Typed/word-processed. Business or personal letterhead.

Style/Tone/Voice: Can be informal or formal. Active tone or voice. [*See Part I for more on these subjects.*]

Structure: (1) Open by giving a full history of the complaint, including actions already taken on your part (e.g., phone calls, letters), (2) State full details of the complaint, including what items of the original agreement weren't met, (3) Tell what you expect to happen and when, (4) Express confidence that you anticipate the matter will be handled with care.

Handy Phrases: After several attempts; I'm truly disappointed; I feel that I am entitled to; I need to inform you; According to our agreement, I am entitled to a full refund; As the contract states; We expect to be treated with courtesy; Please send a service representative to; Am aware that problems do occur; I know you will take appropriate action.

See also: *Part II:* Letters that Require Special Handling; *Part IV:* Requests for Action; *Part V:* Handling a Dissatisfied Customer; *Part VI:* Sensitive Customer Correspondence; *Part IX:* Letters Expressing Dissatisfaction.

August 14, 2003

Dear Herb:

Last September we purchased one of your riding mowers from your Springfield distributor, Blow and Mow. We find now that the starter is defective.

Since Blow and Mow is no longer in business, I am turning to you to honor the lifetime guarantee on this product. I am returning this part for a replacement. Enclosed is a copy of the warranty and my registration number. I understand that I incur no costs with this exchange. I appreciate your service.

Sincerely,

The previous letter is an example of an attempt to get the vendor of a particular good or service to remedy part of the customer/vendor interaction that has gone wrong. While this is the more common purpose for writing a letter of dissatisfaction, it's equally important to state objections clearly when they involve a complaint for which you are not seeking a direct remedy, or in cases where you are not a direct participant.

Dear Jerry:

As the manager of the deli department, I think you should be aware of the horrible language that one of your employees was using as he spoke (yelled) at a customer. The customer was an older woman who was having some difficulty hearing him and it was clearly annoying your employee (probably because there was a long line of other customers waiting to be served).

His identification tag showed the name "John." I was truly shocked to hear the horrible things he was saying to the customer. I couldn't believe my ears. There were other customers present, including some with children! I don't know how many people he has offended, but I found it so offensive that I don't want to go into that part of the store again.

I personally feel he has no place interacting with the public when he lacks the most basic sense of propriety and kindness. Whatever action you decide to take, I am certainly willing to act as a witness.

Sincerely,

Tips for Writing Letters of Dissatisfaction

- Don't just say you are unhappy. Be specific about your complaints.
- As concisely as possible, run through the project history today, stopping to cite every instance where the vendor's performance let you down.
- Tell the vendor how disappointed you are. Ask the vendor how they intend to make things right.

NOTIFYING VENDORS OF DEFECTIVE GOODS

Naturally, if a product doesn't work or has some other defect, that's a good reason to return it. But just don't pack it up and ship it back with no explanation. Be sure to attach a cover letter explaining that you are returning goods purchased and why. Otherwise, your package may get lost in the mailroom, and the return may not be properly credited to your account. The best bet is to return merchandise via a carrier that can trace the shipment, such as UPS.

Format: [*See Appendix A:* Fig. A-1. Simple format for letters and memos.] Typed/word-processed. Business or personal letterhead.

Style/Tone/Voice: Can be either informal or formal. Active tone or voice. [*See Part I for more on these subjects.*]

Structure: (1) Explain why you're writing, (2) Give all details about the defect or your dissatisfaction, (3) Include copies of any relevant paperwork, (4) Explain how you'd like the situation to be handled, (5) Close with an expectation that you will hear back from the reader by a specific date.

Handy Phrases: I am having problems with; Does not work properly; Was delivered on; According to the warranty; Expect you to correct the defect; Please send me return instructions; I am enclosing a copy of my billing statement; The service contract; We look forward to; Need to get this resolved; Wait to hear from you; We are having continual problems with; As it states on the invoice; Credit my account with; Provide a new machine; Please send a service representative to; I know problems do occur; I've been a loyal customer for the past; Please take corrective action.

See also: *Part II:* Letters that Require Special Handling; *Part IV:* Business Requests; Tough Situations; *Part VI:* Sensitive Customer Correspondence.

Dear Carol:

I am a customer of longstanding — my home being almost completely furnished with your appliances, including an electric refrigerator, washing machine, etc. I have always felt that your merchandise was thoroughly reliable, and still do. But unless the mistakes that have been so common in my orders lately are eliminated, I will be forced to take my business to some other concern.

The nuisance of having to send things back is getting to be just a little too much. The last three orders have all had mistakes made in items sent.

The first was a coffee percolator instead of a coffee warming pot. This I sent back, and it was corrected. The second was a three-quart Corningware casserole dish in place of the two-quart I ordered and paid for. I needed the casserole dish, so I gave you the $14.98 rather than wait for the adjustment. The last mistake was sending two jigsaw blades instead of the two saber-saw blades ordered.

These were three successive shipments. Your percentage of error seems to be too high.

For your own information, you have already lost several accounts (my own friends and family) because of similar mistakes. So it might be wise to eliminate the cause of these mistakes, and save more of your customers — including me.

Sincerely,

When goods are ordered from a catalog or online, there is often no retail establishment available to accept returned merchandise. The following is an example of just such a situation.

October 30, 2002

Dear Customer Service Rep:

I recently bought a pair of hiking shoes (item # 4507F) from your catalog. I've tried walking in them twice now and I am unhappy with their performance.

Your catalog states that the shoes "conform beautifully" to the foot. They aren't doing so for me! These shoes have been very uncomfortable and each time I wore them, I've gotten blisters.

Per your 100% satisfaction guarantee, please send me a shipping label so that I can return the shoes to you at no cost to me. Since I do love your other products, I'd be happy if you gave me a credit towards a future purchase.

I look forward to receiving my shipping label sometime next week.

Regards,

Many businesses receive shipments virtually every day. Inevitably from time to time some of the merchandise will arrive damaged or flawed and an exchange or refund will be necessary. Often, these letters need not be as conversational as a personal return since frequently the terms of sale in a business interaction will outline the process you need to follow.

Dear Barbara:

We are in receipt of merchandise shipped to us SPECIAL in pursuant to your invoice no. 813A, dated February 18, 2003.

Certain goods as listed on the attached sheet are defective for the following reasons: Cracked housing; Broken seal ring.

Accordingly, we reject said defective goods, demand credit or adjustment and intend to reship said goods to you at your expense.

Please confirm credit issue and issue instructions for return of defective goods.

Very truly yours,

Tips for Notifying Vendors of Defective Goods

- Don't get angry or rant and rave.
- Explain your complaint. Why are you dissatisfied? Describe what is wrong with the products. Are they broken? Chipped or cracked? Missing the instructions?
- Identify the problem item, what you paid for it, where you bought it, and the date of the purchase.
- With your cover letter, send copies (keep originals) of any paperwork from the purchase (e.g., invoices, warranties, receipts).
- Tell the vendor what you want them to do to fix the problem (e.g., give you a replacement, refund your money, have the vendor send a service technician).
- Specify a date that you expect to hear back from the vendor regarding your problem.

QUALITY CONTROL PROBLEMS

Over the past 100 years or so, quality control (QC) has grown from an art into a science. Customers exact strict quality requirements from vendors. Vendors who fail to meet these requirements usually receive written warnings and requests for corrections.

Format: [*See Appendix A:* Fig. A-1. Simple format for letters and memos.] Typed/word-processed. Business letterhead.

Style/Tone/Voice: Use a formal, active tone or voice. [*See Part I for more on these subjects.*]

Structure: (1) Tell why it is important that the reader take care of the problem — give a full description of the problem, including relevant dates, product identification, invoice number, and a concise summary, (2) State what you expect as a reasonable response — be firm about any agreed-upon warranties or services (your tone should indicate that you presume the reader will take appropriate action, rather than taking a negative, hostile approach), (3) Close with an expression of your confidence or anticipation that the problem will be resolved.

continued

continued

Handy Phrases: Are having continual problems with faulty workmanship; Feel that I am entitled to; Have come to expect; Have received no confirmation; It is important that you; Is placed in jeopardy; Need to call your attention to; Places our working relationship at risk; Regret that I must; The latest problem occurred when; The performance of the; This situation warrants; As a valued customer; As the guaranty states; Provide a new machine; Request a full investigation; Send a service representative; Should refund my; Take appropriate measures to ensure that; The guarantee states that; Will take appropriate action; Am aware that problems do occur; Am confident that this, too, will; Appreciate your position; Bring this to your personal attention; Have been so responsive in the past; Have confidence in your; If we don't hear from you by; Maintain our professional relationship; Responsive to our needs; Take corrective action; Will take appropriate action.

See also: *Part II:* Letters that Require Special Handling; *Part IV:* Business Requests; Tough Situations; *Part VI:* Sensitive Customer Correspondence.

Dear Mr. Graham:

Attached is a sample of box board that your plant manufactured with metal particles embossed in the board. After three previous attempts to resolve this issue, your plant does not appear to be making progress on the elimination of scrap metal.

Metal of this nature, if found in a finished food box, could cause personal injury to a customer and lead to sanctions against my firm by the FDA.

Please let me know what action is being taken to remove this problem. I'd like to know what corrective action is being taken to resolve this issue and have a formal report on this by mid-November. Please respond back with a projected date of completion . . . I'd like to propose 11/17/05.

Sincerely,

Tips for Writing QC Letters

- Specify whether the problem is ongoing and pervasive, periodic, or just involving one particular batch or shipment.
- Say what the exact problem is. Ask the vendor what he is planning to do to fix it and by when.
- Let the vendor know how important his quality is to the overall product or process. For instance, a brake manufacturer who makes bad brakes can cause million-dollar damages to an automaker.

COMPLAINT ABOUT A SERVICE PROVIDED TO YOU

Quality experts talk about the goal of "zero defects" in manufacturing, but in practice it is virtually never achieved. The fact is, mistakes happen.

Achieving zero defects in service industries is even more difficult than in manufacturing. Not only do people make mistakes, but the buyer's opinion of service is based on even more subjective criteria than with products.

When buying a product, such as a refrigerator, it is relatively easy to determine whether the vendor has lived up to expectations. If the model of refrigerator is the one you requested and it works, you — as the customer — are going to be satisfied.

But say you hire an interior decorator to redo your living room, or a graphic artist to design a logo for your company. Whether or not you like their work is based on your individual preferences and subjective judgment. So service businesses have an even more difficult time keeping clients satisfied.

When you have a vendor on retainer, you are slightly less likely to end the relationship than with a vendor from whom you buy on a project or order-by-order basis. One reason is that a lot of time and effort went into evaluating and selecting the vendor, and the buyer does not want to repeat this process. Before showing the vendor the door, spell out your complaints and give the vendor a reasonable amount of time to correct the defects.

Format: [*See Appendix A:* Fig. A-1. Simple format for letters and memos.] Typed/word-processed. Business or personal letterhead.

Style/Tone/Voice: Can be either informal or formal. Active tone or voice. [*See Part I for more on these subjects.*]

Structure: (1) Explain your complaint in full detail, (2) State how you would like the reader to respond to your complaint (i.e., what you want them to do), (3) Close with a statement giving your contact information and a deadline for them to get back to you regarding the issue to be resolved.

Handy Phrases: I'm writing to call your attention to; I have to comment about the way; The latest problem occurred when; The unacceptable behavior of; I've been a valued customer; As it states on the invoice; I expect to be treated with courtesy; Please call to confirm a time; Want a full refund of; Responsive to our needs; Will take appropriate action.

See also: *Part II:* Letters that Require Special Handling; *Part IV:* Business Requests; Tough Situations; *Part VI:* Sensitive Customer Correspondence.

Re: [Account number, service provided etc]

Dear Anne:

On May 18, I rented a 2 hp gas cultivator/tiller at your Rockland location. Joel, the sales clerk, assured me that it was in working condition and that all the parts I needed were included in the box.

I am disappointed because the tiller was useless. The blades were dull, the engine kept sputtering, and the edging attachment was missing. This is in breach of the contract I signed with your company.

When I brought the tiller back to Rockland, Joel was totally unconcerned about my problems and basically did nothing to right the matter. In fact, he made it clear that I was an annoyance. I was very disappointed.

To resolve the problem I request that you refund my money and allow me to rent another tiller that is in good working condition. Enclosed is a copy of my receipt and contract.

I look forward to hearing from you and to a resolution of this problem. I am expecting a call from you next week and if I don't hear from you, I will be contacting the Better Business Bureau. Please contact me at the above address or by phone [give numbers].

Yours sincerely,

The example above shows how to use a letter to resolve a single bad experience. In the example below, the writer is addressing an ongoing concern.

Dear Mr. Weidner:

You will recall that you and I have discussed at least four times in the past eight months the low quality of service provided by your company. After each conversation, service improved for a short time, only to revert back to the old standard that brought about my original complaint.

I will summarize in this letter my previous discussions about your company's performance. You may wish to refer to our contract as you read my comments.

- Windows. According to the contract, all windows are to be cleaned once a month. This is not being done. Often from six to eight months elapse between cleanings. Even when the windows are cleaned, the job is less than satisfactory. But you are aware of this — you've seen the results on several occasions and always promised a better job "next time." It has not happened.
- Floors. The floors throughout the building are to be cleaned after each workday — the carpeting is to be vacuumed and tile and wood floors cleaned with special solvents. Although your servicepeople show up each day, their efforts can only be described as careless.
- Furniture and Equipment. Furniture and equipment are to be dusted or vacuumed daily, and once a month desks, chairs, tables, and other furniture are to be cleaned and polished. Neither of these two contract stipulations is being met to my satisfaction.

- Walls and Drapes. Walls and drapes are to be vacuumed every week. I'm convinced that this is not being done in several offices.
- Miscellaneous. I could mention a dozen other cleaning responsibilities that are not being met satisfactorily — pictures, glass-front cabinets, lavatories, and ashtrays, for example.

I call your attention to paragraph 7c in the contract, Mr. Weidner, in which the provisions for revocation of the contract are described. I do not like to consider such a possibility, but I must unless I have your written assurance that all provisions of the contract will be met.

I will be pleased to meet with you once more to discuss this situation and again point out to you why we are not satisfied with the present arrangement. I assure you that this is a matter of some urgency to me.

Yours very truly,

Tips for Writing Service Complaint Letters

- Reference the contract number or date and the specific services you are unhappy with.

- Compare the agreed-upon requirements to the levels of service actually delivered to date. Be specific. Go item by item.

- Explain the nature of the complaint objectively and calmly. Do not berate or belittle the reader. The person reading your letter may be the person who performed the service, and it does no good to insult him.

- Your key message: "We don't want to terminate our agreement with you, but if you don't shape up — and soon — we will."

- Offer assistance in helping the vendor perform satisfactorily and to clarify any concerns or questions.

- Lay out the next steps and tell the reader what you expect him to do and by when.

NOTICE TO SUSPEND DELIVERIES AND REQUEST FOR RELEASE

Many businesses contract for goods or services to be delivered on a daily, weekly, or monthly basis. Often this is arranged through either informal agreement or a formal contract. The customer gets regular delivery and often some kind of volume discount. The seller gets a steady source of revenue from that account.

If you are unhappy with a vendor under contract, not only must you arrange for the problem with the goods or services to be solved — but you probably will want to suspend ongoing delivery of an additional product or service until the solution is resolved.

Format: [*See Appendix A:* Fig. A-1. Simple format for letters and memos.] Typed/word-processed. Business or personal letterhead.

Style/Tone/Voice: Can be informal or formal. Active tone or voice. [*See Part I for more on these subjects.*]

Structure: (1) State your intention to cancel your contract/service agreement, (2) Provide brief explanation, (3) Give any necessary details about your account to ensure the correct action is taken, (4) Ask for written confirmation of the cancellation, (4) If applicable, end with a note of goodwill.

Handy Phrases: Have decided to; Must cancel our; We will no longer be; Please send me a copy of my last billing statement; Our contract number is; According to my records, my account is paid up to date; Thanks for your help; I hope that we will be able to work together again in the future.

See also: *Part VI:* Contract Termination Letter.

March 16, 1999

Dear Kate:

Your delivery of baseball jackets, which was received by us on March 14, does not meet the specifications as outlined in our contract of November 2, 1998; therefore, we are requesting that you suspend any future deliveries as called for in our contract and release us from that certain contract. Due to our contractual commitments, we must supply our customer with the appropriate goods within a specified period of time, which requires that we now proceed to make our purchases from a different source. We would appreciate receiving your release as soon as possible.

Very truly yours,

Tips for Requesting that the Vendor Suspend Delivery

- Describe the specific problem. Which shipment was late or defective? Which service let you down?
- Tell them that, because of this quality or service problem, you are putting a hold on further orders with them. This hold may be permanent, or you may lift it once the problems are solved to your satisfaction.
- Stress the importance of quality and service to you as a buyer, and that they must deliver this quality and service to get business from you.

Letters Regarding Bids, Contracts, and Agreements

Whenever working with vendors, it is best to put any request in writing. No matter how great your relationship, it's best to have a written confirmation of all transactions so that no one has to rely on memory in case of the inevitable problem or question about services/products. This section covers calls for bids; requests for proposals, contracts, agreements; and other transactions that occur during the beginning phase of hiring a vendor.

CALL FOR BIDS

Typically, people request bids for simple or straightforward products or services. You request a bid for sprinkler systems or a band of musicians for your daughter's wedding as opposed to making a more formal "Request for Proposal" for something detailed and complex, such as hiring a landscape architect or a wedding planner.

Format: [*See Appendix A:* Fig. A-1. Simple format for letters and memos.] Typed/word-processed. Business or personal letterhead.

Style/Tone/Voice: Can be formal or informal. Active tone or voice. [*See Part I for more on these subjects.*]

Structure: (1) Invite vendor to submit a bid, (2) Give details of your requirements (list format will make it easier for the reader to digest), (3) Specify rules or exceptions, if any (e.g., you will only accept limestone blocks for your front landing), (4) Give submission deadline and directions for how to send a bid.

Handy Phrases: We would like to get an estimate of the cost; We are currently seeking bids; Below is a list of specifications; Please let us know what you would charge; Please include the cost of; If you need additional information; Please include installation and other costs; Please have your price reflect freight to; We cannot accept substitutions; Have your bid in our office by; We need your bid in writing no later than; We will announce our decision on.

See also: *Part III:* Job Description; *Part IV:* Requests for Information; *Part IX:* Letters Regarding Bids, Contracts, and Agreements.

TO: Stanley Fromage

September 14, 2003

Dear Stanley:

We are currently accepting bids for replacing the chain-link fence that borders three sides of our property. The job will include dismantling the present fence, cleaning the area, and hauling away the debris. We want to build a new 5-foot-high cedar fence in its place.

Attached to this letter is a detailed sketch of the property. We would also like you to handle all the township approvals, so your estimate should include that as well.

If you are interested in this project, we would appreciate getting your bid on or before September 28. Please mail or deliver your bid to the address at the top of this letter. We hope to hear from you soon.

Sincerely,

Tips for Calling for Bids

- Be specific as to what the job entails and what you want the end result to be.
- Be specific on any other tasks you want the vendor to perform (for instance handling township approvals, as in the sample letter above).
- Give a date by which you must have the bid and how you want it sent to you.

REQUEST FOR PROPOSAL (RFP)

A *cost estimate* is a rough, approximate price. It says to the customer, "This is around what we think it will cost. But we won't know exactly until we have built the item or performed the service. The final bill may be a little more than the estimate, or a little less."

Vendors can usually provide firm price quotations for products and for simple, standard services (e.g., a lawyer charges a flat $200 for creating a will).

For more complex services that are difficult to price, the best the vendor can probably do is give you a tight cost estimate.

The more description you can give about your requirements, the more accurate the vendor's estimate can be. For that reason, it is best to define your requirements and specifications in a tightly written, well-organized request for proposal (RFP).

The vendor analyzes your requirements, and then responds with a proposal detailing (a) his understanding of your requirement, (b) how he intends to solve it, (c) a breakdown of the services and time required to perform each, (d) a cost estimate, and (e) a proposed schedule or completion date.

Format: [*See Appendix A:* Fig. A-1. Simple format for letters and memos.] Typed/word-processed. Business or personal letterhead.

Style/Tone/Voice: Usually more formal than informal. Active tone or voice. [*See Part I for more on these subjects.*]

Structure: (1) Discuss background information and the reason for your request for proposals, (2) Detail all specifics (in outline form, if lengthy), (3) Explain selection criteria, (4) Give due date, (5) Invite reader to contact you with questions.

Handy Phrases: We're interested in; We are planning a program and need your services; Attached are the details of our request for proposal; We require references; Vendors will be selected based on; Please submit your bid by; Please complete the attached form; Please provide the following details.

See also: *Part III:* Job Description; *Part IV:* Business Requests; *Part IX:* Letters Regarding Bids, Contracts, and Agreements.

TO: Frank Benjamin
FROM: Bob Sparrow
RE: Request for Proposal
DATE: 11-6-2000

I am building a new Web site and would like to know what you would charge to do it for me.

Here are the details:

I. DESCRIPTION OF SITE AND THE IDEA BEHIND IT: Please note that this description of the Web site is designed to also be used as copy for the e-mail campaign and other promotional material.

You have a nifty idea for your Web site, like starting a chat group for coin collectors or selling reconditioned antique fountain pens online. But where do you find the vendors who can implement your marketing concept on the Web?

Just click on www.evendorsrus.com, a new online directory of e-business vendors. Tell the site what you need ("collect sales tax on my site," "accept credit cards," "create an incentive program for my customers") by clicking on a drop-down category menu or doing a keyword search. Your screen will display a list of vendors who can handle your requirement, along with their contact information (phone, address, e-mail) and a description of their services.

The majority of e-business applications marketers want to implement on their sites are already available from specialized vendors who have packaged solutions — either software or a service — developed specifically for those applications. By going to these vendors and buying their packaged solutions, Web marketers can get their sites up and running faster while saving hundreds of hours and thousands of dollars.

Until now, there was no centralized source of Web marketing solutions providers. The application you needed might already exist, but you'd never know it. By linking Web marketers with vendors who have exactly what they need, evendorsonline.com solves this problem.

II. SERVICES AVAILABLE ON SITE

Using the www.evendorsrus.com search engine is free. Visitors who register on the site can sign up to receive a free e-zine of Web marketing tips. For a limited time only, visitors who register at evendorsrus.com also receive a free library of downloadable articles on Web marketing, and a small bookstore offering my books on Web marketing with a link to the amazon.com affiliate program for online purchase at the site.

III. BUSINESS MODEL

The content and services of the site are free to users. Revenue will come from vendors listed on the site. Listing will be free, but they can buy an enhanced listing (an HTML page they submit) as well as banner advertising. I will need whoever does this site to place enhanced listings and banners on the site.

IV. SITE OUTLINE/CONTENTS

- Home page explaining the site
- A database of vendor listings — company name, address, e-mail, phone number, optional link to their home page, optional enhanced listing (click to an HTML page submitted by the vendor).
- Search engine to search the vendors (initially 20 to 40) and display appropriate matches by both key word and by predefined categories (probably 10 to 30) in a drop-down menu. The results of the search should be displayed and the viewer should be able to print them out as well
- A contact page
- A registration page
- A small online bookstore (two–eight books)
- A small library of downloadable articles (4–20 articles)
- An FAQ page
- A counter to measure hits

V. YOUR ESTIMATE

Please give me an estimate in writing that includes:

- Cost to put up the site as described
- Cost per hour for changes and updates as required.

Tips for Writing an RFP

- Be detailed. The more clearly the vendor understands exactly what you want, the firmer his cost estimate can be.

- Use bullets, subheads, and numbered lists. Break up the project into discrete tasks, steps, and components. The vendor can price each task, and then add the total to get the project cost estimate.

- Don't forget to ask about the cost of ancillary services. If you are getting an RFP for a new payroll system, your financial department will need training. Tell the vendor to give you a separate cost estimate for each ancillary service.

NOTIFICATION OF WINNING BID

One letter vendors love to receive is notification that they submitted the winning bid — and that you are awarding them a big contract for a lucrative new project. Your notification also helps the vendor prepare the necessary materials (agreements/contracts) for your project, so it's always a good idea to state all the facts and details surrounding the job. And, it's always smart business to have everything in writing — including good news such as your acceptance of the bid.

Format: [*See Appendix A:* Fig. A-1. Simple format for letters and memos.] Typed/word-processed. Business or personal letterhead.

Style/Tone/Voice: Can be informal or formal. Active tone or voice. [*See Part I or more on these subjects.*]

Structure: (1) Affirm that the reader has been awarded the project, (2) Congratulate vendor, (3) Confirm details of project/bid, (4) Attach any necessary paperwork (e.g., contracts, specifications), (5) Close with request for next steps.

Handy Phrases: We're pleased to accept your bid; You are authorized to proceed with; Award your company the job; This letter officially authorizes your company to; According to the terms on the enclosed; Have enclosed your copy of; Here are the documents you'll need; Please review and sign the enclosed contract; Hope to hear from you soon to work out the details; I look forward to working with you; Please sign and return the attached agreement.

See also: *Part II:* Congratulations Letters; *Part III:* Offering a Candidate a Position.

Re: Certification of Award for Snow Removal

Dear Mr. Bentley:

Congratulations! Based on the Board of County Commissioners action on Tuesday, November 14, 2001, please be advised that the Snow Removal Project, Contract PD 45-555-32, was awarded to your company as a lump sum contract of One Hundred Twenty-Four Thousand, Six Hundred Five Dollars ($124,605.00) (including Base Bid of $120,875.00, plus Alternate A of $2,350.00, and Performance and Payment Bond of $1380).

Please provide the Certificate of Insurance, recorded Bond requirements, execute the enclosed two (2) original agreements and return these together with any other submission requirements at your earliest convenience. Once these requirements have been met, we will advise the Contract Administrator for issuance of the Notice to Proceed.

Performance and Payment Bond forms are attached to this letter (six pages). The use of any forms other than these forms shall result in your company incurring additional expense to re-record your bonds on these County forms.

All Project information shall be noted on the bond forms as directed on each form.

Performance and Payment Bonds shall be provided to the Office of Purchasing for review, to assure compliance prior to them being recorded in the Clerk's Office. This may be accomplished by fax or hand-delivering a copy of such bonding paperwork to the Office of Purchasing.

Bonds must be recorded in the Clerk of Circuit Court Recording Office, 1st floor, 223 Palafox Place, Syracuse, New York, 13214, at your expense before the contract is executed. The cost of recording is $6.00 for the first page and $4.50 for each additional page. Checks are to be made payable to Syracuse Circuit Court Recording Office. Original bonds are to be forwarded to the Office of Purchasing.

Your expeditious attention to this matter is greatly appreciated. Please feel free to contact John Clark at xxx-xxx-xxxx if you have any questions, or if you need any assistance.

Sincerely,

Tips for Notifying Bid Winners

- Tell the reader they are being awarded the contract and verify the total dollar amount they will earn from the project.
- Have a positive, enthusiastic tone. Express congratulations. Say how pleased you are to be working with them, and that you anticipate a successful outcome.
- Outline what they need to do next.
- Specify target dates for next steps.

LETTER OF AGREEMENT

Letters of agreement are used to clarify working arrangements between two parties: a homeowner and a contractor; a consultant and a client; a vendor and a customer; a company department and senior management. When the relationship is customer/vendor, a signed letter of agreement may serve as a contract between the parties.

We cannot give legal advice regarding contracts or letters of agreement in this book. However, letters of agreement should accomplish several tasks:

- The letter must identify that it is an agreement to do work.
- The project should be named and described.
- It's also a good idea to thank the customer for choosing you or at least for allowing you to submit the agreement for consideration.

Other important items to include are cost, deadline, schedule, and payment terms. Be detailed and specific. If the agreement is unclear, vague, or ambiguous, it is the vendor, not the client, who is likely to suffer most, although it's generally bad for both parties.

Close by asking for the go-ahead — the return of the signed letter of agreement with any advance payment required.

Format: [*See Appendix A:* Fig. A-1. Simple format for letters and memos.] Typed/word-processed. Business or personal letterhead.

Style/Tone/Voice: Can be informal or formal. Active tone or voice. [*See Part I for more on these subjects.*]

Structure: (1) Express pleasure in working together on the project, (2) Explain all terms, conditions, and contingencies in detail, (3) Add paragraphs to cover conditions likely to arise, (4) Address the subject of expenses, (5) Give any necessary instructions, (6) Close with a request for final comments.

Handy Phrases: This letter confirms our agreement; In accordance with your; Our mutual understanding; Specifically requested that the terms of our; Any changes should be made directly on this agreement; For our records; I have enclosed; Please return a signed copy to; This will apply to; If there is any problem; If you have any questions; Let me know as soon as possible.

See also: *Part VII:* Sales Agreements; *Part IX:* Letters Regarding Bids, Contracts, and Agreements.

The following letter is an agreement sent from the vendor to the customer. As mentioned earlier, agreements are informal contracts and constitute an arrangement between two or more parties. (Contracts tend to be much more formal and are often written and/or reviewed by lawyers.)

Date
Mr. Joe Jones, President
Big Corporation
Anytown, U.S.A.

Dear Mr. Jones:

Thanks for choosing Satisfaction Ad Agency to handle your job #3333. Job #3333 is a series of three capability brochures. I will write these brochures for you and provide such marketing and editorial consulting services as may be required to implement the project.

My base fee for the services I described above is $10,000. That fee estimate is based on 100 hours of working time at my hourly rate of $100, and includes time for copywriting, editing, teleconferencing, meeting, consulting, travel, and research.

Copy revisions are included in my base fee, provided that at such time as the total time devoted by me shall exceed 100 hours, I shall bill you for additional working time at the rate of $100 per hour.

Out-of-pocket expenses, such as toll telephone calls, photocopies and computer printouts, fax charges, messengers, and local and out-of-town travel incurred in connection with the project will be billed to you in an itemized fashion.

Payment of the base fee will be made as follows: One-third of the above-mentioned base fee is due upon my commencement of work; one-third upon delivery of first draft copy; and one-third is due upon completion. Payment for expenses will be made within ten days following receipt of invoice.

If you are in agreement, please sign and date this letter on the lines provided below and fax it to me at xxx-xxx-xxxx or mail it to the address on the letterhead.

Sincerely,

John Brown

ACCEPTED AND AGREED

By: _____ Date: _____

This next sample is an agreement sent by a customer to his company's vendor.

Edgar Wheaton, President
Latitude Media Enterprises, Ltd.
P.O. Box xxxx
Calverton, NY 11933

Dear Edgar,

This letter will confirm our agreement in regards to you and Latitude Media Enterprises, Ltd., becoming a client. As we discussed, these are the terms.

1. Albert A. Butler will provide Latitude Media Enterprises, Ltd. with advertising mail-order copy that can be used for a 7" x 10" space advertisement, to promote a video product.
2. Albert A. Butler can also provide marketing expertise and consulting services for all aspects of this particular promotion at my retainer fee of $400/hour or, at my discretion, barter partial payment for gross profits on ancillary products.
3. All copy, copywriter's layout and design provided will be able to fit a 7" x 10" space ad. Camera-ready mechanicals-type, spacing, copy-editing, proofing, plus two AAs. Estimated $500–$750.
4. If both of us agree the initial test is not sufficiently successful to warrant a roll out in large volume, I will revise the copy up to two additional times at retainer time at $400/hour or any part thereof.
5. The fee for my services is $15,000 in advance plus a royalty of 10 percent of gross sales generated by said mail-order promotion. This royalty is to be paid monthly on or before the 15th. If the promotion is a lead generator, the royalty will be in the form of a mailing fee of 10 cents ($.10) per piece mailed.
6. It is hereby understood and acknowledged by you that I, Albert A. Butler, am relying on the accuracy of the information provided by you, the client, in order to develop the mail-order direct-response advertising. Furthermore, it shall be your responsibility to carefully examine any and all facts, representations, and information in the ad copy, and to delete any inaccuracies or untrue statements. You, as the client, are solely responsible for the contents of any advertising. Nothing in this agreement shall be construed to create or imply a joint venture between you and me and if anything occurs regarding this advertising, which may require the services of an attorney, you are solely responsible for any and all legal fees.

If you are in agreement with everything as set forth in items 1 through 6, please sign where indicated. If there are any changes you wish to discuss, please call me right away.

Sincerely,

Albert A. Butler
President, The Lentil Group

AGREED TO AND ACCEPTED THIS 22 DAY OF APRIL, 200x:

The Lentil Group, Inc.   Latitude Media Enterprises, Ltd.

_____   _____

Albert A. Butler, President   Edgar Wheaton, President

The Lentil Group   Latitude Media Enterprises, Ltd.

Tips for Writing Letters of Agreement

- Use plain English — not legalese. The latter is a turn-off, and your reader may not sign because of it.

- If the subject matter is complex and there are a lot of details and clauses, consider hiring a lawyer to write a more formal agreement in the form of a contract.

- Explain all terms, conditions, and contingencies in detail and have everyone review them. Make any necessary changes and then submit a final document to all parties so that there is a written record.

- Add as many paragraphs as it takes to cover conditions likely to arise. For instance, if you are a roofer, and promise to get the job done in 3 weeks, what happens if it rains for 21 days straight and you are not finished by the agreed-upon date?

- Address the subject of expenses. Is the client paying expenses? Which ones? Are there limits, e.g., meal reimbursement not to exceed $50 a day?

- Provide two copies of the letter of agreement. Tell the client to sign both, return one to you, and keep one for her files. Provide a self-addressed stamped reply envelope or return FedEx label she can use to send the document back to you.

- Develop a standard letter of agreement, using the models provided here, and have your attorney review it. Then use that as a template for your other projects.

- If there are more than three to five items in the agreement, separate these items by numbering them. That way, in discussions you can refer to "point 12."

- Note that the laws of your state govern the agreement. Name the state in the agreement. Know your state laws — ignorance will not protect you in court!

- Require the vendor to provide a federal tax ID number or, if he is an individual, a Social Security number.

NOTICE OF REJECTED BID

A less than pleasant communication for the vendor is to be told that their bid for your account was not successful.

Often it costs vendors a considerable amount of time and money to prepare a proposal in response to your RFP and submit a bid. That time and money is wasted when their bid loses, not to mention they aren't getting the revenue the contract award will generate.

Break the news gently. You want to maintain goodwill with the vendor. Keep in mind that even though you didn't pick them for this job, you may want to buy from them for a future need.

Format: [*See Appendix A:* Fig. A-1. Simple format for letters and memos.] Typed/word-processed. Business or personal letterhead.

Style/Tone/Voice: Normally more formal than informal. Active tone or voice. [*See Part I for more on these subjects.*]

Structure: (1) Express appreciation for the time and effort given to submit the bid, (2) Tactfully describe why the bidder was not selected, (3) If possible, highlight features about the reader's bid and/or company, (4) Close with an upbeat statement of a wish for a future venture together.

Handy Phrases: We appreciate the time you took to create such a detailed bid; Thank you for your excellent work on the bid you submitted to us; Your references and list of previous clients are impressive; Thank you for the well-thought-out proposal on; Afraid I have some disappointing news; After thorough analysis and discussion of the; Due to an unusually competitive response; Because of the overwhelming number of fine proposals submitted; We have decided to award the project to; Better terms than you can offer; Regret to inform you that we have awarded another bidder the; While all of the proposals were of exceptionally high quality; Appreciate the large amount of time and interest you put into; I assure you that we will give you an opportunity to bid again; I hope to have better news for you on the next bid; Likely that we will be able to do business together in the future.

See also: *Part III:* Letter to Unsuccessful Candidate; *Part IV:* Refusing Business Requests.

Dear Edward:

Thank you very much for the proposal you submitted to us on May 16 in response to our request.

We are aware of the great deal of time and work that went into your bid. Therefore, it is with regret that we inform you that we have awarded the contract to another firm. We based our decision on the number of project managers that the other firm can allocate for onsite management.

Edward, your company has a great reputation in our industry. Please know that we will certainly be inviting your firm to bid on our future projects and thank you once again for your proposal.

Very truly yours,

Here's a rejection letter sent to a painting contractor:

Dear Donald:

Thank you for submitting your bid for painting the exterior and interior of the CBAC, Inc. office building. We have decided to accept a competitor's bid instead of the one you submitted. Our board members approved a plan from another vendor based on the vendor's schedule. We do look forward to the possibility of working with you on future needs. We'll also be happy to refer you to other colleagues as appropriate.

Regards,

Tips for Notifying Vendors that Their Bid Was Rejected

- Thank the vendor for submitting their proposal in response to your request.
- Tell the vendor that although they are certainly qualified, you chose another vendor in this instance. Give a reason, if appropriate (e.g., the other firm's fee was lower).
- Assure the vendor that you appreciate the effort that went into their proposal and you will consider them for future projects that are a better fit with their capabilities.

RETAINER AGREEMENT

A specialized type of letter of agreement is an agreement for a monthly retainer for services rendered.

The idea is that the client pays the vendor a regular monthly fee for services, each and every month. In return, they get some concessions or extra service — a discount off the vendor's regular rate; a higher level of service; faster turnaround; priority handling of their requirements.

Some retainer agreements are for fixed periods, such as a year or six months, and carry a stiff penalty for cancellation. Others are month by month, with a small or no penalty for cancellation by either party.

The agreement can call for the client to pay for each month's retainer in advance, or the vendor can bill the client at the end of each month.

Format: [*See Appendix A:* Fig. A-1. Simple format for letters and memos.] Typed/word-processed. Business or personal letterhead.

Style/Tone/Voice: Usually formal. Active tone or voice. [*See Part I for more on these subjects.*]

Structure: (1) State the project, (2) List all the details including start and end dates, any particular do's and don'ts, and fees, (3) Explain payment schedule, (4) Close with a request for a written acceptance of the retainer letter.

Handy Phrases: Thank you for hiring me to; You have agreed; As we discussed, I am being hired as an independent contractor: We have agreed on a $1,000 monthly retainer; As you requested, at the three-month mark, we will review the scope of work and decide; I will send you an invoice each month; I will attach a time sheet each month showing hours worked; The scope of work includes; Please reply to this e-mail to indicate your agreement to these terms.

See also: *Part IV:* Communicating Business Information; *Part VII:* Sales Agreements; *Part IX:* Letters Regarding Bids, Contracts, and Agreements.

Dear Ms. Pauls:

This will confirm that you have retained the services of my private investigative agency to assist you in locating your former high school sweetheart. I agree to use my best efforts in locating the whereabouts of your former boyfriend, Mark L. Greene. The full extent of our agreement is for my agency to locate the whereabouts of this individual and report this information to you.

For my services, you have agreed to pay me $75 per hour. On March 4, I received your initial retainer of one thousand dollars ($1,000) which will be applied against my hourly rate. In the event that I discover his whereabouts before the retainer has been depleted, or you decide to discontinue using my services for any reason, I agree to promptly return the unused balance within one (1) week from my written request. To reiterate our conversation, my hourly rate does not include costs and expenses. These include, but are not limited to, long-distance phone calls, travel, parking, and photocopies (to be billed at 30 cents per copy). They also do not include the fee for my assistant's time, for which I have advised you will be billed at the rate of $45 per hour.

Per our agreement, I will confer in writing with you on all expenses exceeding $100, which you shall approve before they are incurred. In addition, I will bill you monthly with respect to all services performed and costs incurred and shall send you complete, accurate, and itemized monthly statements with receipts to prove same. In the event I spend a sufficient number of hours to deplete the retainer, you will be advised before additional work is incurred to determine if you want me to proceed, and how much additional time you authorize me to devote to this matter. In no event will I incur more than $3,000 to this matter.

As notice of your acceptance of this agreement, please sign below where indicated and return a signed copy to me immediately. I look forward to working with you.

Very truly yours,

Jane Beamer, President
CBAC Private Investigative Agency
Accepted and Agreed to:

By: _____   Date: _____

Tips for Writing Retainer Agreements

- Do not pressure clients into retainer agreements. It's better for you if they ask about it. If they feel you pushed them into it, the chances for dissatisfaction are greater.

- Although agreements should be fair to both parties, err on the side of being less restrictive when it comes to cancellation. Clients do not want to sign agreements they feel limit their options too much.

- Add a paragraph at the close welcoming suggestions for alternative arrangements if the one proposed does not meet the client's needs.

CONFIDENTIALITY AGREEMENT

In working with vendors, customers most often divulge proprietary information that they do not want shared. In such cases, either the vendor or the buyer may provide a confidentiality agreement in which the vendor promises to keep the data confidential and not tell other clients or anyone else about it.

Such agreements typically run to two to three pages or more of single-spaced, densely worded, repetitive text, but they need not. Keep it short and simple.

All the agreement must do is say what information is considered confidential, what the requirements are for handling it, and the penalties for violating the terms, if any.

For extremely proprietary information, consider a patent or work with an attorney to create an agreement. Contract attorneys or intellectual-property attorneys generally charge a couple of hundred dollars for standard agreements.

Format: [*See Appendix A:* Fig. A-1. Simple format for letters and memos.] Typed/word-processed. Business or personal letterhead.

Style/Tone/Voice: Should be formal. Active tone or voice. [*See Part I for more on these subjects.*]

Structure: (1) State what information is considered confidential, (2) Explain your terms of confidentiality, (3) Give the timeframe that the information must kept confidential, (4) Detail information regarding destruction of the information and/or return of the information, (5) Outline legal actions for disclosure, and others.

Handy Phrases: Extremely confidential and valuable information; Will be held confidential; Authorized/unauthorized persons; Agree to the following; These terms are binding.

See also: *Part IV:* Getting Permission to Use an Unsolicited Testimonial; *Part VII:* Sales Agreements; *Part IX:* Letters Regarding Bids, Contracts, and Agreements.

CONFIDENTIALITY AGREEMENT

In consideration of my, the undersigned, being selected for and permitted to review extremely confidential and valuable information to small businesses, I agree to the following:

1. I agree not to share or use this information with any parties without written consent from the Widget Corporation and/or its client, or use it for myself to enter into a competitive venture. The only exception of this commitment will be another member of the project team or the project Coordinator. Furthermore, I agree that at the end of the project, I will destroy all printed documents.
2. I understand that if I reveal the trade secrets to unauthorized persons, I personally may be subject to penalties and lawsuits for injunctive relief and money damages as well as possible criminal charges.
3. I agree that I will not recommend to any business firm or individual requesting assistance for purchase of goods or services from any source in which I or other members of the project team or the sponsors may be interested, nor will I accept fees, commissions, gratuities, or other benefits from any firm or individual.

_____
Printed Name

_____
Signature

_____
Date

Tips for Writing Confidentiality Agreements

- Use short paragraphs, preferably numbered and bulleted. That way, if discussion is needed before signing, you can refer to "definition of work for hire in section 5."

- If applicable, define what effort is required to keep the data secure. You may want to specify technology, such as a firewall protecting the server on which the information is stored, or physical security such as a locked file cabinet.

- Include instructions for the handling of the material once the project is completed. Should it be kept on file, thrown away, shredded, or returned? At whose expense?

- Make penalties and liabilities reasonable. And they should not be incurred without proof of agreement violation.

TERMINATION OF CONTRACT AND/OR AGREEMENT

Contracts are usually more formal than agreements — and have more weight in a court of law because of their language and structure. In any event, there will be times you may need to cancel a contract for a reason other than dissatisfaction. If you cancel in accordance with the terms of the contract, you are not obligated to tell the vendor the reason for the cancellation, although it is a courtesy vendors much appreciate. For example, you would cancel your housecleaning service if you're moving to another state.

Format: [*See Appendix A:* Fig. A-1. Simple format for letters and memos.] Typed/word-processed. Business or personal letterhead.

Style/Tone/Voice: Can be informal or formal. Active tone or voice. [*See Part I for more on these subjects.*]

Structure: (1) Open with a statement of thanks for services/products provided during term of agreement, (2) Explain your intention to cancel your agreement, (3) Briefly state reasons for cancellation if applicable or appropriate, (4) Supply information to help the vendor close your account (e.g., account number), (5) Closing depends on terms of cancellation — extend good wishes if you are canceling on good terms.

Handy Phrases: Although your service has been great; We regret that we must cancel our account; We will not be renewing our subscription [contract, etc.]; We have arranged to take care of this in-house; For your convenience, my account number is; I have enclosed my final payment for the outstanding balance; Please accept our thanks for; If you have any questions; I hope we can work together again in the future.

See also: *Part VI:* Contract Termination Letter; *Part IX:* Notice to Suspend Deliveries and Request for Release.

Dear Ryan:

We're sorry to have to ask you to please cancel our oil service. Our building is undergoing renovation, and with the new plumbing we will be installing gas lines and heaters. Our records show that our account (#45BD) is paid up to date, through this month. Can you send us a final invoice that shows we are paid to date? I understand that per our agreement, there is no cancellation penalty. Please call me when you get a chance so that we can make arrangements to fill the old oil tank by November 30. You've been wonderful to work with all these years — we'll miss you! Please count on us for a referral anytime.

Regards,

Tips for Terminating a Contract or Agreement

- Make reference to the language in the contract that allows you to terminate the agreement at your discretion, and say you are exercising that option.

- Say when the termination goes into effect. Note that you will uphold your end of the contract (which means paying for goods and services) up until that date and no longer.

- Ask the vendor to acknowledge the cancellation in writing.

Letters that Strengthen the Client/Vendor Relationship

Everyone appreciates positive recognition. Here are two great ways to strengthen your bonds with your vendors. You can show your vendors how much you appreciate their business and services by referring them to friends and colleagues. Or send an unsolicited letter of praise — it will truly make someone's day.

LETTER OF PRAISE

If you are pleased with a vendor, take the time to send them a letter telling them so. Vendors love getting such letters, and it help build goodwill for when you want a favor from them. After all, what vendor would risk not delighting the customer whose letter of testimonial hangs on the wall in their office or lobby?

Format: [*See Appendix A:* Fig. A-1. Simple format for letters and memos.] Typed/word-processed. Business or personal letterhead.

Style/Tone/Voice: Can be informal or formal. Active tone or voice. [*See Part I for more on these subjects.*]

Structure: (1) Open with an expression of how pleased you are with the product or service, (2) Give details, if appropriate, (3) Close with a warm expression of thanks and a wish for continued business.

Handy Phrases: We wanted to let you know how satisfied we have been; Our sincere appreciation for the outstanding service; Just a note to let you know; You've provided consistently excellent service; Your team did a great job; You always follow through on your promise; Your staff is knowledgeable and helpful; The wonderful service you provide; Here's to a continued mutually profitable relationship; You've got our whole-hearted appreciation.

See also: *Part II:* Letters That Strengthen Relationships; *Part V:* Change in Employment Status Announcements; *Part VI:* Relationship-Building Letters.

Dear Joel,

On 10-7-00, I signed a contract with your company to have my bathroom remodeled. The work was started as promised on 11-29-00 and completed on 12-11-00. There was not one day when the appropriate work was not done.

The craftsmen were all competent, polite, and respectful of my property. When the work was started, all necessary material was on site.

I am very pleased with the job and would recommend your company to any of my friends or relatives who might be interested in similar remodeling. It is easy to see why your company has been in business since 1938.

As a manager, I appreciate the personal inquiries you made regarding the progress of the work and my satisfaction with it.

Your Design Coordinator, Rich, is one in a million. He has the rare combination of personality, job expertise, coordinating ability, and most of all integrity. What Rich says, you can stake your life on.

As a retired third-level manager with Bell Atlantic, I know a good, competent employee when I see one.

Rich is willing to work long hours to see that the customer is pleased. He also never forgets that he represents the company's interest. A person with that balance is extremely difficult to find.

Your construction supervisor followed the job from start to finish. He also was able to make a decision before it became a problem.

You and your staff made it a pleasure dealing with Monmouth Construction Co. Keep up the good work and Monmouth could be around for another 61 years.

Sincerely,

John A. Edwards

Tips for Writing Letters of Praise

- Tell the vendor you are extremely pleased with them.
- Say specifically what they did that you felt was superior or beyond what you expected.
- Give them permission to use your comments in promotions for their products or services, if you are willing.

VENDOR REFERRAL

From time to time, a colleague, patient, customer, patron, member, neighbor, or friend may ask if you know a supplier who can handle a specific need, such as printing business cards or installing a computer network. You may want to distinguish whether you are just giving a referral, a recommendation, or an endorsement.

A *referral* means you are simply giving a name because you know of a vendor who does the kind of work required. You should make it clear in your referral letter that you are not personally familiar with the vendor's work and cannot vouch for them in any way.

A *recommendation* means you are giving the name of a vendor you have either used or know personally, or who is recommended to you by someone who has used or knows the supplier personally. However, you should let the reader know that you are not vouching for the vendor in any way — you are just passing along information as a lead for the reader.

An *endorsement* means you have used the vendor's service and were pleased. However, your endorsement in no way promises that your reader will be similarly satisfied, and your endorsement should make it clear that you are making no guarantees or warranties as to the vendor's service or quality.

Format: [*See Appendix A:* Fig. A-1. Simple format for letters and memos.] Typed/word-processed. Business or personal letterhead.

Style/Tone/Voice: Can be informal or formal. Active tone or voice. [*See Part I for more on these subjects.*]

Structure: (1) Explain that you're writing to respond to their request for a referral, (2) Give contact information for person being referred, (3) Clarify whether this is a referral, recommendation, or endorsement, (4) Close with an expression of good wishes for a successful project.

Handy Phrases: You indicated that you were looking for someone to; Recently you informed me that you are shopping for; Suggested that you call; Her company has been responsible for; Their services tie in perfectly with; I've worked with; I feel confident they can help you.

See also: *Part III:* Letters of Recommendation and Introduction.

Here's an example of a referral letter:

Dear Steve:

I got your message requesting the name of a Web designer. I know of two through the association I belong to, although I haven't worked with either of them. Here is their contact information — you'll need to ask them for references if you need them and also to get URLs of their work. I hope this information helps! Let me know what happens.

Regards,

This next e-mail is a simple recommendation:

Hi Vince:

I heard through the neighborhood grapevine (i.e., Brigitte!!) that you were looking for a new baby sitter. My friend Jane's daughter, Jennifer, might be a good candidate. I've known Jennifer for all of her 16 years and she's a great kid — very responsible and loves kids. She's done some baby-sitting for the Petersons — why not give them a call to see what they think? Jane's number is xxx-xxx-xxxx. Please let her know I gave you her number. Good luck!

Best regards,

The following is an example of a glowing endorsement:

Dear Linda:

I got your e-mail asking for references for a photographer for a family portrait. I highly recommend Kris Rupp. Our family has used her twice (once for my side of the family and once for my husband's) and all I could say when I saw the proofs was "Wow!" Almost every single picture was a beauty; it was near impossible to pick a photo to use as the final piece. Her prices were reasonable too and she let us keep the proofs (at no cost, which is very unusual). Anyway, her number is xxx-xxx-xxxx. When you call her, please feel free to mention how you got her name.

Also, I know she's got a Web site, so ask her for the URL. If you have time to stop by my house this week, I'd be happy to show you some of the pictures.

Regards,

Tips for Writing Referral Letters

- Give complete contact information for the vendor, including the name of the person you deal with.
- Tell the reader to mention your name when contacting this person.
- If you have used the company and had good results, say so. If you have had some problems, describe those, too.

Common or Possible Client-to-Vendor Requests

This section contains myriad communications that occur during the normal course of handling the administration of business as usual. Among the samples are requests for compliance and additional service, and letters of justification.

REQUESTS FOR COMPLIANCE

Business customers frequently introduce policies and requirements with which they insist vendors comply. New and current vendors should be made aware of these requirements and asked whether they can meet them.

Format: [*See Appendix A:* Fig. A-1. Simple format for letters and memos.] Typed/ word-processed. Business letterhead.

Style/Tone/Voice: Is usually more formal. Impersonal tone, active or passive voice. [*See Part I for more on these subjects.*]

Structure: (1) Make your request, (2) Explain how vendors are expected to comply with the request and give deadline dates, (3) State any penalties or actions taken if vendors do not respond to the compliance request, (4) Close with contact information for vendors to use if they have questions.

Handy Phrases: Enclosed please find; We've restructured; We'll need you to complete and return; You'll find the changes include; All vendors are required; As part of our new accounting system; Please call us if you have questions; We'll need all paperwork by.

See also: *Part IV:* Requests for Cooperation or Assistance.

Dear Vendor,

Enclosed please find the most current Vendor Shipping and Compliance Manual for CBAC RETAILERS. This manual, which was revised January 1, 2003, will be effective immediately. The goal of this manual is to facilitate the process of shipping from the vendor to our Property Warehouses and ultimately to our selling floor.

On November 22, 2002, CBAC RETAILERS employed the service of Bicktech Software to act as our third-party logistics provider, and assist us with our inbound transportation. Please see pages 24 & 27 for detailed instructions.

You will also find included a Vendor Information Sheet for you to update and return with the Response Form.

If you have any questions regarding this packet, please contact the appropriate CBAC Retailers Buyer designated on the contact list. Please fax the Response Form to (xxx) xxx-xxxx to the attention of Corp. Retail Accounting. Please send your Response Form by February 3. Failure to fax the Response Form does not preclude you from receiving a charge back for violations incurred. Thank you in advance for your cooperation.

Sincerely,

Tips for Requesting Compliance with a Policy or Need

- Stress the importance to the vendor of complying with this particular request.

- Spell out the requirements in detail, either in your letter or an enclosed document.

- If noncompliance threatens their status as a preferred vendor, say so in no uncertain terms.

- Say what you expect the vendor to do.

- Give a deadline for responding.

SECOND REQUEST FOR COMPLIANCE

As mentioned in the section above, vendors are tempted to ignore requests that may be important to you but for which they cannot bill you. If the vendor does not respond, send a follow-up letter a week after the deadline passes.

Format: [*See Appendix A:* Fig. A-1. Simple format for letters and memos.] Typed/word-processed. Business or personal letterhead.

Style/Tone/Voice: Can be either informal or formal. Impersonal or personal tone, active or passive voice. [*See Part I for more on these subjects.*]

Structure: (1) Remind vendor of request, (2) Repeat instructions or refer to attached documents, (3) Explain how noncompliance will affect the relationship and current job, (4) Express an understanding of how busy people are, (5) Thank vendor for their time and let them know who to contact if they have questions.

Handy Phrases: As in the previous; Per our first request; Please respond in a timely manner; Please find enclosed; In regard to our previous agreement.

See also: *Part IV:* Requests for Cooperation or Assistance; Requests for Action.

Dear Cameron:

Just a friendly reminder to return the insurance questionnaire (another copy is attached) along with your most current policy. If we don't receive your policy, the project will have to be postponed and, as per our agreement, we will need to turn to another vendor to replace you.

Cameron, I know you're busy, but please do take a moment to complete the questionnaire and fax it back to me at xxx-xxx-xxxx along with your policy. I'll need it by the end of the day on Friday. If you have questions, please call me at xxx-xxx-xxxx. Thanks so much.

Regards,

Tips for Writing Second Requests for Compliance

- Repeat the request.
- Alter the tone from asking to insisting.
- Stress the urgency and importance.
- State the penalties for noncompliance.

REQUEST FOR VENDOR TAX ID OR SOCIAL SECURITY

A standard letter sent out by businesses from December through January each year is a request for their vendors to supply a Social Security or federal tax ID number for preparation of 1099s. You would think that it would make more sense to get this information once and store it in an accounting system database, but no: The same letter goes out to the same vendors from the same customers, year after year after year. Think of all the paper, postage, stuffing, and licking that could be saved!

Format: [*See Appendix A:* Fig. A-1. Simple format for letters and memos.] Typed/word-processed. Business letterhead.

Style/Tone/Voice: Informal/formal (can be both), passive/active voice, impersonal tone. [*See Part I for more on these subjects.*]

Structure: (1) Identify yourself; the recipient may be reluctant to reveal this type of information if there is any ambiguity about who is requesting it, (2) Request information, in this case be sure to indicate how the information will be used, (3) Close with instructions on returning the desired information.

Handy Phrases: In order to ensure that our records are accurate; Current information needed; We must verify; Please supply to ensure prompt payment; Please provide accurate information; Remember to properly sign and date pertinent documents.

See also: *Part IV:* Requests for Information.

TO: All Vendors
RE: Form W-9 (Request for Taxpayer Identification Number and Certification) — needed.
DATE: November 25, 2002.

We are in the process of updating our vendor files in order to ensure that our records properly reflect your Company's current information. Presently we do not have your Federal Tax Identification Number (TIN) or want to verify information we have on file. Internal Revenue Service regulations require that we obtain a TIN for all vendors. If we do not have this number on file, then regulations require us to withhold 31% of each payment released to you.

If your business is a corporation or a partnership, the TIN will be your Employer Identification Number (EIN). If our business is a sole proprietorship, the TIN may be a Social Security Number (SSN) or your EIN if one was issued to your business by the IRS.

These identification numbers are required to facilitate the mandatory annual reporting to the IRS of payments made to noncorporate businesses. Note however, that this form needs to be completed and returned, even if your business is incorporated. (This is our proof that your business is not subject to Form 1099 reporting.)

By January 31st of each year, a Form 1099 will be issued to each noncorporate vendor who received payments from the Widget Corp. totaling $600.00 or more during the prior calendar year. Payments made to attorneys are reported regardless of dollar value.

Please fill out the W-9 form provided, indicate your Federal Tax Identification Number, and make sure the form is signed and dated. Please return as soon as possible to:

Widget Corporation.
Attn: A/P Department
123 ABC Drive
Anytown, NJ 07628

All questions should be directed to the Accounts Payable Department at xxx-xxx-xxxx. Thank you for your cooperation.

Sincerely,

Tips for Requesting Vendor Social Security or Federal Tax ID Numbers

- Have an accountant check the wording of the letter for accuracy.
- If you have more than one person in your company handling accounts payable, have the letter come from a specific individual within that department, who will be the vendor's point of contact concerning all accounts payable questions.
- Give the reader a Form W-9 to complete and return to you.
- Provide a self-addressed, stamped envelope for the return of the signed W-9 to you. It should be addressed to the individual contact, not just "Accounts Payable."

LETTER OF JUSTIFICATION

A "letter of justification" is a letter written to a third party requesting authorization or approval to take a certain action. An accountant, for example, might write the IRS to request an extension of the filing deadline for tax returns he is preparing on behalf of a client. A doctor might write an insurance carrier to explain why a patient needs a certain treatment and that it should be covered even though it was initially denied.

Format: [*See Appendix A:* Fig. A-1. Simple format for letters and memos.] Typed/word-processed. Business letterhead.

Style/Tone/Voice: Is typically formal. Active tone or voice. [*See Part I for more on these subjects.*]

Structure: (1) Make introductory statement about the product/service being requested and why, (2) Give additional information as necessary (e.g., specific information about the event, patient, client), (3) Add details as needed about request (e.g., for a medical justification, you may need to explain why a particular device is the only one that will work as a solution for a patient's situation), (4) Describe any attachments, (5) Give contact information, (6) Discuss next steps.

Handy Phrases: Our patient has a special need for your wheelchair, which; Good reputation; This device will allow; I've attached a letter from John's primary care physician; The estimated requirements include; Please consider this justification for the department to; We certify this information to be accurate [complete, etc.].

See also: *Part II:* Requests; *Part IV:* Business Requests; Tough Situations; *Part VIII:* Working Out Arrangements.

Dear Medical Consultants:

This letter is to request an augmentative communication device (ACD) for Johnnie Doe, a 5-year-old boy with severe dysarthria and apraxia of speech. Johnnie clearly needs this communication device for his health and safety as described below.

Background on the individual:

- **Age:** 5 years, 7 months
- **Diagnosis:** Dysarthria and Apraxia of Speech
- **Prognosis for improvement of speech:** negligible improvement expected in near future, due to the severity of the apraxia
- **Motor control of arms and legs:** mild motor impairment of arms and legs; able to walk, carry the ACD and use direct selection with his hands for access
- **Hearing:** No known hearing impairment
- **Vision (for AAC):** Able to recognize words and symbols as small as 1/2" across
- **Significant surgeries:** none that we know of
- **Other Adaptive Equipment:** none

Medical justification for ACD:

Johnnie's health and safety are constantly jeopardized by his inability to speak. Here are just three incidents that demonstrate the extent of this risk:

- Approximately 1 year ago, Johnnie was playing outside and he came into the house with the remaining bits of some mushrooms. His mother could not tell whether he had eaten any of the mushrooms and Johnnie could not explain where he had found them. His mother had to rush him to the doctor to make sure that he had not ingested any poison. If Johnnie had a communication device, he could have explained to his mother where he found them and whether he had eaten any.
- Recently, Johnnie had some pain in his left leg that was significant enough to make him hop around instead of walking. Because Johnnie was also undergoing serial castings and Botox treatment, his mother felt it was crucial to get details about what happened and where it hurt or the type of pain. However, Johnnie could not explain any of this, so his mother had to take him to see the physician who was conducting the treatment. He was unable to find the source of the problem. If Johnnie had a device, he could have given more details about this pain, to help his mother and physician determine whether a trip to the doctor was truly necessary.
- In addition, Johnnie requires a communication device because of his significant potential risks. He is a bright, cute and very active 5-year-old who is becoming more independent with time. His life between two households puts him in contact with more strangers than most 5-year-olds. He needs a way to communicate in case he should become separated from his parents or in case he was approached inappropriately. He is at risk for abuse simply because he is unable to speak to get attention, to get help, or to report problems with strangers.

Motor access to ACD:

Johnnie has sufficient hand control to access the ACD through conventional direct selection.

Cognitive ability to utilize recommended ACD:

Johnnie has cognitive skills that are above his age level, as demonstrated by receptive language scores and an ability to read that are well above his age level. Johnnie has also demonstrated that he is quick to learn an ACD and immediately applies it to functional communication during the trials at the clinic.

Decision-making based on device features:

In our opinion, it would be inappropriate to recommend a communication device based solely on trials because Johnnie is capable of using a wide variety of devices. Instead, we must base our decision-making on his communication needs and which devices have the features that will meet these needs. Using this approach, we have ruled out the following types of devices for the following reasons:

1. Devices based solely on letter-by-letter spelling: Johnnie's reading and spelling are above age-level, but he cannot spell well enough yet to meet all communication needs for medical necessity. This rules out all devices based primarily on spelling, including: Canon Communicator, LightWriter, etc.
2. Devices with limited vocabulary capacity because Johnnie needs more words/phrases to meet all medical and physical needs (see medical justification above). This rules out devices such as: DynaMo, DigiVox, MessageMates, Macaw, AlphaTalker, Tech/Speak, or any smaller devices.
3. Devices without synthesized speech because Johnnie has emerging spelling skills that will permit him (within two years) to communicate novel messages and vocabulary via spelling. This will reduce his dependence on the programming of others and protect him when he is in situations that he has never encountered before. This rules out: DynaMo, DigiVox, MessageMates, and other devices with only digitized speech.
4. Devices with vocabulary accessible via paper overlays because Johnnie cannot physically change overlays while communicating. This rules out: Holly.com, DigiVox (with levels), Macaw (with levels), AlphaTalker (with levels), Tech/Speak, etc.
5. Devices that rely on encoding for message storage and retrieval: Although we believe Johnnie has the ability to learn sequencing of codes for this method, we do not believe that the school team and family have the time to teach him this strategy. Furthermore, this approach would require months of training before Johnnie could become a proficient communicator. He would be at risk during this time. This rules out: AlphaTalker, DeltaTalker, Liberator and other systems based solely on encoding.
6. Devices that are unreliable due to mechanical failures or frequent software bugs because Johnnie's health and well-being will be jeopardized each time the device requires repair. In our experience, this rules out the following devices: XXXX, XXXX.
7. Devices that are not portable for Johnnie: Johnnie is small even for a 5-year-old. He would be unable to carry any devices that weigh more than a few pounds. This rules out: DynaVox, Optimist and other large devices.

In summary, the only device that will meet Johnnie's needs for communication is the XXXXX, manufactured by XXXXX. This is the only device on the market that can provide the vocabulary and the access that he requires in a truly portable system.

Therapy:

Johnnie receives regular OT, PT, and speech therapy at school. He also receives additional speech therapy twice a week from the clinic.

Justification for each piece of equipment:

These trials and the reasoning above have led us to conclude that the only device that will meet Johnnie's needs is the XXXXX, as listed on the attached quote. In addition, Johnnie will need a backup card to protect his custom vocabulary. Without this additional card, he would be at risk whenever the memory in the device fails and his custom vocabulary is lost. It would ordinarily take any team a month to restore previous custom vocabulary without such a backup card. With the card, Johnnie will be protected daily as he will never lose his vocabulary.

Expectations with ACD:

We expect Johnnie to learn to use his ACD quickly so that within one year he will be able to

- Communicate with a personal physician about a medical condition, complaint, ailment, or symptoms.
- Communicate with personal caregivers about both urgent medical needs and routine personal care needs.
- Develop improved expressive communications skills, vocabulary and understanding.
- Attain specific speech therapy goals and objectives according to the speech treatment or training plan.

Plan of care for the ACD:

- Initial Programming and Training: Under the supervision of XXXXXXXXX
- Ongoing Programming: School team
- Quarterly consultation: XXXXXX
- Yearly re-evaluation: XXXXXX

Team expertise in AAC:

The decision-making regarding this adaptive technology has been done primarily by XXXXX, who will also oversee the implementation. [The letter goes on to describe the experience of this individual in the field of AAC.]

Thank you for considering this request for Johnnie Doe, an excellent candidate for augmentative communication.

Sincerely,

Tips for Writing Justification Letters

- You must prove your case with a preponderance of evidence. Give every important and relevant fact that supports your position.

- Make your case. Explain your position. Make it clear. Anticipate and answer objections the reader is likely to have.

- Offer to answer any additional questions or provide more proof or data.

Letters Regarding Payment Problems

Often we communicate with vendors due to an issue regarding payment. Whether you owe money or are owed money, you may find that a letter is needed to resolve the situation. In these instances, letters also offer the added advantage of providing a written record. In the unfortunate event that any formal action is required, it is usually beneficial to have your attempts to remedy a financial situation documented.

VENDOR PAYMENT TERMS

One problem that arises in business is when a key supplier or vendor changes terms, and you find these new terms unfavorable or unacceptable. If you need them more than they need you, what will you do? You can try to negotiate better terms and then resubmit a new agreement. If the key vendor won't budge, you should write a formal letter stating you are withdrawing future work from them. Then, go find another vendor!

If you have a strong preference for working with this particular vendor, you may be able to come to some kind of consensus for dealing with such situations on a case-by-case basis.

Format: [*See Appendix A:* Fig. A-1. Simple format for letters and memos.] Typed/word-processed. Business or personal letterhead.

Style/Tone/Voice: Can be informal or formal. Active tone or voice. [*See Part I for more on these subjects.*]

Structure: (1) State current situation, (2) Remind reader of original terms or common terms acceptable to you and/or your company, (3) Detail what you can accept as terms, or what you're willing to negotiate, (4) Close with a call to follow up.

Handy Phrases: I just received your invoice; I met with our account manager today; We are not satisfied with your new terms; We need to negotiate; Let's create a win-win situation; According to my records; Received notification that there seems to be an error in; As we discussed over the telephone; Contact me immediately; A review of my records; There appears to be a misunderstanding; If you need any more information; To our mutual satisfaction.

See also: *Part VII:* Change of Terms; *Part VIII:* Working Out Arrangements.

Phil,

Our recent meeting with David Walsh, your senior sales manager, has left us at a crossroads of sorts. I just learned that your company now expects payment within 15-day delivery, citing last year's cash flow crunch as the reason.

I understand your position but, payment problems or no payment problems, 15 days is completely unrealistic. I'd like to talk to you about this. Our current agreement with you is that we pay net 45 days. If you can't accept our orders based on that original arrangement, we will need to find another vendor who will.

Please call me this week when you have a moment. We really want to keep doing business with you.

Tips for Writing Letters about Problems with Vendor Payment Terms

- Describe the dilemma.
- State your position.
- Ask for consensus on what to do about the problem.

WARNING OF DELAYED PAYMENT

If you are not going to pay a vendor's bill on time because you don't have the money, the best way to manage the situation is to let them know in advance, via letter, rather than being silent and letting them think you are a deadbeat.

Format: [*See Appendix A:* Fig. A-1. Simple format for letters and memos.] Typed/word-processed. Business or personal letterhead.

Style/Tone/Voice: Can be informal or formal. Active tone or voice. [*See Part I for more on these subjects.*]

Structure: (1) Open by stating you have unfortunate news to share, (2) Explain your situation, (3) Tell when/how you will pay, (4) If necessary, suggest a call to discuss a payment plan, (5) Close by thanking the vendor for their understanding.

Handy Phrases: Our accounting department failed to notify; The check will be mailed later this week; This letter pertains to an unpaid bill for; You will get our check on; Please accept my thanks and apologies; I'm sorry that this payment is late; We hope the delay has not caused you any inconvenience; We regret that we are late; This was an exceptional circumstance; I assure you that all future payments will be on time; Thank you for your understanding.

See also: *Part VIII:* Working Out Arrangements.

Hi Ted,

I wanted to make you aware of a problem we are experiencing that's affecting our cash flow.

Our biggest account is 90 days past due in paying us, and that's making us late paying our bills. We hope to see a check from this customer this week, and I'm applying all the pressure I can to get this matter taken care of.

Unfortunately, this means we will be late paying you. I hope to have this matter straightened out within 15 days, and I appreciate your understanding.

I will be calling you later today after I have another discussion with our customer. Hopefully, I will have good news, and I'll be able to update you on the situation.

My apologies,

Tips for Warning Vendors of Delayed Payment

- Say that payment will be delayed.
- Give the reason.
- Let the reader know you are making every effort to pay as soon as possible.
- Give the reader an idea of when you think you can send the money.
- If it is a large sum and you cannot come up with it in a reasonable time period, suggest partial payments with a payment schedule.

OVERPAYMENT NOTICE (REQUEST TO SUBMIT A REIMBURSEMENT)

Accounting mistakes happen but when they happen, they need to be addressed promptly before they become a dead issue. If you or someone from your company has overpaid a vendor, it is best to address the problem by asking for a reimbursement in writing.

Format: [*See Appendix A:* Fig. A1-1. Simple format for letters and memos.] Typed/word-processed. Business or personal letterhead.

Style/Tone/Voice: Can be informal or formal. Active tone or voice. [*See Part I for more on these subjects.*]

Structure: (1) Describe the error, (2) Explain what you're going to do or what you want the vendor to do, (3) Close on an upbeat note.

Handy Phrases: Accidentally overpaid you; I've found a mistake in; Please contact our billing department; Please acknowledge and correct the error; I appreciate your time to resolve this; Send me a check for the additional amount; Call if there are further problems; Thanks for your understanding.

See also: *Part VIII:* When the Collection is in Dispute; Credit Adjustments.

Dear David:

As I reviewed my payments for this past month, I realized that I wrote the wrong amount on the check I sent to cover my July charges. I paid $660 for a billing of $460. Rather than crediting my account, please refund the $200 as soon as possible. If you have any questions, please call me at xxx-xxx-xxxx. Thank you for your prompt attention to this matter.

Tips for Writing Overpayment Notices

- Send overpayment notices promptly. The longer you delay, the less likely you are to get money back.
- Explain why the overpayment was made. Did you pay the same invoice by accident twice? Or did the vendor double bill you accidentally?
- Let the reader know you consider this a serious matter and expect prompt action.

Other Letters to Vendors

Like all relationships, there are many times and occasions to communicate with your vendors. Beyond the day-to-day communications we've covered so far, there are lots of reasons to contact vendors — and, in the process, develop and cultivate these very special associations. In this section, we'll cover vendor gift-giving policies, tips on confirming orders, explaining purchasing policies, and inviting vendors to exhibit in trade shows.

VENDOR GIFT POLICY

Vendors like to give their best customers gifts, especially during the holidays, as a way of cementing the relationship, building goodwill, and ensuring future business. If your company has a policy prohibiting the giving of such gifts, notify the vendor in writing at least three to four months prior to the end of the year.

Format: [*See Appendix A:* Fig. A-1. Simple format for letters and memos.] Typed/word-processed. Business letterhead.

Style/Tone/Voice: Can be either informal or formal. Active tone or voice. [*See Part I for more on these subjects.*]

Structure: (1) Thank vendor for their valued relationship, (2) State your no-gift policy, (3) Explain why the policy is in place, (4) End with good wishes for a successful year-end.

Handy Phrases: It's been a great year; Thanks for helping us meet our goals; While we appreciate; We've made it a policy; We feel our policy is fair to all our employees; In the past; Please accept our best wishes for the holiday season.

See also: *Part IV:* Giving a Business Gift; *Part VI:* Free Gifts.

October 17, 2002

Dear Jerry:

With the holidays fast approaching, we want to take the time to thank you for the excellent creative work and dependable service you have provided to the Widget Corp. over the past year.

We also want to remind you that our policy regarding gifts is a clear and firm one: We prohibit the sending of gifts of any kind to our people — at the office or at home. We feel this ensures an equitable and fair treatment of all of our Widget people.

Thank you, again, for the excellent work you've been doing. Please do not hesitate to contact us with any suggestions you may have to further increase our effectiveness.

Sincerely,

Michele Wolk
Director of Marketing Promotion

Tips for Writing a Gift Policy Letter

- Spell out the gift policy. Some companies prohibit any gifts. Others prohibit gifts above a certain dollar amount, typically $25.
- Explain the reason for your policy.
- Remind readers that you expect them to comply with this policy (it is non-negotiable) and that there will be penalties if they don't.

CONFIRMATION OF ORDER

Smart buyers confirm their orders in writing. That way, if there is a dispute (e.g., the vendor says they never received the order), you can document your actions in writing.

Format: [*See Appendix A:* Fig. A-1. Simple format for letters and memos.] Typed/word-processed. Business or personal letterhead.

Style/Tone/Voice: Can be either informal or formal. Active tone or voice. [*See Part I for more on these subjects.*]

Structure: (1) Review what was agreed on — reiterate all details of the order including order number, pricing, expected delivery date, (2) Add, if applicable, any new information that affects the order, (3) Close with a note of thanks and an expression emphasizing your pleasure in working together.

Handy Phrases: As we agreed; To review, here are the items; Per my telephone order of; I'd like to confirm; I've made a complete listing; Please note the change in; Please send the order by; Let's proceed with; As our contract stipulates; I've enclosed 50% of the payment; Please send a detailed invoice to; I'd be happy to address any questions; I appreciate working with you: please call me at.

See also: *Part VI:* Order Acknowledgment.

October 15, 1999

Ms. Laura Johnson
Executive Meeting Manager
Baltimore Orioles Hotel
Batter Street
Baltimore, MD 21201

Dear Laura:

Enclosed is a signed copy of the Banquet Event Order for the Widget Company's October 25 seminar being hosted by your hotel.

Laura, I wanted to let you know how much I enjoy working with you. Of all the hotel meeting managers I've been in contact with for our company's many meetings, you have been the most responsive. You've always replied to my letters promptly, and I appreciate your calls and follow-up.

As a new meeting planner, I'm still faced with learning all the ropes — you are certainly making my job a little easier.

Thanks for your help, and I'll talk to you in a few days to give you the guaranteed number of attendees.

Sincerely,

Tips for Writing an Order Confirmation

- Confirm the order (goods or services purchased, price, terms, conditions, delivery date) in writing — either in the letter itself or an enclosure.
- Convey your enthusiasm about the project.
- Let the vendor know you are looking forward to working with them and will provide whatever help they need to make the project a success for your organization.

PURCHASING POLICY LETTER

Outlining your company's purchasing policy can help start a relationship with a new vendor on the right foot. Your letter needs to supply all of the terms and conditions of payment for goods or services rendered. Some businesses have their purchasing policy outlined in a separate document. If this is the case, you don't need to outline all of the terms in your letter, instead discuss the reason you are writing and request that they review the enclosed policy statement. If you do not have this type of documentation, be sure that all of the relevant terms are spelled out in the letter. Take a look at this example.

Format: [*See Appendix A:* Fig. A-1. Simple format for letters and memos.] Typed/ word-processed. Business letterhead.

Style/Tone/Voice: Can be either informal or formal. Active tone or voice. [*See Part I for more on these subjects.*]

Structure: (1) Welcome vendor, (2) Explain your company's policies and procedures, (3) Elaborate on terms (or refer reader to an enclosure), (4) Close with an invitation to call or write with questions or clarifications.

Handy Phrases: According to the following terms; Please review and agree to the verbiage below; You will need to supply a certificate; Under this agreement; Establishes the basis for; Statement of work; In an effort to make our invoice procedure more efficient; Designate a name or number for; Enclosed is a copy of the terms of our agreement; Don't hesitate to.

See also: *Part VI:* Routine Customer Correspondence.

September 16, 2002

Dear Supplier,

The purpose of this letter is to inform you of MerrySign, Inc., Purchasing and Accounts Payable policies and procedures relative to the procurement of goods and services, including payment of Supplier invoices.

Only the Purchasing Department staff has the authority to make financial commitments on behalf of MerrySign for the purchase of all goods and services. We make these commitments by issuing a Purchase Order to document all transactions. The Purchase Order number must appear on all packing slips, invoices, and correspondence pertaining to the purchase.

As a Supplier to MerrySign, it is imperative that your packing slips and invoices match the Purchase Order by description, quantity, and total cost, on a line-item basis. You must coordinate the matching details with the Buyer from MerrySign's purchasing department who issued the Purchase Order.

Failure to send the ORIGINAL invoice, or an electronic invoice, directly to the Accounts Payable department will result in delayed payment. If electronic invoices are submitted to address below, do not send a paper copy as back up, Please note that all invoices must be on company letterhead, with the invoice number, related Purchase Order number, and other pertinent information clearly indicated. All original invoices must be sent to:

MerrySign, Inc.
Attn: Accounts Payable
xxxx Flattop Circle
Tides, Virginia, xxxxx

Or via e-mail to, accountspayable@merrysign.com

If MerrySign receives an invoice that does not reference a valid Purchase Order number, or does not match the Purchase Order, the following will occur:

1. A delay in invoice payment processing time.
2. You will be contacted by Purchasing and/or Accounts Payable to discuss MerrySign policy.
3. The invoice will be returned to you for correction and resolution.
4. Invoice aging will not commence until the date a corrected invoice is received at the MerrySign office noted above.
5. You could jeopardize future business with MerrySign.

If you have any questions in regard to this policy, please contact any of the undersigned:

Mike Jones, Purchasing Manager   703-555-5555
Dorcas Johnson, Purchasing Manager   650-555-5555
Pauline Jackson, Accounts Payable Manager   703-555-5555

Very truly yours,

MerrySign, Inc.

Tips for Writing Purchasing Policy Letters

- Give complete instructions to the vendor on getting authorization for the work. If they should not proceed without a purchase order number, say so.

- Tell the vendor how and where to submit invoices for payment.

- Be clear about the need for procedures to be followed and the penalties they may incur for not complying.

INVITATION TO EXHIBIT

If your company or organization has major events — sales rallies, annual meetings, exhibitions — you may invite vendors or business partners to participate, either by exhibiting or attending.

Format: [*See Appendix A:* Fig. A-1. Simple format for letters and memos.] Typed/word-processed. Business or personal letterhead.

Style/Tone/Voice: Can be either informal or formal. Active tone or voice. [*See Part I for more on these subjects.*]

Structure: (1) Open with an invitation to exhibit at the event — give details about date, time, place (if there are a lot of details, put them on a separate sheet and refer reader to the sheet for complete details), (2) Mention benefits of exhibiting (number of attendees, highlights from previous events), (3) Give any additional information available (e.g., URL, contact to call for more info), (4) Close with a call to respond.

Handy Phrases: Here's an opportunity; Thanks for your interest; Our association is proud to announce; Have you join your colleagues; Gain valuable face-to-face; You'll have a chance to meet; Enclosed is a breakdown of attendees by; Exhibit hours; Your fee includes; The cost for a booth is; Look forward; For more information; The enclosed reply card.

See also: *Part II:* Invitations to Events*; Part IV:* Invitations; *Part VII:* Selling By Invitation.

Thank you very much for your interest in the 1998 CBAC Conference to be held in Birmingham, October 17th–20th. We are very excited about our opportunity to host this conference and we need the help of companies like yours to make it a success. Your company, of course, will also benefit.

The cost of an exhibitor booth at this year's conference is $1,000. This price includes two conference registrations for attendance of all conference functions, an 8' x 10' booth with table and seating, and security guard protection during all nonshow hours. Between the Exhibitor Show and the conference functions, your employees will have a wonderful opportunity to network with all of the CBAC members.

Beyond the support you show to CBAC by participating in our Vendor Fair, we need your sponsorship for various conference functions. Your sponsorship of these functions will be recognized with additional advertisement at the conference and if you choose to sponsor a breakfast, lunch, or dinner function, the opportunity to address the membership about your company. We will be happy to assist in funding the sponsorship level that fits your company.

In addition, we have the opportunity for your company to give our membership the advantage of your company's expertise. We will be having several educational seminars on October 19th and 20th and we would like your company to consider presenting a topic. We are taking suggestions on educational topics right now, so if you have a topic you would like to present, let us know.

Attached is everything you need to reserve your exhibit space, decide the event(s) you wish to sponsor, and recommend your educational seminar topic. Just follow the instructions on the forms and return them as soon as possible; space is very limited. If your company would like to step up and provide sponsorship for a conference function, please contact me and I will get your sponsorship set up.

Thank you so much for your support!

Sincerely yours,

Darryl H. Simmons
Public Relations

Tips for Inviting Vendors to Exhibit at an Event or Show

- If participating in the event gives the vendor an edge or inside track in winning future business from you or others within the organization, say so.
- Describe the event, the audience, and why the vendor will benefit by gaining visibility and exposure in front of this audience.
- If there is a cost to exhibit, say so. Give pricing as well as exhibit requirements.

PART X

E-MAIL AND FAX CORRESPONDENCE

In American business, the use of e-mail is exploding, with 110 million Americans having access to e-mail. The typical office worker sends and receives an average of 40 e-mails daily, according to a Gallup poll. Too few business people recognize that this revolution in communication has resulted in a need to flush away old-fashioned phrases, get to the point quickly, keep messages brief, and motivate the recipient to read the message itself.

Suddenly R&D professionals, engineers, technicians, biologists, chemists, mathematicians and others are being asked to "send an e-mail" rather than pick up a telephone. Without that greater "bandwidth" of face-to-face communication, a technician may have trouble letting his words speak for him.

Make no mistake: An e-mail message cannot replace the personal touch of a phone call. Use the telephone to judge the nonverbal clues your listener is giving you. On the phone you might be able to recognize when a listener is resisting or rejecting what you have to say. Not true with e-mail.

Many e-mails are filled with extra words; many could be cut in half . . . if their writers were trained to write carefully and to care about the reader's attention span.

Differences Between E-Mail and Regular Letters

There are more similarities than differences between e-mail and postal mail; at least as far as letter writing is concerned.

- Both are a form of correspondence between two individuals: the recipient and the sender.
- Both are essentially letters and most follow the same structure and format.
- Both are read by people who are accustomed to reading standard written English, not Internet shorthand or jargon.
- Both often contain an element of persuasion. The goal is to get the reader to take action.

But there are definite differences, too, when it comes to online versus offline writing.

Readers who are online have a shorter attention span than readers who are offline. Why? Text is more difficult to read on a screen than in print, and also, attending to your e-mail forces you to halt other tasks you want to do on your PC. Therefore, e-mails are usually shorter than postal letters.

Another reason for the brevity of e-mail is that e-mails typically deal with a short, single subject (e.g., answering a simple question, such as "Where do you want to meet for dinner?). Letters, by comparison, often address multiple and complex subjects — one of the reasons the person wrote a letter in the first place rather than made a phone call or sent an e-mail.

A third reason e-mails are concise is that they are more interactive than letters. When you answer someone's e-mail, your answer may contain the text of his or her previous message. There's no need to recap or remind them of what they said in the first place, as there is with postal mail.

E-Mail Structural Components

E-mail and postal mail have similarities and differences. Let's start with the similarities.

Basically, e-mail has much the same structure and style as a business letter. There is a beginning or introduction, a middle, and an end or close. That's why we don't have a whole section of this book of sample e-mail messages versus sample letters. Most of the letters in Parts II through VIII can, with minor modification, work perfectly well in the message area of an e-mail.

As for the major differences, e-mails have some requirements postal mail does not. These include a "from" line, subject line, electronic distribution list, embedded links, and sig files.

THE "FROM" LINE

ISPs (Internet Services Providers) set up customer accounts so that every e-mail a user sends carries his particular "from" line. Typically the "from" line is your name ("Joe Schmo") or more commonly your e-mail address ("joeschmo@joeschmo.com).

People tend to open e-mail from people they know, and delete e-mail from people they don't know. Therefore, your "from" line will gain the attention of people you already have a relationship with. If the reader doesn't know you, the only hope you have of him opening and reading your message is a compelling subject line (see below).

THE DISTRIBUTION LIST (CC AND BCC)

Your ISP's e-mail account service probably allows you three options with regards to recipients:

- **To:** Specifies the main recipient.
- **cc:** Selects people who get a copy and are identified as getting a copy. The initials "cc" stand for "carbon copy," back in the days when duplicate copies of letters were made on carbon paper.
- **bcc:** Selects people who get a "blind carbon copy" — that is, they receive a copy but their names do not appear on the distribution list.

Business-writing handbooks published a decade or more ago stressed the importance of listing cc people alphabetically. The importance of this in postal letters has diminished, and it is even a less common practice with e-mail.

The cc list not only distributes the e-mail to these other folks, but it also lets the main recipient (the person named in the "to" line) know they are getting the copy. So the cc list would include team members and others officially involved with the project being discussed.

The bcc list also distributes the e-mail to people, but the main recipient is not aware of this transmission. So the bcc list would include people who you want to get a copy of the e-mail without telling your correspondent about it. For instance, when complaining about a problem to your account rep at a vendor company, you might bcc his boss as extra insurance that your complaint will be handled swiftly.

THE SUBJECT LINE

Next to the "from" line, the most important part of your e-mail is the subject line. These are the words the reader sees when the e-mail hits her in-box. Based on the "from" line and "subject" line, readers make a quick decision whether to open the e-mail, save it for later reading, or delete it. The less likely the recipient is to recognize your "from" line, the more important your subject line.

The best subject lines contain a few words that arouse the reader's interest or promise a reward for opening and reading the e-mail. A worker with a suggestion on how to improve process efficiency might send an e-mail to the plant manager with the subject line, "New idea for cutting production costs." [*For more information on writing compelling subject lines, see* Writing E-Mail Messages that Get Opened and Read, *later in this chapter.*]

Since e-mail programs cut off subject lines, keep your subject lines short. Thirty to 40 characters is the recommended length for subject lines, with 50 the absolute maximum (that count includes spaces). This often necessitates encapsulating the subject of the message in a few short words (e.g., "CTP/AP guidelines missing" or "Need template for container design").

Later in this part, we'll look at the "4 U's" method of making your subject lines more appealing and attention-getting.

THE MESSAGE AREA

The message area is that big, blank area on the screen where, when you hit the button to create an e-mail, you type the message you want to send. You will notice that the message area is limited, so that when you type a longer e-mail, it often scrolls down onto two or more screens. E-mail experts use the term "above the fold" to refer to the part of your message visible on the first screen.

E-mail marketers always make sure they cover the most critical information (i.e., what they are writing about and why you should reply) above the fold. They know if they don't, response falls off dramatically.

Therefore, if you are writing longish e-mail messages, make sure you lead with your most important points above the fold. A good way to do this is to use the "inverted pyramid style" taught in journalism school.

A pyramid has the foundation at the base, which supports the other parts of the building that rest on top of it. In the inverted pyramid, the base or foundation of your document — the most important information — is at the top, or beginning. Subsequent paragraphs present additional information, in decreasing order of importance. That way, if your reader only reads the first paragraph, she at least gets all the key facts.

Salutations and Closes

Personalized salutations in the message area are optional. You can simply begin your message in the message space. Or you can type in "Dear Bob," first. Some people feel the latter warms up the message.

The only exception we see is that people who would not be reluctant to use "Dear Bob" as the opening of a letter are leery of carrying "Dear" into the somewhat more intimate realm of e-mail. And, although "Dear" has, traditionally, not carried any connotation of extra intimacy in a business letter, it does sometimes seem a bit chummy for e-mail style, so let the use of "Dear" in your e-mail be governed by what feels comfortable to you.

A close is also optional. You can simply end your message with the last sentence. Or you can type "Sincerely," leave a few spaces, and then type your name. It's up to you.

The Sig File

A signature (sig) file is an "electronic letterhead" that automatically appears at the bottom of every e-mail message you send. A sig file contains information similar to letterhead: your name, company name, street address, city, state, ZIP code, phone number, fax number, and Web site, for instance. Some people like to add the company slogan under the company name.

There are two reasons why you should set up a sig file for all your outgoing e-mail. First, it saves you from having to type all that information each and every time. Second, the sig file makes it easy for the recipient to contact you through channels other than e-mail — phone, postal mail, fax — when you include that information on all your communications.

Your e-mail software likely has a feature to allow you to customize your own sig file. If you have difficulty understanding how the feature works, ask your ISP for help.

Here is a sample e-mail combining all of the features discussed above:

From: somebody@somewhere.com
To: nobody@nowhere.net
Subject: Bob Walton contract
Date: Sat, May 3, 2003, 11:12 a.m.

Hi Merton:

I'm Bob Walton's project manager. He asked me to send you a boilerplate
copywriting project template. Below my signature is what we use.
(Currently, we e-mail it to people as a regular text e-mail. I am looking into
converting it into a PDF and attaching it to an e-mail.)

Please call or e-mail me if you have questions.

Regards,

Ellen Fremont

Your Copy Needs
20 Fortieth Street
Hoboken, NJ 07030
Phone 888-888-8888
Fax 888-888-8889
assistant@somewhere.com

Attached Files

Be careful about sending attached files, especially to people you don't know. People worry about catching a computer virus from files. If they don't know you and your e-mail includes an attached file, they are likely to delete the whole message without opening it.

Be sensitive, also, when it comes to sending large, multimedia files — such as big PowerPoint presentations — as attachments, even if the person is a coworker or colleague. Some people do not like to open, store, and print these large files, and would rather get your presentation mailed to them as hard copy.

Also, the recipient's computer might not have enough memory to download the files easily. The download could take a really long time and tie up the recipient's computer such that you really tick them off big time! When in doubt, ask people whether they mind getting large files before sending them.

Another thing to remember is to make sure that the people at the other end of your communications have similar programs for opening and understanding your messages. If you write your attachment in Lotus WordPro and the recipient does not have this program installed on his computer, he won't be able to read your attached file.

Writing E-Mail Messages that get Opened and Read

The following suggestions are designed to help you improve your e-mail style, make sure that your e-mail is clear, and ensure that the recipient reads and opens your important message. (*See Appendix A: Fig. A-4.*)

- **Use the Subject line to capture attention and motivate the reader to read on.** The Subject line should not only summarize what you are about to say, but should, when necessary, motivate the reader to take action. Very short "Re" lines can be mysterious or meaningless (e.g. "Training"). Instead, be more specific — e.g., "Subject: Ideas for new training course." [*See also* The Subject Line, *earlier in this part.*]
- **Summarize your message in your first paragraph.** Answer the question "What do I want the reader to know, do, or believe as a result of this e-mail?" in the first paragraph. With e-mail being traditionally short, readers expect a first paragraph to do more than just introduce a thought. They expect it to summarize why you are writing — what you want the reader to know, do, or believe. E-mail messages often ramble; they work up to their main subject, and, in the process, alienate readers. Note: If you get the reputation of being a "rambler," people are going to put off reading your e-mails until they have more time — which means they may never get to them at all.
- **Keep your message short.** While letters should, in general, be kept to one page, e-mail — because of its volume, the scrolling involved, and the expectation of brevity — should almost never be more than a few paragraphs. Anything longer can and should be sent as a separate file.
- **Use standard, grammatical English.** Avoid the "staccato" style of incomplete sentences and other shortcuts. As a carryover from when computer memory was scarce, some people still write e-mail in "Saw sub. Sank same" prose.

There's no need to write in phrases or half sentences. Grammar, punctuation, and clarity still count.

- **Resist the temptation to "dress up" your e-mails.** Most business correspondence e-mails are simple text messages. But as regular users master HTML and other graphics programs, they are tempted to dress up their e-mails with visuals — banners, borders, animation, flashing lights, pictures, video, and audio (an e-mail message with audio or video is called "rich media").

  Adding a lot of special effects to your message is like putting glitter and gold stars on your report cover in grade school to impress the teacher and get an A. The teacher, of course, was more interested in the content and how you expressed yourself in grading — the gold glitter ploy never worked.

  Avoid "gold glitter" in your e-mail. Not only does it irritate some readers, but it also means slow downloading for users with older systems and slower Internet connections. Remember, just because you are in a big corporation with T1 lines doesn't mean your customer has the same level of technology. Always write and design e-mail so the widest number of recipients can read it.

- **Proofread every e-mail.** Use your e-mail program's spelling checker before hitting "Send." As in the early days of television, we are still a bit awed by the fact that we can send e-mail so quickly and easily around the globe. Often we tend to forget that e-mail messages define us in the same way other communications do.

  That being the case, don't allow a single misspelling or typo in your e-mail. Use the spelling checker and also recognize that spelling checkers are far from perfect. They cannot read your mind, so if you write "hear" and you meant "here," you need to proofread your work to catch the problem.

Reply Wisely

The discussion so far applies to all e-mails, both those you send out as well as your replies to e-mails you have received. Here are a few extra considerations to keep in mind when replying to the messages in your in-box.

Don't Reply to a Corporate Group

Be careful when replying to a message sent by someone from an organization. Even though your reply may be meant for his eyes only, if you hit the Reply button, you may send your reply both to him as well as everyone on his cc list (the bcc list does not get your reply). One solution: Send a sanitized reply, suitable for everyone on the cc list, when you hit the Reply button. Then compose a separate outgoing e-mail, with additional detail, and send it only to your main recipient.

BE CAREFUL WHO YOU INCLUDE ON A STRING

Within large organizations, e-mail messages are often routed back and forth between various team members. This creates a long string of back-and-forth replies, since all previous e-mails can be included in each new outgoing one. Confusion can result: Sometimes it's difficult to tell who's asking what, and whether you are supposed to reply or are just getting a copy "for your information."

There are two solutions: First, think about whom you add to e-mail cc and bcc lists. If they don't absolutely have to see it, don't put their name on it. Being cautious in this manner will cut down on the length of e-mail strings (also known as threads or "threaded discussions") and the number of contributors to the discussion. Also, everyone already gets too much e-mail, and you don't want to add to his or her burden.

The second solution is to break the thread by composing a new, original e-mail rather than simply hitting Reply. Hitting Reply continues the thread automatically, carrying along the carload of all messages. Composing a new message allows you to jettison the past messages as well as drop unnecessary recipients from the string.

THINK BEFORE YOU PRESS "SEND"

If you receive an inflammatory message, resist the urge to "return fire" with a hasty (or angry) response.

Be diplomatic. E-mail's convenient reach can be a drawback because it can memorialize your hurt feelings instead of giving you time to calm down and regain your objectivity. Remember that e-mail is permanent and irrevocable. Don't write in anger, and stay away from profanity.

Reread your response to make sure that none of the phrases you've written inadvertently reveal testiness or impatience. In particular, avoid sarcasm, annoyance, and rudeness.

Moreover, reread your work aloud because your ear will catch a negative tone faster than your eye will.

Cool down before pressing the Send key! One effective tactic: Compose your reply and save it as a draft. Reread it the next morning when you are in a calmer state of mind, and you'll quickly catch and eliminate any phrasing the reader might find offensive.

Tip: Beware Being *Too* Personal

E-mails, more so than letters, are easy to distribute widely and they also have a habit of being stored in computers long after they are written. For these reasons, be careful that you don't indulge in writing personal e-mails on the job or that you don't insert too many personal comments in business e-mail. More than 50 percent of America's corporations keep some track of — or watch over — employee e-mails. There is a fuzzy line between an employer's right to keep tabs on e-mail usage and an employee's right to privacy. It's best to be cautious and not to write anything that you wouldn't want seen by your whole department, your manager, or by an outsider.

Know the Emotional Connotations of Punctuation and Grammar

Punctuation adds body language to writing. While we all use punctuation to construct our sentences, we rarely think of these marks as adding emotion to our message. But they do.

An em dash (—) can add special emphasis to a thought, guiding the reader to what you feel is most important. Ellipses (. . .) shows hesitation or omission. And parentheses ( ) can show your reader what you consider to be a secondary thought.

Just as punctuation conveys shades of emotion, emoticons (symbols such as :) the popular smile face) and acronyms (e.g., BTW for *by the way*) also add breadth to your messages. Appendix B contains a list of popular e-mail acronyms.

While some users are not given to using the types of abbreviations and acronyms popular in on-line chat rooms, they should at least be familiar with emoticons and acronyms that can, on occasion, add levity, lighten the tone of a message, or merely underscore the urgency or lack of urgency in an e-mail.

"Emoticons" help communicate someone's mood or indicate when someone's joking. The most typical smiley is :), which, if you tilt your head to the left, is two eyes and a smiling mouth. Although they are not used frequently for business dealings, they are used frequently online and should be recognizable to e-mail users.

While your high school teachers may frown, you should know that certain points of grammar previously forbidden are okay in e-mail:

- Occasionally, one-sentence paragraphs are acceptable and can rivet the reader on a particular idea or provide a transition between lengthy paragraphs.
- Contractions (I'll, don't, we'll) add a certain warmth to writing and should be encouraged in informal messages like letters or e-mail.
- Long paragraphs (more than ten lines) usually turn online readers off, even if each idea belongs in the paragraph.
- Starting the occasional sentence with "and" or "but" is not a hanging crime. Starting with a conjunction adds a natural flow to your writing.

Despite e-mail's informality, letter-writing style considerations continue to hold: Keep sentences and paragraphs short, and eliminate wordiness, redundancy, and old-fashioned words. Write to express, not to impress. E-mail has even less tolerance for phrases like "pursuant to," "enclosed please find," and "under separate cover" than do memos or regular letters.

Consider the Look of Your Message

In cyberspace, as in written communication elsewhere, you need to be aware of anything that can influence a reader's perception of you and your message. Use appropriate type styles, sizes, formats and colors to reinforce your message. Increasing the size of the type adds importance to a phrase, while decreasing the size sends a message of demoting a particular thought or section. ALL CAPS CONNOTE SHOUTING. Too much boldface can come across as stern and schoolmarmish.

Each typeface has its own personality, connoting everything from businesslike (use Arial or Times New Roman) to playful (use Braggadocio or Benguiat Frisky). Look at each typeface offered by your PC software and decide whether a new typeface will epitomize the tone you are trying to convey. If you are creating a message on replacing antiquated phrases with more modern equivalents, for example, you might want to put each old-fashioned phrase in Algerian to convey "old fashioned." The substitute phrase could be in a more modern face, such as Desdemona.

Colors also can influence people's perception. While most people stay with black for messages that are strictly business — black having a "bottom-line" concreteness to it — be aware that colors can create moods. Blue, for example, can connote serenity; green sends off a signal of "go" or "money"; and red can imply passion, danger, or "stop."

Internet Direct-Mail Marketing Messages

Internet direct mail, also known as "e-mail marketing," is the sending of promotional e-mails to prospects and customers. ("Direct mail" refers to promotional postal mail, or advertising mail, sometimes known as "junk mail" — a term frowned upon by industry insiders.)

E-mail marketing messages typically generate a response rate between 1 and 10 percent, although some do better and a few do worse. The copy in your e-mail plays a big role in whether your e-marketing message ends up at the bottom or the top of that range.

How does Internet direct mail work? You send the reader an e-mail message advertising your product. The e-mail contains an embedded link the reader can click on (e.g., "for more information on Product P, click on www.PPP.com").

Clicking on the link takes the reader to a Web site or page containing more information on the product, and also a form the reader can submit to either buy the product or request a quote, pricing, or other details.

E-mail marketing is measured in terms of "click-through" rates. The click-through rate is the percentage of people who received your e-mail who clicked on the embedded link to get to your Web site or page. A click-through rate of 1 percent means out of every 100 receiving the e-mail, 1 clicked to get more information.

E-mail marketing to prospects whom you don't know is relatively expensive, because you must rent an "e-list" (a list of opt-in names with e-mail addresses). This can cost anywhere from $100 to $400 per thousand names, and there is usually a 5,000-name minimum.

So how do you make money? When the people who click through either order your product or request more information by completing and submitting the online reply form on your Web page, you automatically capture their e-mail addresses. Now you can e-mail to these leads or customers again and again, as often as you like, without paying a dime in list rental fees.

It is repeat marketing to the "house list" (your list of customers or leads and their e-mail addresses) that makes the bulk of the profits in e-mail marketing, for two reasons. First, your marketing cost is close to zero. And second, the response rates from e-mailing to this house e-list are typically two to ten times higher than you get from e-mailing to a cold rented e-list.

How Long Should an E-Mail Marketing Message be?

What works best in e-mail marketing — long copy or short copy? It's a quandary for direct marketers much more so than general marketers. Here's why:

There's a widely held viewpoint that, on the Internet, the less copy the better. Web marketing experts tell us that the Internet is faster-paced than the "snail mail" world, that attention spans are shorter, and long messages get zapped into oblivion with the click of the mouse. "Keep it short!" they extol in countless advisory e-zines.

General advertisers, for the most part, also believe that when it comes to copy, the shorter the better. Often their print ads have large pictures and only a handful of words. So they have no trouble embracing the "people don't read" mentality the Web marketing gurus say works best.

But traditional direct marketers — newsletter publishers, seminar promoters, magazines, book clubs, insurance, audio cassettes — whose products are typically sold with long copy direct mail packages and self-mailers have a problem. It goes something like this:

> "In print, I have to use long copy to make the sale . . . or I just don't get the order. We've tested short copy many times — who *doesn't* want a cheaper mailing piece with less ink and paper? But it has never worked for our product. Now my Web marketing consultant says the e-mail should be just a few paragraphs. If a few paragraphs won't convince people to buy offline, why should things be any different online?"

And these marketers are right: Just because a person buys online doesn't change the persuasion process. If he needs the facts to make a decision, he needs them regardless of whether he is ordering from a paper mailing or a Web site.

Yet the Web marketing gurus have at least a clue as to what they are talking about. You might intuitively sense that your four-page sales letter, if sent word for word as a lengthy e-mail, wouldn't work. People would click away long before they got to the end. So what's the answer?

First, you need to quantify what is meant by "short" versus "long." When a Web marketing guru talks about "short" e-mail, she probably means only three or four paragraphs. So when she says long copy doesn't work, she is against e-mails of more than a few paragraphs. If, in this context, a traditional marketer says, "Long copy *does* work," he'd mean long compared to the typical e-mail — not compared to the typical direct mail letter on paper. A "long" e-mail, which may fill several screens, is closer in length to a two-page letter — "short" by direct mail standards — than to a four-page letter. And it doesn't even come close to an eight-page letter.

Second, you need to quantify how much shorter online copy is than offline. Should you translate your entire package, word for word? Should you compress it to half its length? Less? Kathy Henning, who writes extensively about online communication, says, "In general, online text should be half as long as printed text, maybe even shorter." Not a precise formula, but a good starting point for estimation.

Third, and most important, we need to remember that the copy for e-mail marketing campaigns is not wholly contained within the e-mail itself. It is really in two parts. The first half of the message is in the actual e-mail. The e-mail contains a link to a page on a Web site or server. When you click on that link, you jump to the page, where the remainder of the message is presented, along with the online order mechanism.

In a traditional direct-mail package, on the other hand, the message is unevenly split. Consistently, 98 percent of the copy is in the letter and brochure, with the remaining 2 percent on the order form. In e-mail marketing campaigns, the division is less balanced and more varied.

The bottom line: E-mail marketing can work without having e-mails competing with *War and Peace* in word count. By strategically splitting your copy between the front-end e-mail and back-end response page, you can get your message across without having time-pressured Web surfers fleeing in terror.

TECHNIQUES FOR EFFECTIVE E-MARKETING MESSAGES

Here are a dozen or so proven techniques for maximizing the number of your e-mail recipients who click-through to your Web site or page. (*See Appendix A, Fig. A-4.*)

- **At the top of the e-mail, put a "FROM" line and a "SUBJECT" line.** The "FROM" line identifies you as the sender if you're e-mailing to your house file. If you're e-mailing to a rented list, the "FROM" line might identify the list owner as the sender. This is especially effective with opt-in lists where the list owner (e.g., a Web site) has a good relationship with its users. Some e-marketers think the "from" line is trivial and unimportant; others think it's critical. Internet copywriter Ivan Levison says, "I often use the word 'Team' in the "FROM" line. It makes it sound as if there's a group of bright, energetic, enthusiastic people standing behind the product." For instance, if you are sending an e-mail to a rented list of computer people to promote a new software product, your "SUBJECT" and "FROM" lines might read as follows: "FROM: The Adobe PageMill Team / SUBJECT: Adobe PageMill 3.0 limited-time offer!" Your ISP can show you how to change subject lines for different messages.

  The "SUBJECT" line should be short, attention-grabbing, and curiosity-arousing, compelling recipients to read further without being so blatantly promotional it turns them off. Example: "Your input needed by Thursday," "Do grid circuits work?"

- **Lead off the message copy with a killer headline or lead-in sentence.** You need to get a terrific benefit right up front. Pretend you're writing envelope teaser copy (see Part VII) or are writing a headline for a sales letter.

- **In the first paragraph, deliver a miniversion of your complete message.** State the offer and provide an immediate response mechanism, such as clicking on a link connected to a Web page. This method appeals to Internet users with short attention spans as well as users who are busy and can give each e-mail only a second or two get the whole story.

- **After the first paragraph, present expanded copy.** This copy should cover the features, benefits, proof, and other information the buyer needs to make a decision. Expanded copy appeals to people who need more details than a short paragraph can provide.

- **Close by repeating the offer-and-response mechanism, as in a traditional direct-mail letter.**

- **Limit the number of click-through links in your e-mail to three.** John Wright, of the Internet marketing services firm MediaSynergy, says that if you put multiple response links within your e-mail message, 95 percent of click-through responses will come from the first two. Therefore, you should make three click-through links your limit. An exception might be if you are writing an e-newsletter or "e-zine" broken into five or six short items, where each item is on a different subject and therefore each has its own link.

- **Use wide margins.** You don't want to have weird wraps or breaks. Limit yourself to about 55 to 60 characters per line. If you think a line is going to be too long, insert a character return. Internet copywriter Joe Vitale sets his margins at 20 and 80, keeping sentence length to 60 characters, and ensuring the whole line gets displayed on the screen without odd text breaks.

- **Take it easy on the all-caps.** You can use WORDS IN ALL CAPS but do so carefully. They can be hard to read — and, as mentioned previously, in the world of e-mail, all caps give the impression that you're shouting.

- **Shorter is better.** This is different from classic mail-order selling where as a general principle, "The more you tell, the more you sell." E-mail is a unique environment. Readers are quickly sorting through a bunch of messages and aren't disposed to stick with you for a long time [*see* How Long Should an E-Mail Marketing Message Be? *earlier in this part.*]

  Get the important points across quickly. If you want to give a lot of product information, add it lower down in your e-mail message. You might also consider an attachment, such as a Word document, PDF file, or HTML page. People who need more information can always scroll down or click for it. The key benefits and deal should be communicated in the first screen, or very soon afterward.

- **Make your message's tone be helpful, friendly, informative, and educational, not promotional or hard-sell.** "Information is the gold in cyberspace," says Vitale. Trying to sell readers with a traditional hyped-up sales letter won't work. People online want information and lots of it. You'll have to add solid material to your puffed-up sales letter to make it work online.
- **Refrain from saying your service is "the best" or that you offer "quality."** Those are empty, meaningless phrases. Be specific. How are you the best? What exactly do you mean by quality? And who says it besides you? And even though information is the gold, readers don't want to be bored. They seek, like all of us, excitement. Give it to them.

THE "4 U's": 4 WAYS TO SPICE UP YOUR SUBJECT LINES

When prospects get your e-mail marketing message, they make a quick decision, usually in a couple of seconds, to open or delete it based largely on the subject line. But given the glut of promotional e-mail today, how can you convince a busy prospect — in just a few words — that your message is worthy of attention?

The "4 U's" copywriting formula — which stands for urgent, unique, ultra-specific, and useful — can help. Originally developed by copywriter Michael Masterson for writing more powerful headlines, the 4 U's formula works especially well with e-mail subject lines. According to this formula, strong subject lines are:

- **Urgent:** Urgency gives the reader a reason to act now instead of later. You can create a sense of urgency in your subject line by incorporating a time element. For instance, "Make $100,000 working from home this year" has a greater sense of urgency than "Make $100,000 working from home." A sense of urgency can also be created with a time-limited special offer, such as a discount or premium if you order by a certain date (e.g., "Free home appraisal: this week only").
- **Unique:** The powerful subject line either says something new, or if it says something the reader has heard before, says it in a new and fresh way. For example, "Why Japanese women have beautiful skin" was the subject line in an e-mail promoting a Japanese bath kit. This is different than the typical "Save 10% on Japanese Bath Kits."
- **Ultra-specific:** Boardroom, publisher of *Bottom Line Personal* and other newsletters, is the absolute master of ultra-specific bullets, known as "fascinations," tease the reader into reading further and ordering the product. Examples: "What never to eat on an airplane," and "Bills it's okay to pay late." They use such fascinations in direct mail as envelope teasers and in e-mail as subject lines.

- **Useful:** The strong subject line appeals to the reader's self-interest by offering a benefit. In the subject line "An Invitation to Ski & Save," the benefit is saving money. In "UNIX data recovery — once difficult, now easy," the promise is to simplify data recovery in UNIX environments.

When you have written your subject line, ask yourself how strong it is in each of these 4 U's. Use a scale of 1 to 4 (1 = weak, 4 = strong) to rank it in each category. Rarely will a subject line rate a 3 or 4 on all four U's. If it doesn't rate a 3 or 4 on at least *three* of the U's, however, it's probably not as strong as it could be and can benefit from some rewriting.

A common mistake is to defend a weak subject line by pointing to a good response. A better way to think is as follows: If the e-mail generated a profitable response despite a weak subject line, imagine how much more money you could have made by applying the 4 U's? Here's an example:

4 U's Example

A software marketer recently sent out a successful e-mail marketing campaign with the subject line "Free White Paper" (see glossary in the appendix). How does this stack up against the 4 U's?

- **Urgent:** There is no urgency or sense of timeliness. On a scale of 1 to 4, with 4 being the highest rating, "Free White Paper" is a 1.
- **Unique:** Not every software marketer offers a free white paper, but a lot of them do. So "Free White Paper" rates only a 2 in terms of uniqueness.
- **Ultra-specific:** Could the marketer have been less specific than "Free White Paper"? Yes, he could have just said "Free Bonus Gift." So we rate "Free White Paper" a 2 instead of a 1.
- **Useful:** I suppose the reader is smart enough to figure the white paper contains some helpful information he can use. On the other hand, the usefulness is in the specific information contained in the paper, which isn't even hinted at in the headline. And does the recipient, who already has too much to read, really need yet another "Free White Paper"? I rate it a 2. Specifying the topic would help, e.g., "Free White Paper shows how to cut training costs up to 90% with e-learning."

Go through this exercise with every e-mail subject line you write. You can also apply the formula to other copy, both online and offline, including direct-mail envelope teasers (see Part VII), ad headlines, letter leads, Web page headlines, subheads, and bullets.

Rate the line you've written in all four U's. Then rewrite it so you can upgrade your rating on at least 2 and preferably 3 or 4 of the categories by at least 1. This simple exercise may increase readership and response rates substantially for very little effort.

Where to Get Your E-Marketing Lists

Your customer-and-prospects lists can come from one of three sources:

- **House files.** As with traditional direct mail, e-mail marketing works best when sent to your house list of customers and prospects. If your house files don't have e-mail addresses, there are several ways to obtain them. You can run your file through an e-mail address appending service, and expect to find e-mail addresses for between 10 percent and 30 percent of the records. You can also make e-mail address collection part of your ongoing marketing and customer service records. For instance, one of my vendors that awards gifts based on bonus points offered to add 300 bonus points to my account in exchange for my e-mail address.

- **E-zine subscribers.** Theoretically you will get high response rates mailing to people who have signed up for your free e-zine [*see* Appendix A, Figure A.7]. However, these folks are often freebie seekers, and may not be qualified prospects. Therefore, results vary. Some e-zine lists are pure gold. Others generate less sterling results.

  Another option is to run classified ads in other people's e-zines with a link to your landing page or micro site. This lets you get your message to people at a far lower cost per thousand than solo e-mails. However, the circulations of many e-zines are unqualified and unaudited; therefore the quality of the audience you reach can be questionable. Again, you have to test. To run short ad in someone's e-zine typically costs $20 to $40 per thousand subscribers.

- **Rented opt-in e-lists.** You can rent e-lists for e-mail marketing campaigns at costs ranging from $100 to $300 per thousand. As with traditional direct mail, test lists in small quantities before expanding your e-mail campaign to the entire list.

E-mail Marketing Warning

Be careful about e-mailing people you do not know. If you e-mail strangers, make sure the content is informational or conversational, and contains no sales pitch or commercial message. Sending an unsolicited promotional e-mail to an individual whom you do not know, and who has not agreed to receive such messages, is called "spam." It is illegal and can have many negative consequences, from a nasty response to having your ISP shut down your account. Avoid spamming.

When renting e-mail lists, make sure the list is an "opt-in" list. That means people on the list have agreed to receive promotional e-mails.

continued

continued

How is this done? Have you ever registered on a Web site or submitted a reply form where you checked a box that said, essentially, that you give permission for the Web site to send you occasional e-mails of interest? If so, you have opted in, and the Web site owner is likely intending to rent your name on the commercial list market.

By the same token, avoid "spam" lists. These are lists of e-mail addresses collected from the Web without the recipient's permission.

How can you tell the difference? One way is price. If you see a list advertised as "millions of names for $25," it's a spam list. Don't buy it! Legitimate opt-in lists rent for $100 to $400 per thousand names.

Include an opt-out statement in order to prevent flaming from recipients who feel they have been spammed by stating that your intention is to respect their privacy, and making it easy for them to prevent further promotional e-mails from being sent to them. All they have to do is click on Reply and type "UNSUBSCRIBE" or "REMOVE" in the subject line. Example: "We respect your online time and privacy, and pledge not to abuse this medium. If you prefer not to receive further e-mails from us of this type, please reply to this e-mail and type 'Remove' in the subject line." (*Flaming* is when recipients of promotional e-mail express their displeasure by replying and sending you nasty messages.)

E-mail privacy also is a delicate issue for anyone on the receiving end of "spam" and other unwanted e-mail messages. When you respond to an e-mail message from someone selling something, you run the risk of becoming a permanent part of that person's database and may receive time-consuming, unwanted e-mails far into the future. It's best to follow instructions for removing unsolicited e-mails, despite the hassle, so that you save yourself from endless future e-mails from people who pitch to you solely because you haven't actually told them to stop.

Fax Correspondence

For hundreds of years, the only way to communicate at long distance was postal mail. With the invention of the telegraph and telephone, people could communicate conversationally in a two-way mode thanks to electricity. Then as now, telephone calls were spontaneous and off the cuff; telegraphs were typically limited to very short messages, e.g., "SOS (save our ship)." Letters remained the only medium, however, for written, thought-out, lengthy communication.

A fax works by optically scanning a printed document, translating the image into data, and transmitting the data over a phone line. The receiving machine reassembles the data into the image, which it prints on the paper using laser or ink-jet technology.

When the fax machine became popular, people thought it would revolutionize communication since a letter could be sent and received in less than a minute using the fax machine versus days through the mail. Indeed, the fax would have revolutionized written communications, except that almost immediately it was replaced by the faster, more-efficient method of online communications: first PC-to-PC communications via modem, quickly followed by today's standard, e-mail and the Internet.

With more than 100 million Americans accessing the Internet, e-mail has replaced fax for the vast majority of transmitted written communications. It is simply easier to write and send a message online than to fax it. As a result, the use of the fax machine is limited primarily to transmitting documents that already exist as hard copies, but are not available in an electronic file format that can be sent over the Internet.

Some software programs allow you to send and receive faxes through your personal computer. In this case, the software has a template, which automatically generates the cover sheet. The receiving computer prints the cover sheet, followed by the message of the document being faxed.

FORMATS

Unlike e-mail, which has some special formatting requirements (see samples in this chapter), faxes have none. Faxes are either written in standard memo or letter format (*See Appendix A: Fig. A-1 and Fig. A-1A*). Simple format for letters and memos.). The letter or memo is then transmitted to the recipient with a fax cover sheet. Using the fax cover sheet (see sample below) eliminates the need to specially format your letter or memo for fax transmission.

COVER SHEETS

There is nothing terribly fancy about a fax cover sheet. It should be one page and include the following information: date sent, time sent, name of recipient, fax number of recipient, and the sender's name and contact information. It should also inform the recipient of the total number of pages being sent (be clear about whether the cover sheet is included in this total) and the topic.

The bottom half has space for any custom message that should be added in addition to the materials being sent. A simple fax cover sheet is shown as follows.

Priority Fax Transmission

Date_____ Time_____

To_____

Fax_____

FROM: Bob Zed, CTC   phone 888-888-8888

37 W. Crackerbox Avenue   fax 888-888-8889

Hoboken, NJ 07030

We are transmitting _____ pages including this cover sheet. If you do not receive all the pages or they are not legible, please call back as soon as possible. Thank you.

SUBJECT_____

MESSAGE:

If the document you are sending is self-explanatory, just write a short description of the topic on the "Subject" line of the fax cover sheet (e.g., "local area networks") and send. You should include text under the "Message" heading only if you feel the need to explain what you are sending, otherwise leave it blank.

The message text is short, typically only a few sentences, or at most a couple of paragraphs. Its main purpose is to either draw attention to the material being faxed, or to highlight the portions of it that are most important to the reader. A couple of sample fax cover sheet messages appear as follows.

MESSAGE:

Jessica:

Take a look at this cost estimate. It seems reasonable, except the monitor is more than we want to spend. We could save $200 per desktop switching from the 19" to the 17" model, which has a totally acceptable resolution for our purposes. What do you think?

— Richard Johnson

MESSAGE:

Bergen County CHADD now has its own Web site. Please help us spread the word. Thanks.

FAX COURTESY, LEGALITY, AND CONFIDENTIALITY

For routine correspondence, you can use fax, but use it sparingly. When you send a fax, you tie up the recipient's fax machine, and the recipient is paying for the ink and paper. Because of this, many people do not like to receive long faxes. You may want to send long, nonurgent documents at night, so as not to tie up the recipient's fax machine during business hours. If you have more than half a dozen pages or so, you might call or e-mail the person first, and ask whether they would prefer to get the material sent via fax, mail, or overnight delivery.

For marketing to existing customers and prospects, the law does allow you to send promotional faxes to people with whom you have an established prior relationship. But again, use fax marketing sparingly, if at all. Be especially sensitive when marketing to people at home or who work in small businesses. They often sit near the machine and resent it being used for marketing purposes.

For marketing to generate inquiries or acquire new customers, avoid using the fax. Sending promotional faxes to people whom you do not know and with whom you have no existing relationship is in most instances illegal, with stiff fines for violation of the law.

If you have a small business or are self-employed, you should have a separate phone line and number for your fax machine. It annoys people to get a busy signal when trying to send you a fax because you are on the phone talking. Ideally you should have three lines and numbers: one for the telephone, a second for the fax machine, and a third for your Internet connection.

When faxing to employees in large corporations, be aware that in most cases, many employees share a single fax line and machine. Therefore, anyone walking past the fax machine can see your message before the recipient picks it up. For this reason, if your message is confidential, e-mail or postal mail are better options than fax when communicating with a corporate reader,

Tips for Effective Fax Communication

- Beware of reducing a larger page to 8½" x 11" for faxing. The reduced type may be too small for the recipient to read.

- Material printed on colored paper does not fax well because of the colored background. Fax is best used for transmitting documents that are black ink printed on white paper.

- Number the pages of the document you are faxing. Faxed pages are often accidentally dropped or shuffled, making it difficult for the recipient to review them in the order you sent them.

- Periodically have your fax machine cleaned and serviced to eliminate lines and smudging when transmitting documents.

- If you want the recipient to sign a document and return it via fax, say so on your cover sheet and indicate your fax number.

- If a live signature is required for legal reasons, you can send the document as a fax, but you should also send the original by postal mail.

FORMATS

Which form of written correspondence should you choose? As a rule, letters, postcards, faxes, or e-mails are sent to people outside the company. Letters are appropriate for dealing in a slightly more formal manner with important items. Faxes can be less formal than letters, but are considered by most companies to be the equivalent of a signed letter with regards to confirming orders or agreeing to negotiated terms and/or conditions. Because of their lightning speed, e-mails tend to be informal, brief, and to the point. [*See Part X for more about e-mails and faxes.*]

Postcards are great for service reminders or change-of-address announcements. People can put them on the bulletin board or stick them in their daily planner. Handwritten notes, because of their personal feel and because they are so unusual in today's harried business world, work well for networking purposes.

Letters are effective for communicating information or making a persuasive argument. They are also best for sensitive/confidential information that is not intended for a mass audience. Traditional letter paragraphs, however, are not always the best way to transmit detailed information. Consider alternative ways to communicate data. If you have a lot of numbers or specifications, consider putting them in a table or numbered list rather than writing them as narrative text.

A fax is a good alternative to a letter when speed is more essential than formality. As previously noted, faxes are nearly universally accepted for correspondence related to ordering, shipping, and paying for merchandise since signatures are included in the document. A fax is best in circumstances where an immediate "hard copy" of information is necessary due to the work environment, such as warehouses, loading docks, factories, etc. And faxes will remain the fastest method for providing graphical information such as drawings, advertising layouts, pictures, directions, etc., until the majority of PC users have the ability to scan documents at their desks.

E-mail is typically used when responding to someone else's e-mail, with short and informal messages, or when speed of delivery is of the essence. Also use e-mail when your recipient is likely to share your message with other decision-makers in her organization; an e-mail is faster and easier than a printed letter or memo to distribute.

RULES AND OPTIONS

Decades ago, letter-writing books agonized over the proper rules for presenting information in letters, second sheets, envelopes, and so on. In today's fast-paced world, however, people pay less attention to such niceties, and adherence to rigid format rules is not so important: Your reader really doesn't care whether the left margin is ½ inch or ¾ inch.

The rules of desktop design for letter writing are simple: Keep it neat, clean, and readable. Here are some tips:

- Type size for letters ranges from 8 to 12 point, depending on the typeface used. Times Roman is a popular typeface for letter body copy, although both Prestige Elite and New Courier make the letter look typewritten, which for many has a warm, almost quaint look.
- Word processing gives you several fonts, including boldface and italic, which can be used to add emphasis or create headings and subheads. On typewriters, asterisks were used for bullet lists and to make boxes. Word processing software offers a selection of bullets and can place a variety of borders around text to make boxes.
- Letters are frequently typed single space, with double spacing between the paragraphs.

SAMPLE FORMATS

There are several different letter formats you can choose from, depending on your needs:

- Simple format (Fig. A-1). In simple format, all parts of the letter are flush left. The letter is informal, without salutation or close.
- Memo (Fig. A-1A). Memos typically use the simple format, but with the heading format shown in the figure.
- Block format (Fig. A-2). A formal letter with all elements flush left. It includes a heading, inside address, salutation, body, close, and signature. Spacing between the elements is shown in Fig. A-2A.
- Semi-block format (Fig. A-3). Similar to block format, but with more indenting to make the copy easier to read. Paragraphs are indented five spaces at the beginning instead of flush left. The close and salutation are to the right of the page instead of the left.
- E-mail format (Fig. A-4). An e-mail is similar to a letter in many respects, but it has some parts — usually a from line and a subject line — a letter does not. Also, the close and signature on an e-mail are optional, and many people don't use them. Another difference is that e-mail often contains links the reader can click to hyperlink to a page on the Web, such as a Web site home page or landing page.

- Press release format (Fig. A-5). When communicating news to the editor of your local newspaper, industry trade publication, or other media, the preferred format is the press release. Text at the top of the page indicates the organization issuing the release, the person the editor should contact for more information, and when the story may be released or printed. The rest of the release is written as an article, with a headline and paragraphs in block style.
- Résumés (Fig. A-6). When writing to inquire about employment, the details of your employment history and education are communicated in a separate résumé, not in the cover letter.
- E-zine (Fig. A-7). For many companies, monthly or biweekly electronic newsletters, or e-zines, are used in place of cordial contacts and other print letters to keep in touch with customers, suppliers, and business partners. These are not written in traditional e-mail or letter format. Typically they are written as newsletters, except the articles are much shorter (often just a paragraph or two) than in traditional printed promotional newsletters.

FIGURE A-1
Simple format for letters and memos.

444 West Wilson Street
Madison, Wisconsin 53715
July 9, 2002

Cambridge Camera Exchange, Inc.
Seventh Avenue and 13th Street
New York, NY 10011

INCOMPLETE SHIPMENT

_____
_____
_____
_____
_____
_____
_____
_____
_____
_____
_____
_____

Marilyn S. Conway

FIGURE A-1A

Memo.

To: Elsie Brennen

From: Bob Bly

Date: May 4, 2002

Subject: CBAC presentation

Thanks for sending the PowerPoint. It looks great, and I have no changes.

Can you send one copy to Leslie White at Bicktech? Be sure to let her know it is for my presentation at the Marketing Roundtable next month.

Thanks again for the good, prompt work.

P.S. When you have a minute, please give me a call to discuss how we might turn this presentation into a CD-ROM.

FIGURE A-2

Block letter format.

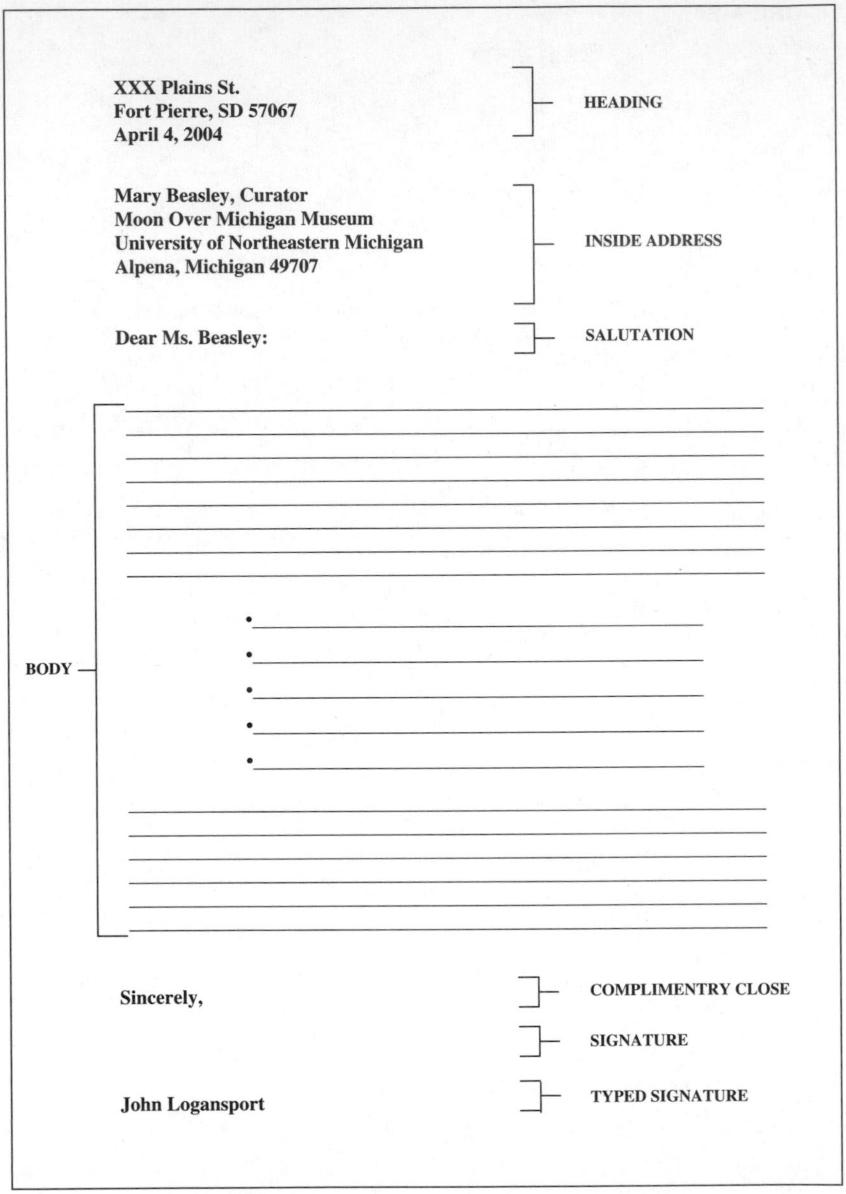

XXX Plains St.
Fort Pierre, SD 57067
April 4, 2004 — HEADING

Mary Beasley, Curator
Moon Over Michigan Museum
University of Northeastern Michigan
Alpena, Michigan 49707 — INSIDE ADDRESS

Dear Ms. Beasley: — SALUTATION

BODY

Sincerely, — COMPLIMENTRY CLOSE

— SIGNATURE

John Logansport — TYPED SIGNATURE

FIGURE A-2A

Spacing of elements in a business letter.

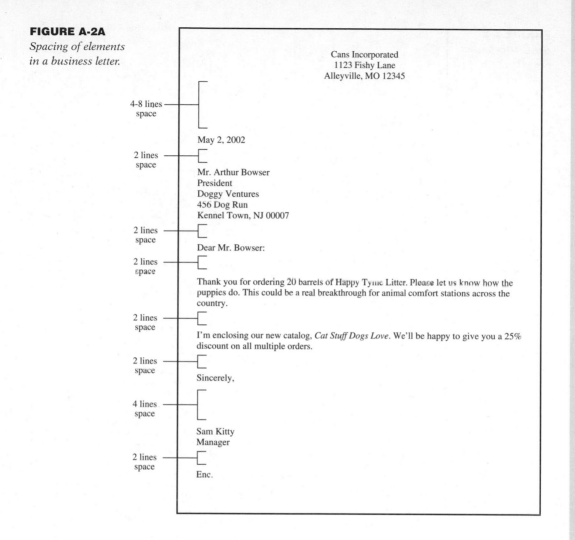

Cans Incorporated
1123 Fishy Lane
Alleyville, MO 12345

4-8 lines space

May 2, 2002

2 lines space

Mr. Arthur Bowser
President
Doggy Ventures
456 Dog Run
Kennel Town, NJ 00007

2 lines space

Dear Mr. Bowser:

2 lines space

Thank you for ordering 20 barrels of Happy Tyme Litter. Please let us know how the puppies do. This could be a real breakthrough for animal comfort stations across the country.

2 lines space

I'm enclosing our new catalog, *Cat Stuff Dogs Love*. We'll be happy to give you a 25% discount on all multiple orders.

2 lines space

Sincerely,

4 lines space

Sam Kitty
Manager

2 lines space

Enc.

FIGURE A-3
Semi-block letter format.

FIGURE A-4

Email format.

Link in first
2 paragraphs

Lead (what it is and
why I should care)

Subject: "Revitalizing your e-business"

In a forested, seaside conference center just minutes from Monterey, a select group of top-level executives and prominent e-business consultants will be having — on Sept. 7-10 — a meeting that will redirect their businesses for long-term success.

And if you click on [LINK] now, you may be able to get in on these sessions while there are still a few seats available.

In this revolutionary course, "Revamping for New E-Business Success," these executives will be learning how to redefine their companies e-business strategies to compete in the new business economy of the mid-2000s.

You too can learn — from some of the nation's top e-business experts and consultants — the following keys to successfully compete and prosper in today's international post-recession business arena:

— How to construct a new e-business strategy for your company.
— What necessary changes your company must make to gain a competitive e-business edge.
— How to realign your company culture to attract international Web customers.
— How to create topnotch, cost-efficient Web solutions and services.
— What financial assessments are necessary to avoid costly mistakes. Bullets
— How to determine and realize your company's e-commerce potential.
— How to gain opportunities for global partnerships.
— How to deal-make in a virtual universe.

If you want to successfully redirect your company's e-business in order for it to prosper immediately and in the years ahead, please click on [LINK] to sign up now. Registration is limited and we will be accepting no more applicants after July 31st. If you sign up before July 1st, however, as an added bonus, you will be able to take advantage of a one-on-one consultation — scheduled just for you and your company's needs, on the topic of your choosing — with a select team of e-business specialists.

We respect your online time and privacy. If you prefer not to receive further e-mails from us of this type, please reply to this e-mail and type "Remove" in the subject line.

Close with link
and offer

Opt-out language

FIGURE A-5

Press release format.

FROM: CBAC Technologies

CONTACT: Herb Carter, phone (201) 888-8888 | Who to call for more information |

| Release Date |

FOR: <u>Immediate Release</u>

| Headline |

New PTA plasma welding system has deposition

Speeds up to 3X faster than conventional technologies

| Lead |

Hoboken, New Jersey--CBAC Technologies has introduced a new plasma-transferred arc (PTA) system that performs at deposition speeds up to three times faster than competing technologies, announced Herb Carter, a Vice President with the firm.

| Claims attributed to a source |

CBAC's high-tech PTA welding system, the only one of its kind in North America, deposits metal alloys on metal surface at rates up to 55 pounds per hour, compared with 20 pounds per hour for conventional plasma, gas-tungsten, and oxy-acetylene welding technologies. The PTA system can work with metal powder, wire, powder filled wire, and rods.

The key to the PTA system's greater speed is a new plasma arc transfer system consisting of a solid state DC power source, process controller, and unique plasma torch with hermetically sealed cooling and gas-flow systems. No torch sealing is needed, eliminating micro-leakage in the ionization zone. High-speed flow of the cooling medium enables the PTA system to handle extremely high thermal loads.

| Proof |

------- more -------

| Indicates a Second Page |

FIGURE A-6

Résumé.

John Lewkowski
848 Plains Street
Fort Pierre, South Dakota 57067
605-555-9745

Employment Objective

A museum staff position leading eventually to a curatorship.

Education

B.A. Earlham College, Richmond, Indiana, 1988.
Major: history   Minor: biology   GPA: 3.85/4.00 = A

Experience

Museum volunteer, Joseph Moore Museum, Earlham College, 1986-88. Assisted director of small natural history museum. Developed traveling museum program for four local elementary schools. Identified and cataloged specimens, maintained exhibits.

Summer intern, Tippecanoe County Historical Museum, Lafayette, Indiana, 1987. Wrote grant proposal resulting in $10,000 award for archeological dig at 18th century French and Indian trading settlement. Worked with state and federal agencies, university faculty, museum staff.

Laboratory assistant, Earlham College, spring term 1988. Supervised freshman biology lab, prepared lab materials and specimens, answered students' questions, and graded lab reports. Was selected Outstanding Teaching Assistant in the Natural Sciences.

Honors and Activities

Earlham Alumni Scholarship,   1985-88
Outstanding Teaching Assistant,   1988
Earlham College tennis team,   1985-88

Personal Data

Speak and write French. Interests: travel and photography

FIGURE A-7

E-zine format.

From: Bob Bly
Subject: Bob Bly's Direct Response Letter

Resources, ideas, and tips for improving response to business-to-business, high-tech, industrial, Internet, and direct marketing.
October 3, 2002

You are getting this e-mail because you subscribed to it on www.bly.com or because you are one of Bob's clients, prospects, seminar attendees, or book buyers. If you would prefer not to receive further e-mails of this type, go to www.can'tfind.com, enter your e-mail address, and hit Unsubscribe.

FOR SOFTWARE MARKETERS ONLY
I'll be presenting a Webcast called "Secrets to Selling Software By Mail" on 10/17 at 1 pm. Attendees will learn how to craft compelling copy and create irresistible offers for direct mail packages selling software products of all kinds.

You can register for the event here:
https://www.registerforevent/here

HIRING A SPEAKER FOR YOUR NEXT MEETING OR SEMINAR? WATCH OUT!

What can go wrong with something so innocuous as hiring a well-known keynote speaker?

** One speaker used a naughty word in his PowerPoint presentation to 300 top executives; another listed the competitor's name and contact information throughout his handouts.

** A novice meeting planner hired a speaker for a 3-hour keynote and then found out the speaker only had material to speak for 90 minutes on his topic.

** A speaker's invoice included unexpected expenses such as his $7,000 first-class ticket, his pro shop charges, and his fee for copying his handouts onsite (600 pages copied at the hotel at 20 cents per page).

For tips on how to avoid these and other common meeting planning pitfalls, see the next mailing!

STAMP OUT BAD POWERPOINT PRESENTATIONS!

If you are going to use PowerPoint, don't let ho-hum slides detract from the value of your message, or cause you to miss a precious opportunity to make a winning impression.

PowerPoint pro Mary Taylor can help you deliver your business message – whether it's to your internal or external customers – with slide design for your presentation. With over 25 years' experience in marketing communications, she can help you make your message come alive.

She'll "pretty up" boring text slides, add pizzazz to dry statistical charts, and create the positive impression with your audience that you're looking for. For more information, contact Mary Taylor at XXX-XXX-XXXX, or visit www.website.com

----

KNOCK, KNOCK

For a writing project, I need engineering jokes (jokes about engineers and engineering) -- good, bad, or terrible. Please e-mail your jokes to ppppp@ppp.com. Thanks!

60-SECOND COMMERCIAL FROM FERN DICKEY, PROJECT MANAGER:

Bob is available on a limited basis for copywriting of direct mail packages, sales letters, brochures, data sheets, white papers, ads, e-mail marketing campaigns, PR materials, and Web pages. We recommend you call for a FREE copy of our updated Copywriting Information Kit. Just let us know your industry and the type of copy you're interested in seeing (ads, mailings, etc.), and if Bob is available to take your assignment, we'll tailor a package of recent samples to fit your requirements. Call Fern Dickey at xxx-xxx-xxxx or e-mail pppp@can'tfind.com.

More...

USEFUL LETTER WRITING AIDS

ADDRESSES, ENCLOSURES, AND CC'S

Mr.	For addressing a man.
	Mr. George Rowland
Messrs.	For addressing two or more men. Often used to address members of a professional firm (not a business organization) composed of men.
	Messrs.— Jones and Hitchcock
Ms.	For addressing a woman.
	Ms. Gloria Smith
Mesdames.	For addressing two or more married or unmarried women.
	Mesdames Stone and Myers
Esquire. (Esq.)	For addressing lawyers. It follows the name. Daniel Mummaugh, Esquire
	Harold Lang, Esq.
Honorable (Hon.)	For addressing high officials in federal, state, and local government. It is spelled out when preceded by "the."
	The Honorable Harry Shirk
	The Honorable Mr. Shirk
	Hon. Harry Shirk
Reverend (Rev.)	For addressing ministers and priests of religious organizations. It is spelled out when preceded by "the."
	The Reverend Paul Eric
	The Reverend Dr. Troll
	Rev. O. Osgood Brown

Rabbi	For addressing Jewish clergy in the United States, not abbreviated.
	Rabbi George Levy
	Rabbi Levy
Doctor (Dr.)	For addressing anyone who holds a doctorate. Abbreviate it when it is followed by a full name. Write it out when it is followed by a surname only.
	Dr. Jennifer Hill
	Doctor Hill
Professor (Prof.)	For addressing college teachers who hold professional rank. You may abbreviate it before a full name in an address.
	Professor Lewis G. Jennings
	Prof. Lewis G. Jennings
	Professor Jennings
Sr. and Jr.	These abbreviations are, in effect, titles. They follow a full name and are separated from it by a comma.
	Dr. Paul R. Rosenblatt, Sr.
	Mr. Henry M. Narducci, Jr.
Enclosure.	If any material other than the letter is to be mailed in the envelope, the word Enclosure is typed two lines below the signature, flush with the margin. The abbreviation Enc. Or Encl. Is often used.
	Sam Smith
	Enclosure
Indication for carbon copies.	Write "Copy to" or "cc" and the name of anyone who will receive a copy of the letter two lines below the signature. (The term "cc" is an abbreviation for "carbon copy," referring to the now-obsolete practice of using carbon paper to make a copy of a letter as it was being typed.)
	cc: Harry Carter
	cc. Susan Ritnor

TWO POEMS

Versions of the following two anonymous poems have been posted in offices and floating around the Web for years. They offer a humorous look at common gaffes that you should try to avoid.

The Nature of the Typo

The typographic error
Is a slippery thing, and sly.
You can hunt it till you're dizzy
But it somehow will get by
Till the forms are off the presses
It is strange how still it keeps;
It shrinks down in a corner
And it never stirs or peeps.
The typographic error
Is too small for human eyes,
Till the ink is on the paper . . .
When it grows to mountain size.
The Boss, he stares with horror,
Then grabs his hair and groans;
The copy reader drops his head
Upon his hands and moans.
The remainder of the issue
May be clean as clean can be,
But the typographic error
Is the olny thing you'll see.

–Anonymous

Spell Checker

Eye halve a spelling chequer
It came with my pea sea
It plainly marques four my revue
Miss steaks eye kin knot sea
Eye strike a key and type a word
And weight four it two say
Weather eye am wrong oar write
It shows me strait a weigh.
As soon as a mist ache is maid
It nose bee fore two long
And eye can put the error rite
Its rare lea ever wrong.
Eye have run this poem threw it
I am shore your pleased two no
Its letter perfect awl the weigh
My chequer tolled me sew.

–Anonymous

CAPITALIZATION

The following are ordinarily capitalized	Examples
The first word in a direct quotation within a sentence.	He asked: "Are you going to help?"
Proper nouns and some adjectives formed from proper nouns unless use has made them so familiar that they are no longer associated with the original name.	London, Rockefeller Center, France, Maine, Fifth Avenue, Impressionism But: diesel, ampere, hertz, ohm
The names of organizations, institutions, government agencies, businesses, and holidays.	Lever Brothers Company, U.S. Small Business Administration, Library of Congress
An official title used before the name of the person holding it.	President James Johnson, founder of the Acme Company; President Bush, Governor Cuomo But: "Mr. Cuomo was elected governor of New York"; "James Johnson, president and founder of the Acme Company"
Geographical terms when they are part of a proper name.	Long Island Sound, Mt. Hood
Sections of the country and world and adjectives derived from them when they refer to a specific geographical area.	They live in the West. He is a Northerner. Southern California
When they indicate direction, don't capitalize north, south, east, and west.	Chicago is east of Denver.
Registered trademarks.	Formica, Frisbee, Scotch Tape
The first and last word and all nouns, pronouns, verbs, adjectives, and all other words of five or more letters in titles and subtitles of books, magazines, newspapers, articles, essays, etc.	His article is called: "Ten Tips to Better Business Writing and Technical Writing."

PUNCTUATION MARKS

COMMA ,	Separates dependent clauses; a dependent clause doesn't present a complete thought. Separates elements in a series.	Mr. Smith, a lawyer, was at the party. As I mentioned in my letter, we need to hire three secretaries.
	Can be used after salutation in a personal letter.	We need action, not words.
SEMICOLON ;	While commas separate dependent clauses, semicolons separate independent clauses that closely relate to each other.	Hundreds of tests are conducted to determine product safety; accidents still occur regularly.
COLON :	Announces that something follows. Usually precedes a series or an explanation.	Go to the stockroom and bring me these items: pens, ribbons, and folders.
	Also used after the salutation of a business letter.	Hospitals exist for one reason: to heal the sick.
HYPHEN -	Links words. Usually links two or more words modifying a noun.	This is a state-of-the-art course.
	Can divide the syllables of a word at the end of a line of text.	We need to go through a two-stage process.
ELLIPSIS ...	Shows hesitation or omission of letters or words. Often used when only part of a quotation is used.	"I...am...guilty," he stammered. "This is the best report I've seen..."
PARENTHESES ()	Adds information. Often the information is of secondary importance.	Acme Co. had great revenues (see fig. 5). I'm sending you the two checks (No. 1246 and No. 1249) you requested.
DASH —	Highlights or interrupts a thought. A dash SHOUTS; parentheses whisper.	The Dow Jones Average closed at 6,960 — a new low for the year — confirming that we are still in a bear market. The seminar — which includes a text, handout materials, and a workbook — costs $3,000.

APOSTROPHE '	Shows possession or contraction.	The boy's pen is on his desk.
		We'll see you soon.
		The employees' rights are protected by OSHA.
		Mr. Dickens's book is open.

GRAMMAR GUIDE

	INCORRECT	CORRECT	WHY
Subject and verb disagreement	In reference to your recent letter, your address in our files are correct.	In reference to your recent letter, your address in our files **is** correct.	The subject of the sentence is "address," not "files."
	An order form, as well as a post-paid envelope, are enclosed.	An order form, as well as a post-paid envelope, **is** enclosed.	
Noun and pronoun disagreement	Each supervisor must complete their personnel reviews by Friday.	Each supervisor must complete **his or her** personnel reviews by Friday.	"Supervisor" is singular, so it takes a singular verb.
		Or Supervisor**s** must complete their personnel reviews by Friday.	Make "supervisors" plural to avoid cumbersome "his" and "her."
Problematic pronouns	John, George, and me met to discuss the job.	John, George, and **I** met to discuss the job.	Remove the first subjects and read the sentence: "me met"? Obviously not.
	We met with Mr. Brown, Mr. Smith, and yourself in New York.	We met with Mr. Brown, Mr. Smith, and **you** in New York.	
Dangling modifiers	After finding the missing report, the search was ended by the secretary.	After finding the missing report, the secretary ended the search.	Since the "search" didn't do any finding, the secretary had to find the report.

	INCORRECT	CORRECT	WHY
Misplaced modifiers	The payroll teller recommended First Carrier over Federated, whose delivery service is very prompt.	The payroll teller recommended First Carrier, whose delivery service is very prompt, over Federated.	If First Carrier is recommended, it must be the prompt company, not Federated.
Run-on sentences	Your projected cost for fiscal 1991 is $650,000, however, this figure may vary because of a variety of factors.	Your projected cost for fiscal 1991 is $650,000; however, this figure may vary because of a variety of factors.	The "however" is the start of a whole new thought with its own subject and verb.

CLICHES TO AVOID

a few well-chosen words
abreast of the times
acid test
agree to disagree
almighty dollar
among those present
ancestor
at one fell swoop
bated breath
beat a hasty retreat
beg to say
best-laid plans
bolt from the blue
bountiful repast
break the news gently
breakneck speed
budding genius
but that's another story
by leaps and bounds
captain of industry
center of attraction
checkered career
commercial pursuits
conspicuous by this absence
day of reckoning
description
die is cast

doomed to disappointment
down through the ages
each and every one
endorse the sentiments
equal to the occasion
every walk of life
exception that proves the rule
fast and furious
goes without saying
gone but not forgotten
greatness thrust upon
his paternal (maternal)
host of friends
impenetrable mystery
in any way, shape, or form
irony of fate
last but not least
looking for all the world like
lull before the storm
made a pronounced success
misguided youth
nipped in the bud
no sooner said than done
perfect in every detail
powers that be
profound silence
psychological moment

riot of color
ripe old age
sadder but wiser
seething mass of humanity
silence reigned supreme
skeleton in the closet
the scene beggars
vale of tears

venture a suggestion
veritable avalanche
view with alarm
words are inadequate
words fail me
work with Trojan
worse for wear

SOUND-ALIKE WORDS

Words	Meaning
Accept	to receive
Except	to exclude
Adapt	to suit
Adept	proficient
Adopt	to tailor, modify
Advise	to counsel (verb)
Advice	(noun) counsel
Affect	to influence, to change (verb)
Effect	a result; (verb) to bring about
All ready	prepared
Already	previously
Assent	consent
Ascent	rise
Cite	to summon, to quote (verb)
Sight	a view
Site	(verb) to see a location

Words	Meaning
Coarse	common, rough
Course	a direction of progress
Commence	to begin
Comment	(noun) a remark; (verb) to remark
Correspondents	writers
Correspondence	letters, other written communication
Counsel	(noun) advice; (verb) to advise
Council	a group, an assembly
Decent	proper, respectable
Descent	(noun) act of descending
Descend	(verb) to come down
Dissent	(noun) disagreement; (verb) to disagree
Deposition	testimony
Disposition	disposal, temperament
Digression	deviation
Discretion	judgment, prudence
Dissolution	termination, breaking up
Disillusion	to free from false impression
Enforce	to force, to compel
In force	in power, in effect
Elicit	to draw out
Illicit	illegal, improper

Words	Meaning
Enclose	to place within
Inclose	in legal use, preferred in speaking of land
Exceed	to surpass
Accede	to agree
Formally	ceremoniously
Formerly	in times past
Forth	away, forward
Fourth	the number: 4
Farther	in space
Further	in thought, in space
Later	comparative form of late
Latter	second of two mentioned
Loose	unattached, free
Lose	to suffer loss
Precede	to go before
Proceed	to begin, to continue
Release	(noun) liberation; (verb) to free
Relief	aid, comfort
Relieve	to ease, to remove burden
They're	contraction of they are
Their	possessive pronoun
There	adverb showing location

TIPS ON TONE

Prefer positive to negative words.	Instead of "John has neglected to show up at the last three meetings," try: "John has not attended…"
Put negative news first in a sentence that has both positive and negative news.	By putting the "good news" last, the reader ends with it and the thought lingers (e.g. "Although I can't hire you, I'm sending your résumé to someone who can.")
Don't write when you're angry.	…You'll probably regret it in the morning. You have no control over who your communication will be shown to and what consequences might develop.
Don't use value judgments designed to make readers feel bad about past mistakes.	Instead, try to motivate your reader to improve behavior in the future. So, don't write, "Your problems stem from improper management of your time" when you can write, "You could benefit from improving your time-management skills," or "I suggest you improve your time-management skills."
Use contractions to warm up your message.	It's perfectly fine to use contractions in memos and letters. After all, we use them in speech.
Give your reader a reason to comply before making a request.	Don't just say, "Send me the check today," give a reason: "To make sure you get your order by Christmas, send me your check today."
Be courteous, but don't overdo humility.	"Thanks for taking five minutes from your schedule" sounds like pleading. You're putting yourself down when you use this. Instead, write "I enjoyed meeting with you."
Apologize completely.	Don't write, "I'm sorry about what happened, but you shouldn't have…" Instead, apologize without ifs, ands, or buts.
Empathize before stating an opinion.	Spend a sentence or two reflecting the customer's feelings, empathizing with what the customer is experiencing: "It sounds as if you're worried about your staff's lack of computer literacy."

ONLINE ACRONYMS

BFN	bye for now
BTSSOOM	beats the [stuffing] out of me
BTW	by the way
CUA	commonly used acronym(s) OR common user access
FAQ	frequently asked questions
FU	[fouled] up
FUBAR	[fouled] up beyond all recognition
FUD	(spreading) fear, uncertainty, and disinformation
FWIW	for what it's worth
FYI	for your information
GR&D	grinning, running, & ducking
HTH	hopes this helps
IAE	in any event
IANAL	I am not a lawyer (also IANAxxx, such as IANAMD or IANACPA)
IMCO	in my considered opinion
IMHO	in my humble opinion
IMNSHO	in my NOT so humble opinion
IMO	in my opinion
IOW	in other words
LOL	lots of luck or laughing out loud or (sometime) lots of love
MHOTY	my hat's off to you
NFW	no [bleeping] way
NRN	no reply necessary
OIC	oh, I see!
OOTB	out of the box (brand new)
OTOH	on the other hand
OTTH	on the third hand
PITA	pain in the [...]
PMFJI	pardon me for jumping in
ROTFL	roll(ing) on the floor laughing (also, ROF,L, ROFL)

RSN	real soon now (which may actually be a long time away)
RTFM	read the [full] manual (or message)
SITD	still in the dark
SNAFU	situation normal, all [fouled] up
TANSTAAFL	there ain't no such thing as a free lunch
TIA	thanks in advance
TIC	tongue in cheek
TLA	three-letter acronym (such as this)
TTFN	ta ta for now
TTYL	talk to you later
TYVM	thank you very much
W4W	(WP4W, etc; all the various products, such as...)
WYSIWYG	what you see is what you get
7/24	all day long, seven days a week, 24 hours a day

BIG WORDS

Instead of:	*Use:*
abbreviate	shorten
aggregate	total, whole
amorphous	shapeless
anomalous	abnormal
antithesis	opposite
aqueous	watery
ascertain	find out
autonomous	independent
beverage	drink
cessation	stop, pause
circuitous	roundabout
coagulation	clotting, thickening
comestibles	food

Instead of:	*Use:*
commencement	start, beginning
concept	idea
conjecture	guess
contiguous	near, touching
currently	now
deficit	shortage
demonstrate	show
discourse	talk
disengage	free
duplicate	copy
eliminate	cut out
elucidate	clarify
expedite	hasten, speed
facilitate	ease, simplify, help
feasible	possible
gradient	slope
homogeneous	uniform, similar
impairment	injury, harm
incision	cut
incombustible	fireproof
inundate	flood
maintenance	upkeep
minuscule	tiny
nomenclature	name, system of terms
obtain	get
optimum	best
orientate	get your bearings
parameter	variable, factor

Instead of:	*Use:*
posterior	rear
potentiality	potential
requisite	needed, necessary
segregate	set apart
subsequent	next
sufficient	enough
terminate	end
verification	proof
viable	workable
vitreous	glassy

WORDY PHRASES

Instead of:	*Use:*
a large number of	many
along the lines	like
as a general rule	generally
as shown in table 6	table 6 shows
as yet	yet
at all times	always
at this point in time	at this time, now
at your earliest convenience	now, soon
by means of	by
despite the fact that	although, even though
during the course of	during
even more significant	more significant
exhibits the ability	can
has been widely acknowledged as	is
has proven itself to be	has proved, is
have discussion of	discuss

Instead of:	*Use:*
hold a meeting	meet
inasmuch as	since
in many cases	often
in order to	to
in some cases, in other cases	sometimes
in the course of	during, while
in the event that	if
in the form of	as
in the majority of instances	usually, generally
in the near future	soon (state approximate or exact date)
in the process of tabulating	in tabulating
in the vicinity of	near
is equipped with	has, contains
it is clear that	clearly
on a daily basis	daily, every day
on a weekly basis	weekly
on an annual basis	yearly
on the basis of	by, from
on the occasion of	when
prior to that time	before
start off	start
subsequent to	after
take action	act
the necessity is eliminated	you do not need to
the reason why is that	because
until such time as	until
with reference to	about
with the result that	so that

REDUNDANCIES

Redundancy	Substitutions
absolutely essential	essential
absolutely perfect	perfect
actual experience	experience
adding together	adding
advance plan	plan
all of	all
an honor and a privilege	an honor
any and all	any
balance against one another	balance
basic essentials	essentials
by means of	by
cancel out	cancel
combine into one	combine
consecutive in a row	consecutive
continue on	continue
cubic meters in volume	cubic meters
current status	status
different varieties	varieties
equally as well	equally
final outcome	outcome
first and foremost	first
first introduction	introduction
first priority	priority
goals and objectives	goals
Gobi Desert	Gobi
honest truth	truth
in close proximity	close

Redundancy	Substitutions
isolated by himself	isolated
joined together	joined
main essentials	essentials
mixed together	mixed
mutual cooperation	cooperation
necessary requisite	requisite
one and the same	the same
open up	open
overall plan	plan
past history	history
personal opinion	opinion
physical size	size
point in time	time
rain shower	shower, rain
reason why	reason
refer back to	refer to
repeat again	repeat
small in size	small
take action	act
this particular instance	this instance
this particular time	now
triangular in shape	triangular
true facts	facts
uniformly consistent	consistent
whether or not	whether
wrote away for	wrote for
you may or may not know	you may know

FREQUENTLY MISSPELLED WORDS

Here are some words that are commonly misspelled and some mnemonic devices (memory aids) that will help you spell them correctly.

WORDS	REMEMBER
accidentally	keep a "tally" in "accidentally"
accommodate	accommodate "accommodates" 2 c's and 2 m's
acknowledgment	Think "GM"
already	not "All ready"
appearance	put a "pear" in appearance"
attorney	put a "torn in atTORNey
authoritative	take the "rat" out of "authoritative"
bargain	You "gain" when you bargain
beginning	think "beg-inning"
benefited	keep "fit" in "benefited"
calendar	put "lend" in "caLENDar"
canceled	cancel the second "l" in "canceled"
committee	"committee" is made up of 2 "m's", 2 "t's," and 2 "e's"
controversy	put a second "O" in contrOversy
describe	2 "e's" on "describe"
develop	no final "e" in "develop"
disappoint	if you use 2 "p's" you'll never "disaPPoint"
embarrass	2 "r's" and 2 "s's"
endeavor	endeavor to put an "a" in "endeavor"
environment	don't forget the second "n" in "enviroNment"
exercise	sound it out "ex-er-cise"
familiar	"familiar" has 2 "I's"
February	put the "br" in FeBRuary
foreign	foreign rulers "reign"
guarantee	a "U" in guarantee suits you to a tee
immediately	immediate + ly

WORDS	REMEMBER
its	"its" for possessive
	"it's" for contracting "it" + "is"
judgment	1 "e" in "judgment"
manageability	manage/ability
noticeable	there's no "cable" in noticEable"
occasion	every "oCCasion" has 2 "c's"
occurred	two "c's" and two "r's" in "occurred"
omission	o + mission
preferred	two "r's" is "prefeRRed"
privilege	no "ledge: in "priviLEGE"
questionnaire	two "n's" in "questioNNaire"
receive	"i" before "e" EXCEPT AFTER "c"
renown	Kick the "k" out of "renown"
separate	there's no "per" in "sePARate"
stationary	you gEt stationEry at a store;
	you stAy "stationAry" in your seat
supersede	"superSEDE" not "CEDE"
they're/their	"they're" (they are) certain of "their" knowledge
unnecessary	think "un-necessary"
until	u-n-t-i-l = five letters
Wednesday	forget pronunciation think WED-NES-Day
whether/weather	"wHether" implies hesitation
	"wEather" makes you wet
write/written	"write" has one "t"
	"written" has two

ANTIQUATED PHRASES

Instead of:	*Use:*
kindly	please
advise us	tell us, let us know
tender	offer, send
this will acknowledge your	as you requested
endeavor	try
in view of the fact	because
in lieu of	instead of
in the amount of	for
we deem it advisable	we suggest
state	say
not in a position to	can't
in compliance with your request	as you requested
it is our opinion	we think
at the present time	now
under separate cover	separately
in the event that	if
in the near future	soon
similar to	like
inadvertent postponement	delay

MORE ANTIQUATED PHRASES

The following are antiquated business phrases. They sound stuffy and old; use them sparingly, if at all! Read your copy out loud; if it doesn't sound like something you would say in a normal conversation, rewrite it.

according to our records	as captioned above
acknowledge receipt of	as per
acknowledge with pleasure	as regards
acknowledging yours of	as stated above
	assuring you of

at all times

at an early date

at hand

at the present time

at the present writing

at this time

at your convenience

attached hereto

attached herewith

attached please find

awaiting your further wishes

awaiting your order

awaiting your reply

beg to acknowledge

beg to advise

beg to assure

beg to call your attention

beg to confirm

beg to state

beg to suggest

carefully noted

check to cover

complying with your request

concerning yours of

contents noted

contents duly noted

continued patronage

deem (for think)

desire to state

due to the fact

duly noted

enclosed find

enclosed herewith

enclosed please find

esteemed favor

esteemed order

esteemed request

favor us with your order

favor us with your reply

for your files

for your information

hand you herewith

has come to hand

have before us

hereby advise

hereby insist

herewith enclose

herewith find

herewith please find

hoping for your order

hoping to receive

I am (ending last sentence)

I beg to advise

I have your letter of

I trust

in accordance with

in answer to same

in answer to yours

in conclusion would state

in connection therewith

in due course

in due course of time

in re

in reference to

in receipt of

in reply would advise

in reply would wish

in response to yours

in the amount of

in the near future

in this connection

kind indulgence

kind order

kindly advice

kindly be advised

kindly confirm same

looking forward to

may we suggest

may we hope to receive

meets your approval

of above date

order has gone forward

our Mr._____

our line

our records show

per

permit us to remind

please accept

please advise (be advised)

please find herewith

please find enclosed

please note

please rest assured

please return same

pleasure of a reply

proximo (prox.)

pursuant to

re

recent date

referring to yours of

regarding the matter

regarding the above

regarding said order

regarding yours

regret to advise

regret to inform

regret to state

said (the said regulation)

same (regarding same)

soliciting your advise

soliciting your indulgence

soliciting your patronage

take the pleasure in

take the liberty of

thank you kindly

thanking you in anticipation

thanking you in advance

thanking you kindly

the writer

this is to acknowledge

this is to advise

trusting to have

trusting to receive same

ultimo (ult.)

under separate cover

up to this writing

valued favor

valued order

valued patronage

we are (ending last sentence)

we are pleased to advise

we are pleased to note

we have before us

we remain (ending last sentence)

we take pleasure in advising

we trust

wish to advise

wish to state

with kindest regards

with reference to

with your kind permission

would advise

would state

would wish to

your esteemed order

your favor has come to hand

your future patronage

your kind indulgence

your letter of even date

your letter of recent date

your Mr._____

your valued patronage

yours of even date

yours of recent date

yours duly received

yours kindly

yours with regard to above

yours with respect to same

Sexist Terms

Instead of:	*Use:*
anchorman	anchor
advertising man	advertising executive
chairman	chairperson
Englishman	Brit
fireman	firefighter
foreman	supervisor
a man who	a person who
man the booth	staff the booth
mankind	humankind
manpower	labor
manmade	manufactured
man-hours	hours
Mrs., Miss	Ms.
newsman	journalist
mailman	mail carrier
policeman	police officer
salesman	salesperson
stewardess	flight attendant
waitress	server
weatherman	meteorologist
workman	worker

Abbreviations

Instead of:	*Use:*
as soon as possible	ASAP
carbon copy (to)	cc:
cash on delivery	c.o.d.
company	Co.
credit	cr.

Instead of:	*Use:*
department	dept.
district	dis.
doing business as	DBA
each	ea.
fiscal year	FY.
for example	e.g.
for your information	FYI
Incorporated	Inc.
manufacturing	mfg.
merchandise	mdse.
postscript	P.S.
quarter	qtr.
that is	i.e.
East	E
North	N
South	S
West	W
Doctor of Medicine	M.D.
Doctor of Philosophy	Ph.D.
Esquire	Esq.
General	Gen.
Governor	Gov.
Honorable	Hon.
Lieutenant	Lt.
Manager	mgr.
Master of Arts	M.A.
Master of Science	M.S.
Mechanical Engineer	M.E.
Private	Pvt.

Instead of:	Use:
Registered Nurse	R.N.
Reverend	Rev.
Saint	St.
Saint (feminine)	Ste.
Secretary	sec.
Senior	Sr.
Sergeant	Sgt.
Treasurer	Treas.
Vice President	V.P.
Alabama	AL
Alaska	AK
Arizona	AZ
Arkansas	AR
California	CA
Canal Zone	CZ
Colorado	CO
Connecticut	CT
Delaware	DE
District of Columbia	DC
Florida	FL
Georgia	GA
Guam	GU
Hawaii	HI
Idaho	ID
Illinois	IL
Indiana	IN
Iowa	IA
Kansas	KS
Kentucky	KY

Instead of:	*Use:*
Louisiana	LA
Maine	ME
Maryland	MD
Massachusetts	MA
Michigan	MI
Minnesota	MN
Mississippi	MS
Missouri	MO
Montana	MT
Nebraska	NE
Nevada	NV
New Hampshire	NH
New Jersey	NJ
New Mexico	NM
New York	NY
North Carolina	NC
North Dakota	ND
Ohio	OH
Oklahoma	OK
Oregon	OR
Pennsylvania	PA
Puerto Rico	PR
Rhode Island	RI
South Carolina	SC
South Dakota	SD
Tennessee	TN
Texas	TX
Utah	UT

Instead of:	*Use:*
Vermont	VT
Virgin Islands	VI
Virginia	VA
Washington	WA
West Virginia	WV
Wisconsin	WI
Wyoming	WY

MAILING AND SHIPPING

Your three main choices for sending letters, postcards, and other printed matter is the United States Postal Service, United Parcel Service, and FedEx. Here's a little information about the three major players in the mailing/shipping field:

UNITED STATES POSTAL SERVICE (WWW.USPS.COM)

The United States Postal Service's Website has lots of great information and tools about mail — from an instant ZIP code finder to calculating postage to printing shipping labels. One of the best features of the site are the free downloadable forms and reports. Their postage rate page (http://www.usps.com/common/category/postage.htm) has several documents that list the most current postage rates (one report is for domestic mail, one is for international mail). You can view it on your screen, print it out, or download to your hard drive.

Another interesting section of the site is "Grow Your Business" (http://www.usps.com/grow/welcome.htm).

UNITED PARCEL SERVICE (WWW.UPS.COM)

Did you know that the United Parcel Service (UPS) was founded in 1907 as a messenger company? According to their Website, they are the world's largest package delivery company. You can go online to www.ups.com and set up an account, find out their rates, order supplies, and schedule shipments.

Their site has lots of helpful documents (see http://www.ups.com/content/us/en/resources/index.html) on interesting topics such as tariff information and how to properly prepare packages for shipping. You can download special software onto your computer so that you can easily work with UPS for shipping, reporting, tracking, etc.

FEDEX (WWW.FEDEX.COM)

In the movie *Castaway*, FedEx efficiency manager (Tom Hanks) manages to survive four years on a deserted island when his plane carrying FedEx packages crashes into the ocean and he gets washed to shore. As days, weeks, and months pass, his life is saved, in part, as each intact FedEx package after intact FedEx package floats onto the island. How can we not love FedEx?

You can set up an account on the FedEx Website, get supplies, schedule pickups, find rates, and helpful shipping advice. They also offer international shipping tools.

Businesspeople might be interested in FedEx's supply chain and transportation management services (see http://www.fedex.com/us/supplychain/services/?link=1).

All three services offer online package tracking services — a very useful and timesaving tool.

GLOSSARY

A

active voice   the verbs in the active voice show the subject acting. Example: "The dog bit the boy."

adjective   the part of speech that modifies a noun or other substantive by limiting, qualifying, or specifying, and distinguished by one of several suffixes, such as -able, -ous, -er, and -est, or syntactically by position directly preceding a noun or nominal phrase.

adverb   a word used to modify the sense of a verb, participle, adjective, or other adverb, and usually placed near it. Example: "He writes *well*" or "Make the border *extremely* bright."

apostrophe   the superscript sign (') used to indicate the omission of a letter or letters from a word, the possessive case, or the plurals of numbers, letters, and abbreviations.

B

block style   the most common layout of a business letter where the entire letter is left-justified and single-spaced except for a double space between paragraphs.

body   the portion of the letter below the salutation and above the close.

boldface   type with a heavier, darker appearance. Often used to introduce important new terms.

border   a box placed around text.

bullets   a type of character, the most common being a large dot, that is used to separate text or to begin paragraphs, especially in lists.

business reply card   a postage-paid single card used for product registration, product ordering, or customer survey.

business reply envelope   a self-addressed, specially formatted, bar-coded envelope/postcard that enables a business to pay postage for responses received from customers.

business reply permit   a method whereby a business reply permit holder may authorize individuals and activities to send First-Class matter to the permit holder and have the postage and fees paid by the permit holder.

C

close the part of the letter after the last paragraph and above the signature, typically "Sincerely."

closing paragraph at the end of a letter that brings it to a polite, businesslike close.

conjunction the part of speech that serves to connect words, phrases, clauses, or sentences. Any of the words belonging to this part of speech, such as *and*, *but*, *as*, and *because*.

copy the words to be printed or spoken in an advertisement or in the body of a business letter.

copyedit to correct and prepare (a manuscript, for example) for typesetting and printing.

cover letter a letter sent with other documents to explain their contents more fully or provide more information.

customer service correspondence or letters relating to the status of a customer's account, order, and other business with the company.

D

dangling modifier a word or phrase apparently modifying an unintended word because of its placement in a sentence. Example: "when young" in the sentence "When young, circuses appeal to all of us."

direct mail advertising circulars or other printed matter sent directly through the mail to prospective customers or contributors.

dunning to request a past-due payment from a customer or other debtor.

E

edit to prepare written material for publication or presentation, as by correcting, revising, or adapting.

e-mail a system for sending and receiving messages electronically over a computer network, as between personal computers. A message or messages sent or received by such a system.

F

first person the grammatical category of forms that designates a speaker or writer referring to himself or herself. Examples of forms in the first person include the pronouns "I" and "we."

flush left text that is aligned vertically on the left side of a page.

flush right   text that is aligned vertically on the right side of a page.

"from" line   in e-mail, where the name of the sender is found.

G

grammar   the study of how words and their component parts combine to form sentences.

greeting   see *salutation*.

H

heading   the segment, most often of a memo, that indicates the topic of the memo, who it's from, and to whom it is being sent. In a letter, the return address (usually two or three lines) followed by the date.

headline   a line at the head of a page or passage giving information such as the title, author, and page number, usually set in large print.

hedge phrase   a phrase uttered after a statement that implies uncertainty. Example: "I'd like to go to the movies . . . I *think*."

HTML   a markup language used to structure text and multimedia documents and to set up hypertext links between documents, used extensively on the World Wide Web.

I

indicia   markings on bulk mailings used as a substitute for stamps or cancellations.

inside address   the address you are sending your letter to.

italics   a style of printing type patterned on a Renaissance script with the letters slanting to the right: *This sentence is printed in italic type.*

J

johnson box   a block of text at the very top of a fundraising, sales, or direct-mail letter's first page, above the salutation. This copy may or may not actually be boxed copy. Color, larger type, a distinctive font, italics, a border, even a graphic image serve to make the copy jump out at the reader.

K

kerning   a measurement of the spacing between letters in a word.

key code   the code that enables the user to take advantage of special discounts or promotions.

L

leading   the space between lines of text.

letter   a written or printed communication directed to a person or a organization.

letterhead   the heading at the top of a sheet of paper, usually consisting of a name and an address. Stationery imprinted with such a heading.

M

mailing list   a list of names and addresses to which advertising and other mail is sent, either via postal mail or e-mail.

marketing   the process or technique of promoting, selling, and distributing a product or service.

memo   a written record or communication.

meter   a postage meter is a mailing system that prints postage directly on the envelope (or on an adhesive tape) for any type of mail — first, second, third, or fourth class; air mail, registered mail, special delivery, or other special services.

monarch envelope   envelope with the specifications 3.87" by 7.5".

N

noun   the part of speech that is used to name a person, place, thing, quality, or action and can function as the subject or object of a verb, the object of a preposition, or an appositive.

number 9 envelope   envelope with the specifications $3\frac{7}{8}$" x $8\frac{7}{8}$".

number 10 envelope   envelope with the specifications $4\frac{1}{8}$" x $9\frac{1}{2}$".

P

paragraph   a distinct division of written or printed matter that begins on a new, usually indented line, consists of one or more sentences, and typically deals with a single thought or topic or quotes one speaker's continuous words.

passive voice   verbs in the passive voice show something else acting on the subject. Example: "The boy was bitten by the dog."

PDF (portable document format)   the file format for documents containing any combination of text, graphics, and images in a device-independent and resolution independent format. The reader cannot alter the file.

prefix   an affix, such as *dis-* in disbelieve, attached to the front of a word to produce a derivative word or an inflected form.

pronoun   the part of speech that substitutes for nouns or noun phrases and designates persons or things asked for, previously specified, or understood from the context.

proofread   to read copy or proof for purposes of error detection and correction.

proposal   a document submitted to a potential customer proposing the rendering of a service or another business arrangement.

P.S.   a message appended at the end of a letter after the writer's signature. Additional information appended to the manuscript, as of a book or article. The abbreviation **P.P.S.** means an additional message appended after the p.s.

punctuation   the use of standard marks in writing to separate words into sentences, clauses, and phrases.

Q

quotation mark   either of a pair of punctuation marks used primarily to mark the beginning and end of a passage attributed to another and repeated word for word. Also used to indicate the unusual or dubious status of a word. They appear in the form of double quotation marks (" ") and single quotation marks (' '). Single quotation marks are usually reserved for setting off a quotation within another quotation.

R

ragged left   text that is not full-justified. The left edge of the text is uneven, or "ragged."

ragged right   text that is not full-justified. The right edge of the text is uneven, or "ragged."

re: in reference to; in the case of; concerning.

report   a written record or summary.

résumé   a brief account of one's professional or work experience and qualifications, often submitted with an employment application.

S

sales   the exchange of goods or services for an amount of money or its equivalent; the act of selling.

salutation   begins with the word "Dear" followed by the recipient's name.

second person   the grammatical category of forms that designate a speaker or writer referring to the person addressed. Examples include pronouns such as "you" and "yours."

second sheet   in a letter with multiple pages, the second piece of stationery is referred to as the second sheet.

sentence   a word, clause, or phrase, or group of clauses forming a syntactic unit that expresses an assertion, a question, a command, a wish, an exclamation or the performance of an action.

sig file   a personal footer that is automatically attached to e-mail.

signature   the author's name handwritten at the end of a letter.

signature line   the author's name typed below the handwritten signature.

spam   unsolicited e-mail, often of a commercial nature, sent indiscriminately to multiple mailing lists, individuals, or newsgroups; junk e-mail.

style   the way in which something is said, done, expressed, or performed: a style of speech and writing.

subject line   in e-mail, a brief summary of what the message is about.

suffix   an affix added to the end of a word or stem, serving to form a new word or functioning as an inflectional ending, such as *-ness* in gentleness, *-ing* in walking, or *-s* in sits.

T

teaser   short attention-grabbing, curiosity-arousing text on the outside of an envelope, compelling recipients to read further.

tense   any one of the inflected forms in the conjugation of a verb that indicates the time, such as past, present, or future, as well as the continuance or completion of the action or state.

text   the main body of printed or written matter on a page.

third person   the grammatical category of forms that designates a person or thing other than the speaker or the one spoken to. Examples of forms in the third person include pronouns such as "she" and "they."

tone   refers to the writer's attitude toward the reader and the subject of the message.

V

verb   the part of speech that expresses existence, action, or occurrence in most languages.

voice   verbs can be used either in the active or passive voice. Most writers consider the active voice more forceful and tend to stay away from passives.

W

white paper   a marketing brochure written and designed in the format of a special report or informative article.

INDEX